PRAISE FOR *UNDERSTANDING DIGITAL MARKETING*

P9-DEO-165

'*Understanding Digital Marketing* accomplishes well the difficult feat of assembling current practical strategies from leading experts in the digital marketing field.'
Carol Stuckey, Executive Director, Strategic Growth Initiatives, Harvard University Division of Continuing Education

'Comprehensive, contextualized and current. Does a great job of balancing solid overview with specific, insightful case examples. An essential addition to any marketer's bookshelf.'
Dr Agnes Nairn, Dean, Hult International Business School

'This is a great handbook on the world of digital marketing, a world that can seem quite overwhelming at times, especially with the speed of change. A practical guide, it makes a great case for the importance of digital marketing in *any* marketer's toolbox. Updated to include some of the latest challenges in digital marketing, what I like most is that it remains people-centric, to help ensure that any digital marketing activities you undertake have a fair chance of success.'
Tara Beard-Knowland, Senior Director, Ipsos Connect

'A no-nonsense, clearly written book which you can dip in and dip out of depending on your digital needs. Excellent to see that the human side of digital has a clear presence throughout.'
Dr Sarah Warnes SFHEA, Senior Teaching Fellow, UCL School of Management

Fourth Edition

Understanding Digital Marketing

Marketing strategies for engaging the digital generation

Damian Ryan

First published in Great Britain and the United States in 2009 by Kogan Page Limited
Second edition 2012
Third edition 2014
Fourth edition 2017

2nd Floor, 45 Gee Street	MPHC Marketing	4737/23 Ansari Road
London EC1V 3RS	122 W 27th St, 10th Floor	Daryaganj
United Kingdom	New York NY 10001	New Delhi 110002
www.koganpage.com	USA	India

© Damian Ryan, 2009, 2012, 2014, 2017

The right of Damian Ryan to be identified as the author of this work has been asserted by him in accordance with the Copyright, Designs and Patents Act 1988.

ISBN   978 0 7494 7843 8
E-ISBN   978 0 7494 7844 5

British Library Cataloguing-in-Publication Data

A CIP record for this book is available from the British Library.

Library of Congress Cataloging-in-Publication Data

Names: Ryan, Damian, author.
Title: Understanding digital marketing : marketing strategies for engaging
   the digital generation / Damian Ryan.
Description: Fourth edition. | New York : Kogan Page Ltd, 2016. |
   Revised edition of the author's Understanding digital marketing, [2014] |
   Includes bibliographical references and index.
Identifiers: LCCN 2016037268 (print) | LCCN 2016037831 (ebook) | ISBN
   9780749478438 (paperback) | ISBN 9780749478445 (e-ISBN) |
Subjects: LCSH: Internet marketing. | Social media. | Strategic planning. |
   BISAC: BUSINESS & ECONOMICS / Marketing / General. | BUSINESS & ECONOMICS
   / E-Commerce / Internet Marketing. | BUSINESS & ECONOMICS / Advertising &
   Promotion.
Classification: LCC HF5415.1265 .R93 2016 (print) | LCC HF5415.1265 (ebook) |
   DDC 658.8/72–dc23

Typeset by Graphicraft Limited, Hong Kong
Print production managed by Jellyfish
Printed and bound by CPI Group (UK) Ltd, Croydon, CR0 4YY

CONTENTS

Bonus online-only chapters and contributor views are available at the following url (please scroll to the bottom of the web page and complete the form to access these):

www.koganpage.com/understanding-digital-marketing

Bonus online-only chapters:
Measurement and data: is it working?
Going global – internationalization: cross-border digital marketing
Digital transformation 101: a journey of change towards a transformed customer experience

Bonus online-only contributor views:
Also included at the above url are three other contributions to this edition that were too good to omit!

PREFACE

Digital marketing is dead... long live digital marketing!

I love this business. I love its energy, passion and soundbytes too, just like the one above.

Digital attracts some of the brightest minds and ideas and sometimes attracts people desperately seeking a sensationalist headline (just like the one above!).

Last week at an industry event I heard that not only had digital marketing well and truly snuffed it but in fact advertising was dead too. A miserable start to the event but it did make me think what truth, if any, lay within...

Every day there are more ways to engage, more tools to try out, more facts, figures, infographics... not forgetting seminars, webinars, events with cool acronyms – and then of course there are sites, apps, channels, clips, magazines and (ahem) other sorts of publications... let's not ignore the experts, the gurus, the white papers, PowerPoints and shares, likes, comments, emoticons, tweets and retweets... it's a noisy old world.

And yes it is flawed but it's still alive and...

Anything that evolves and moves like lightning has already set off a few speed cameras. No omelette was ever made without breaking a few eggs and digital is no stranger to this fact, but it's showing no signs of slowing down... shedding its immortal coil, well not yet anyway.

Since the last time I sat down to work on this book (about two years ago) the digital marketing world has changed. It has become more scientific and taken several leaps forward, particularly with programmatic and mobile. But the audience has changed too – in fact I feel that the audience is now more elusive than ever. Sure it's a bigger audience and we can all run around waving stats, but there is a fundamental difference: while advertisers and technologists battle on with new formats, new tools and fab ways of measuring stuff, the consumer has been ignored.

The desire for digital marketing has, in my opinion, forsaken the fundamental objective of digital marketing... to engage our digital generation in an appropriate, mutually agreeable and profitable manner, whereby the consumer feels loved and has received value for money and value for their time.

This IS the marketplace. If you are an agency or brand and are not prepared to subscribe to this objective, well then, it's not digital marketing that is dead, it's you my friend.

Is it any wonder that adblocking has become such a major issue for publishers and brands? Is it any surprise that marketers struggle to maintain audience and engender loyalty? The consumers have been left out of the conversation for too long and it will now start to show.

Be under no illusion… digital marketing is not dead… BAD digital marketing is dead and bad digital marketers and their bad agencies are dead too.

Disrespecting privacy, irritating consumers and making the mistake of copying what you do online with what you do offline is dead.

Being intrusive, awkward, inconsistent with crappy online forms that don't scroll down properly and archaic interfaces that wouldn't know UX if it bit them in the BX… you're dead too!

Simply put, if your friends spoke to you the way some digital marketers speak to you then you would probably punch them in the face or leave them waiting outside in the rain…

If marketers want to be part of this brave, new and exciting landscape then we have to get our act together and start being more inclusive and emphatic towards the interests of consumers – marketers in the coming years will be judged on the experience they provide for their customers. We used to talk about the four Ps of marketing… price, place, promotion and product. E Jerome McCarthy, the originator of the four Ps, sadly passed away a few months ago. He wasn't wrong about the four Ps – it is just what we knew and understood at that time.

I have rewritten the four Ps to apply to our current generation of stakeholders. Please consider the 10 Ps:

1 PERFORMANCE: how is your activity measured against objectives and against competitors? The internet has shrunk the world but mammothed the available number of service and product providers. How you perform in relation to digital engagement consigns you to success or failure.

2 PRESENCE: how is yours? Online, mobile, search engines, social media? Are you there? Do you look good? Is it working?

3 PLEASURE: how do your customers rate their user and customer experience with you versus your competitors? Who does this better than anyone? If you know that answer then BE LIKE THEM… do not settle for second best.

4 PROXIMITY: are you there when your customers need you? Are you on hand 24/7? This generation wants it all and wants it now.

5 PERTINENT: are you relevant? Are your marketing and outreach relevant to their needs at this time? Do you know? Well if you don't then go and find out – ask them, they won't bite!

6 PROCESS: how is this working out for your customers... how you engage is one thing but the actual process of delivery and payment (another P?) is not to be overlooked.

7 PERSONAL: not sure why I just thought of this but I fly to Dublin every 10 days or so and there's a guy on passport control who checks my passport and says, 'Thanks, Damian.' It makes me smile and I like him. That is what we need online – not Mrs Ryan or Dear Sir... when used in the right way, personalization is very powerful.

8 PREFERENCES: and if your customers don't want to go too personal then provide them with preferences so you can all learn and all get the best from your relationship.

9 PROFIT: weirdly this was not part of the original four Ps but it should have been. Everything you do should be measurable and return on investment (ROI) is often a crucial part of this measurement.

10 PEOPLE: ones and zeroes are all very useful but let's not forget we are dealing with people – ignore this at your peril!

The past, the current and the future are and always have been about the customer. Never losing sight of that fact. Regardless of technology, competition, media... now is the time to engage with customers on their terms, to listen and show that you love them – and if digital media can help to achieve that then digital marketing is very much alive and well.

In the pages that follow I take you on a journey into the world of digital marketing. I will show you how it all started, how it got to where it is today, and where thought leaders in the industry believe it is heading in the future. Most importantly of all, I'll show you – in a practical, no-nonsense way – how you can harness the burgeoning power of digital media to engage with consumers and drive your business to the crest of this digital marketing wave, and how to keep it there.

This book will:

- help you and your business to understand that digital marketing is all about people – the customers that your business relies on for success and the people in your team who are responsible for engaging and delighting these customers by understanding that the new currency is EXPERIENCE;

- help you and your business to choose online advertising and marketing channels that will get your ideas, products and services to a massive and ever-expanding market;

- give you that elusive competitive edge that will keep you ahead of the pack;

- future-proof your business by helping you to understand the origins of digital marketing and the trends that are shaping its future;

- give you a concept of the scale of the online marketplace, the unfolding opportunities and the digital service providers who will help your business to capitalize on them;

- provide practical, real-world examples of digital marketing successes – including leading brands that have become household names in a relatively short space of time;

- offer insight through interviews, analysis and contributions from digital marketing experts;

- … ultimately, give you the tools you need to harness the power of the internet in order to take your business wherever you want it to go.

As you travel into this digital world the book will reveal how leading marketers in sectors as diverse as travel, retail, gambling and adult entertainment have stumbled on incredibly effective techniques to turn people on to doing business online, reaping literally millions as a result. The book will show you how to apply their experience to transform your own digital enterprise.

Whether you are looking to start up your own home-based internet business, work for a large multinational or are anywhere in between, if you want to connect with your customers today and into the future, you need digital channels as part of your marketing mix.

The internet has become the medium of choice for a generation of consumers: the first generation to have grown up taking for granted instant access to digital information. This generation integrates digital media into every facet of its daily life, in ways we could never have conceived in even the recent past. Today this generation of digital natives is entering the workplace and is spending like never before. This is the mass market of tomorrow, and for business people and marketers the challenge is to become fluent in this new digital language so that we can talk effectively to our target audience.

Television froze a generation of consumers to the couch for years, now digital media is engaging consumers and customers in ways that the early architects of the technology could never have dreamed. The advent of 'two-screen' or even 'three-screen' marketing is now becoming a real consideration

– just look at how our own lives are changing and how we soak up data…
How many of us regularly sit in front of the television with our laptops,
tablets and mobile phones all on the go at the same time?!

When the Apple Mac came along it opened up the art of publishing and,
as a result, print media boomed. Today the same thing is happening online,
through the phenomenon of user-generated content (UGC) and social
networking: ordinary people are becoming the directors, producers, editors
and distributors of their own media-rich content – the content that they,
their friends and the world want to see. But that is only the start.

Prime-time television audiences are falling, print media is coming under
increasing pressure to address dropping circulation figures – and while the
old school sits on the sidelines, bloated and slowly atrophying, digital media
has transformed itself into a finely tuned engine delivering more power,
opportunity and control than any other form of media could dream of.

In other words – it's time to follow the smart money!

Over the last 23 years I have had the absolute pleasure of working at the
coalface of this burgeoning and insistent new media. I have met lots of smart
people and spoken to literally hundreds of organizations with massively
diverse and challenging agendas. The one common factor was a hunger for
data and knowledge: anything that would give their particular brand that
elusive competitive edge.

When putting this book together I wanted to make it as informative and
practical as possible. Each chapter begins with a summary of its content,
so you can easily browse through the chapters and select the one that
addresses the topic you're interested in. I've purposely left out the jargon –
and where technical terms have been absolutely necessary I've supplied a
clear definition in the text, backed up by a complete glossary at the back of
the book that explains in plain English all of the terms that digital marketers
use. The result, I hope, is a book that is clear, informative and entertaining,
even for the complete digital novice.

The book has morphed since the first edition, which was published in
2009. Then the book was more focused on very basic techniques with
a lathering of common sense. I feel the second edition was quite similar
in many ways but succeeded in demonstrating more points of proof by
incorporating some really exciting and provocative case studies. In 2014
I finished the third edition and in doing so realized that I am no longer an
expert in digital marketing – Marshall McLuhan, the inspiration behind my
work, once famously said: 'I'm not here to explain, I am here to explore.'
This has been one of the most influential quotes governing not just this
edition but the previous three editions of *Understanding Digital Marketing*.

We cannot dwell for very long on what we don't know because it will become irrelevant or obscure – the best we can hope for is to gain an understanding and be able to apply that understanding to our everyday challenges.

The techniques were becoming so complex and technology was moving so fast that I had to pull together a group of real experts to help me provide you – the reader – with the best possible content. And now it is the fourth edition, or 4.0 (which sounds cooler) – so what's different?

Lots!

First there are a series of new chapters, some of which are included in the book and some are bonus chapters that will appear online only (at www.koganpage.com/understanding-digital-marketing):

- Exploration and explanation into programmatic: it has come of age and marketers need to understand what it means and how they can apply it to their advantage.

- Internet of things (IoT): I was tempted to run this piece in the last edition but wanted more case studies – now is the right time for this piece.

- Digital transformation: everyone is talking about it but what does it mean to marketers?

- Internationalization: digital marketers have always been interested in new geographical markets but the need to understand new customers is now paramount.

And of course a chapter on how marketers can optimize the customer and user experience – after all, this is the source of my earlier pontification (another P?!).

So you hold in your hands what marketers around the world have been crying out for: a book that shows you how to successfully use the internet to sell your products or services. It begins with the origins of the medium and takes you through the various disciplines of digital marketing campaigns. The book travels around the world collecting facts, figures, comment and opinion from acknowledged experts, brands and organizations in different fields, getting them to spill the beans on how the internet delivered the goods for them.

Aside from these pillars of purpose, I have also revisited every other chapter from the first three editions and ensured they are up to date and include valid, practical examples of digital marketing in action.

Writing a book about this subject has always been too great a challenge without adopting a collaborative approach. The book sets out to democratize the digital marketing knowledge that exists in the world. While I believe I have gone some way to achieving this objective, I now believe that the best path from here is to open up this challenge to digital marketers everywhere, to create a place where they can connect with one another, collaborate on all digital marketing-related subject matter and, ultimately, build knowledge and prosper as a result. Over the last three years, together with colleagues from all over the world, and a super team in London, I have been putting together a platform to achieve this objective and now invite you to get on board. Please visit www.gogadm.com and join the movement.

And remember... digital marketing is NOT dead... BAD digital marketing IS dead. Welcome to the book and welcome to a world where your customers expect to have a positive and rewarding experience!

Damian Ryan

ABOUT THE AUTHOR

Damian Ryan started writing about "advertising" at the age of 15. A career in media, journalism and publishing followed, until one day in 1993, while visiting Chicago, he first witnessed the internet. Convinced of its potential, he moved out of publishing and in 1996 established ICAN, the first digital advertising business of its kind. Ryan built and sold ICAN and then repeated the process with two other digital businesses, before embarking on a career in corporate finance in 2006.

Ryan combines his passion for digital with dealmaking – it's a unique perspective that sets him apart from other authors and financiers, while keeping him up to speed with the never-ending march of technology.

He started writing the 'digital marketing' series of books in 2007 (formerly with co-writer and friend Calvin Jones).

He lives in London with his partner Tamara, is father of twin daughters and can be contacted at **dryan@mediaventura.com** or **damian@gogadm.com** or via social media.

CONTRIBUTORS' BIOGRAPHIES

Anna-Marie Odubote, creative copywriter, Social Chain

Anna-Marie Odubote is a London-born, Manchester-based creative copywriter at Social Chain, Europe's largest social media marketing agency, with experience writing for everything from *Dazed and Confused* magazine to Coca-Cola billboard copy. At just 24 Anna-Marie has been a published writer for 15 years.

Anne Tulloch, marketer

A results-driven marketer with 15+ years' experience in developing marketing strategies for high-profile brands such as Virgin and BSkyB. Able to hit challenging business KPIs utilizing the full digital media mix alongside in-house online and on-air media. Taking ownership responsibilities of website platform strategy, optimization and reporting she enables end-to-end audience attraction, engagement and retention.

Bhavna Mistry

Bhavna came into PR via 20 years in journalism on titles including the *Guardian, Management Today, Design Week, Marketing* and *Campaign*. Her editorial talents and contacts, an eye for strategy, understanding the big picture and appreciating where PR fits in, are highly prized by clients across the marketing communications sector.

Bradley Nickel, direct response copywriter and digital content strategist

Bradley is a direct response copywriter and digital content strategist living in the United States. He helps million-dollar businesses to generate more leads and sales through the power of the written word.

Brandon Carter, content specialist, Outbrain

Brandon is a content specialist at Outbrain. He began his career as a staff journalist for the Maine weekly *The Coastal Journal* before moving to New York and joining the product licensing divisions of Peanuts Worldwide and Sesame Workshop.

Brian O'Kelley, co-founder and CEO, AppNexus

As co-founder, chief executive officer of AppNexus and chairman of the company's board of directors, Brian has more than a decade of leadership experience in the online advertising sector, including his tenure as chief technology officer (CTO) of Right Media (later sold to Yahoo! in 2007), where he led the creation and commercialization of

(Continues overleaf)

multiple real-time bidding technologies. This also includes the invention of the world's first online advertising exchange – the engine that powers and optimizes the real-time purchase and placement of digital advertising. Brian is an inventor of patents that enable AppNexus's technology to power innovative trading solutions and marketplaces for internet advertising. He has been an active investor in, and early-stage advisor to, start-up businesses such as Invite Media (acquired by Google in 2010), MediaMath, Dstillery and Solve Media. Brian is also a regular contributor to Forbes on technology-related topics, and among other honours he has been named in Crain's 40 Under 40, Adweek 50 and Silicon Alley 100 lists, and was recognized as an E&Y Entrepreneur of the Year in the New York region in 2012. Brian holds a BSE in computer science from Princeton University, where he is an active alumnus. He lives in New York City with his wife and daughter.

Bruce Clayton, co-founder, Optimus Performance Marketing

Bruce has extensive experience in both online and offline marketing, having worked in TV, radio and for online media owners before moving into affiliate marketing in 2003. Gaining experience with both general and specialist networks, Bruce joined forces with an industry-leading affiliate and founded Optimus Performance Marketing, a multi-award-winning company delivering performance management solutions and consultancy to a wide variety of clients. Bruce and his co-founder bring years of experience in delivering results for their client base. This focus on results since conception has been the cornerstone of their success, and the agency is now one of the leading performance marketing agencies in Europe.

Bryndis Sadler, marketing executive and office manager, GADM

Bryndis is a marketing executive and the office manager at GADM, implementing all outgoing communications and incoming engagement on behalf of GADM and its collaborators – via different marketing streams, social media channels and the GADM website. She also oversees the ongoing development of the website and membership packages. Alongside the event and strategy teams, she plays a part in curating all GADM events, content strands and helps to support the new business function of GADM to prospective clients. Bryndis can often be found exploring London for new places to eat and more books to buy when she hasn't finished any of the ones she already owns.

Chris Bishop, founder, 7thingsmedia

Chris founded 7thingsmedia in 2009 and is responsible for the overall strategy and direction of the global business. He is the creative vision behind the agency and regularly gets involved in client strategy and development.

7thingsmedia clients boast global superbrands such as Graziashop.com, kate spade new york, NET-A-PORTER and TK Maxx. 7thingsmedia's services include strategic digital consultancy and media planning and buying across affiliates, display, lead generation, mobile, pay per click, search engine optimization and social media.

Chris holds a plethora of accolades acknowledging his contribution to marketing, including the prestigious title of 'Marketer of the Year' from *The Drum Magazine* plus places in VOGUE.com's 100 Most Influential People in Fashion and BIMA's Digital Hot 100.

Craig Brown, senior account manager at NMPi

Having joined NMPi in July 2013, following his studies in genetics at Newcastle University, Craig has moved through the ranks to senior account manager. A passionate, driven and innovative individual, Craig leads the team to ensure accounts are market leading, proved in the shortlisting of a client in 2015 for the retail award at the Performance Marketing Awards, and his nomination at the European Search awards for Young Search Professional of the Year.

Dale Lovell, chief digital officer, Adyoulike

Dale is chief digital officer at Adyoulike, Europe's leading native advertising technology platform. Based in London, Dale has worked in online journalism, digital publishing, content strategy and creative content marketing for over 15 years. Previously as a journalist, he had contributed to over 50 leading publications, and was listed as a BIMA Hot 100, alongside Adyoulike UK MD Francis Turner, in recognition as a digital leader striving to push the industry forward. He sits on the IAB UK's Content and Native Council and is a regular commentator in the digital marketing industry press in the UK.

David Harvey, co-founder, Altair Media

David's career has spanned TV, press and digital media, with the last eight years specializing in digital media. Voted as one of *The Drum*'s Top 100 most influential people in digital, one of the crowning moments of David's digital career was winning the Marketing Engage Award for Automotive, beating multimillion campaigns with a very modest budget. Having sat on the board of agenda21, David moved to the Publicis-owned Razorfish where he headed up the media department across EMEA, after which he set up Altair Media, delivering on the promise that all clients deserve amazing work.

Epiphany

A Jaywing agency full of creative, talented individuals who connect powerful ideas, rich data and new technologies. Epiphany creates high-performance campaigns for its clients

that change their businesses and meet the needs of their consumers online. They understand the importance of useful content, great user experience, clean code, platform choice and targeting people by extracting the maximum value from clients' paid, owned and earned channels. Founded as a search specialist in 2005, Epiphany helps clients to create successful digital marketing through the use of search engine optimization, pay per click, display, content, conversion rate optimization and website development.

FCB Chicago

FCB is the oldest and newest advertising agency in Chicago. Founded in 1873 as Lord & Thomas and reintroduced as Foote, Cone and Belding, they create big transformative ideas that drive change. With over 700 employees, they have an entrepreneurial spirit, with scale and best-in-class capabilities all under one roof.

Fiona Morrissey, events and marketing manager, GADM

Fiona manages all of GADM's events and marketing, including sector, skill, private members session and bespoke. From organizing logistics to guaranteeing the audience, she works alongside clients to ensure that the content fits the correct message. Fiona has been working in the marketing industry for six years and achieved a first-class BA Honours in business and marketing.

A results-orientated, high-energy, marketing and events professional, Fiona enjoys a challenge and exploring new possibilities at every opportunity.

Fran Cowan, marketing director, InSkin Media

Fran is responsible for driving InSkin Media's brand development, product marketing, internal and external communications, and events programme across its global operations. Fran joined the company in 2012 as marketing and communications manager. She was previously marketing manager at Specific Media, and a founding marketer at MySpace International.

Greig Holbrook, founder, Oban Digital

International digital marketing and the importance of cultural intelligence are at the core of Oban Digital, the specialist agency that Greig founded in 2002. Greig's passion lies in helping businesses to realize the full global potential of the web and e-commerce. He regularly speaks on the subject at events and contributes to media debate. Greig has worked with a number of forward-thinking brands including Dell, BBC World Service, Etsy, AXA PPP, Rapha and De Beers.

Iolo Jones, CEO, TV Everywhere

Iolo has degrees in radio, film and television and educational broadcasting and started his career as a technician in the film and TV industries. He went on to work for major ad agencies and formed his first multimedia company in the 1990s. He founded early webcaster Web Channels, and then early stage cloud TV

company Narrowstep, which he took public on the NASDAQ market. For the past decade, Iolo has been the CEO of TV Everywhere and the chair of rights management software company Rights Tracker. Iolo also sat on the course board for leading film and TV college Ravensbourne. He runs a popular industry blog at http://www.iptvtimes.net.

James Bailey, UX consultant, internet of things

James is a UX consultant with a passion for user-centred design, leading projects that include the internet of things (IoT), websites, mobile, TV, print and events. James has experience working in a range of sectors such as local and global, B2B and B2C. He has developed a framework for the IoT, which applies user-centred design to the creation of connected products and services. James also gives talks around the UK and leads IoT research projects.

Jeff Ortegon, creative director, Undertone

Jeff Ortegon is the creative director at Undertone, where he leads the PIXL Studios creative team. Obsessed with challenges, he works day-to-day on curating and executing ideas in order to refine and improve them. Jeff has a passion for bringing ideas to life in surprising, innovative and, ultimately, effective ways that move people to feel differently and act accordingly. Prior to joining Undertone, Jeff held several positions at world-class creative agencies including MRY and

mcgrarrybowen, where he created on-brand, on-strategy compelling creative for many Fortune 500 brands.

Jessica Stephens, CMO, SmartFocus

Jess is a 2x entrepreneur and digital marketer with a focus on e-mail and mobile technologies as well as a near-obsessive preoccupation with data and the stories data can tell. E-mail and mobile have been at the core of Jess's career. For more than a decade she has been involved in everything from client-side programme delivery, to vendor-side product development. Jess's most recent

start-up was proximity marketing platform TagPoints, which she sold to SmartFocus, gaining the role of CMO of the acquiring company in the process. Jess has experience of both the bootstrap start-up world and corporate marketing for FTSE 100 brands.

Jo Sensini, founder, Velvet

Jo founded Velvet in 2003, after a career that spanned banking, management training and senior roles at PR agencies including Leedex, The Rowland Company and Republic, with roles in France, Italy and Japan.

Jocelyn Le Conte, PPC team leader, Periscopix

A PPC team leader at Periscopix, a Merkle Company, Jocelyn oversees a range of clients of all sizes from a wide range of sectors, directing paid search, social and display strategies for brands such as Tesco and OVO Energy. Knowing pay-per-click platforms – such as Google AdWords, Bing Ads and DoubleClick Search – inside out, and working closely with providers to test out new features before they are released to the public, she is a performance marketer at the  forefront of the industry and a member of Google's Channel Partner programme, providing training and support for companies who wish to utilize any of the DoubleClick Digital Marketing products.

Jon Dodd, co-founder, Bunnyfoot

Jon holds a DPhil in visual and computational neuroscience from Oxford University. As an academic he researched – amongst other things – how you and your brain judge attractiveness, discern the shapes of shampoo bottles, and make decisions when shown visual illusions (he can also tell you a thing or two about how faces indicate age, gender and trustworthiness and why caricatures work so well). Shortly after this, he  escaped the cosy confines of academia and co-founded Bunnyfoot. The premise was (and still is) to help people to create great experiences by applying the brainy bits from science and psychology, along with best practice and techniques from disciplines such as usability, human–computer interaction, ergonomics and user-centred design.

Kerry Gaffney, global director of communication and community, MOFILM

Kerry is the global director of communication and community for MOFILM, a people-powered marketing agency and part of the world's first Brandtech company, You and Mr Jones. MOFILM connects emerging film and creative talent from around the world to big brands to create award-winning content. A disruptive model based on the tenets of crowdsourcing, it provides video content strategy, production and distribution for brands such as Coca-Cola, PlayStation, Airbnb and Netflix.

Kerry is a digital marketing specialist and leads the company's digital and traditional marketing programmes. She manages a geographically dispersed team to deliver an unfailing positive experience for MOFILM's creator community.

Before joining MOFILM, Kerry helped to establish the Porter Novelli global digital team, with the remit to make every public relations practitioner in business intrinsically digital. As well as developing new digital products, Kerry created and delivered digital training, both in-house and to clients. She worked with a broad spectrum of businesses including The Royal Mint, BT, HP, Braun, AstraZeneca and Procter & Gamble on a range of local, regional and global digital initiatives.

Kevin Gibbons, managing director, BlueGlass

Kevin Gibbons is the managing director of BlueGlass, a digital marketing agency specializing in search engine optimization and content marketing. With offices in London, Zurich and Tallinn, BlueGlass helps clients such as Expedia, Totaljobs and the *Financial Times* by acting as an extension to their digital teams, in order to achieve the very best content marketing results.

Laura Taylor Burge, senior data scientist, Marketing Metrix

A senior data scientist, Laura has an in-depth knowledge of a wide range of statistical methods and coding languages. As well as specializing in intelligent data manipulation and data-driven strategy, she also enjoys writing thought-provoking white papers on mathematical processes, technological initiatives and recent market issues. Laura has worked for Marketing Metrix for five years, applying her skills to deliver unique requirements for a range of business and consumer brands such as the Financial Conduct Authority, Which? and the Samaritans. She continues to provide Marketing Metrix's clients with the evidence-based insight that drives business forwards.

Lyndsey Best, co-founder, Altair Media

Lyndsey is a pure digital expert, having spent over 13 years working for some of the best digital agencies in the world. She has been recognized and awarded as one of the best in the industry on numerous occasions including *The Drum* Digerati Top 100 Most Influential Digital Marketers, *Media Week* and *The Drum* 30 under 30; she was shortlisted for the Revolution Digital Rising Star and was voted as one of the Top 10 digital planners by *Campaign*. Lyndsey was appointed to the board of agenda21 at just 27 years of age, and set up Altair Media in 2014, in response to the demand from clients for an independent and transparent digital agency partner.

Martin Doyle, CEO and founder, DQ Global

Martin is CEO and founder of DQ Global, a data-quality software company based in the UK. With an engineering background, Martin previously ran a CRM software business. He has gained a wealth of knowledge and experience over the years and has established himself as a data quality improvement evangelist and an industry expert.

Matt Brocklehurst, platforms marketing lead APAC, Google

Matt is the platforms marketing lead APAC at Google, previously being the UK product marketing lead for search and mobile. He has also worked for Yahoo!, leading the EMEA marketing team and has held senior management positions at AdMob, Latitude Search Marketing, Thomson Reuters, *Financial Times* and Euromonitor. Connect on Twitter @brocklehurst.

Meriem Nacer, head of paid search, VisualSoft

Meriem has spent over six years within paid search, her love for numbers and Excel has continued to be an asset throughout the ever-changing market. Working with some fantastic brands across a wide variety of industries, from global high-street fashion brands to finance, entertainment and charities has allowed her to continue to develop the skills to further her career to become head of paid search at VisualSoft.

MullenLowe

MullenLowe is a creatively driven integrated marketing communications network with a strong entrepreneurial heritage and challenger mentality, operating in more than 65 markets. They work with some of the world's most innovative market- ers: clients who always think like challengers. Whether it is defying category norms, breaking

conventions, talking to an audience in a new way or across new channels, or whether it is changing behaviours through innovation, doing something that has never been done before or even challenging the client's brief – this way of thinking helps them to reach their most creative, exciting and effective work.

Nick Fettiplace and Jonathan Verrall, head of earned media and associate SEO director, Jellyfish

Nick Fettiplace is the head of earned media at Jellyfish Digital Marketing Agency, heading up a team of search engine optimization (SEO), social and content marketing practitioners across the UK, United States and South Africa. With over 10 years of experience within organic search, he is a regular contributor to industry publications and is an active public speaker at training, roundtable and thought leadership events.

Jonathan Verrall is an associate SEO director at Jellyfish with a specialism within technical search engine optimization. He leads search campaigns for large global brands across the globe and is integral in maintaining standards across the business's organic offering.

Ogilvy & Mather

In 1948, David Ogilvy founded the agency that would become Ogilvy & Mather. Starting with no clients and a staff of two, he built his company into one of the eight largest advertising networks in the world. Today it has more than 450 offices in 169 cities.

Its history is the evolution of one man's thoughts, talents and work ethic translated into a company culture, a defining business strategy, a destiny.

Pete Campbell, managing director, Kaizen

Pete Campbell is the managing director of Kaizen. They have worked with global brands including River Island, Symantec and 888.com on innovative search engine optimization (SEO) and content marketing campaigns. Pete built his first website at age 11, pretends not to be totally addicted to video games and is a regular speaker at digital marketing conferences, including SMX, BrightonSEO and SEMDays. He also received a Travolution award for 'Rising Star of the Year' for his SEO work on travel brands.

Phillippa Gamse, professor of digital marketing and social media, Hult International Business School

Phillippa Gamse, CMC is a digital marketing strategist with over 25 years' experience, and the author of *42 Rules for a Web Presence That Wins*. She is professor of digital marketing and social media at Hult International Business School.

Remon Pepers, CTO and shareholder, Targetoo

Remon Pepers is chief technology officer (CTO) and a shareholder at Targetoo. He has seven years' experience in the advertisement business, the last two of which are related to mobile advertisement. He is delighted to have made the right decision to join this mobile advertisement movement, which he considers a great step forward in advertising technology. Remon's beliefs are that with the right people next to you and with the right attitude you can reach any goal you have in mind, which is further reflected at Targetoo. Targetoo's aim is to create and sustain a dynamic and enthusiastic team, and establishing a positive attitude. Targetoo's ethos is to look far beyond their own success and well-being, believing the true power lies in making the client happy.

Ricky Wallace, marketing manager, ClearPeople

Ricky is marketing manager for ClearPeople, an award-winning Consultagency™. He is responsible for creating, developing and implementing the delivery of ClearPeople's marketing strategy and working with in-house designers, developers and clients to improve the customer experience with brands. Ricky has over 11 years' experience in marketing, having started his career at the global advertising agency JWT. He has a first-class degree in media and advertising, and recently completed the IDM postgraduate diploma in direct and digital marketing, keeping abreast of the latest challenges and opportunities in digital marketing.

Rob Welsby, director of search and insight, Further

Rob is director of search and insight at award-winning independent search agency Further, heading up the data analytics, conversion and search side of the business. In his 15 years in digital marketing Rob has worked on effective strategy and campaigns for such brands as AVG, Expedia, Beko, Aetna and Mazda. He is passionate about digital marketing, which certainly helps when it comes to keeping up with the pace of change by Google, and the latest online marketing trends. When not reading search and social marketing blogs, travelling to speak at conferences or client workshops, you can find him riding his Kona mountain bike on whatever hills he can find in Norfolk, or enjoying a decent Dark 'n' Stormy at the nearest pub.

Roy Graff, author, *China, the Future of Travel*

Roy Graff is an 'old China hand' with over 20 years of experience working in and with China in the tourism, hospitality, luxury retail and digital marketing sectors. Based in London, Roy heads Digital Jungle's UK and European business, offering full-service digital marketing support for the Chinese audience. He is author of the book *China, the Future of Travel* (2015) (www.chinafutureof travel.com). Roy has held senior management and director roles at multinational travel companies (wholesale/retail and online) in business development, marketing, sales, distribution and product development. Since 2005 he has delivered strategic advice, business development, market research, marketing and distribution services to a range of travel, hospitality, luxury retail and transportation companies as well as government organizations. Among them: VisitBritain, UKinbound, Eurostar, Tourism Ireland, PromPeru, Ghana Tourism Board, Peninsula Hotels and Resorts, CitizenM Hotels, Skyscanner, Bulgari Hotel London, Gemfields PLC, Lastminute.com, OKtogo, Viator, G Adventures, ELLE Magazine, and many others.

Simon Kingsnorth, digital marketing leader and author of *Digital Marketing Strategy* (Kogan Page)

Simon Kingsnorth is a digital marketing leader and author of the book *Digital Marketing Strategy*, published by Kogan Page in 2016. He has built digital strategies for many leading organizations and led teams at large multinationals and start-ups. He has also consulted to businesses globally and specializes in all areas of digital including search engine optimization, content  strategy, pay per click, user experience, social media, analytics, e-mail and affiliate marketing.

Stephanie Ryan, senior writer, We Are Social

Stephanie Ryan is a digital content creator and writer with a passion for social. Stephanie is experienced in social media content strategy, copywriting, design, research and project management. As a senior writer at We Are Social, Stephanie works with clients including Netflix and First Direct, helping create compelling content that people actually want to read. She  was previously a content and community manager at We Are Social in Sydney, working across a number of global and local brands.

Steve Waite, managing director, Americas GlobalSign Inc

Steve Waite is CEO for GlobalSign's North and South American operations. Steve is also one of the founding board members for the GlobalSign group of companies. He is responsible for GlobalSign's enterprise and channel strategy, commercial direction, technology vision
and execution of product strategy throughout the North and South American region. Prior to joining GlobalSign Steve was the co-founder of the European arm of GeoTrust Inc, RapidSSL.com, and a key strategist for launching the GeoTrust brands into Europe, where he established the brand recognition and value proposition that helped catapult GeoTrust into number one SSL provider positions in a number of European countries, prior to GeoTrust being acquired by VeriSign.

Steve Walker, head of SEO, STEAK

Steve has worked in the search engine optimization (SEO) industry for over six years, spanning numerous roles across both technical and content disciplines, and during his career having the opportunity to work with brands such as JD Sports, Beagle Street, Kwik Fit Insurance Services and G4S. Using his background in strategic marketing and strong technical know-how, Steve has been able to continually develop STEAK's SEO offering during his tenure as head of SEO, resulting in award-winning SEO campaigns and increased client growth. When offline, Steve enjoys
keeping fit with Muay Thai training and is an avid movie fan.

Steven Woodgate, marketing, Microsoft

Steven works in marketing at Microsoft. A communicator at heart with a creative PR mind in a marketing and advertising world, and a developing leader in trying to bring storytelling and 'story-doing' to marketing, PR and advertising campaigns, Steven is also a part of Marketing Academy Alumni programme, after being a scholar in 2014, and selected as one of '70 Rising Social Media Stars' in a global survey. He is also a mentor for We Are Squared, as well as being a member of the Digital Action Group for ISBA and a judge for DMA.

Trenton Moss, founder, Webcredible

Trenton started Webcredible with no money, no office, no clients, no contacts... but a lot of drive and determination to help brands sort out their customers' digital experiences. He's a recognized pioneer and industry leader in customer and user experience. As CEO, he is responsible for leading and driving forward Webcredible's three-year plan. He is also ultimately responsible for company revenue targets and Webcredible's short-, medium- and long-term commercial activities, as well as maintaining its unique culture of collaboration, trust and empowerment.

ACKNOWLEDGEMENTS

My thanks to Charlotte, Jenny, Helen, Sonya, Mark and all the team at Kogan Page – we've produced seven books in nine years now. I won't say it gets easier with time but there is no way any of this would happen without your support and guidance.

Thanks to the GADM team and in particular Stacey Riley who spent many hours editing contributions, harvesting case studies and listening to my rants over the last six months. Special thanks to Fiona Morrissey and Bryndis Sadler, Simon Fitchett, Dennis Hobbs, Nigel Paul, Martin Scovell, Barry Flaherty and David Williams (super photographer) too.

Thanks to my business partners and collaborators; Howard Block in particular. To all the contributors – thanks so much. There is no way this book could be produced without the expert input of more than 60 of you in this single edition. Your details are included earlier in these preliminary pages of the book but I am so honoured to have worked with you on this, thank you once again. Big shout out to James Jones, Graham Wylie and Josh Zeitz of AppNexus, and Steve Waite, Paul Tourret and Christian Simko of GlobalSign.

And, finally, no piece of work gets published without special mention and thanks to the three most important ladies in my life: Tamara Jane Williams for your love and support but also for pushing me along the path when I needed it… Alannah and Katie, my lovely daughters, soon to be turning 13 and writing about far more interesting topics than digital marketing!

Damian Ryan
damian@gogadm.com

For Dad
Our north our south our east and our west
1933–2015

Digital marketing... the origin of...

01

OUR CHAPTER PLEDGE TO YOU

When you reach the end of this chapter you will have answers to the following questions:

- How did we reach the dawn of a digital age in marketing?
- What are the similarities between the internet and historical global communications revolutions?
- How many people are on the internet and how quickly is it growing?
- How is digital technology influencing consumer behaviour?

In the beginning...

Once upon a time, etched on a dusty curbstone amidst the ruins of the ancient Roman city of Pompeii, you'll find an engraved penis, strategically carved to point the way to what, at the time, was one of the most popular brothels in the area. Guides will tell you it is the 'oldest advertisement in the world, for the oldest business in the world'. While the truth of that claim is debatable, the phallic ad is certainly very old.

The Pompeii penis was buried by the eruption of Mount Vesuvius, which destroyed the city on 24 August AD 79, but the true origins of marketing go back much further than that. Although, according to business historians, marketing as a discrete business discipline was not born until the 1950s, marketing activities have played a fundamental role in the success of businesses from, well, the very first business. There are few certainties in the world of business, but one thing is for sure: if you don't let customers know about your business, you won't stay in business for very long.

But this is a book about marketing in the digital age – the present and the future

That is true. We're here to talk about the exciting world of digital marketing as it has emerged from relative obscurity in the late 1990s into the mainstream of business in 2016. We are going to look at how businesses just like yours can harness the power of this online revolution to connect with a new wave of consumers: consumers who take this pervasive technology and integrate it seamlessly into their everyday lives in ways we could never have conceived of as recently as a decade ago.

This book is about the future of marketing. So why are we starting by looking backwards? In the 1960s classic *Understanding Media: The extensions of man*, Canadian communications theorist and philosopher Marshall McLuhan noted: 'It is instructive to follow the embryonic stages of any new growth, for during this period of development it is much misunderstood, whether it be printing or the motor car or TV.' As is so often the case, having a basic grasp of the past can help our understanding of the present, and ultimately illuminate our view of the future.

So buckle your seatbelt as we take a whistle-stop tour of how marketing has evolved over the years, and how advertising and technology have converged to define a new marketing landscape that has changed the world of marketing in the last 20 years and will continue to do so in the years ahead.

The changing face of advertising

Advertising can be intoxicating. The spin, the story, the message, the call to action, the image, the placement, the measurement, the refinement – it all adds up to a powerful cocktail that can ultimately change the world. At its core, advertising is all about influencing people – persuading them to take the actions we want, whether that is choosing a particular brand of toothpaste, picking up the phone, filling in a mailing coupon, downloading an app or visiting a website. Done well, the power of advertising can achieve amazing things, and if you are in business you're already doing it, and will continue to do so.

Advertising through the ages

Advertising, an essential component in the marketing of any business, has been around for a long time. The Pompeii penis is positively modern compared to some of the advertising relics that archaeologists have unearthed in ancient Arabia, China, Egypt, Greece and Rome. The Egyptians used papyrus to create posters and flyers, while lost-and-found advertising (also on papyrus, and often relating to 'missing' slaves) was common in both ancient Greece and Rome. Posters, signs and flyers were widely employed in the ancient cities of Rome, Pompeii and Carthage to publicize events such as circuses, games and gladiatorial contests.

People have been trying to influence other people since the dawn of human existence, utilizing whatever means and media they had at their disposal at the time. The human voice and word of mouth, of course, came first. Then someone picked up a piece of stone and started etching images on a cave wall: enduring images that told stories, communicated ideas and promoted certain ways of doing things.

The first advertising? That is debatable, but these images, some of which are around to this day, certainly demonstrate an early recognition of the power of images and messages to influence the perception and behaviour of others.

The development of printing during the 15th and 16th centuries heralded a significant milestone in advertising, making it more cost-effective for marketers to reach a much wider audience. In the 17th century, adverts began to appear in early newspapers in England, and then spread across the globe. The first form of mass-media advertising was born.

The 18th and 19th centuries saw a further expansion in newspaper advertising, and alongside it the birth of mail-order advertising, which would evolve into the massive direct mail/direct response industry that has been utterly disrupted by the internet but still exists today. It also saw the establishment of the first advertising agency, set up in Philadelphia in 1843 by the pioneering Volney Palmer. Initially ad agencies acted as simple brokers for newspaper space, but before long they developed into full-service operations, offering their clients a suite of creative and ad-placement services.

The 20th century saw the dawn of another new advertising age, with the advent of radio offering a completely new medium through which advertisers could reach out to prospective customers. Then came television, which shifted the advertising landscape yet again, and towards the end of the century a new force – the internet – began moving out of the realm of 'techies' and early adopters to become a valuable business and communication tool for the masses. The era of digital marketing was born.

Technological advances have punctuated the evolution of advertising throughout history, each fundamentally altering the way that businesses could communicate with their customers. Interestingly, however, none of these groundbreaking developments superseded those that came before.

Rather they served to augment them, offering marketers more diversity, allowing them to connect with a broader cross-section of consumers. In today's sophisticated age of paid search placement, keyword-targeted pay-per-click advertising and social media, you will still find the earliest forms of advertising alive and well.

Stroll through any market, practically anywhere in the world – from the food markets of central London to the bazaars of North Africa, to the street markets of India – and you will be greeted by a cacophony of noise as vendors use their voices to vie for the attention of passing customers. The human voice, the first marketing medium in history, is still going strong in the digital age. And if you get as far as the final chapter in this book, you will read why I think 'voice' is about to make a massive resurgence in the years ahead.

The technology behind digital marketing

As I have already mentioned, developments in technology and the evolution of marketing are inextricably intertwined. Technology has underpinned major milestones in the history of marketing since its inception. The process tends to go something like this:

- New technology emerges and is initially the preserve of technologists and early adopters.
- The technology gains a firmer foothold in the market and starts to become more popular, putting it on the marketing radar.
- Innovative marketers jump in to explore ways that they can harness the power of this emerging technology to connect with their target audience.
- The technology migrates to the mainstream and is adopted into standard marketing practice.

The printing press, radio, television and now the internet are all examples of major breakthroughs in technology that ultimately altered forever the relationships between marketers and consumers, and did so on a global scale. But of course marketing is not about technology, it is about people: technology is only interesting, from a marketing perspective, when it connects people with other people more effectively.

There are plenty of examples of technology through the ages having a significant impact on various markets – technology that may seem obscure, even irrelevant today. How about Muzak – the company that brought elevator music to the masses back in the 1930s? The technology for piping audio over power lines was patented in 1922 by retired Major General George O Squier, and exclusive rights to the patent were bought by the North American Company. In 1934, under the corporate umbrella of 'Muzak', they started piping music into Cleveland homes.

Muzak seemed to have hit on a winning formula, but the advent of free commercial radio sounded the death knell for the company's chosen route to market. With free music available on shiny new wirelesses, households were no longer prepared to pay for the Muzak service. Undeterred, the company focused its efforts on New York City businesses. As buildings in New York soared skywards, the lift/elevator became practically ubiquitous. Muzak had found its niche, and 'elevator music' was born.

You might think 'So what?'

It is true that, compared to behemoths of contemporary media such as radio, television and now the internet, elevator music is small potatoes. But back in its heyday this was cutting-edge stuff, and it reached a lot of people. Muzak had the power to sway opinions and influence markets – so much so that, for music artists of that era, having your track played on the Muzak network practically guaranteed a hit.

The point is that technology has the ability to open up completely new markets, and to radically shake up existing ones. The mainstream adoption of digital technology – the internet, the software applications that run on it, and the devices that allow people to connect to both the network and each other whenever, wherever and however they want to – promises to dwarf all that has come before it. It heralds the single most disruptive development in the history of marketing.

Whether that disruption represents an opportunity or a threat to you as a marketer depends largely on your perspective. I hope the fact that you are reading this book means that you see it as an opportunity.

Note to reader

Check out McLuhan's 'tetrade of media effects' – it's a great sanity check for all new media.

https://en.wikipedia.org/wiki/Tetrad_of_media_effects

The first global communications network: 'the highway of thought'

To understand the explosive growth of the internet we need to look back at how early communications technology evolved into the global network of interconnected computers that today we call the internet. The story of electronic communication begins with the wired telegraph – a network that grew rapidly to cover the globe, connecting people across vast distances in a way that seemed almost magical, and changed the world forever.

Tom Standage, in his book *The Victorian Internet* (1998), looks at the wired telegraph and draws some astonishing parallels between the growth of the world's first electronic communications network and the growth of the modern-day internet. Standage describes the origins of the telegraph, and the quest to deliver information from point to point more rapidly in the days when speedy communication relied on a fast horse and a skilled rider:

> On an April day in 1746 at the grand convent of the Carthusians in Paris about 200 monks arranged themselves in a long, snaking line. Each monk held one end of a 25-foot iron wire in each hand, connecting him to his neighbour on either side. Together the monks and their connecting wires formed a line over a mile long. Once the line was complete the abbot, Jean-Antoine Nollet, a noted French scientist, took a primitive battery and, without warning, connected it to the line of monks – giving all of them a powerful electric shock.

These 'electric monks' demonstrated conclusively that electricity could transmit a message (albeit a painful one) from one location to another in an instant, and laid the foundation for a communications revolution.

In 1830 Joseph Henry (1797–1878), an eminent US scientist who went on to become the first Director of the Smithsonian Institute, took the concept a step further. He demonstrated the potential of the electromagnet for long-distance communications when he passed an electric current through a mile-long cable to ring an electromagnetic bell connected to the other end. Samuel Morse (1791–1872), the inventor of Morse code, took Henry's concept a step further and made a commercial success of it: the electronic telegraph was born.

In 1842 Morse demonstrated a working telegraph between two committee rooms in Washington, and congress voted slimly in favour of investing US $30,000 for an experimental telegraph line between Washington and Baltimore. It was a very close call: 89 votes for the prototype, 83 against and 70 abstentions by congressmen looking 'to avoid the responsibility of spending the public money for a machine they could not understand'.

Despite the reservations of the congressmen, the new network was a huge success. It grew at a phenomenal rate: by 1850 there were more than 12,000 miles of telegraph line criss-crossing the United States, two years later there was more than twice that, and the network of connected wires was spreading rapidly around the globe.

This spellbinding new network delivered news in moments rather than the weeks and months people were used to. It connected people over vast distances in ways previously inconceivable, and to many remained completely incomprehensible.

Governments tried and failed to control this raw new communications medium. Its advocates hailed it as revolutionary, and its popularity grew at an unprecedented rate. Newspapers began publishing news just hours rather than weeks after the event, romance blossomed over the wires, couples were married 'online', gamblers used the new network to 'cheat' on the horses, and it transformed the way that business was conducted around the world. In the space of a generation, the telegraph literally altered the fabric of society.

Does any of this sound familiar…?

A *New York Times* article published on Wednesday 14 September 1852 describes the telegraph network as 'the highway of thought'; not much of a stretch from the 'information superhighway' label that we apply to our modern-day revolutionary network. If anything, the communications revolution instigated by the telegraph must have represented more of a cultural upheaval than the explosive growth of the internet today.

For the first time, people grasped that they could communicate almost instantly across continents and even oceans. They felt a sense of closeness, a togetherness that simply had not been possible before. The telegraph system was hailed by some as a harbinger of peace and solidarity: a network of wires that would ultimately bind countries, creeds and cultures in a way hitherto unimaginable. Others, of course, used the network to wage war more efficiently. The sheer expansion of ideas and dreams that ensued must have been truly staggering, the opportunities and potential for change bewildering.

For rapid, long-distance communications the telegraph remained the only game in town until 1877, when two rival inventors battled to be the first to patent another new technology set to turn the world of electronic communications on its head. Its name, the telephone; the inventors, Elisha Gray and Alexander Graham Bell. They submitted their patent applications within hours of one another – but Bell pipped Gray to the post, and a now famous legal battle ensued.

The first words ever transmitted into a telephone were uttered by Bell, speaking to his research assistant, Thomas Watson, in the next room. He simply said: 'Mr Watson – come here – I want to see you.'

Early networks

The internet story really starts in 1957, with the USSR's launch of the sputnik satellite. It signalled that the United States was falling behind the Russians in the technology stakes, prompting the US government to invest heavily in science and technology. In 1958, the US Department of Defense set up the Advanced Research Projects Agency (ARPA) – a specialist agency established with a specific remit: making sure the United States stayed ahead of its Cold War nemesis in the accelerating technology race.

In August 1962 a computer scientist, Joseph Carl Robnett Licklider (1915–90), vice president at technology company Bolt Beranek and Newman, wrote a series of memos discussing the concept of an 'intergalactic computer network'. Licklider's revolutionary ideas, amazingly, encompassed practically everything that the internet has today become.

In October 1963, Licklider was appointed head of the Behavioral Sciences and Command and Control programmes at ARPA. During his two-year tenure he convinced the agency of the importance of developing computer networks, and although he left ARPA before work on his theories began, the seed for the Advanced Research Projects Agency Network (ARPANET) – the precursor to the internet – had been sown.

In 1965 researchers hooked up a computer at Massachusetts Institute of Technology's (MIT) Lincoln Lab with a US Air Force computer in California. For the first time, two computers communicated with each other using 'packet'-based information transmitted over a network.

ARPA (since renamed Defense Advanced Research Projects Agency (DARPA) – www.darpa.mil) started the ARPANET project in 1966, claiming that it would allow the powerful computers owned by the government, universities and research institutions around the United States to communicate with one another and to share valuable computing resources. IBM and other large computer companies at the time were sceptical, reportedly claiming that the network proposed by ARPA could not be built.

ARPA ploughed on, and on 21 November 1969 the first two computers were connected to the fledgling ARPANET, one at University of California, Los Angeles, the other at Stanford Research Institute. By 5 December the same year, the network doubled in size as they were joined by two other computers: one at University of California, Santa Barbara, the other at University of Utah's graphics department. The new network grew quickly. By 1971, 15 US institutions were connected to ARPANET, and by 1974 the number had grown to 46, and had spread to include overseas nodes in Hawaii, Norway and London.

You've got mail

E-mail, which is still often described as the internet's 'killer application', began life in the early 1960s as a facility that allowed users of mainframe computers to send simple text-based messages to another user's mailbox on the same computer. But it wasn't until the advent of ARPANET that anyone considered sending electronic mail from one user to another across a network.

In 1971 Ray Tomlinson, an engineer working on ARPANET, wrote the first program capable of sending mail from a user on one host computer to another user's mailbox on another host computer. As an identifier to distinguish network mail from local mail Tomlinson decided to append the host name of the user's computer to their user login name. To separate the two names he chose the @ symbol.

'I am frequently asked why I chose the "at" sign, but the at sign just makes sense,' writes Tomlinson on his website. 'The purpose of the at sign (in English) was to indicate a unit price (for example, 10 items @ US $1.95). I used the at sign to indicate that the user was "at" some other host rather than being local.'

E-mail, one of the internet's most widely used applications – and one of the most critical for internet marketers – began life as a programmer's afterthought. Tomlinson created e-mail because he thought it 'seemed like a neat idea' at the time: 'There was no directive to "go forth and invent e-mail". The ARPANET was a solution looking for a problem. A colleague suggested that I not tell my boss what I had done because e-mail wasn't in our statement of work.'

From ARPANET to internet

The term 'internet' was first used in 1974 by US computer scientist Vint Cerf (commonly referred to as one of the 'fathers of the internet', and now a senior executive and internet evangelist with Google). Cerf was working with Robert Khan at DARPA on a way to standardize the way that different host computers communicated across both the growing ARPANET and between the ARPANET and other emerging computer networks. The transmission control program (TCP) network protocol they defined evolved to become the TCP/IP (transmission control program/internet) protocol suit that is still used to this day to pass packets of information backwards and forwards across the internet.

In 1983 the ARPANET started using the TCP/IP protocol – a move that many consider to signal the true 'birth' of the internet as we know it. That year, too, the system of domain names (.com, .net, etc) was invented. By 1984 the number of 'nodes' on the still fledgling network passed 1,000 and began climbing rapidly. By 1989 there were more than 100,000 hosts connected to the internet, and the growth continued.

Making connections – birth of the web

It was in 1989 that Tim Berners-Lee, a British developer working at CERN (the European Organization for Nuclear Research) in Geneva, proposed a system of information cross-referencing, access and retrieval across the rapidly growing internet, based on 'hypertext' links. The concept of a hypertext information architecture was nothing new, and was already being used in individual programs running on individual computers around the world. The idea of linking documents stored on different computers across the rapidly growing internet, though, was nothing short of revolutionary.

The building blocks for the world wide web were already in place – but it was Tim Berners-Lee's vision that brought them together. 'I just had to take the hypertext idea and connect it to the TCP and domain name system (DNS) ideas and – ta-da! – the world wide web,' Berners-Lee comments on the W3C (World Wide Web Consortium) website.

The first web page on the internet was built at CERN, and went online on 6 August 1991. It contained information about the new world wide web, how to get a web browser and how to set up a web server. Over time it also became the first-ever web directory, as Berners-Lee maintained a list of links to other websites on the page as they appeared.

The wild wide web – a new frontier

Up to this point, the internet had been the realm of technologists and scientists at research institutions. But the advent of the web changed the landscape, making online information accessible to a much broader audience. What happened next was explosive. Between 1991 and 1997 the web grew at an astonishing 850 per cent per annum, eclipsing all expectations. With more websites and more people joining the online party every day, it was only a matter of time before innovative tech-savvy marketers started to notice the web's potential as an avenue for the marketing message.

The mid-1990s saw an explosion in new online ventures as pioneering entrepreneurs, grasping the burgeoning potential of this exciting new medium, scrambled to stake their claim on this virtual new frontier. In August 1995 there were 18,957 websites online; by August 1996 there were 342,081

('15 Years of the Web, Internet Timeline', www.bbc.co.uk). Note that at the time of writing there are over 1 billion websites online. Actually the number is 1,009,525,265 but that will have been eclipsed by the time this book comes out.

Silicon Valley was awash with venture capital as investors bet big bucks on the internet's next big thing – some with viable business plans, others with charismatic founders riding on the coat tails of the prevailing net mania. New ventures sprung up almost daily, selling everything imaginable – or selling nothing at all. Fledgling companies spent vast amounts of money, growing quickly with scant regard for turning a profit, betting their future on building strong online brands that could win the hearts and minds of net consumers. The profits would come later... at least, that was the theory. Some of these companies were destined to become household names in a few short years; others would vanish into obscurity just as quickly.

These were heady, almost euphoric times. The internet had acquired the mythical Midas touch: a business with .com in its name, it seemed, was destined for great things. Initial public offerings (IPOs) of dot.com companies made millionaires of founders, and made the headlines, fuelling further mania. It was an era that saw the birth of some of today's most well-known online brands: sites such as Amazon.com, Yahoo!, eBay... and, in September 1998, Google Inc.

Boom, boom... bang!

For a time it seemed like the halcyon days of the late 1990s would continue forever, that the dot.com bubble was impervious to bursting. Fuelled by speculative investment and high-profile high-tech IPOs, the Nasdaq Composite stock index continued to rocket upwards. Each new dot.com success fuelled the fervour for technology stocks, blowing up the bubble a little more. On 10 March 2000 the Nasdaq index hit an intra-day high of 5,132.52 before settling to an all-time closing high of 5,046 points.

And then it went into free fall.

What happened to the railways in the 1840s, radio in the 1920s and transistor electronics in the 1950s had finally hit the dot.com boom. Between March 2000 and October 2002 some US $5 trillion in all was wiped off the market value of technology stocks. Speculative investment suddenly stopped, venture capitalists were less cavalier with their cash, and high-risk start-ups with dubious business plans ran out of places to source funding. With profits still a distant dream, even for high-profile internet start-ups, the coffers soon began to run dry. It signalled the end of the road for many.

Despite the occasional 'blip', both the stock market index and the fortunes of internet businesses continued to wane until 2003 when, slowly but surely, the tide turned and things started to look up. Although there had been some high-profile closures, mergers and acquisitions in the wake of the crash, the reality is that, for the internet industry as a whole, the inevitable 'readjustment' had a positive impact. It essentially cleared the decks – sweeping away a plethora of unviable, poorly conceived and poorly managed businesses – and served as a poignant reality check to those who remained. Yes, there were casualties, but overall the industry emerged stronger, more focused and both optimistic and, crucially, realistic about the future.

Two other critical elements helped fuel the recovery, and to some extent the public fascination with the internet: one was the meteoric rise of Google from relative obscurity to dominate the world of internet search, the other was the accelerated roll-out of high-speed, always-on broadband access for residential users.

People could suddenly find what they were looking for online – could get access to what they wanted, when they wanted it – without having to go through the frustrating rigmarole of a dial-up connection. It transformed the online experience, turning it from a passing curiosity into a useful everyday tool for a much wider demographic of users. And the more people who used the internet, the more indispensable it became.

The sheer size of the major internet players now has surpassed all previous understanding of both scale, power and value too. In February 2016 Google, albeit briefly, became the most valuable company in the world – for a few moments it edged above Apple and closed the day on a value exceeding $533 billion.

Digital marketing has become the most powerful form of marketing ever known to mankind – that is about the height of it!

Enough technology... let's talk about people

If you're non-technical the world of digital marketing may seem a bit daunting at first. All that technology must be really complicated... right? Not necessarily.

One of the key things to remember if you are new to digital marketing is this: digital marketing is not actually about technology at all, it's all about people. In that sense it is similar to traditional marketing: it is about people (marketers) connecting with other people (consumers) to build relationships and ultimately drive sales.

Technology merely affords you – the marketer – new and exciting platforms that allow you to connect with people in increasingly diverse and relevant ways. Digital marketing is not about understanding the underlying technology, but rather about understanding people, how they are using that technology, and how you can leverage that to engage with them more effectively. Yes, you have to learn to use the tools at your disposal – but understanding people is the real key to unlocking the potential of digital marketing.

A huge and growing market

Although internet companies suffered bruised finances and a tarnished public image in the wake of the dot.com crash, the internet itself never stopped growing, both in terms of the number of websites online and, crucially from a marketing perspective, the number of people with internet access. In March 2000, when the dot.com bubble burst, there were an estimated 304 million people in the world with internet access. By March 2003 that figure had doubled to 608 million, and in December 2005 the global online population passed 1 billion. As of November 2015 the figure sat at 3.4 billion people. That is nearly half the global population... and it's still climbing (see Figure 1.1).

Figure 1.1 The global distribution of the world's 2.1 billion internet users by region (according to Internet World Stats, November 2015)

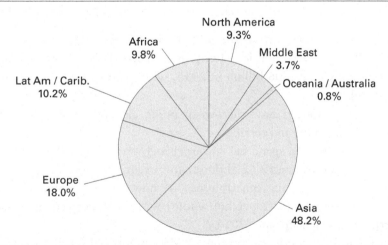

SOURCE: Internet World Stats (www.internetworldstats.com/stats.htm); basis: 3,366,261,156 internet users on 30 November 2015; copyright © 2015, Miniwatts Marketing Group

At GADM (www.gogadm.com) we recently identified that within one year of this book's publication there will be more people online than offline – an important rubicon but also a time when we should be excited to see what the newcomers will teach us!

As global and local online populations have spiralled upwards, so too have the levels of broadband penetration, which means that not only are there more people online, but they are also online more often, for much longer periods of time and can do much more with that time – all of which means that the market penetration of digital channels is growing rapidly. As the potential audience grows, so too does the allure of digital marketing. Marketers around the world are sitting up and taking notice, and big-name brands are taking the internet and other digital marketing channels seriously: loosening the purse strings and redistributing their advertising spend.

As detailed in an extract by Warc (2015) using data sourced by eMarketer:

> Digital advertising is continuing to show strong growth, with eMarketer estimating that global digital adspend will increase 18 per cent this year to $170.17 billion, accounting for almost 30 per cent of total adspend.
>
> The United States, which has the world's largest overall ad market, worth $195.26 billion, will also have the largest digital ad market in 2015, with advertisers in the region expected to spend $62.07 billion on digital formats this year, up 16.8 per cent since 2014.
>
> The United States also has the largest mobile internet adspend in the world, which eMarketer values at $31.53 billion for 2015, or 43.8 per cent of all global mobile adspend. (https://www.warc.com/News/PrintNewsItem.aspx?ID=35405)

Recent figures released from the joint survey of the Internet Advertising Bureau UK (IAB UK) and PricewaterhouseCoopers (PWC) show that digital ad spend grew to £8.606 billion in 2015, which is up 16.4 per cent, and a record high.

Consumer goods is now the top-spending display sector, followed by travel and transport, and retail.

Mobile advertising spend has unsurprisingly soared, up 60.3 per cent to reach a record breaking £2.627 billion, now accounting for 30.5 per cent of all UK digital advertising. Smartphones are now the most popular internet device (an average of 2.1 per household) with a 21 per cent increase in smartphone ownership since 2014.

Meanwhile, stateside, according to ZenithOptimedia's 2016 forecast, global ad expenditure will grow 4.6 per cent in 2016, reaching US $579 billion by the end of the year. Global mobile advertising expenditure will increase by US $64 billion between 2015 and 2018, growing by 128 per cent.

Introducing consumer 2.0

Unless you have been hiding under a rock in the Outer Hebrides since about 2004 you will be familiar with the Web 2.0 (pronounced two-point-oh) moniker. It is bandied about with alacrity by the web-savvy elite, but what exactly does it mean?

Let's start off with what Web 2.0 is not: it is not a new version of Web 1.0. Web 2.0 is not a revolution in technology, it is an evolution in the way that people are using technology. It is about harnessing the distributed collaborative potential of the internet to connect and communicate with other like-minded people wherever they are: creating communities and sharing knowledge, thoughts, ideas and dreams.

If you have ever shared photos on Instagram, read and commented on a blog, looked for friends on Facebook, watched a video clip on YouTube, tried to find your house on Google Maps, video-called friends or family abroad using Skype or looked up an article on Wikipedia, then you have used Web 2.0 technologies.

Suddenly it seems we have been inundated with version 2.0 of anything and everything as different sectors of society seek to demonstrate that they are current and progressive. We have Business 2.0, Government 2.0, Education 2.0, Careers 2.0... and, of course, Marketing 2.0. Well, not to be outdone, we would like to introduce you to the new, improved, Consumer 2.0.

Once upon a time, consumers were quite happy to sit in front of passive broadcast media, accepting whatever was being peddled their way by editors and programme schedulers. Yes, there was an element of choice – you could buy a different newspaper, listen to a different station or choose a different channel – but the ultimate decision in terms of the content available to you rested with someone else.

Then along came the web, and changed all the rules. Now, with Web 2.0, broadband and rich media content, today's consumers are in control like never before. They can choose the content they want, when they want it, in the way that they want it... they can even create their own and share it with their friends, their peers and the world – for free.

'Consumers are becoming better informed, better connected, more communicative, and more in control than ever', highlights Julian Smith, an analyst with Jupiter Research writing for the ClickZ network. 'They are better informed through the increased ability to access and sift an abundance of information any time, anywhere. They are better connected through the ability to instantaneously communicate with others across time zones and social strata. They are more communicative through the ability to publish and share their ideas and opinions. They are more in control through the ability not only to personalize their information and entertainment consumption, marketing messages, and the products and services they buy, but also to gain satisfaction on demand.'

Analysts at Jupiter Research identified seven key ways in which the increasingly widespread adoption of technology is influencing consumer behaviour:

- *Interconnectivity*: networked digital technology is enabling consumers to connect with each other more readily, be it through e-mail, instant messaging (IM), mobile messaging, or web-based social networking platforms such as Facebook, Twitter and LinkedIn – or more likely a combination of all of these platforms. Consumers are interacting with like-minded people around the world, paying scant regard for trifling concerns such as time zones or geography. Peer-to-peer interaction is reinforcing social networks, and building new virtual communities.

- *Technology is levelling the information playing field*: with digital technology, content can be created, published, accessed and consumed quickly and easily. As a result, the scope of news, opinion and information available to consumers is broader and deeper than ever. Consumers can conduct their own unbiased research, comparing and contrasting products and services before they buy. Knowledge is power... and digital technology is shifting the balance of power in favour of the consumer.

- *Relevance filtering is increasing*: with such a glut of information available to digital consumers, they are through necessity learning to filter out items relevant to them and to ignore anything they perceive as irrelevant. Increasingly digital consumers look to have their information aggregated, categorized and delivered (whether through e-mail or really simple syndication (RSS) feeds – a way to automatically retrieve updated posts/ articles from a website). They use personalization features to block out irrelevant content and increasingly employ software solutions to exclude unsolicited commercial messages.

- *Niche aggregation is growing*: the abundance and diversity of online content allows consumers to participate and indulge their specialist interests and hobbies. Aggregations of like-minded individuals congregate online; the homogeneous mass consumer population is fragmenting into ever smaller niche groups, with increasingly individual requirements.

- *Micropublishing of personal content is blossoming*: digital media's interactive and interconnected nature allows consumers to express themselves online. Publishing your own content costs little more than a bit of time and imagination, whether through discussion forums, message boards, feedback forms, voting platforms, personal photo galleries or blogs. Users are posting their opinions online for all to see, and are consulting the opinions of their online peers before making purchasing decisions. How often do you check an online review before booking a table at an unknown restaurant, a weekend break at a hotel, or even buying a new car?

- *Rise of the 'prosumer'*: online consumers are getting increasingly involved in the creation of the products and services they purchase, shifting the balance of power from producer to consumer. They are letting producers know what they want in no uncertain terms: the level of interaction between producer and consumer is unprecedented. Individuals are more involved in specifying, creating and customizing products to suit their requirements, and are able to shape and mould the experiences and communications they receive from producers. Traditional mass-production and mass-marketing concepts are rapidly becoming a thing of the past.

- *On-demand – any time, any place, anywhere*: as digital technology becomes more ubiquitous in people's lives, the corresponding acceleration of business processes means that consumers can satisfy their needs more quickly, more easily and with fewer barriers. In the digital economy, trifling concerns such as time, geography, location and physical storage space are becoming irrelevant. It is a world of almost instant gratification – and the more consumers get of it, the more they want it... now, now, now! David Black, head of Branding and Consumer Markets for Google UK, recently referred to 'WWW' as: 'what we want, where we want and when we want'!

For marketers this evolution of the marketplace, and the shift in consumer mindset that it heralds, presents a plethora of new challenges. As consumers increasingly embrace new ways of communicating, take greater ownership of the information and entertainment they consume, and aggregate in increasingly specialized niche online communities, marketers must *engage* in new ways. And the first step on their journey is to understand what is digital marketing.

And that is what the rest of this book is all about.

CASE STUDY   Dulux

Dulux is the UK's leading paint brand, with a wealth of products and services designed to help customers find the perfect colours for their home. They provide expert knowledge to help their customers achieve great results.

Location

Global.

The challenge

Dulux wanted to increase engagement with their full product range, increasing sales of testers and paint and engaging with customers earlier in their purchase cycle.

To do this, they needed to overcome the biggest barriers to purchase: consumer confidence around picking the right colour, and uncertainty regarding the potential end result.

Target audience

Couples and families making big decisions around painting their newly purchased home.

Action

- User experience (UX) design agency Webcredible was chosen to manage the project.
- Webcredible followed a user-centred design approach to identify an innovative solution to match the natural behaviours of Dulux customers and ensure long-term use of the app.
- They carried out initial user research to uncover Dulux customers' needs and goals – the research clearly demonstrated that a visualization feature would be a great fit.
- Having validated the idea, they generated detailed, overarching design principles to ensure they created an inspiring, functional user experience. The principles were to:
  - Avoid a prolonged journey by allowing people to colour a room in two taps – tap on a colour, then tap on a wall.

- Inspire experimentation by allowing people to pick different colours and instantly see the wall colour change.
- Move people along the decorating journey by encouraging them to order testers once a colour has been tried on a wall.
- Offer 'just enough' fidelity so that the solution did not compromise on the user experience to create a pixel-perfect room mock-up.
- Ensure the visualizer user interactions were simple and could be used holding up a phone/tablet and looking through it.

- Guided by these principles, Webcredible began designing the app, its interface, visual design and user journeys.
- Throughout this process they carried out numerous rounds of user testing to ensure that the journeys and interactions were not only beneficial to users but brought them real joy.

Results

Since launching in 60 global markets the app has been an unbelievable success with over 5 million downloads; app users increased by 143 per cent, usage increased by 247 per cent and visits to the saved-items page have risen by 242 per cent.

Most importantly, the number of users searching for a stockist rose by an incredible 92 per cent and tester sales increased by 65 per cent.

The app also won Innovation of the Year at the Digital Communication Awards, Innovative Mobile App of the Year at the UK IT Industry Awards and Best Hi-tech Gadget at the House Beautiful Awards.

Links to campaign

https://www.dulux.co.uk/en/articles/the-dulux-visualizer-app

About the creator

Trenton Moss is chief executive officer (CEO) and founder of Webcredible, a UX design agency based in London.

Have a plan and stick to it... strategy!

02

> **OUR CHAPTER PLEDGE TO YOU**
>
> When you reach the end of this chapter you will have answers to the following questions:
>
> - What is a digital marketing strategy and why do I need one?
> - How do I know if digital marketing is right for my business?
> - How do I formulate a digital marketing strategy?
> - Are my customers ready for digital marketing?

Why you need a digital marketing strategy

Why do you need a digital marketing strategy? The simple answer: because without one you will miss opportunities and lose business. Formulating a digital marketing strategy will help you to make informed decisions about your foray into the digital marketing arena, and ensure that your efforts are focused on the elements of digital marketing that are most relevant to your business. It is a crucial first step towards understanding how the constantly evolving digital marketplace relates to you, and how it affects the relationship between your business or brand, and your customers and prospects.

It doesn't matter what business you're in, it is a fairly safe bet that an increasing number of your target market rely on digital technology every day to research, evaluate and purchase the products and services they consume. Without a coherent strategy of engagement and retention through digital channels your business is at best missing a golden opportunity, and at worst could be left behind, watching your competitors pull away across an ever-widening digital divide.

Unlike conventional forms of mass-media marketing, the internet is unique in its capacity to both broaden the scope of your marketing reach and narrow its focus *at the same time*. Using digital channels you can transcend traditional constraints such as geography and time zones to connect with a much wider audience. At the same time, digital technology allows you to hone your marketing message with laser-like precision in order to target very specific niche segments within that wider market. Implemented effectively it can be an incredibly powerful combination.

It is often stated that the internet puts consumers in control like never before. But it is important to remember that the internet also delivers an unprecedented suite of tools, techniques and tactics that allow marketers to reach out and engage with those same consumers. The marketing landscape has never been more challenging, dynamic and diverse.

And therein lies the crux of our need for a cohesive digital marketing strategy. If you are going to harness the power of digital marketing to drive your online business to dizzying new heights, you need a thorough understanding of your market, how your customers are using digital technology, and how your business can best utilize that same technology to build enduring and mutually rewarding relationships with them, while optimizing the experience between you and your customers.

As digital channels continue to broaden the scope available to us as marketers, so they add to the potential complexity of any digital marketing campaign. Having a clearly defined strategy will help to keep you focused, ensure that your marketing activities are always aligned with your business goals and, crucially, that you are targeting and engaging the right people.

Your business and digital marketing

Whether or not your business is suited to digital marketing depends very much on the nature of that business, where it is now, and where you want it to go in the future. If, for example, you are a dairy farmer in rural Ireland, have a fixed contract to supply milk to the local co-operative, and have little, if any, scope or ambition to diversify and grow your business year on year, then digital marketing probably is not for you. Likewise, if you are a local butcher with an established client base in north London and simply want to maintain the status quo, then again you will probably do just fine without digital marketing.

If, however, you are a north London butcher looking to diversify your product offering, broaden the scope of your business and want to start selling your quality organic produce to restaurants and hotels around the country... well then, welcome to the world of digital marketing.

In truth, there are very few businesses today that would not benefit from at least some degree of digital marketing – even if it is just providing a basic online brochure telling people what you do, and sending out the occasional update to existing customers via an e-mail newsletter or RSS feed.

Whether you are running a home-based 'lifestyle' business selling hand-embroidered cushion covers, are a small-scale artisan food producer, an up-and-coming restaurateur or managing a large multinational corporation, a growing proportion of your customer base is already online, with more joining them every day (see Figure 2.1). Obviously, the more your target market comes to rely on these online channels for its information, research and purchasing needs, the more critical digital marketing will become to the ongoing success of your business.

Digital marketing – yes or no

There are really only two key questions you need to answer when it comes to deciding whether or not your business needs a digital marketing strategy. They are:

- *Is my audience online/is it going to be online?* If your customers use digital technology to research and/or purchase the products and services you provide, then you absolutely need to embrace digital marketing now in order to engage with them and retain them. If they don't, then you don't. It really is that simple. Just bear in mind that as the next generation of consumers start to become your new customers, they are likely to demand more digital interaction from your business. If you are not in a position to deliver that, they could well choose to spend their money elsewhere.

- *Are my products/services/brands suited to digital marketing?* This can be a tricky one – but the answer is usually yes. Typically it doesn't matter what your product, service or brand is: as long as you have established that there is a viable online audience for it (see question 1), then you should be promoting it online. While some products and services are obviously more suited to online purchase and fulfilment than others (digital files, such as e-books or music, spring to mind), you will also find being marketed effectively through digital channels plenty of items that few people would ever dream of actually purchasing over the internet. Consumers go online to research, evaluate and compare their choices. They make purchasing decisions based on the quality of their online

Figure 2.1 Are your customers online? Figures from the Pew Internet & American Life Project April–May 2013 showing the proportion of US adults now online, and a breakdown of their demographic make-up

Demographics of internet users
% of adults in each group who use the internet (the number of respondents in each group listed as 'n' for the group)

		Use the Internet
All adults (n = 2,252)		85%
a	Men (n = 1,029)	85
b	Women (n = 1,223)	84
Race/ethnicity		
a	White, Non-Hispanic (n = 1,571)	86^c
b	Black, Non-Hispanic (n = 252)	85^c
c	Hispanic (n = 249)	76
Age		
a	18–29 (n = 404)	98^{bcd}
b	30–49 (n = 577)	92^{cd}
c	50–64 (n = 641)	83^d
d	65+ (n = 570)	56
Education attainment		
a	Less than high school (n = 168)	59
b	High school grad (n = 630)	78^a
c	Some College (n = 588)	92^{ab}
d	College + (n = 834)	96^{abc}
Household income		
a	Less than $30,000/yr (n = 580)	76
b	$30,000–$49,999 (n = 374)	88^a
c	$50,000–$74,999 (n = 298)	94^{ab}
d	$75,000+ (n = 582)	96^{ab}
Urbanity		
a	Urban (n = 763)	86^c
b	Suburban (n = 1,037)	86^c
c	Rural (n = 450)	80

SOURCE: Pew Research Center's Internet & American Life Project Spring Tracking Survey, April 17 – May 19, 2013. N = 2,252 adults. Interviews were conducted in English and Spanish and on landline and cell phones. Margin of error is +/– 2.3 percentage points for results based on internet users.

NOTE: Percentages marked with a superscript letter (eg, ^{a}) indicate a statistically significant difference between that row and the row designated by that superscript letter, among categories of each demographic characteristic (eg age).

experience, then head to a bricks-and-mortar store to hand over their cash. Boats, cars, houses, apartments, horses, tractors – you name it – they are all being actively and successfully marketed online.

Defining your digital marketing strategy

Once you have decided that you do, in fact, need to pursue some form of digital marketing, the next step is actually to sit down and define your strategy. Unfortunately, there is no 'one size fits all' strategic panacea here. We don't have a magic recipe to ensure your digital marketing success, and neither does anyone else (despite some of the online hyperbole you may read on the subject).

Basically, every business needs to 'bake' its own unique strategy based on its own particular set of circumstances. While the available ingredients are the same (we will cover the major ones later in the book), the resulting strategies can be radically different.

It's common sense really. If you sell apples to local grocers by the truck load your strategy will bear little resemblance to that of a company selling downloadable e-books and reports on financial trading, which will in turn be very different to the strategy adopted by a sports clothing manufacturer who wants to cut out the middle man and sell directly to consumers over the web.

Different products, different markets, different needs... different solutions. What it ultimately boils down to is this: the best people to define your digital marketing strategy, curiously enough, are the people who best know your business.

Laying strong digital foundations

The good news is that you have almost certainly already started the process of defining your digital marketing strategy. Before even picking up this book you have probably been thinking about digital marketing in the context of your business, about what your competitors are doing online and why, about how your customers and prospects are integrating digital technology into their lives, and about how you can best exploit these new and exciting digital channels to foster longer, more productive relationships with them. These are the components that will form the foundation of your digital marketing strategy:

- *Know your business*: is your business ready to embrace digital marketing? Are your products/services suited to online promotion? Do you have the right technology/skills/infrastructure in place? How will digital marketing fit into your existing business processes? Do those processes need to change, and are you and your staff ready to accommodate those changes?

- *Know the competition*: who are your main competitors in the digital marketplace? Are they the same as your offline competitors? What are they doing right (emulate them)? What are they doing wrong (learn from them)? What are they not doing at all – and is there an opportunity there for you? How can you differentiate your online offering from theirs? Remember, competition in the digital world can come from just around the corner, or from right around the globe. The same technologies that allow you to reach out to a broader geographical market also allow others to reach in to your local market. When you venture online you are entering a global game, so don't limit your analysis to local competition.

- *Know your customers*: who are your customers and what do they want from you? Are you going to be servicing the same customer base online, or are you fishing for business from a completely new demographic? How do the customers you are targeting use digital technology, and how can you harness that knowledge to engage in a productive and ongoing relationship with them?

- *Know what you want to achieve*: if you don't know where you are going, there is a fair chance you will never get there. What do you want to get out of digital marketing? Setting clear, measurable and achievable goals is a key part of your digital marketing strategy. Are you looking to generate online sales, create a source of targeted sales leads, improve your brand awareness among online communities, all of the above or perhaps something completely different? Your goals are the yardsticks against which you can measure the progress of your digital marketing campaigns.

- *Know how you are doing*: the beauty of digital marketing is that, compared to many forms of advertising, results are so much more measurable. You can track everything that happens online and compare your progress against predefined goals and key performance indicators (KPIs). How is your digital campaign progressing? Are certain digital channels delivering more traffic than others? Why is that? What about conversion rates – how much of that increased traffic results in tangible value to your business? Measure, tweak, refine, remeasure. Digital marketing is an ongoing iterative process.

The process of formally defining your digital marketing strategy forces you to sit down and analyse with a critical eye the market in which you are operating, and to really think about the different components of your business and how digital marketing can help you to achieve your business goals.

Don't get too bogged down in the technical details – remember, digital marketing is about people communicating with other people, the technology is just the bit in the middle that helps it to happen. Your strategy should provide you with a high-level framework – a bird's-eye view of the digital marketing landscape with your business centre stage – the details will come later.

Understanding the digital consumer

There is a notion that pervades marketing circles today, a notion of mysterious ethereal creatures who exist in a hyperconnected, multifaceted cyber world of their own. They are an enigma: they speak a different language, communicate in ways we don't understand, and they are turning the world of marketing on its head. These are the ephemeral, wraith-like 'digital consumers', who slip effortlessly through the marketer's grasp. Digital consumers are different, we're told... but are they really?

The digital consumer revealed

The first thing to realize about digital consumers is that there is basically no such thing. The customers and prospects you encounter online are the very same people who walk into your store every day, call you on the telephone, or order something from your mail-order catalogue. There is nothing dark, sinister or mysterious about them. They are people – like everyone else.

'There is no great mystery about how [digital consumers] think and what they want,' maintains interactive marketing expert Giles Rhys Jones of Interactive Marketing Trends (http://interactivemarketingtrends.blogspot.com):

> These consumers are doing exactly what people have been doing for thousands of years – communicating with each other.
>
> The fact that technology is enabling them to communicate with each other faster, over distance, over mobiles and in 3D worlds is being perceived as something dangerous, unique and extraordinary, something that needs to be controlled and pinned down. People talk to each other – they always have. They are talking the same language and saying the same things, they are just not necessarily sitting in the pub talking to one person or five people, but doing it online to 15 or 5,000.

Making the web their own

Consumers, whatever their 'flavour', do not care about the way that marketers define what they do. Concepts such as above the line, through the line, below the line, digital, traditional, experiential, linear, analogue, mobile, direct, indirect – or any other 'box' we care to slip our marketing endeavours into – are completely meaningless to them. All consumers care about is the experience – how the marketing available to them can enhance the experience and help them to make more informed decisions.

People are the single most important element in any form of marketing. That is just as true in the digital space as it is in any other sphere of the discipline. As a marketer you need to understand people and their behaviour – and here is where the notion of the digital consumer does carry some weight, because consumer behaviour is changing, and it is changing because of the pervasive, evocative and enabling nature of digital technology (see Figure 2.2).

'The majority of today's consumers are actively personalizing their digital experiences and sampling niche content and video with increasing frequency,' said Dave Friedman, president of the central region for Avenue A | Razorfish, writing in an article for Chief Marketer (www.chiefmarketer.com).

'We've reached a collective digital tipping point as a majority of consumers are tapping into a variety of emerging technologies and social media to increasingly personalize their digital experiences,' said Friedman. 'From recommendation engines, to blogs, to customized start pages, today's "connected consumer" navigates a landscape that is much more niche and personalized than we ever expected.' The practice of broadcasting generic advertising messages to the mass market is rapidly being usurped by specifically targeted, narrow-cast marketing, through digital channels, to an increasingly diverse and segmented marketplace. Even, ultimately, to a target market of one. Digital marketing allows us to build uniquely tailored ongoing relationships with individual customers. This is a conversation, not a lecture. Marketing in the digital age has been transformed into a process of dialogue, as much about listening as it is about telling.

I don't know you and you don't know me

On the internet, no one knows you are a dog... right? Perceived anonymity is another online trait that can have a profound effect on consumer behaviour. It liberates consumers from the social shackles that bind them in the real world; online they are free to do and say as they please, with scant regard for the social propriety that holds sway in 'real life'. In a bricks-and-mortar store, shoppers will wait patiently for service, and will often endure a less than flawless shopping experience to get what they want. Online they won't; they demand instant gratification and a flawless customer experience. You

Figure 2.2 Digital consumption survey

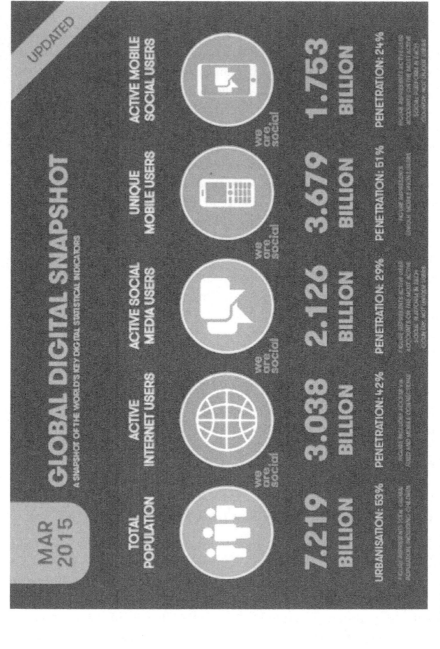

SOURCE: Used with permission from We Are Social

have to deliver, first time, every time. If you fail to engage, retain and fulfil their expectations on demand, they are gone, vanishing into the ether of cyberspace as quickly as they came; the only trace a fleeting, solitary record on your web server's log file...

And then they will tell all their online friends about their less than stellar experience.

Key traits of the online consumer

We are all familiar with the old road-rage analogy of the congenial, neighbourly man or woman who suddenly becomes a raving speed demon when they get behind the wheel of a car. Well, there is something about the immediacy and anonymity of the digital experience that has a similar effect on people.

It is always risky to generalize and make assumptions about people – especially in a field as dynamic and fast moving as this one. The only real way to know your market intimately is to conduct original research within your particular target group. That said, a lot of research work has been done (and continues to be done) on the behavioural traits of online consumers, and a broad consensus has emerged around the key characteristics that epitomize the digital consumer:

- *Digital consumers are increasingly comfortable with the medium*: many online consumers have been using the internet for many years at this stage – and while the user demographic is still skewed in favour of younger people, older users are becoming increasingly internet savvy. 'It's almost like a piano player who plays faster once they know the instrument. In the beginning people "pling, pling, pling" very carefully, and then they move on to playing symphonies,' said web usability guru Jacob Nielsen in an interview with the BBC. As people become more comfortable with the medium they use it more efficiently and effectively, which means they don't hang around for long: your content needs to deliver what they want, and it needs to deliver quickly.

- *They want it all, and they want it now*: in the digital world, where everything happens at a million miles per hour, consumers have grown accustomed to getting their information on demand from multiple sources simultaneously. Their time is a precious commodity, so they want information in a format that they can scan for relevance before investing time in examining the detail. Designers and marketers need to accommodate this desire for 'scanability' and instant gratification when constructing their online offering. Think about 'value for time' as well as 'value for money'.

- *They are in control*: the web is no passive medium. Users are in control – in the Web 2.0 world more than ever before. Fail to grasp that simple fact and your target audience will not just fail to engage with you, they will actively disengage. We need to tailor our marketing to be user-centric, elective or permission-based, and offer a real value proposition to the consumer in order to garner positive results.

- *They are fickle*: the transparency and immediacy of the internet do not eradicate the concept of brand or vendor loyalty, but they do erode it. Building trust in a brand is still a crucial element of digital marketing, but today's consumer has literally at their fingertips the power to compare and contrast competing brands. How does your value proposition stack up against the competition around the country and across the globe? Your brand identity may be valuable, but if your *overall* value proposition does not stack up then you will lose out.

- *They are vocal*: online consumers talk to each other... a lot. Through peer reviews, blogs, social networks, online forums and communities they are telling each other about their positive online experiences... and the negative ones. From a marketing perspective this is something of a double-edged sword – harness the positive aspects and you have incredible viral potential to propagate your message; get it wrong and you could just as easily be on the receiving end of an uncomfortable online backlash.

---

21 minutes in my digital life

Contribution by Stacey Riley, GADM assistant editor, 5 April 2016

It is 7 am. I wake to the sound of my iPhone alarm going off. After several attempts scrambling in the dark I manage to find my phone and turn my alarm off. Bleary-eyed, I check the messages I've received overnight: a couple of iMessages from my boyfriend (he's a night owl), a WhatsApp from my flatmate (who is currently in Atlanta) and an update of Facebook messages on our hen-party group chat. I reply to each, then check my Facebook, Instagram and Twitter accounts. I scroll briefly though each, pausing on my Twitter feed to click through and read an article by *New Humanist* magazine. I read one-third of the article, enjoy it and retweet the link for myself to read in full later.

I get up and put the kettle on to make a cup of tea. Whilst waiting for the kettle to boil, I check my work e-mails ahead of the day. Content from our collaborators, updates on projects and other e-mails fill my inbox. I mentally prioritize them before checking my g-mail calendar to look at today's schedule.

Cup of tea in hand, I wander back to my room to plan what to wear today. I check the weather app on my phone to gauge today's temperature and chance of rain: 14 degrees and sunshine – I choose a dress to wear.

A ping goes off, it's my boyfriend sending me a gif of a puppy falling asleep. He's obviously struggling to get up this morning.

... it's 7.21 am, time for a shower, then breakfast.

Welcome to the world of me, a digital native. One evening, my phone had run out of battery and I had left my charger at work. I hadn't realized how much I relied on it – everything from setting my alarm, to checking the weather and the best route to a meeting. Yet I am only on the cusp of generation Y. For anyone under the age of 25 it is a completely different experience – a hyperconnected, high-octane world of instant access and gratification with digital technology at its core. To young people today, these are not merely digital tools, they are essential, seamlessly integrated elements of their daily lives. These are digital consumers, the millennials, generation Y... call them what you will. They are insistent, impatient, demanding, multitasking information junkies. They are the mass market of tomorrow – and, as marketers, it is absolutely imperative that we learn to speak their language today.

The four Ps of marketing and the 10 Ps of digital marketing

In earlier editions of this book I talked about the famous four Ps of marketing (product, price, promotion and place). And I think all of these still apply as solid foundations to any marketing strategy, digital or otherwise. In the preface of the book I have devised a refresh of the four Ps to apply to the changing consumer in the digital age and to be aligned to the technical possibilities too. This is called the 10 Ps of digital marketing and I strongly recommend that before embarking on a digital strategy you sense-check your ideas and plans against these 10 Ps prior to investment.

Eyes on the prize

Another crucially important area of your digital marketing strategy is setting realistic goals. Your strategy should explicitly define the business goals that you want your digital marketing efforts to help you achieve. As with any other journey, you can only plan an effective route if you have a clear, unambiguous destination in mind from the start. Or to put it another way, you might be the world's best archer – but if no one gives you a target to aim at, what good will it do you?

To measure your progress towards those goals, you also need to set milestones along the way, consistently measuring your achievements and steering your digital campaign towards your ultimate destination. Here, again, the digital realm offers a raft of tools and techniques to help marketers reap a better return from their investment.

We will be examining the topic of web metrics and website intelligence throughout this book, but the crucial thing to remember here is that digital marketing is an iterative process of continuous improvement and refinement. You can monitor and analyse the effectiveness of your digital marketing campaigns in practically real time. You can measure everything, and even run alternative ads and strategies side by side to see what works best before committing to a given course: test, refine, retest and then decide where to make your investment, based on real data from real customers.

Tracking accountability

When a computer or mobile phone – in fact let's call it a digital media device – hits a site, a record is created in the web server's log file based on the unique IP address of that user, and tracks their navigation through the site. Software on the web server also sends a small, unobtrusive file to the user's browser known as a 'cookie', which essentially allows the web server to recognize the same user when they come back to the site again.

Based on information in the log file, marketers can tell a surprising amount about the user's activity on the site:

- We know the user's broad geographical location based on the digits in the IP address. We know when they arrived and from where.

- We know what type of browser and operating system they are using.

- So far we know very little but we can already start to be more accountable. For example, we can now order our advertising and marketing messages to be delivered only to people with a Mac who live in Ireland and do not like working before lunchtime but are seriously interested in sports.

Now let's make things a little more interesting. By adding specific 'page tags' to our website (with the help of a website developer, webmaster and analytics partner) we can start to do some very clever things – following website visitors to the purchase point and beyond. For example, say we choose to run a banner ad campaign. We can detect not only the people who click on the banner and go through the site to become purchasers, we can also detect those people who do *not* click on the banner, but then go ahead and buy the product anyway a few weeks later.

This is really exciting stuff for marketers, because ultimately it dispenses with our whole fascination with the value of the click-through. Not long ago, digital marketing metrics were all about clicks, clicks, clicks. Today, while clicks remain an important guideline, ultimately they are about as useful as saying '230 people noticed my ad today, isn't that great'. Well, in a word, no. Today's online marketing investment is about tangible returns, it is about conversion and ROI; ultimately it is about the accountability of the brand, the price, the ad campaign and the job of the marketer. Which scenario would you rather: a warm post-campaign glow when the research company pats you on the back and says well done for achieving a 10 per cent increase in brand recall among 18–24-year-olds, or 1,293 enquiries about your product and the names and addresses (e-mail, of course) of the 233 new customers who now own your product?

Online marketing is very like direct marketing in that regard. You invest, you sell, you weigh up your ROI, you learn, you adapt, you move on. Except that, online, the process is much accelerated. Yes, of course there is still value in brand-based advertising. The big problem with it is its lack of accountability. The truth is that digital is simply more accountable. You have far more control and can make far more informed decisions based on the feedback and information that the technology provides. It is easy to control the pace and flow of your marketing budget, to turn it up or down and to channel it in different directions. If you are selling holidays, for example, you already know enough about your customers to realize that certain times of the year (holiday season) are less effective for advertising than others (freezing winter days). But how cool would it be if you could target your holiday advertising so that your ads start to run when the temperature drops below 10°C in a particular region? What about being able to advertise your currency-exchange services based on the performance of the markets? Well, in the digital world, you can do that. The potential is boundless.

Bringing it all together

There is a lot to think about when defining your digital marketing strategy but, in the end, the process is about researching, analysing and understanding three things that are crucial to your success: your business, your competition and your customers. Your strategy lays the foundation for everything you do as a digital marketer, and will guide the decisions you make as you implement some of the techniques outlined in the coming chapters – and choose not to implement others, precisely because they do not fit with your chosen strategy.

Effective digital marketing is about boxing clever. You pick and choose the elements that are specifically relevant to your business. Going through the process of defining a clear strategy, based on a thorough analysis of where your business is now, and where you want digital marketing to take it, puts you in the ideal position to know what is likely to work for you and, just as importantly, what probably will not.

CASE STUDY   Kwik Fit

Kwik Fit opened their first centre in 1971 and are now the leading experts in automotive parts repair including tyres, brakes, exhausts, MOT testing, car servicing and air-conditioning recharge.

They are the leading fast-fit supplier of tyres in the UK and carry stocks of over 600,000 products from leading manufacturers including Pirelli, Goodyear, Michelin, Continental and Dunlop. They have over 600 centres in the UK.

Location

National, UK.

The challenge

- To deliver a revenue growth of 24 per cent.

- To deliver a cost of sale below 10 per cent.

- To deliver a concise strategy that works within supplier restrictions and Kwik Fit brand guidelines.

- To achieve the maximum share of voice amongst competitors and rapidly increase Kwik Fit's market share.

Target audience

- All ages, both male and female, who own a car.

- Cars that have an upcoming MOT or are in need of servicing.

Action

One of the first activities that the team at Optimus implemented on the Kwik Fit programme was to introduce a seasonal MOT strategy during the months of March and September to coincide with the new registration plates and to target new customers and audiences during peak times for sales.

Timings and seasonality underpinned the success of this programme. For example, when the weather was unpredictable and cold during winter months, deals on winter tyres and batteries were prevalent, whilst during the hot summer months, as the public were planning to travel or take long journeys, offers for air-con servicing and pre-holiday car preparations were more commonplace.

Multiple and concurrent exclusive voucher codes and cashback incentives were introduced for the Kwik Fit brand in order to attain maximum exposure and coverage, as well as regularly planted generic codes put in place to sustain merchant page exposure and conversion results.

The unique rotation of offers and promotions on behalf of Kwik Fit means that a spread of deals is constantly available, appealing to a wide age range of motorists with varying requirements and consistently communicating the Kwik Fit brand value proposition. This maximizes the volumes of what are essentially distress or planned purchases in most cases, as car repairs are often essential and MOTs are a legal requirement.

Results

The activity implemented by Optimus exceeded the growth target of 24 per cent and delivered a substantial 63 per cent growth in revenue.

Another key objective was to reduce the cost of sales to below 10 per cent and Optimus delivered a cost of sales below 7 per cent.

Furthermore, each of the key service areas showed double digit growth: MOT at 63 per cent, services at 77 per cent, tyre fitting at 86 per cent and mobile fitting at 114 per cent.

For every £1 spent on affiliate activity, Kwik Fit noted a £15.60 return on investment.

About the creator

Optimus is a digital agency specializing in online retail marketing. With offices in Devon and London, they work both nationally and internationally with the single purpose of driving online growth and sales for their e-commerce clients.

Links

https://www.kwik-fit.com
www.optimus-pm.com

Comment

We engaged Optimus to launch and run the Kwik Fit affiliate programme. The programme has exceeded our initial targets as well as delivering outstanding ROI well within our cost-of-sale targets. This means we have the necessary flexibility of budget and all the key relationships in place, allied to a proven strategy to deliver future targets.

Danny Macro, online marketing manager at Kwik Fit

Crouch, touch, pause... engage...

03

Note: If you're a fan of rugby you will understand the title of this chapter. For non-rugby fans, 'crouch, touch, pause, engage' is what the referee says as he instructs the players forming a scrum. A scrum is... oh, never mind!

OUR CHAPTER PLEDGE TO YOU

When you reach the end of this chapter you will have answers to the following questions:

- Why is my website so important?
- How do I build an effective website?
- How should I structure the information on my website?
- What is usability, and why should I care?
- Why are accessibility and web standards important?
- What is responsive web design (RWD)?
- How do I create compelling web content?

Your website – the hub of your digital marketing world

Before we get going on this chapter we need to agree something together – whether your website appears as a shop window on a person's 'connected' television set or it materializes as a mobile site enabled for a smartphone, or is just a simple old-fashioned home page on a computer screen, it is still a shop window to your digital world and it is still a website. Later in the chapter you will read about developments in the world of 'responsive web design' that are impacting the creation and evolution of sites, but now this is all we need to agree on: a website is increasingly *everywhere* and as long as you can access and acquire your products and services do we really need to get into semantics?

As a digital marketer, your website is your place of business. You may have all sorts of campaigns out there, tapping the far-flung reaches of cyberspace for a rich vein of new customers, but ultimately everything will be channelled back through a single point: your website. That makes your website incredibly valuable. In fact, it is the single most valuable piece of digital real estate that you will ever own. Get your digital marketing strategy right, and who knows, it could well end up being the most valuable piece of real estate you own: period.

We cannot stress this point enough. In an uncertain and constantly evolving digital world, your website is the one thing over which you have complete and explicit control. You can change anything and everything on your website; you can tweak it, tune it and manipulate it in any way you want; you can build in ways to track and measure *all* of the activity on your website. You own it – it is yours, and it is the yardstick by which your entire online business will be measured.

A conversion engine for traffic

All of the digital marketing techniques we discuss in the coming chapters have one thing in common: they are designed to drive targeted, prequalified traffic to your website. But *traffic on its own does nothing but consume internet bandwidth*: it is your website that converts that traffic into prospects and customers – taking the numbers and transforming them into something of tangible value to your business.

As a digital marketer your website is not just an online brochure to let people know who you are and what you do. Granted, some of the information you provide on your site will serve that purpose – but only in a peripheral capacity. Nor is it simply there to garner search engine 'mojo' and generate huge volumes of traffic. Think of your website primarily as a *conversion engine* for the traffic you garner through all of your other digital marketing endeavours.

Yes, you need to provide information about your business, products and services – but always with your conversion goals in mind. Everything on your website should be geared towards achieving those conversion goals, either directly (products and service information, online ordering/sales functionality, sales-focused copy and calls to action, enquiry forms, newsletter sign-up, etc) or indirectly (business and brand information that builds trust, content that encourages repeat visits and/or establishes your authority/ reputation in your field).

Your conversion goals could be anything from an actual online purchase (a sales transaction) to an online query (lead generation), to subscribing for your online newsletter (opt-in for future marketing)... or whatever else you decide is important for your business and appropriate for your customers. You can, of course, have multiple, tiered conversion goals. Your primary goal might be an online sale or booking, your secondary goal could be online lead generation and your tertiary goal could be to harvest opt-in e-mail addresses for your mailing list.

It doesn't matter what your goals are, or whether your website is a small information/brochure-type site or a huge online store, the important thing is that you keep your goals in mind when you design (or redesign) your website. Remember, conversion is the key to digital marketing success; your website, and the user experience you deliver through it, is what will ultimately drive that conversion.

Building an effective website

An effective website is essentially about the convergence of two things: your business goals and the needs of your target market. Build something that aligns the two and you will end up with an effective website. Broken down like that it sounds simple, but achieving that convergence can be a tricky process – and a quick surf around the web will soon demonstrate that it is easier to get it wrong than to get it right.

You will note that we used the word effective, rather than successful. For a website to be successful people need to be able to find it (which we cover in Chapter 4), but if you build your site to cater for the right people's needs you significantly increase the chance that, once they arrive, they will become more than just a passing statistic.

First, let's state here and now that this is not a definitive guide to website development. This is a book about digital marketing. In this chapter we explore how to approach your website with digital marketing in mind. Our focus is to maximize the effectiveness of your website with a view to your digital marketing endeavours.

What follows is a high-level overview of the important elements to consider when designing your website from a digital marketing perspective. It is not meant to be an exhaustive guide. Most of the topics we touch on here would warrant an entire book to themselves. In fact, if you surf on Amazon you will find a swathe of titles available in each category. You will also find an avalanche of relevant (and, of course, irrelevant) information on the web.

Here, our aim is to arm you with the high-level knowledge you need to make informed decisions about your website design in a digital marketing context, and to communicate exactly what you need in order to engage with your web design partners when it is time to construct your digital hub.

The main steps of building your website

Different businesses will follow different processes involving different groups of people when designing, developing and implementing a website, but regardless of the approach you choose to take, how formal or informal the process, there are a number of key stages that generally form part of any web development project:

- *Planning*: establish your goals for the site; analyse the competition; define who your target market is, how they will find you online and what they will be looking for when they arrive; map out a schedule and decide who will do what and when.

- *Design*: decide on the 'look and feel' of the site – colours, graphics, information architecture (the arrangement or structure of the information), navigation, etc. The way that information is arranged can have a big impact on a site's usability and its perceived relevance and authority both for users and search engines.

- *Development*: putting it all together, taking the agreed design and constructing the actual pages of the site, crafting the content, links and navigation hierarchy.

- *Testing*: making sure everything works the way it should before you let it out on to the big bad internet.

- *Responsive web design (RWD)*: if your customers are mobile then you would probably be wise to design your site with mobile screen sizes and functionality in mind (more on this later in this chapter).

- *Deployment*: your new site becomes live on the internet for the whole world to find... or not, as the case may be.

Before you start

Know why you are building a website

'What is my website for?' It's a simple enough question, yet you might be amazed at how many businesses have never asked it. They have a website because everyone else has one and it seemed like a good idea at the time. The result is a site – invariably an isolated little island in the backwaters of cyberspace – that brings nothing to the business but the expense of annual hosting and maintenance. Ideally you should have a clear idea of exactly what your organization wants to achieve from a website *before* you start to build it.

Know who your website is for

Knowing who exactly you are creating your website for is also crucial to its success. Yet, surprisingly, it is another thing that is often overlooked in the process. Far too many websites end up being designed to appeal to the committee of executives who ultimately sign off on the project, instead of the people who will actually be using them. Don't fall into that trap. For your website to succeed it needs to appeal to one group of people, and one group of people only: your target market.

Think about how your users will access your website, what they will want to find when they get there, and how your site can fulfil those needs. Put yourself in their shoes, or better still, ask them directly what they want to see/do on your website. Try conducting some informal market research with people who would potentially use your website (online and/or offline). The results may be illuminating, and could be the difference between a successful website and an expensive online experiment.

Build usability and accessibility into your website design

Usability and accessibility are central to good web design and yet both are frequently ignored, or at least are not given the weighting they warrant when it comes to making design decisions. They are about making sure that your site content can be accessed by the widest possible audience, and delivering the information and functionality that users want in a way they are comfortable and familiar with.

No doubt you will have heard the acronyms UX and CX (user experience and customer experience) and in fact this latest edition of the book features a separate chapter on this subject for the first time – this underlines how singularly vital both UX and CX have become. Why? Well, because digital marketers and their developers have come to terms with the importance of that big P word – *people*.

Usability

The theory behind web usability is straightforward enough: simple, elegant and functional design helps users to achieve what they want to achieve online more effectively. It is about taking the frustration out of the user experience, making sure things work intuitively, eliminating barriers so that users accomplish their goals almost effortlessly. Your goal is to help the user to do what they want to do in the most efficient and effective way possible. Everything else is just web clutter. Achieving a simple, elegant design that delivers what the user wants with a minimum of fuss is not easy, but putting in the effort can pay huge dividends.

Expert view

Optimizing your mobile presence
Contribution by Matt Brocklehurst, Product Marketing at Google

Many brands ask, 'Should we create a mobile site or an app?' If you have to choose, your first priority should be a mobile-optimized site. Improving mobile site-load time by one second can increase conversion rates by 27 per cent. Once it is live, then consider launching an app to cater to loyal users.

Designing a site for mobile demands more than taking content from your desktop website and fitting it into a small screen. First, understand how customers interact with your existing site, paying particular attention to mobile visitor habits. From here, adapt your value proposition to mobile by tailoring content to specific audiences. Get input from your agency about implementation options: building using responsive web design, dynamically serving different HTML on the same URL, or creating a separate URL for mobile. Check out progressive web apps that give you much of the functionality of an app with all the advantages of a mobile site. Tag your mobile site to track and analyse user behaviour. And be aware that the work is never finished – evaluate site performance and iterate based on insights about user interactions.

To enrich relationships with users, next you can think about building a branded app – but be clear about its purpose. Will it offer entertainment, utility or both? Don't be tempted to just port your mobile site into the app. Instead, design a made-for-app experience using features such as notifications, camera integration or one-click purchasing. If resources require prioritization, design for mobile platforms that represent the majority of the smartphone-installed base. You could also consider developing a single hybrid app that automatically adapts its layout to tablets and smartphones. Once your app has launched, encourage downloads through site links, in-app ads, mobile search ads and PR activity.

Of course, you are still not done; think past the install and contemplate how to actively engage the user base to drive incremental transactions. For example, new remarketing technologies make it possible to reach app users by serving targeted search and display ads tailored to those individuals who have downloaded your app. Meanwhile, many analytics packages can now measure app engagement and model lifetime value for app users. By tapping into these insights and optimizing accordingly, you can deliver a consistently great mobile experience for your users.

For a step-by-step guide to usability, and a comprehensive downloadable e-book of research-based web design and usability guidelines, check out the US government's usability website at www.usability.gov.

Accessibility

The term accessibility, in relation to the web, refers to the process of designing your website to be equally accessible to everyone. A well-designed website should allow all users equal access to the information and functionality they deliver. By adhering to accessibility guidelines when designing your site you are basically making sure that it is useful to as broad a cross-section of your target audience as possible.

If your site complies with accessibility guidelines it will also work seamlessly with hardware and software designed to make the internet more accessible to people with disabilities. For example, by making sure you include descriptive text alternatives to images and multimedia content on your website you can help visually impaired or even completely sightless visitors to access your site through special text-to-speech software and/or text-to-Braille hardware. How stringently you choose to adhere to these accessibility guidelines will depend on several factors, including the nature of your site, your target audience and, in some circumstances, the requirements of local accessibility legislation.

With both accessibility and usability, very small and simple steps can make a big difference; even something as small as ensuring that the text on your website resizes according to the user's browser preferences can have a huge impact on some people's ability to use your site effectively.

A more detailed look at website accessibility, including all of the most current accessibility standards and guidelines, can be found on the W3C website at www.w3.org/WAI/.

Words make your website tick

The world of the web is dominated by words. Audio, video, flash and animation may seem to be everywhere online, but even in an era where multimedia content seems to be taking over, at its core the web is still all about text, and the connections between different words and phrases on and between websites. As a digital marketer, some of those words and phrases are more important to you than others, and knowing which words are relevant to your business is essential to building an effective website.

These are your keywords or key phrases, and in the search-dominated world of the digital marketer they are, in a word, key. Exactly what they are will depend on your business, the digital marketing goals you defined as part of your overall strategy, and on the online behaviour of your target market. But you need to know what they are.

Keywords are practically synonymous with search, so we cover the basics of keyword research and selection in the 'Search' chapter (Chapter 4). But it is a very good idea to have your list of target keywords in mind from the very beginning. It is much easier to optimize a site for search engines as you build it, than to retro-fit search engine optimization after the fact. Your keywords will help to guide everything, from your site design to your information architecture and navigation, right down to the content on the individual pages of your website.

Know your competition

Identifying your competition, analysing what they are trying to achieve with their websites, where they are succeeding and where they are failing, can be a great way of getting ideas and looking at different ways to compete online. Take the keyword phrases you have identified for your website and type them into leading search engines – the sites that rank highly for your keywords are your online competition.

What are they doing well, and how easy would it be for you to emulate and improve on those things? Put yourself in the user's shoes. What sort of user experience are they offering? How could it be improved upon? What about the content?

A thorough analysis of your online competition can reveal a lot, not just about them and what they offer online, but about the direction you choose to take with your website in order to compete effectively.

Choosing your domain name

Every website on the internet has a unique address (a slight simplification, but we don't need to get into the complexities here). It is called an IP address, and is not very interesting, informative or memorable to most humans. It consists of a series of numbers something like 209.85.143.99 (type that address into your browser and see where it takes you).

While this is fine for computers and the occasional numerically inclined tech-head, it's not much use to the rest of us. So, back in the early days of the internet, the domain name system was developed to assign human-readable names to these numeric addresses. These domain names – things like digitalmarketingsuccess.com, google.com, wikipedia.org or harvard.edu – are naturally much more useful and memorable to your average human than the IP addresses they relate to.

You need your own domain name

If you don't have your own domain name, you need to register one. As a business, if you want to be taken seriously online, piggybacking on someone else's domain is completely unacceptable. An address like www.mysite.someothersite.com or www.someothersite.com/mysite/ looks unprofessional, makes your web address difficult to remember, will not do you any favours with search engines and generally tarnishes your business image wherever you publicize it, online and off.

The good news is that registering a domain is cheap (less than US $10 per year, depending on the domain registrar you choose) and easy. It may be included as part of the package offered by your website developer, or you can easily register a domain yourself. You can check availability, select your domain and register it in minutes online (www.mydomain.com is the registrar we used to register the domain associated with this book; there are plenty more to choose from, just type 'domain registration' into your favourite search engine and you will be presented with plenty of options).

It is worth noting that while most domains operate on a first-come first-served basis, some country-specific domains (such as Ireland's .ie domains) have special eligibility conditions that need to be satisfied before the registration is confirmed. Check with the relevant country's domain name authority to see if any country-specific conditions apply to the domain(s) you are interested in.

Some things to bear in mind when choosing your domain name are:

- *Make it catchy, memorable and relevant*: choose an easily identifiable domain name that is relevant to your business and easy for people to remember.

- *Use a country-specific top level domain (TLD) to appeal to a local audience*: the TLD is the element of an internet domain name that comes after the 'dot'. For instance, in the domain name understandingdigital.com the top-level domain is com or COM. If your market is local, it often pays to register the local version of the domain (.co.uk or .ie, for example) instead of (or as well as) the more generic .com, .net or .org. If you are appealing to an international audience, a generic TLD may serve you better. Of the generic TLDs .com is by far the most universally accepted and popular – making it the most valuable one to secure. The variety of TLDs has literally exploded in the last year or so – now you can buy lots of different suffixes for your site (such as .tickets, .office or .shop). However keep it relevant… don't land yourself in a situation where you have a really smart and creative name like www.understandingdigitalmarketing.book and then find out that no one can find you because they are looking for you elsewhere…

- *You can buy multiple domain names*: there is nothing to stop you buying more than one domain in order to prevent others from registering them. You can then *redirect* the secondary domains to point to your main website. Another option is registering country-specific domains to give yourself an online 'presence' in each country you do business in. You can then deploy a regionally tailored version of your website to each of those domains (the preferable option), or redirect them to a localized section on your main website.

- *Consider different suffixes*: there are so many available these days – .mobi, .insurance, .sport and so on. Maybe one of these suffixes is a cool idea for your particular brand?

- *Keywords in a domain name can be beneficial*: you may decide to incorporate one of your keyword phrases into your domain name. Opinion varies on the significance of this in terms of its impact on your search engine ranking, but it may help both search engines and users to establish right from the start what your site is about.

Hosting – your website's home on the internet

The other bit of housekeeping you need to take care of before your site goes live is hosting. Your finished site will consist of files, applications and possibly a database, all of which sit on a computer that is permanently connected to the internet. This computer is your web server, and it will be running special software that will accept requests from users' web browsers and deliver your web pages by return. It is a bit more complicated, but basically that is what it boils down to.

Unless you belong to a large organization with its own data centre that has a permanent connection to the internet backbone, it is highly unlikely that you will host your site in-house. A much more likely scenario is to arrange a hosting solution through a specialist hosting provider.

Different types of hosting

There are basically three different types of hosting offered by web-hosting companies – all of which are perfectly acceptable for your business website. The option you choose will depend largely on your budget, how busy you anticipate your website will be (in terms of visitor traffic) and the amount of control you want over the configuration of the server (whether you need to install your own custom software, change security settings, configure web server options, etc).

A word of warning here: avoid 'free' hosting accounts. While they may be tempting for a small business site to begin with, they tend to be unreliable, often serve up annoying ads at the top of your site, do not offer the flexibility or functionality of a paid hosting account, may not support the use of your own domain name, offer limited (if any) support, and present a greater risk that you will be sharing your server with some less than desirable neighbours – which can hurt your search engine rankings.

Shared hosting accounts

With shared hosting you are essentially renting space on a powerful server where your website(s) will sit alongside a number of other websites (typically hundreds, sometimes thousands on a single server). Each hosting account has its own secure virtual space on the server where you can upload your site's files. A dedicated control panel for account administration offers some degree of control over server configuration and usually provides access to a suite of additional software and tools to help you (or your webmaster) to manage your website(s). All of the websites on a server typically share system resources such as CPU, RAM, etc.

Shared hosting is the most common and cheapest form of hosting, and it is how the majority of websites – particularly for small to medium-sized businesses – start out. Most shared hosting accounts have space restrictions and a monthly bandwidth cap. They are ideal for small to medium-sized businesses and websites with average levels of traffic. In most instances this is the most cost-effective form of hosting.

Virtual dedicated hosting

With virtual dedicated hosting a single server is 'split' into a number of virtual servers. Each user feels like they are on their own dedicated computer, when in fact they are sharing the resources of the same physical machine. The users will typically have complete administrative control over their own virtual space. This is also known as a virtual private server (VPS). While virtual dedicated hosting offers complete flexibility in terms of the administration, software and configuration options available, you are still sharing server resources with other users/websites.

Dedicated hosting

Dedicated hosting solutions provide a dedicated, high-powered server for your website(s), and your website(s) alone. You do not share space or system resources with anyone else – which means you don't share the cost either, making dedicated hosting comparatively expensive.

Dedicated servers offer much more power and flexibility, because changes made to the server affect only your website(s). That means that you (or your webmaster/technical team) have complete control over server configuration, security, software and settings. They also typically offer much more capacity in terms of space and bandwidth than shared hosting – making them suitable for high-traffic sites.

Because of the flexibility and control offered by dedicated hosting solutions (complete control over the host computer), they tend to require more technical ability to administer than shared hosting environments.

Server co-location

Co-location is essentially the same as dedicated hosting, except that instead of the hosting company providing a preconfigured dedicated server for your website, you buy and configure your own server, which is then hosted at their dedicated hosting facility. This offers perhaps the ultimate in flexibility, because you have complete control not only over the software and setting on the server, but also over the hardware specification, operating system, software, security… everything. Co-location is essentially the same as hosting your own server in your own office – except that your server is plugged in to a rack in a dedicated hosting facility, with all of the bells and whistles you would expect.

Cloud-based hosting

Cloud-based hosting is different to traditional hosting models in that you pay for your hosting based on the resources you use, rather than paying for a fixed hardware resource and monthly allowance of space and bandwidth. Essentially, when you are hosting in the 'cloud' your web server is a virtual entity, it does not exist on a single physical server – it is distributed across multiple clustered servers, sharing resources between them. In theory, cloud-based hosting can be cost-effective because you only pay for the resources you use; instantly scalable, because you can tap into practically limitless computing resources on the fly; and inherently reliable, as there is no single point of failure. If one physical machine keels over, the others share the load until another comes on stream to replace it. That is a very simplistic explanation of how cloud computing works… but you get the idea.

Cloud computing, which encompasses cloud-based hosting, is not without its issues. These largely revolve around data ownership, privacy and security; the debate, as always, is ongoing. That said, cloud-based hosting is really gaining traction in the marketplace, and increasing numbers of hosting providers are now offering a cloud-based 'pay for what you use' option as part of their portfolio. As always, you need to weigh the merits of what is on offer and decide what works best for your business.

Choosing your hosting company

Your website developer will be able to help you decide which web hosting option is right for you, based on the size, design, functionality and configuration of your website, and your anticipated levels of traffic based on your business goals. They should also be able to recommend a reliable web-hosting company that will serve your needs.

When choosing your web host, bear the following in mind:

- *Choose a host in the country where your primary target market lives*: this is important, because search engines deliver local search results to users based in part on the geographical location of the server on which the web pages reside (which they can infer from the server IP address).

- *Make sure the host is reliable*: do they offer guaranteed uptime/levels of service? Many hosts publish live server statistics that demonstrate the reliability of their services. You should expect a service level approaching 100 per cent from a high-quality hosting service.

- *What sort of support do they offer*: make sure the hosting you choose includes efficient and effective support 24/7. If your website goes down you need to be confident you can call on your host for assistance whatever time of the day or night.

- *Backup and disaster recovery*: if the worst happens and the server goes belly up, what sort of disaster recovery options does the host have in place? Ideally your host should take several daily snapshots of your entire account/server, allowing them to restore it and get your site back up and running as quickly as possible, should the worst happen.

- *What do others think*: find out what other customers think. Read testimonials, and search for discussions on webmaster forums and social media sites relating to the hosts you are considering. Are other people's experiences good or bad? Post a few questions.

- *Shop around*: hosting is an incredibly competitive industry, so shop around for the best deal – but bear in mind that the cheapest option *is not always the best choice*.

How to choose a web designer/developer

Unless you are a web designer yourself, or have access to a dedicated in-house web development team, you need to bring in a professional web design firm to help with your website project. You will find a host of options out there, offering a range of services that will literally boggle your mind. The good news is, if you have done your preliminary work you should already have a fair idea of what you want from your website, who it is aimed at and the sort of features you want to include. Armed with that knowledge, you can start to whittle down the list of potential designers to something more manageable.

Look at their own website: in trying to assess the relative merits of a web design company, the best place to start is with their own website. What is their site like? Examine it with a critical eye. Does it look professional? Is it functional? Think about what they are trying to achieve, and how well the site addresses the needs of its target audience (you, in this case). Is it easy to find what you want? Does it meet or exceed your expectations? If not, do you really want the same people working on your website?

Examine their portfolio: practically every web design firm offers an online portfolio showing recent website projects they have worked on. Look at these – but go beyond the portfolio pages and click through to the actual websites themselves. Again, put your analytical hat on and ask what the sites are trying to achieve, who they are aimed at and how well the designers have achieved those goals.

That should give you enough of a steer to produce a reasonable shortlist of potential candidates. Now you can dig a little deeper:

- *Ask their customers for recommendations*: go back to the best of the portfolio sites for your shortlisted designers. Go to the 'contact us' page and drop them a line by e-mail or pick up the phone to ask for some honest feedback on their web design experience. Would they recommend the firm?

- *What is their online reputation like?* Web forums, online communities and peer review sites are another good place to look for information about your shortlisted web design firms. Is the online vibe positive or negative? What are people saying about them?

- *Are they designing sites to be found?* Your website is only as good as the quality traffic it gets. Are your shortlisted designers search engine savvy? Go back to the portfolio sites you looked at, and pick out some of the keyword phrases you would expect them to rank for in a search engine. Now go to the search engines and type in those keyword phrases. Have those sites been indexed? Where do they rank on the search results page? Low ranking does not necessarily indicate a problem with their web design – there are many components that contribute to search engine ranking (see Chapter 4), but it may be something you should ask them to clarify before making your decision.

- *Do they adhere to web standards?* Go to the W3Cs website validation page (www.w3.org/QA/Tools/) and run the web addresses of your shortlisted web designers through the MarkUp Validator, Link Checker and CSS Validator. Do the sites validate as web-standards compliant? You should not necessarily discount your favourite designers because of this – but it is something else you should ask them about before making your final decision.

By now you should have whittled down your shortlist to a few competent and professional companies that you want to quote/tender on your website project. The final decision is, of course, up to you.

Arranging your information

Your site structure – the way you arrange and group your information and how users navigate their way around it – can have a massive impact on its usability, its visibility to search engine spiders, its rank in search engine results pages (SERPs – a term in search engine marketing that refers to the results pages returned when a user submits a query to the search engine) and its potential to convert traffic once it arrives. Getting your information architecture right is absolutely critical to the success of your website.

It can be difficult to know where to start. You know what information you want on your site, but what is the best way to arrange it so that users can access it intuitively, at the level of granularity they desire, while also providing you with maximum exposure in the search engines for specific keywords? The answer, as is so often the case in digital marketing, is that it depends. It depends on the sort of business you're in, the type of site you're building, your target audience, your business goals and a whole host of other variables.

Start with your keywords

The keywords your potential users are searching on should give you a good indication of both the content they are looking for and the search terms you want your site to rank for in the SERPs. Take those keywords and arrange them into logical categories or themes. These themes, along with the staple 'home page', 'about us' and 'contact us' links, give you the primary navigation structure for your site.

Define your content structure

Look at your main themes, the keywords you have associated with each of them and the corresponding information or content you want to include beneath each. Now define a tiered hierarchy of subcategories (your secondary, tertiary navigation levels, etc) within each theme as necessary until you have all of your targeted keywords covered. Arrange your content so that the most important information is summarized at the highest levels, allowing the user to drill down to more detailed but less important information on the specific topic as required. Try not to go too deep in terms of navigation subcategories – it is rarely necessary to go beyond three, in exceptional cases four, levels deep from the home page (see Figure 3.1).

Figure 3.1 A simple website information hierarchy

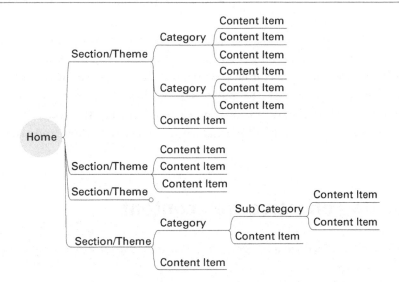

Your home page

The home page is often perceived as one of the most important pages on your site, but is potentially one of the least useful, both to your business and to your site visitors. For a start, home pages tend, by necessity, to be relatively generic – too generic to answer a user's specific query or to instantly entice the conversion you crave. Indeed, many of your visitors – especially those arriving from a search engine, or by clicking on a link from another website or an online advertisement – will tend to land on a much more focused internal page, one that deals with the specific topic that they have searched for or clicked on. This deeper page should be much better at satisfying their immediate requirements.

Where a home page comes into its own is as a central reference point for navigating your content. A breadcrumb trail or navigation path along the top of your site can tell a user at a glance exactly where they are on your site in relation to a fixed point: your home page. It is also a convenient central location that users can easily return to. No matter where they wander on your site, users are always only one click from home, which reassures them that they cannot get lost.

Your home page should be a 'jumping off point' for the rest of your site, offering intuitive one-click navigation to all of your main sections or themes, and telling people immediately what your site is about, and how it can help them. It is also a good place to highlight new products and services, special offers, incentives, news or anything else you want to promote on your site.

Avoid splash screens that simply show your company logo and a 'click here to enter' button – they offer no benefit at all to your users or to your business – they are web clutter at its worst. Likewise, flash intros – the 'skip intro' button is one of the most widely clicked buttons on the web. Remember: you want to make it as easy as possible for your visitors to achieve their goals, so avoid putting obstacles between them and your real content.

Writing effective web content

Now you have defined a structure for your information you are ready to put together your content.

Stop! Don't make the mistake that often happens with new websites. You cannot simply take your offline marketing collateral and paste the same copy into your web pages and expect it to work.

The golden rule of writing effectively in any medium is to know your audience – the more your writing is tailored to your audience, the more effective it is. It is exactly the same on the web. The difference between effective web writing and effective print writing reflects the core difference in the nature of the audience. Print is a linear medium, the web is random access; people read through printed material from beginning to end, on the web they scan and skip; offline readers are patient, online readers want the information they are looking for now, now, now.

We already know a bit about the characteristics of online users from our look at online consumer behaviour in Chapter 2 – writing effective web content is about taking what we know about web users in general, and the target audience of our website in particular, and applying that knowledge to deliver our information in a format that meets those readers' needs:

- *Grab attention*: web users are impatient – forget flowery introductions and verbose descriptions. Make your writing clear, concise and to the point from the start.

- *Make it scannable*: avoid large blocks of uninterrupted text. Use headings, subheadings and bullet points to break up the text into manageable, scannable stand-alone chunks.

- *Make it original*: unique, original content is a great way to engage your users and establish your relevance and authority – and search engines love it.

- *Use the inverted pyramid*: the inverted pyramid writing style often used for newspaper stories tends to work well on the web. Aim to deliver the most important points of your story first, going on to deliver supporting details in order of decreasing importance down the page. Ideally, the user should be able to stop reading at any point and still get the gist of the content.

- *Be consistent*: use a simple, easy-to-read writing style, and keep things consistent across the site. If you have a number of people creating your content, consider developing a style guide or house style to help maintain consistency.

- *Engage with your reader*: use a conversational style, and write as if you were talking to an *individual* rather than an audience. It will help your writing to engage with the reader on a much more personal level.

See our chapter on content marketing in this edition of *Understanding Digital Marketing* (Chapter 8) – this is certainly going to be one of the hottest growth areas online in the years ahead.

Expert view
Top 12 web design mistakes to avoid
Contribution by Pauline Cabrera (http://www.twelveskip.com/
guide/website/966/12-top-web-design-mistakes-to-avoid)

1. The design does not speak for itself

If you are a police officer and you want yourself to be identified as one,
then you must always wear the right uniform and the right badge. The
same principle goes with web design: you have to wear the right 'tie'
for your users to know who you are and what you do. If you are selling
e-books and tutorials, then you don't want to let people think that your site
is that of a local restaurant they are familiar with.

Start asking if you have solid branding. Do the colours, the font styles
and the objectives of your company reflect your website design, and vice
versa? Do you use only the necessary and the right elements for your
company to be clearly identified? Do you use trigger keywords to make
people understand at once what you offer? People don't take more than
a minute to guess what your website is about, so you had better show
the right face at once.

2. Noisy, unorganized visuals

Since design is about visuals, you must show how user-friendly your
website is. User-friendliness is just another technical way of understanding
user-centredness, and if your design is poor in this respect, then it is
another way of saying that you don't deserve a user.

Noisy and unorganized visuals here mean that your content is not
properly laid on the surface. Do you have clear navigation? Do the
elements of your website fall on the right sections or areas of the page as
a whole? Do your posts have a clear readability, ie are they well-spaced,
scannable and friendly to the eyes? Do your ads and banners fall on the
right areas, so as not to be mistaken for something else? Are there too
many distracting elements, such as flashy banners and animated texts?

3. Your design manipulates or prohibits users from spontaneity

This may sound very harsh, but you may not be aware of it yet. You know
these terms for sure, but for web design, this means that a part or the
whole of your design forces users to do something or not to do something.
If people don't want to enter into your survey, don't force them to do so in
exchange for access to something they are asking for.

How about a pop-up window? Any sudden music playback? Do any links of yours require a new window? We all know that these things are annoying. How about access to some materials or pages? Do you require your users to sign up first? If you are really strict with your content, at least you make yourself clear about why things should be kept that way.

4. Unclear or broken navigation and structure

People hate it when they click a broken link, or worse, a link that leads them to somewhere else. More so, despite the fact that you have a navigation bar, sometimes people want to look for something immediately and specifically without scrolling on your hover buttons one by one. The question now is, do you have an internal search engine and a link to your site map?

It is always a failure for websites if their goals are naturally and usually not met. People are being led to your site for a reason, and you only want to satisfy their need. If they cannot find what they are looking for in the first few minutes, then all your efforts and planning fail.

5. Confusing and misleading links

Links are but the circulatory system of the internet. These are the necessary elements wherein all (relevant) pages meet and are anchored upon. Knowing how important links are, you should treat links with respect, and so your users as well – let the links say what they are about to see and nothing else.

Make a clear distinction also of the differences between your underlined or coloured words or phrases with your links. Make sure also that your links at different states (hover, on, off, etc) portray a different visual cue so as to aid people in knowing which links they have already clicked or not. Lastly, buttons should appear as buttons, and those that are not should not appear as such.

6. 'Long' pages

The word 'long' here equates to two aspects of a web design: length and time. In length, your website should not be so long (vertically or horizontally) that people get sick of going back to some key areas they find important. If you are providing a single-page website, make sure that you give assistance to your users by anchoring links that will help them to jump from one section to another, or even back to the top of the page.

Long texts and content should also be broken down into pieces or 'chapters'. You can lay out these chapters in separate pages, which is done in a lot of designs. If you are about to integrate a presentation or a PDF, be sure that at least you provide the first few pages or slides first

▶

– those that don't take the most amount of time to load or download. Afterwards, always give users the link to the whole file.

Additionally, you must realize that people hate it when their data connection is slow, and worse, when the website they are in need of connecting to is slow and even non-responsive. That's where optimization comes in, and that's where you really need to learn to trim your content to a loadable limit. If you are really a good resource, then be a good resource.

7. User filtration

I have discussed manipulative web designs, but I would like to give more space to user experience as a whole. Remember that readers are impatient, and you cannot blame them if they are seeking only convenience. Do any of your pages or resources need a 'higher clearance level' for them to get access to, such as a required membership? If you are really serious about membership, and if you want to take control of and grant access to specific content, at least you must make it easy and clear.

Users will not be happy if they are required to fill in personal information over and over again; they are lucky if their browsers have an auto-fill feature. How about you allow other quicker registration methods, such as linking a Facebook or Google account? The same also goes for purchases and payments. Do you provide prices at once? Do you make them feel safe when they enter credit card details, or at least provide a PayPal assurance? Does your captcha look too blurry or is it illegible, meaning that people will just get frustrated making too many attempts?

Remember that making that utmost appeal to your potential clients or customers is not enough; you must actually guide them along up to the last step and not leave them coughing in the middle. User filtration comes in when they are about to bite what you offer, but turn away frustrated in the middle of the process.

8. Unreachable contact details

Do not forget to include contact details that are visible, comprehensive and offer a lot of options. Make sure also that the options you offer on your contact area are all working fine and that someone is ready to respond. Remember that your contact information is what makes your users feel assured that they are understood by humans, so you don't want to compromise it by letting users call an offline channel.

9. Designs that will only work when...

If someone is knocking on your door, you don't want to send them back to their homes just to put on the right pair of sandals. The same goes with a healthy design. You don't want to use any programming languages that will require every user of yours to get a specific plug-in or software first. Aside from the fact that many of these plug-ins are suspicious nowadays, it is really annoying and inconvenient.

The same also goes for browser compatibility. Did you make sure that your design works and displays well when viewed in a different browser? How about making your website flow and respond to different screen sizes, which are already ongoing norms? Is your domain good for all countries, and won't blacklist an IP address, preventing access to your site? Checking all these factors will make your website a lot friendlier for ordinary people.

10. Using splash pages

No, this is not really a sacrilege to web design, but you must understand that using splash pages will create a very rigid barrier between search engines and your site. If you are really worried about search engine optimization (SEO) stats and reports, then removing the barrier will lead to better results.

Using splash pages can often be seen as an amateur way of advertising: it is the equivalent to a shout-out. Do your marketing the natural way, and people will visit you naturally as well.

11. Old design and content

Carefully look at how your website is designed. Is it already out of date? Is the content updated at least regularly? Will there still be someone looking for your old product?

Always consult a professional if you are not sure if your site needs a redesign. If you have trouble loading your site with content, you can always outsource for talented individuals. If you are really serious about your site's goals, then you need to do something.

12. No further analytics

That's why analytics are there: to let you know what is going on with your website and its content. If you are serious about what you have planted, you should be more than excited with how it is growing (or shrinking) and, of course, take necessary action. You don't want to throw corn pellets on the ground without checking if the birds have come or not.

Your website is your investment, and you should consider it as such at all times. Avoid the above-listed mistakes, and you will gain a better-functioning website that people will love to use.

That's it: your new site is ready, it is live online… it's there for all the world to see, and it looks great. Now all you need is traffic, and in the chapters that follow we show you exactly how to get it!

CASE STUDY   TotallyMoney.com

TotallyMoney.com is the UK's credit eligibility and comparison specialists, committed to helping people get accepted. They help you to get the credit you deserve by building an eligibility check that matches people to credit cards/loans that have the highest percentage chance of acceptance.

Location

UK.

The challenge

TotallyMoney.com is one of the UK's leading credit comparison sites, a highly competitive vertical. They wanted to increase their SEO visibility and brand awareness by creating data-driven, impartial content that helps users to make informed decisions in a simple and fair way.

They asked Kaizen to create an innovative content marketing campaign to earn authoritative backlinks and press coverage referencing the TotallyMoney.com website.

Target audience

- UK adults.
- Low to middle income.
- People who want to/need to improve their credit rating but keep facing rejection.

Action

- The objective was to create a complex data visualization that informed users on the best commuter towns and cities surrounding London, which could genuinely help people to make an informed decision on the best places to live – avoiding the rising London property prices.
- First, Kaizen had to determine which metrics would define a town or city as one of the best.

- The metrics that were agreed upon were average house prices; average season ticket prices; the journey time to/from London; and the average gross disposable income.

- Kaizen used Zoopla.co.uk as their main source for determining the average house price in each town; the National Rail website for season ticket costs and commuting times to/from the city; and the Office for National Statistics on gross disposable income.

- The next step was to figure out an accurate way to effectively rank the best commuter towns.

- For each location they assigned a score out of 40 based on the four available metrics. Each metric was scored between 1 and 10 using the following linear equation:

Table 3.1

	Score	House Price	Commuting	Trave Time (mins)	GDHI
Worst	1	£1,190,287.00	£6,076.00	45	£17,709.00
Best	10	£165,851.00	£1,872.00	19	£23,341.00

- Each location was then ranked from 1st to 89th based on its total score out of 40.

- Kaizen then built an interactive tool based on the data, which led to the visualization of a map with each town featured on a 'train line'. When initially viewed it shows you all of the towns based on the ranking, but a user can then use sliders to change each of the metrics. For example, they could use the sliders so they could just see the towns with a commuting time of less than 20 minutes.

- To support the interactive tool, Kaizen also created a static infographic version, along with multiple press releases summarizing the findings.

Results

As a result of the campaign, Kaizen gained 53 pieces of coverage (and still counting), including 44 links. These came from national newspapers including the *Daily Mail, AOL* and the *Metro*, along with the regional newspapers from the towns featured on the map.

The data also features in a number of regional print publications such as the *Surrey Mirror* and the *Gravesend Messenger.*

Links to campaign

http://www.totallymoney.com/commuter-hotspots/tool/
http://www.totallymoney.com/commuter-hotspots/infographic/

Comment

Our key aim was to create a beautiful, unique data visualization so that a user would instantly 'get' what the best commuter towns were. We worked really hard on that, with multiple design iterations, and it paid off. This is what I believe made the campaign such a strong success.

Pete Campbell, managing director, Kaizen

About the creator

Kaizen is a digital marketing agency based in London. They provide both SEO and content marketing campaigns for global brands that deliver significant growth in earned traffic as a result of innovative, industry-leading marketing campaigns (https://www.kaizensearch.co.uk/).

Bonus online-only chapter

Measurement and data: is it working?

Our chapter pledge to you – by the end of this chapter you will understand:

- The importance of measurement.
- The differences between owned, paid for and earned media.
- Why testing is vital.
- What attribution modelling is all about.

For this chapter I had the pleasure of working with data and analytics experts DQ Global, Marketing Metrix and Philippa Gamse. My thanks to each of them for their time and attention for this book.

To read this chapter, please go online to:

www.koganpage.com/understanding-digital-marketing

Search: being found online

OUR CHAPTER PLEDGE TO YOU

In this chapter you will discover answers to the following questions:

- Why is search important?
- What is a search engine, and how does it work?
- How big is search?
- How do I optimize my website for the search engines?
- What is paid search marketing and how does it complement SEO?
- What is black-hat SEO and why should I avoid it?

Search: *still* the online marketer's holy grail

When the first edition of this book was published in 2009 I called search the online marketer's holy grail. Back then search was essentially the panacea that, if harnessed effectively, would drive sustainable waves of targeted traffic to your website and, ultimately, generate more revenue for your business. For many businesses it still is.

Over the years our digital consumption habits have changed dramatically as we rely less on home pages and search engines, instead discovering content through social media and direct messaging on mobile apps. According to a report by Shareaholic in January 2016, collectively the top eight social networks drove 31.24 per cent of overall traffic to sites in December 2014, up from 22.71 per cent the same time the previous year.

That is pretty impressive, but it is important to remember that visitor volume is only part of the equation when it comes to choosing an effective platform for marketing your business. When it comes to getting your information in front of a highly targeted audience at the precise moment *when they are looking to buy your products or services*, search engines still reign supreme. To discount their importance to your online business based on the fickle barometer of online 'buzz' would certainly be a mistake.

In Chapter 3 we discovered how your company's website forms the hub of your digital world. Your website is much more than a shop window to a huge and growing global marketplace: a well-designed and implemented website is a place where you can interact with your customers, a virtual meeting place where you can do real business, with real people, in real time. The commercial potential is, quite simply, unparalleled.

But if you are going to realize even a fraction of that potential then you need to make sure that people can *find your site*. Even in this age of rampant online engagement, peer recommendation and reviews, the way that the vast majority of people find the things they need online is by typing a phrase into that little empty box on the home page of their favourite search engine.

On the internet there is really no such thing as passing trade. The chances of a potential customer stumbling across your site while randomly browsing the web are approaching negligible. That means your visitors have to learn about your site from somewhere else: by word-of-mouth recommendations (online or off), through conventional advertising and branding channels, by following a link from another website or (and still by far the most likely scenario) by clicking on a link in a search engine results page (SERP).

Think about the way you use the internet. Where do you go when you are looking for information, products or services online? If you are shooting the virtual breeze with your friends you head for Facebook, Twitter or Instagram, but if you're trying to find something specific you are much more likely to head for your favourite search engine.

About the engines

Why is search engine marketing so important?

In 2015, US businesses spent a staggering $27.3 billion on search marketing, according to the Winterberry Group. Why spend so much?

Simple: because search engines give those businesses a prime opportunity to put their products, services or brands in front of a vast and ever-growing market of prospective customers *at the precise time* those customers are looking for exactly what the business is selling. That is a pretty evocative marketing proposition – especially when you consider the volumes involved.

During January 2016, in the United States alone, search engines fielded more than 17.5 billion search queries (comScore qSearch). That is more than 2.5 searches for every living person on the planet in a single month!

Some important points to note:

- 70–80 per cent of users ignore the paid ads on any given search, focusing on the organic results.

- 75 per cent of users never scroll past the first page of search results.

- Companies that blog have 434 per cent more indexed pages. Companies with more indexed pages get far more leads.

- SEO leads have a 14.6 per cent close rate, while outbound leads (such as direct mail or print advertising) have a 1.7 per cent close rate.

- While this varies between different verticals, a study from Caphyon in 2014 shows that of Google searches 31 per cent of organic clicks go to the #1 position, 14 per cent of organic clicks go to the #2 position, and 10 per cent of organic clicks go to the #3 position.

How do search engines work?

It is important to understand at this point that search engines are interested, first and foremost, in delivering timely, relevant, high-quality search results to their users. The search engines are constantly researching, developing, testing and refining ways to enhance the service that they provide – looking to optimize the relevance and quality of the results they serve back to the user on every single query.

The rationale is simple: the better the search experience for the user, the better the reputation of the search engine and the more users it will attract. The more users a search engine has, the more alluring it is to advertisers, ergo the more ad revenue it can pull in.

Putting users first makes search engines richer... and that makes search engine shareholders happy. In that respect the internet is no different to traditional marketing channels like commercial television, radio and print publications. It is the viewers, listeners and readers that these channels look after first – because it is the audience that brings in the advertisers. Without an audience, they have no advertisers, and without advertisers they have no business.

From a marketer's perspective the search engines' constant quest to improve the search experience for users is something of a double-edged sword. Yes, it means that the best search engines have a bigger pool of potential prospects for your paid search advertising and your organic SEO efforts. But equally, the fact that things keep changing makes the process of optimization a continuous, uncertain and labour-intensive process.

Scouring the web

To deliver accurate, relevant, high-quality search results to their users, search engines need to gather detailed information about the billions of web pages out there. They do this using automated programmes called 'bots' (short for robots) – also known as 'spiders' – which they send out to 'crawl' the web. Spiders follow hyperlinks and gather information about the pages that they find.

Once a page has been crawled by a spider, the search engine stores details about that page's contents, and the links both into and out of it, in a massive database called an index. This index is highly optimized so that results for any of the hundreds of millions of search requests received every day can be retrieved from it almost instantly.

It is a mammoth task. While no one knows the real number of unique web pages out there, and search engines typically don't publicize the size of their indices, a post on Google's official blog (25 July 2008) gave some rare insight into just how big the web is:

The first Google index in 1998 already had 26 million pages, and by 2000 the Google index reached the 1 billion mark. Over the last 16 years, we've seen a lot of big numbers about how much content is really out there. Recently, even our search engineers stopped in awe about just how big the web is these days – when our systems that process links on the web to find new content hit a milestone: 1 trillion (as in 1,000,000,000,000) unique URLs on the web at once! Source URL: https://googleblog.blogspot.co.uk/2008/07/we-knew-web-was-big.html

Search engines do not index every one of those trillion URLs, of course. Many contain similar or duplicate information, or are not really relevant to search (think of a dynamically generated online event calendar, for example, with links to 'next day' and 'previous day' – in theory you could keep clicking forever, but only pages containing event information are of any relevance in search results), so some don't make it into the index.

The list of results for any given search query, which often contains many millions of pages, is then run through the search engine's complex ranking algorithms: special programs that use a variety of closely guarded proprietary formulas to 'score' a site's relevance to the user's original query. The output is then sorted in order of relevance and presented to the user in the SERPs.

Search engines process a huge volume of searches, scanning billions of items and delivering pages of relevant, ranked results in a fraction of a second. To the user the process seems quick, straightforward and seamless; but there is a lot going on behind the scenes.

Optimizing your site for the engines

To many, SEO appears to be something of an arcane art. It is a world that is shrouded in high-tech mystery, a complicated world full of secrets that mere mortals haven't a hope of understanding. One of the best places to start for tips on improving your site's ranking with the search engines is with the search engines' own guidelines, tips and resources for website owners (see Table 4.1).

Table 4.1 Links to webmaster resources for major search engines

Search engine resource	URL for webmasters
Google Webmaster Central	**http://www.google.com/webmasters**
Bing Webmaster Tools	**http://www.bing.com/toolbox/webmaster**
Yahoo! Web Publisher Tools	**http://tools.search.yahoo.com/about/ forsiteowners.html**

We asked Chris Bishop, an expert in SEO, to give us his advice on how to maximize your SEO efforts.

Expert view
An SEO survival kit: a field guide to Google's algorithms
Contribution by Chris Bishop, expert in SEO

For some, Google's algorithms are mysterious animals – hard to predict, difficult to understand and always ready to penalize the unwary. But start thinking about Google as an ecosystem kept stable by these algorithms, and it becomes easier to understand their behaviour and avoid the penalties they can impose.

All of these algorithms exist to make search better for your customers; their evolution contributes to the healthy growth of the internet as a tool for safely exploring, learning, buying and selling. If your content supports

▶

their specific objectives, then the algorithms will reward your site with higher ranking in organic search returns; if not, penalties will be imposed and your ranking will be suppressed.

There are five categories of Google algorithm, which have evolved to serve separate and specific functions:

1   *Penguin* improves user experience by looking at the quality of links to websites. It seeks out and removes spammy-looking sites from search returns, discouraging the kind of reckless link building that diminishes the accuracy of search.

2   *Panda* is all about website content. With a huge territory to crawl over and control, its job is to clear search returns of sites that have 'thin' or low-quality content. It is wise to all the 'black hat' activities – such as 'keyword stuffing' and 'cloaking' – that unscrupulous developers have used to build traffic in the past.

3   *Pigeon*, famous for its homing powers, looks after local search, providing the best matches for your query according to location.

4   *Hummingbird* is the Google search algorithm itself. It is precise and fast in the execution of its role. It ensures the quick sharing of ideas and content on the web.

5   The *mobile* algorithm, on the other hand, governs a whole separate, device ecosystem, promoting mobile-friendly sites on mobile-specific SERPs through enhanced ranking, as well as sensing where links to apps could be served appropriately.

How can we stay on top of the SERPs?

The Google ecosystem thrives through the automated scanning and promotion of websites with good content, using the systems outlined above – it aims to push up the ranking of sites that are well written, device specific, user friendly and authoritative. By the same token, it penalizes websites with poor content – those that appear badly maintained, laden with spammy or broken links, stuffed with keywords and duplicate pages.

What do penalties mean for me?

Penalties can mean the immediate demotion of your site far down the SERP rankings, making it almost impossible to find in natural search and causing your site traffic to dwindle. It is easy to see how the imposition of

Google penalties can ruin the growth and profitability of your internet business, and why you need to act quickly if you suspect there is a problem.

How are penalties imposed?

Google's delicate balance of promotion and penalty through search ranking is actually kept in place through a combination of algorithmical and manual operations. Manual and automated penalties are detected and dealt with in different ways – so, if you suspect you have been hit you will first need to work out which you are dealing with.

Often, the first indication you will have that a penalty of either kind has been imposed is a sudden drop in your site's traffic, since no prewarning system exists. It is important , therefore, that you regularly monitor traffic and be prepared to do some detective work if you think something is wrong.

Detecting and dealing with a manual penalty

You can check to see if you have been hit by a manual penalty by looking in the Google Webmaster Tools. If you have, there will be a 'manual actions report' describing where you have fallen foul of the rules.

Manual checks on sites by human operators are, in fact, quite common. According to Matt Cutts, former head of Google's webspam team, Google hands out more than 400,000 manual penalties every month. The good news is, they are relatively easy to handle.

Manually enforced penalties last for a defined period of time, eg one month. After that time, the penalty is lifted regardless of whether the issue has been fixed. But if you have fixed the problems before that window expires, you can submit a reconsideration request direct to Google to get the penalty lifted. There is great advice on how to do this on Google's own help pages.

Detecting and dealing with an automated penalty

The penalties imposed by the Google algorithms are more difficult to detect, since they do not tell you what you have been hit with and when. But they are mainly imposed by the Penguin and Panda algorithms. As discussed, Penguin deals with the quality of links to your site and Panda is concerned with the content of the site itself.

In the event of an unexplained dip in site traffic your webmaster will need to carry out date analysis to find out if you have been hit by a known algorithm update. They might have to match up the Moz update history with your traffic decline in order to be sure.

▶

Sort out your backlinks

If you've been hit by a penalty due to the quality of your links you will need to carry out an urgent backlink analysis and clean up. Export all links and rank them from the most authoritative to the least using a tool such as MajesticSEO. Get a sense of which sites are the issue and contact the webmasters of the sites where low-quality links appear, in order to remove them. Store a record of the e-mails you have sent in Google Docs, to show (for any future appeals) that you have made a reasonable effort. Create a disavow file for the remaining links domains.

Dealing with low-quality content on your website

For content issues, your focus should be on quality. Eradicate duplicate content where possible and deploy canonicals or robot.txt to remove confusion for search engine crawlers. Ensure each page on your website has keyword-optimized content and create unique, authoritative content with no spelling or grammatical errors.

Winning on penalties

Taking this kind of remedial action will not only mean penalties should be lifted on the next Panda update, but your website may rank even higher than before.

Recovering from Google penalties is possible, but following this best-practice advice with regular spring cleaning of links and content will make you battle-ready for future updates, too.

Evolving with Google

Google's algorithms are always evolving. They are getting better all the time, adapting to new digital threats and new market conditions with every update. And the lesson is that your web strategy should change and develop, too.

Don't get stuck in a pattern of repeating old SEO tactics, even if they seem to offer short-term gains of traffic. They are invariably evolutionary dead ends. So be strategic and long term in your view. Favour quality, expert content for your website, focus on *attracting* links rather than blindly building or buying them. That way, you will stay on top of the SEO food chain.

Make your site easy to crawl

If you are looking to attract search engine traffic, the last thing you want to do is make it difficult for search engines to index your website. Make sure your site design does not present unnecessary obstacles to search engine spiders.

While some 'window dressing' is obviously important to make your site appeal to real people when they arrive, to get enough of them to your site in the first place it is vital that your design does not unwittingly alienate search engine spiders (see Table 4.2). Make sure your site works for both, and that each page includes relevant text-based content; avoid flash-only sites and frames, which are difficult for spiders to crawl effectively; and make sure that every page on your site can be reached via a simple text-based hyperlink.

Table 4.2 Spider traps: web design features that can hurt your search engine visibility

Website feature	Why it's bad for your SEO
All flash website	Difficult for spiders to crawl. While search engines have improved their ability to index text-based content within flash files, excessive dependence on flash is still a bad idea for both SEO and usability.
JavaScript navigation	Spiders often don't activate JavaScript code, so unless you implement an alternative they may struggle to reach other pages on your site via script-based navigation. Make sure you have at least one *regular, text-based hyperlink* to every page on your site.
Frames	Frames are notoriously difficult to implement effectively from a user experience perspective, are very rarely necessary, and often cause indexing problems for search engine spiders.
Image maps and other non-text navigation	Some spiders may have problems following these links. If you use image maps for navigation on your pages, make sure you have *alternative text-based hyperlinks* leading to the same pages.
Dynamically generated pages	Less of a problem than it used to be, but some spiders can have trouble with very long dynamically generated URLs that contain too many parameters (?W=XYZ). Try to configure your site to use 'Search Engine Friendly' URLs where possible, or at least restrict dynamic URL parameters to a maximum of three.
AJAX	See notes for JavaScript above.

Words are the foundation for SEO

The starting point for effective SEO is knowing what the people who are looking for your products, services or information are typing into that little box on the search engine home page. Known as keywords or keyword phrases (which consist of two, three or more keywords), these form the foundation of your SEO efforts. Effective keyword selection should always be the very first thing that is carried out, as it permeates every aspect of SEO activity. Keywords are used to differentiate site architecture and will also inform the content marketing strategy.

Choosing effective keywords

So how do you go about choosing the right keywords for site optimization? Well, a good place to start is with the people you are hoping to attract. Knowing your target audience is a critical component of any marketing campaign – and it is the same here. Put yourself in your prospect's shoes, sitting in front of your favourite search engine looking for information on the product or service you are selling. What would you type into the box?

These are your 'seed' keywords. They give you a starting point to work from. Take these keywords and play around with them. Imagine the various combinations of search terms that your prospects might use to find your site. Type these into the engines and look at the results. Examine the sites that are ranking highly for your chosen keywords. Analyse them and try to work out how they are achieving those rankings.

You can also use a wide range of automated keyword suggestion tools such as the free tools provided by Google AdWords (http://bit.ly/GoogKWTool) and on the SEO Book website (http://bit.ly/UDMSEOBook); or Wordtracker (www.wordtracker.com) and Trellian's (http://bit.ly/KWDiscovery) keyword tools, both of which offer a free basic service with paid upgrades for a more comprehensive version. These tools typically provide insight into the search traffic volumes for the most popular phrases relating to seed keyword phrases you provide.

There are a lot of different keyword research tools and services available on the web. Perhaps the best way to research your options is to look for things like 'keyword research tool' or 'keyword suggestion' in your favourite search engine.

Jocelyn Le Conte, SEO expert from Periscopix, gives us her expert view on how to target your consumers using keywords.

Expert view

Targeting the consumers behind the keywords

Contribution by Jocelyn Le Conte, SEO expert from Periscopix

Whilst the world of paid search has typically revolved around keywords and search terms, there are now many other audience signals that can be used to ensure you are reaching the right person at the right time, thereby increasing the chances of targeting consumers at the correct stage in their decision making. We can look beyond the keyword to identify trends and opportunities in user behaviour, which can then be used to improve campaign performance. Not only does this allow advertisers to be more selective about who sees their ads, but it also improves the overall user experience, as the most relevant landing page can be chosen alongside tailored ad messaging.

What audience signals are readily available?

- demographics (age, gender, parental status etc);
- geographical location;
- time (hour of day and day of week);
- device (computer, tablet or mobile);
- remarketing;
- first-party customer relationship management (CRM) data.

Who is this user?

Knowing what you know about your target audience, does this user fall into the same demographical buckets? If so, it is possible to increase keyword bids to be more competitive on the search engine results page. If not, there are now more options available to increase the chances of turning that user into a loyal customer. Age, gender and other identifiers – such as whether they are a parent or not and their household income bracket – allows a campaign manager to provide the most relevant and appealing messaging possible. A fashion retailer, for example, can tailor ad messaging based on that user's gender signals. If a female user is searching with generic keywords such as 'winter jackets', showing an ad featuring women's fashion terms and using a landing page specific to

▶

a female range of jackets is likely to increase both traffic and sales versus options that try to cover all bases and cater for both men and women.

Where are your users and what are they doing?

Thinking about where the user is and what they are doing at the time they make a search can provide vital insight into their current mindset and likelihood to convert. Is the user near your store and likely to make their purchase offline rather than online? Are they searching during opening hours, or doing research in the evening to follow up on once you are open again? What device are they using? On a mobile device users are probably looking for directions or a phone number and are less likely to fill out lengthy online forms.

Rather than pausing or removing keywords because they don't provide the desired return, signals such as these provide you with other options to trial first. For example, a restaurant in central London that uses paid search to generate web bookings may choose to narrow down the audience exposed to their ads to people within three miles of the restaurant's location. They may also then choose to tailor their ad messaging for users searching on mobile phones in order to encourage phone calls rather than booking-form completions, as this action is more easily carried out on a smaller screen.

Has this user been to your site before?

Using remarketing, returning site visitors can be treated differently to new users. If a visitor spent several minutes browsing multiple pages of your site a couple of days ago, they are more familiar with your offering and brand and are therefore more likely to complete their transaction if they return. Did they make it all the way through the purchase process just to drop off at the payment details page, perhaps because they decided to wait until pay day before treating themselves to a new leather jacket? Increasing bids to be front-of-mind next time they are searching for one will raise the chances of securing that sale, and extra incentives can be provided by offering a coupon code in the next ad they see. Did they browse the catalogue pages for shoes but didn't purchase? When you launch a new range, let them know that there are new products to look at that might better suit their style or price range, in case they are more in line with what they were looking for.

Do you want to pay for that user's click again?

It is also possible to identify audiences that you may want to exclude from search campaigns. If your campaigns have small daily budgets or the main focus is on customer acquisition, users who have already visited your website but not converted can be prevented from seeing your ads again in the future. If a user has already provided their contact information via a newsletter signup or web form, in order to save your budget you can exclude these users and follow up instead via other means to nurture the lead, such as e-mail marketing.

Similarly, if bounced straight off your site last time they came, save your budget and don't target them again in the future if they didn't like what they saw first time around.

What do you know about your own customers that you can use to your advantage?

Using your internal CRM data, users you already have a relationship with can be treated accordingly. New customers? Be front of mind with more competitive bids next time they are looking for another of your products. Regular purchasers? Push delivery subscriptions or VIP packages in the ad messaging. Cold leads? Offer them a discount code in the ad next time they search for one of your keywords in order to get them to re-engage.

You may also be able to identify opportunities for upselling or cross-selling. A retailer with a list of users who have recently purchased a TV can ensure their ads are placed first should that user then go on to search in the future for a TV stand or Blu-ray player. Similarly, anyone who signed up for a 30-day free trial may be looking to upgrade to a paid subscription once the time period is up, in which case an advertiser can increase keyword bids for their most competitive keywords and amend ad copy – just to these users around day 28 – to promote the benefits of using their service.

For online consumers 70 per cent agree that the quality, timing and relevance of a brand's message influence their perception of a brand. Analysing and layering user-intent signals over keywords allows advertisers to build campaigns tailored specifically to their audience, personalizing ad messaging and blocking uninterested users from future exposure. It is not just about the keyword any more, so adapt your audience targeting to get the best out of your paid search campaigns.

Analyse the competition

Other tools on the web can provide you with insight into how your leading competitors are doing in terms of search engine traffic for particular keywords. Services on sites like SEO Toolset (www.seotoolset.com) and Compete (www.compete.com) can provide information on which keywords are driving traffic to your competitors' websites from the major search engines, and which of your competitors' sites are ranking for which keyword phrases – all of which can inform the choice of keywords you want to optimize for.

While automated tools are a good guide, don't underestimate the value of people as a source of inspiration for keyword selection. What you believe people will search for and what they actually type into the search box are often two very different things. Get a group of people together – if possible, representative of your target market – and start brainstorming keywords. The results will probably surprise you.

I have my initial keyword list, now what?

The first thing you want to do is narrow your initial list down to a more manageable size. What constitutes a manageable size will depend on your situation – on how much time, money and resources you have available for your SEO effort. Remember, there is nothing wrong with starting small: optimize a few pages for what you believe are your main keywords, and monitor the results on ranking, traffic and conversion for those pages. That will give you a solid foundation from which to build your optimization efforts, and your SEO expertise.

To whittle your list down to size, start by eliminating all of the words or phrases that are too general. Broad single-word terms such as 'shoes', 'mortgages', 'bottles' or 'computers' tend to be both very difficult to rank for (because they are high-traffic terms that can apply equally to a huge number of sites across the net), and at the same time are far too generic to drive valuable targeted traffic to your site.

Suppose you are an independent mortgage consultant based in Camden Town, London. If you choose to optimize a page based on the keyword 'mortgages' you will find yourself competing with a raft of mortgage providers, mortgage advisers, mortgage brokers, mortgage industry news sites, etc, from all over the world. Even if (and it's a big if) your page does make it to those coveted elevated positions in the SERPs for that keyword, the chances that people searching for the term 'mortgages' will be looking for an independent consultant in Camden are slim at best.

Phrases such as 'mortgages in Camden' or 'mortgage consultant north London', on the other hand, are potentially much less competitive, and generate much lower search volumes, but are much more valuable to your business, because the people who search on those terms are far more likely to be interested in the products and services you offer.

In other words, the more general a keyword, the less likely it is that your site will contain what the searcher is trying to find. Effective SEO is not just about generating traffic volume, it is about finding that elusive balance between keyword search volume and keyword specificity that drives the maximum volume of *targeted traffic* to your site.

Long-tail versus short-tail keywords

Keywords in SEO fall into two broad categories. Short-tail keywords are simple one- or two-word phrases that are typically very general in nature and attract a large volume of individual search requests. Long-tail keywords, on the other hand, are more complex queries that contain more words, and are much more specific in nature. Individually they attract a much lower volume of search traffic than their short-tail counterparts, but cumulatively these long-tail-type queries account for the lion's share of internet search traffic.

Martin Murray, the former head of Google's small and medium business channel for EMEA, sums it up like this:

In any keyword domain there are a small number of highly trafficked keywords or phrases and a large number of low-trafficked keywords or phrases. Often, the keyword domain approximates to the right-half of a normal curve with the tail of the curve extending to infinity. Low-trafficked keywords are therefore also known as 'long-tail keywords'.

The highly trafficked [short tail] keywords have the following characteristics: highly competitive, consist of one or two words, have a high cost per click and may have low conversion rates as they tend to be quite general. Examples from the accommodation sector might include 'hotel', 'London hotel' or 'cheap hotel'.

Low-trafficked [long tail] keywords are not so competitive, often consist of four, five or more words, have a lower cost per click and can have a higher conversion rate as they are quite specific, indicating that the searcher is further along the online purchasing cycle. Examples might include 'cheap city-centre hotel Dublin', 'stags weekend hotel temple bar Dublin' or 'business hotel with gym and spa Wexford'.

Effective search marketing campaigns tend to put a lot of effort into discovering effective long-tail terms, particularly for use in sponsored listings (pay-per-click) campaigns.

Successful keyword research should ultimately allow the marketer to find and focus on phrases that satisfy:

- volume: the number of people actually using that term to search;
- competitiveness: the number of other sites competing for the same phrase relevance;
- profitability: based around the products or services with the best margin.

Typically it makes sense to take a balanced approach, and work with a mixture of general short-tail keywords and more specific long-tail keywords as part of your organic SEO effort, while focusing on highly specific long-tail search terms is likely to yield a higher return on your investment for pay-per-click (PPC) campaigns (see later in the chapter).

Tracking the effectiveness of keywords has become more difficult since Google began to encrypt the referring terms, which now show as 'not provided' in analytics platforms. Keyword research therefore needs to be managed using other methods such as historical SEO data, webmaster tools, paid search data and site search data.

Focus on one page at a time

The list of keywords you are left with is very important. It essentially provides you with an SEO 'template' for your website. One of the key things to remember when you are approaching SEO is that you will be optimizing your site *one page at a time*. While you will look at some site-wide factors as part of your SEO effort, SEO is not a straightforward 'one-size-fits-all' operation, and each of the existing pages on your site will need to be optimized independently. It is also highly likely you will want to create new pages to maximize your potential search engine exposure for as many of your chosen keyword phrases as possible.

Think about it: when a search engine presents results to a user, it is not presenting whole sites, it is presenting the individual pages that, according to its algorithms, best match a user's query. That means each individual page on your website gives you an explicit opportunity to optimize for specific keywords or phrases – and that is important.

Your goal, then, is to isolate the important keywords and phrases in your particular market, and then to ensure your site includes individual pages with unique, relevant content optimized for a small number (ideally one or two, no more than three) keyword phrases. The more individual pages you have, the more opportunities you have to get your business in front of your prospects in the SERPs... and at the end of the day that is what SEO is all about.

Choose your page <title>s carefully

There is a small but very important HTML tag that lives in the header section of the code on each of your web pages. It is called the 'title' tag, and the text it contains is what appears in the title bar at the top of your browser window when you visit a web page. It is also, crucially, the text that appears as the 'clickable' blue link for a page when it is presented to users in the SERPs.

This means that what you put in the title tag is incredibly important for the following reasons: 1) The title tag is one of the most important on-page factors used by the search engines to rank your page. At this stage most, if not all, SEO experts agree that appropriate use of the title tag is a key factor in ranking well in the SERPs, and advise weaving your primary keyword(s) for a page into the title tag whenever possible (see Figure 4.1). Just remember not to sacrifice readability for your human audience. 2) The title is the first glimpse of your content that a search user will see. Giving your pages concise, compelling and informative titles will entice more users to click through to your page when it appears in search results.

Figure 4.1 Screenshot showing title tag and meta-description as they appear in HTML source code, and the same page as it is rendered in the Firefox browser, showing the start of the same title tag in the active tab

Give each page a unique meta-description

Another HTML tag that used to be very important for SEO, but is now pretty much obsolete, is the meta-tag. Meta-tags contain information that is accessible to browsers, search engine spiders and other programs, but that does not appear on the rendered (visible) page for the user. This meta-data was once used extensively by search engines to gauge what a page was about – especially the once obsessed-over meta-keywords tag.

There is, however, one HTML meta-tag that is still worth including as part of your SEO, and that is the meta-description tag. As with most things in search, the opinion of leading experts in the SEO community is divided as to just how valuable the meta-description tag is in terms of search engine optimization. While it is widely acknowledged that the tag does little, if anything, to improve your page ranking, it can help to boost your click-through rate (CTR) when your page does appear in the SERPs.

Depending on the query and the page content, leading search engines will often use the contents of your meta-description tag as the descriptive 'snippet' of text that appears below your page title in the SERPs. A well-written description for each page can, in theory at least, entice more users to click through to your page when it is returned in search results.

Use of the meta-description text by search engines is inconsistent. The rules applied vary from engine to engine, and even between different types of query on the same engine. However, having compelling, informative meta-description tags is something that search engines encourage – it certainly won't hurt your rankings, is beneficial to users and may well boost traffic to your site.

Use HTML mark-up for page headers

The actual difference that using specific HTML mark-up for page headings (eg <h1>, <h2>, etc) makes is marginal. However, the heading of a page should summarize its content and will therefore determine the types of keywords that it will be optimized around. Using HTML heading mark-up will not do any harm and will also provide users with a snapshot of content when they arrive at that page.

Make navigation easy for visitors and search engines

Search engines use a site's structure to determine the relative importance of pages within it, so pages linked from the main navigation are given a higher priority than deeper, secondary- or tertiary-level pages. The words used within the navigation are also key for engines, allowing them to determine the themes of linked pages – so it is important to use specific terms rather than generic, non-specific terms such as 'products', 'services' or 'solutions'.

CSS-based drop-down navigation systems can help to provide flexible, search-engine-friendly links to internal site categories and pages.

Both users and search engines benefit from the use of breadcrumb navigation when exploring website structures. For users, breadcrumb navigation provides a quick and easy way to determine exactly where they are within the site and navigate up a site structure easily. For search engines, breadcrumb links provide an overview of the site's structure and direct access to related pages.

Tag visual content for search engines

Page-specific images make sites much more appealing for visitors, and search engines are becoming much better at recognizing the content of photos. However, it is still important to properly tag and describe visual content for search engines and visitors. This includes adding an ALT description to all key images and, if relevant, a caption. This is vital for linking images as their ALT tags act like anchor text, so are given much more weight than for non-linking images.

Enhance search engine listings

Structured data mark-up is a way of providing additional meaning and context to the search engines about the content of a page, so they can create 'rich snippets' that enhance its listing on the SERPs. The main standard for structured data is ratified by www.schema.org and can be applied to a huge variety of data: for example, reviews, locations, people, events and products. When properly tagged, structured data can enhance search engine listings with star ratings, dates and additional information that benefits users and can also improve click-through rates. It is worth exploring the information contained in Google's Webmaster Guides as well as Schema.org to see which data types within a site can be tagged to enhance the user experience.

Another way to enhance search engine listings is through Google Authorship. When a connection is established between an author and the content they create through Authorship, Google displays the author's profile picture, name and a link to their Google+ profile (see Figure 4.2).

Figure 4.2 Screenshot showing Google Authorship

WordPress › Google+ Author Information in Search Results (Free ...
wordpress.org/.../**google**-author-information-in-search-results-w... ▾
by Florian Simeth
25 Oct 2013 - A) Set up **authorship** by linking your content to your Google+
profile. Create a Google+ Profile (http://plus.**google**.com); Follow this link to
open ...

Content – the most important thing on your site

Content is the single most important thing on your website: period. Unique, relevant, informative content is what sets your site apart from the competition. It is the reason users want to visit you, why other sites will want to link to you and, of course, why search engines will want to suggest your site to their users in search results.

When writing content for your site the key thing to remember is that you are writing it, first and foremost, for a *human audience*, not for search engine spiders. Yes, your pages need to be 'search-engine friendly', but the spiders should *always* be a secondary consideration: put your human audience first.

We asked Kevin Gibbons, managing director of BlueGlass, a digital marketing agency specializing in SEO and content marketing, to give us his expert view on the current landscape and future of SEO.

Expert view
The landscape and future of SEO
Contribution by Kevin Gibbons, managing director of BlueGlass

The one thing you can always be certain of in SEO is that the only constant is change! Ever since Google launched in 1998, they have kept us on our toes. They shook up the search engine landscape very quickly with their PageRank-based algorithm, which ranks pages in their search engine results based upon their link authority.

This development significantly increased the relevancy of search results. As a result, Google quickly started to build their market share to become people's search engine of choice.

Links, links, links

Of course, if you were looking to become a leading site and drive high-quality traffic and revenue from search engines, an obvious way to do this would be by link building.

Back in the 1990s the algorithm was in an early phase; quite often the site with the highest amount of links won. In some respects this is fine, but it meant that in a high-stakes game where everyone is looking for the quick win, it led to a lot of manipulation in order to make your website appear to be the best site in the eyes of Google...

And the biggest problem was that it worked!

The rise of content marketing

As Google clamped down on what they saw as SEO tactics, people already afraid of link building – and SEO in general – now found that previously successful tactics came with an important word attached: risk.

The one thing that we all knew Google loved – and was widely seen as the right thing to do, whether focusing on SEO or not – was to build a brand. Content marketing became a high-growth industry, when marketers realized that they could increase their natural search performance by providing the best content experience for a given keyword or topic, and earn links and social engagement. The focus shifted to authority publishers and influencers offering quality over quantity.

Of course content marketing is not new – people have been doing it for hundreds of years. The difference is that it now had quickly become a technique that marketers were adopting towards strengthening the organic performance of websites.

Typically I like to break this down into three pillars, so that you can make sure you are focusing on the right areas, and to ensure that you understand where you are at each stage:

- *Content strategy*: in order to achieve success, you first need to know what it looks like. Having a clear content strategy can help you to identify the gaps that are missing in your SEO strategy and customer journey. By visualizing the potential of what can be achieved, you can then start to put a plan into place on how to target those keyword and content-topic opportunities.

  Content is king! The most important thing for content today is to write it for the target audience. Google, Bing, Yahoo!, etc are *not* your target audience. If you write content for your target audience – thinking about the types of terms they will be searching for – you will begin to show up naturally in their searches, and your ranking and traffic will start to rise.

- *Creativity*: having a great idea is one thing, seeing it come alive is quite another. Content can take a number of different forms. The key to success is to start with the story you want to tell. Once you know this, it is easier to start piecing it together in terms of how to tell it – whether that is as a blog post, in-depth article, visual image or infographic, interactive guide, e-book/white paper, video or a slideshow presentation.

▶

There are multiple forms this could take – and you might want to use a combination of them together – keeping in mind that different people will prefer to consume content in different ways. However, the key thing is that your content gets your message across effectively and that it is the highest quality it can be in order to resonate and engage with your target audience.

Aim big and try to create the best piece of content created on the web for the subject you are writing about.

- *Promotion*: once you have your content ready to go, now you need to get it seen. However, if you are only just thinking about promotion now, chances are it might already be too late.

  You should be thinking about your target audience from the very start: who is your target audience? What are their persona profiles/demographics? Where do they go online? Who are their social influencers? What publishers/blogs do they read?

  Once you know this it is easier to craft your content towards them – so that when it comes to promotion, they are already on board, and because you involved them early they are more than happy to promote you.

  You can start researching the type of results you want to achieve with your promotion. Analyse what content your favourite bloggers love to write about. Ask what your customers would love to see more of. Seek out publishers/influencers who like to share and ask them what they think about your ideas.

  If you can target this well, everything else becomes so much easier. Once you have begun to generate coverage, you can reach out to new bloggers, promote to your e-mail newsletter list, run paid social media campaigns and look to drive more attention, engagement and coverage for your content.

SEO measurement

Perhaps the most important thing in content marketing is that you don't forget why you are doing it in the first place! At first, you might be looking towards KPIs such as social media engagement, authority links, PR coverage, referring/organic traffic, search rankings etc. However, over the longer term, if your ultimate goal is SEO, the way you would probably like to measure this is by the uplift in organic revenue or leads.

This is why it is so important to have that clear content strategy in place from the start, because then you can prioritize your content ideas and themes by value to the business. From there, you can then begin to work backwards in terms of measuring the organic uplift to the site – specifically for key pages/categories you have been focusing your content upon – so that you can demonstrate the impact made.

Remember that SEO is not an overnight thing, it improves over time. It takes time, it takes work, and it is important to have realistic expectations. The mindset that 'this one content campaign is going to change everything' could do more damage than good. You need a sustained effort and well-planned content strategy in order to make sure that you are constantly moving in the right direction. The best long-term results are rarely seen from big spikes in traffic – it is the gradual month-on-month small wins that build up into much bigger wins.

What's next?

It is always important to look not just at what is working now, but also where SEO is going next.

You can always get caught up in the latest tactics, which can give you a small gain here or there. You can read endless articles on recent updates. Right now the topical ones would be changes to Google's search layout, the RankBrain algorithm, or further Panda/Penguin roll-outs. But this can change on an almost daily basis. When it does, you have to decide if you are going to react or hold. Sometimes the best thing to do is nothing – carrying on as you were and seeing if the situation works itself out. Otherwise you'll be chasing Google's changes endlessly, while not allowing adequate time for back-end analysis.

Google's aim has always been to provide the best/most relevant results for a given query to a search. Rather than chasing the algorithm and targeting the small wins it is much more beneficial to focus on the bigger ones.

The biggest winners in organic search are inevitably the ones who are looking much further ahead, trying to provide the best experience possible for their audience. Additionally, by now you have to be thinking not just as a website, but as a platform available across all devices.

Keywords in content

The subject of keywords in content is something that generates a lot of debate in SEO circles: where to place them, when and how often they need to appear on the page and lots more besides. As with most things SEO, opinions tend to vary significantly on the subject.

There is no magical number of words per page or number of times to use your phrases in your copy. The important thing is to use your keyword phrases only when and where it makes sense to do so for the real people reading your pages.

Links – second only to content

As you have read, the critical importance of links in securing a high page ranking is one of the few things that has universal consensus in the world of SEO. Popular opinion maintains that nothing, but nothing, is more important than high-quality inbound links from 'authority' websites in achieving high rankings in the search engine results.

But wait a minute... if nothing is more important than links, why did we just say in the heading that links are second only to content? Simple: because creating outstanding content is the most effective way of attracting high-quality inbound links from authoritative online sources. And there is no doubt that those are the links that have the biggest impact on your search engine rankings.

The role of internal and external links

Internal links and external links are both important for boosting the ranking of individual pages within your site. First let's define exactly what we mean by internal and external links:

External links: these are links that reside on pages that do not belong to your domain – in other words, links from other websites.

Internal links: these are the links that reside on pages that belong to your domain or subdomains – in other words, links between pages on the same website, or pages that reside in subdomains of the primary domain.

All of these links are important. Links from reputable external sources boost your site's perceived authority with the search engines, which in turn helps your more popular pages to rank higher in the SERPs. Internal links give you a way of distributing the 'authority' accrued by your more popular pages (like your home page, for example) to other important pages that you want to rank for. Internal links can also help to group pages of related content. For example, using a 'related posts' list helps to make site content more engaging, and encourage visitors to explore the site rather than bounce off a page as soon as it has been visited.

Getting good links

There are a huge number of ways that you can encourage people to link to your site. But building quality natural links is not easy, and it takes time. It depends on creating high-quality content, and building a reputation for excellence (or notoriety – which can work well for links, but might not project the right image to your customers) in your chosen field, which in turn encourages other website owners to link to you.

There are, of course, some quicker, easier ways to secure incoming links, but such links tend either to be of poor quality (hence of little SEO value), or violate search engine guidelines. Search engines take a dim view of anyone trying to artificially manipulate search results. Remember, they are trying to deliver the most relevant, highest-quality results to their users – and see any attempt by a less relevant or lower-quality site to leapfrog up the rankings as 'search engine spam'.

Harvesting links purely for the purpose of boosting your site's rankings in the search engines is frowned upon, and while it may work in the short term, it is a risky strategy at best that will ultimately harm your rankings, and may even result in your entire site being blacklisted and removed from the search engines' indexes altogether. If you are trying to build a sustainable, long-term online business it simply is not worth the risk.

For sustainable long-term rankings, focus instead on building high-quality links through ethical means, concentrate on your content, and build your site with your end user in mind. Working within search engine guidelines may mean that it takes a lot longer to achieve the rank you are looking for, but in the end it is generally better that way.

Link-building tips:

- *Generate truly valuable content that other sites will want to link to*: these one-way unsolicited links are by far the most valuable kind. Search engines love them, and see them as a genuine endorsement of one site by another. As your site becomes more visible, the content will organically attract more links, which in turn will improve your visibility, attracting even more links. When it works, this process is self-perpetuating, leaving you free to concentrate on quality content, while the links look after themselves.

- *Let people know your site is out there*: people can only link to your site if they know it is there. Promote your site at every opportunity, especially in places where you know there are other website owners. Use the medium to your advantage. Online communities, forums, social networking sites and e-mail lists all offer great opportunities to get your site URL out in front of people who can link to it. Blogs are another source of potential links – some blogs are incredibly popular, and bloggers are noted for their affinity to linking. Try submitting a few poignant comments to high-ranking blogs in your sector (do this responsibly; aim to add real value to the discussion rather than simply promoting your site).

- *Create your own blog*: a blog can be an incredibly powerful promotional and link-building tool, if used wisely. If you have strong opinions, or a high level of knowledge in your industry, and you are happy to write regular posts, setting up a blog is easy and can be a great way to increase both visibility and incoming links.

- *Network, network, network*: use your network of contacts both online and offline to promote your site and encourage people to link to it, and pass it on to their own network of contacts in turn. If people look at your site and like what they see, they may well link to it.

- *Ask the people who link to your competitors to link to you*: use tools such as Moz Open Site Explorer, SearchMetrics, LinkDex or MajesticSEO to find out who is linking to your main competition for your selected search keywords. Approach those sites and ask them if they would be willing to link to your site too. After all, if they link to your competitors, why wouldn't they?

- *Encourage links within content and with descriptive anchor text*: links within content are preferable to links on a page that just lists links. Surrounding content helps to put a link in context, both for the user and for the search engines. You should also encourage descriptive anchor text that, if possible, includes one or two of your chosen keywords.

- *Submit your site to high-quality directories*: getting your site listed in high-quality, well-respected online directories such as the Open Directory Project (www.dmoz.com, which is free) and Yahoo! Directory (dir.yahoo.com, which charges an annual fee for commercial listings) can be a great way to get your link-building started. These links will help both search engine spiders and that all-important human traffic to find your site. As leading directories are also considered 'authority' sites by the major search engines, links from these sites will also help boost your ranking.

- *Use link bait*: link bait is anything that will entice incoming natural links from other websites or users. Link bait can be an interesting or controversial article, a downloadable document or report, a plug-in that improves the functionality of a piece of software or useful widgets (small snippets of code) that other website owners can embed into the sidebars and content of their pages that include a link back to your landing page. Link bait is really *anything* that could entice someone else to link to your content. Be creative! Just stay within the search engines' published guidelines.

- *Offer to swap links with a select few relevant, high-quality sites*: these are called reciprocal links. Although they are less useful than they used to be in terms of SEO value, they can still be used effectively in moderation. While the power of reciprocal links to boost your rankings has been diluted, they do help to establish relevance and authority in your subject area – just be sure that you link to relevant, high-quality sites, and only swap links with a few of them. As a rule of thumb, you should *never* – just for the sake of a reciprocal link – link to a site that you would not genuinely recommend to your site visitors.

Submitting your site URL and site map

Submitting your site URL, strictly speaking, is not necessary any more. If you have followed the advice above, and have managed to secure some inbound links, it will not be long before the spiders find you. That said, all of the major search engines offer a free submission process, and submitting your site won't hurt. If you want to kick-start the indexing process, then by all means go ahead and manually submit your home page and one or two other important pages.

The other thing you can do that will help search engines to crawl all relevant pages on your website is to submit an XML site map that adheres to the site map protocol outlined on www.sitemaps.org. Submitting a site map will not do anything to up your pages' rankings, but it will provide additional information that can help search engines to crawl your site more effectively. It is one more thing you can do to improve the odds, so ask your webmaster, web developer or SEO to include a site map for your site, and to either manually submit it to the major search engines, or to add an entry in your robots.txt file (a file that sits in the root directory of your webserver that contains instructions for automated crawlers) that lets them pick it up automatically.

Local SEO

Any business that gets some or all of its customers or clients locally should consider local SEO. That could be a local restaurant, retail outlet, doctor, dentist or lawyer, but it could just as easily be a local ad agency. If you have a physical address in a city and expect people to go there, you should be doing local SEO for that location.

While all of the factors that apply to regular SEO also impact local SEO (on-page factors, links, content, indexing, etc), local comes with a few unique elements. The first and probably most important is that for local SEO you need to create and claim a local profile on Google (and other platforms as desired). Your local listing is what will usually show for localized search results.

The second most important thing is called a NAP citation, which is any place online that uses your company name, address, phone number. Google views NAP citations in the same way as regular SEO views links – citations from authoritative and relevant sources can help improve your ranking. While Google is very smart, it is important that all citations use the same format as far as possible. Don't abbreviate in one and not the other (St versus Street, for example).

Third, you need reviews – lots and lots of reviews (preferably really good ones). The quantity and quality of reviews left for your business on your Google Places page is one of the most important local ranking factors.

The three biggest factors in local listings appear to be the number of citations, the number of reviews (primarily on your Google Places listing, although other places do count) and how positive the reviews are overall. From what we have seen, positive reviews will trump citations, so persuading your customers and clients to recommend you on your Google local page is the single most important thing you can do.

And start all over again...

Now you have your site optimized, it is time to sit back and start reaping the rewards, right?

Unfortunately not! The ever-changing nature of the search environment means that there is no magic bullet in SEO. It's not a one-size-fits-all discipline, and it never ends. You have to work hard to find the right blend of targeted keywords for your particular business, operating within your particular market at the current point in time. You have to optimize your pages based on those keywords, and deliver compelling, high-impact content. You have to attract incoming links.

Then you have to measure, monitor and refine continuously, tweaking and tuning your optimization efforts based on changing conditions in the marketplace, the search engines and your customers. Take your foot off the gas, and that high ranking you have worked so hard to achieve will gradually (and sometimes not so gradually) start to slip away.

Optimization is a dynamic and iterative process – and if you want sustained results it needs to be ongoing. In this section we have barely scratched the surface of the wonderfully dynamic, often frustrating but potentially incredibly rewarding world of SEO. To learn more, check out some of the free and subscription-based SEO resources online such as SEO Book (http://bit.ly/UDMSEOBook), visit www.gogadm.com... or just 'Google' it. After all, it is reasonable for you to expect that the best people to advise you on your SEO will be up there near the top of the SERPs.

Advertising on the search engines

According to figures released by the Interactive Advertising Bureau (IAB), paid search revenue for the United States came in at US $20.5 billion for 2015, a figure that accounted for just over 34 per cent of total online advertising spend.

What is paid search engine advertising?

Paid search marketing refers to the paid-for advertising that usually appears alongside, above and occasionally below the organic listings on the SERPs or on a partner site. These are usually labelled with something like 'sponsored links' or 'sponsored results' in order to make it clear to users that they are, in fact, paid-for ads and not part of the search engine's organic listing.

Typically, you pay each time your ad is clicked, hence 'pay per click' or PPC. PPC is the most common form of paid search marketing, but you can also buy ads on a 'cost per thousand' (CPM) basis.

How does paid search advertising work?

When a user enters a search query into the search engine, the engine returns a list of organic search results. It also determines which ads to show that are relevant to the search query. These ads, which sit adjacent to or above the organic listings, used to be small, unobtrusive text-based ads, but now may come with enhanced listings that include images and other data such as price and merchant name. While high ranking in the organic listing is the ideal that most webmasters are striving for (because it is 'free' and because users see organic results as impartial: they trust, and therefore click on, organic listings in preference to paid ads), optimizing a page to rank in organic search results can be difficult, and getting a consistently high and sustainable ranking takes a substantial amount of effort and a lot of time.

Time without traffic, of course, is a missed opportunity for your online business, and that is where paid search advertising comes in. By agreeing to pay the search engines a fee per click for your ads to show up as sponsored result when a user types in your chosen keywords, you can put your site in front of your prospect in the SERPs almost immediately. When the user clicks on one of your ads, you get a new visitor and the search engine bills you for the click: everyone is happy, at least in theory.

PPC keywords are bid on by advertisers in an auction-style system: generally the higher the bid per click, the higher the ad's placement in the SERPs. Most PPC systems also employ a 'quality' quotient into their ad placement rankings, based on the popularity of the ad (its click-through rate, or CTR) and the perceived quality of both the ad content and the landing page it points to (eg Google's AdWords Quality Score).

Why use paid search marketing?

There are a lot of reasons to use PPC search marketing. Here are just a few:

- *Generate traffic while you are waiting for your SEO to kick in*: it can take months to get your site to the top half of the first page of organic search results through SEO. PPC ads can get your site in front of your audience almost immediately.

- *Highly targeted ads mean a better chance of conversion*: you are not broadcasting your message to the masses as you would be with a display ad or banner ad – your search marketing ad will only appear in front of users who have prequalified themselves by typing your chosen keywords into the search engine in the geographical regions you have selected.

  It can be an incredibly effective way to advertise. You only pay for your ad when a prequalified user clicks on it and is taken to your site. If they don't click, you don't pay. Providing your keywords are highly targeted and your landing pages convert well, it can generate a very healthy ROI. Some of the specific benefits of PPC advertising are:

– Full financial control: there is no minimum spend, you can set maximum monthly budgets on an account-wide basis or on individual campaigns, and you specify the maximum amount per click that you are prepared to pay for each ad.

– Full editorial control: you are in complete control of every aspect of your campaign – from the title and ad copy, to the keywords and keyword matching option to apply, to the URL of the page you want users sent to.

– Testing, tracking and tweaking on the fly: there are tools that allow you to run real-time comparison tests to see how differences in your ads affect your click-through rate, and a host of reporting options that let you track your campaign and tweak it to achieve better results.

– Improve your reach: target different keywords to those you rank for in the organic search, and broaden your reach for those more specific long-tail keywords that yield small volumes of high-value traffic.

– Transcend the boundaries of the SERPs: for even broader reach you get to select whether you want your ads to appear only on the search engine's own sites, on their advertising affiliate sites, or even on specific affiliate sites of your choosing.

Sounds great, how do I get started?

Unsurprisingly, the search engines have made setting up PPC campaigns really easy. There are automated wizards to guide you through the sign-up process, and plenty of tools to help you establish, monitor and optimize your campaign. It is all very slick, and from a standing start you can have your first ad appearing next to search results and driving traffic to your site in under 15 minutes.

But hold your horses... just because you can, doesn't necessarily mean that you should. Rushing headlong into your first PPC advertising campaign might yield great results for you 'out of the box', and then again it might not. As always, it pays to do a bit of preparation first.

Sarah McCormick, brand manager for Visual Soft, offers us her expert view on the importance of knowing your audience in order to run an effective campaign.

Expert view

The importance of knowing your audience
Contribution by Sarah McCormick, brand manager for Visual Soft

As more people turn to the world of online retail, the requirement for running an effective marketing campaign to deliver your message on the web has significantly increased. Digital marketing techniques including SEO, PPC and affiliates are all avenues that should be explored to drive visitors, and ultimately revenue.

Since the introduction of the AdWords system in 2000, PPC has been a constantly evolving form of online advertising. It has become one of the core channels for most companies and even sole traders, and in the last five years alone we have moved away from how many keywords you have in your account and ad copy stating 'buy' or 'sign up', to being strategic with just about everything we do, from match types, bid changes, landing-page testing and looking at the bigger digital picture for cross-channel and cross-device.

Know your audience

It is quite easy to drive traffic to your site, but is it the right traffic? Understanding your audience is a key aspect for a strong advertising campaign across any media channel, as in order to persuade them to consider, try or purchase your products, you must beyond all other requirements know 'that' audience.

As an example, a fashion retailer could have numerous audiences, including:

- the regular purchaser;
- the quarterly wardrobe refresher;
- the inspiration searcher;
- the offline purchaser;
- the cross-device purchaser;
- the app users.

With so many different audiences, it is important to know your key objective and understand how to obtain the right traffic for the objective you are trying to achieve.

How PPC can help

Pay-per-click (PPC) advertising is a great testing ground to understand what works with such metrics as click-through rate (CTR) and conversion rate (CR). Using tools such as Google Analytics to understand bounce rates, number of pages visited and time on site can give you the direction to achieve or refine your goals.

Experiment testing has been around in AdWords for a while, allowing you to A/B test campaigns, using different landing pages, bids etc. This is basically splitting your traffic however you require, ie 50/50.

However, moving away from the A/B test campaigns you also have remarketing lists for search ads (RLSAs), demographic and customer match – all key attributes to test, which can help drive your accounts forwards.

Using RLSAs

In 2013 Google introduced remarketing lists for search ads (RLSAs) – allowing a great testing ground to expand account reach and understand your customers better. However, not so exciting for clients who had difficulty implementing tracking code. Since then, in 2015 Google introduced a way of using Google Analytics (GA) to create RLSAs.

RLSAs allowed you to move away from the usual bid methods to allow for more in-depth targeting methods that combined website behaviour with the search queries within the Google SERP. As long as more than 1,000 people visit your website in 540 days, you will meet the minimum audience size requirement to run an RLSA campaign.

RLSAs are extremely powerful, but also extremely underutilized. These can be used across both keyword and shopping campaigns. It is a big opportunity for any small business with a limited marketing budget.

There are two ways of using RLSA, 'Target and Bid' and 'Bid Only'.

'Bid Only' is used for when you want to modify a bid to selected audiences lists but still continue to be seen by everyone else too across your selected search terms or product listing ads (PLAs). Below are a few examples of how to use this:

- I am willing to be in a higher position across generic terms if the person has previously visited the site as they could be further down their purchase cycle.

- I want up-weighting previous visitors to the 'Dresses' category if they search for generic 'accessories' or 'footwear' – well, a girl needs to complete her outfit.

▶

- I don't want to pay as much for a returning customer, so down-weighting bids on previous purchasers across specific adgroups, ie branded terms.

Not only can you down-weight, but you can also completely exclude audiences, so by excluding you would not show to anyone within that audience list, ie previous purchasers across brand terms. Again this would depend on what you are trying to achieve – and also remember to monitor the SERP if you are planning on doing this. As always with advertising, where there is an opportunity, competitors are monitoring. This is why we test and refine strategies.

'Target and Bid' allows you to show only to your chosen target audience lists. This enables you to potentially target terms that you previously have not been able to due to budget restrictions, or due to previously testing high traffic levels and low performance.

Below are a few examples of use:

- duplicate campaign to target specific audiences;
- previous site visitors across generic terms, ie Black Friday;
- previous site visitors on competitor terms;
- running a new customer/returning customer account strategy.

There are a lot of different ways to use these, and the best way to start is 'Bid Only' in order to understand your audience across the keyword set you have.

RLSAs are also now available on Bing; however, tracking code will need to be implemented.

Implementing demographic for search ads

It goes without saying that being able to modify bids to increase visibility when your key demographics are searching is a no-brainer, as is excluding demographics that are not the right fit:

- Age ('18–24', '25–34', '35–44', '45–54', '55–64', '65 or more' and 'Unknown').
- Gender ('Female', 'Male' and 'Unknown').
- Parental status ('Parent', 'Not a parent', and 'Unknown').

As you can see there is an 'Unknown' demographic group. To be able to make the most out of using these within your paid search strategy, make sure you test before defining the core direction in order to understand what you have now, then modify and continue to test. Remember, without doing it you will not know if this is a positive or negative for your account.

Demographic targeting is also available within Bing too, and has been for some time.

Customer match

At the end of 2015 Google introduced 'Customer Match'. This enables you to reach your highest-value customers across Google search, as well as YouTube and Gmail. Customer Match allows you to upload e-mail addresses, in customer lists, which can be matched to signed-in users on Google in a secure and privacy-safe way.

Like with RLSAs you can up- or down-weight these lists and also gather insight from these lists depending on your account structure, ie you obtained leads that went cold over six months ago. If these were a Customer Match list, from implementing this across your account you would be able to see if they are still searching and in the market.

Although not available on shopping campaigns just yet, there are key indicators to suggest that it could be coming soon, so it is worth taking into consideration if you are reviewing your CRM segmentation.

Where next?

If you haven't started using RLSAs or demographics for search ads (DFSAs), the best way to start is 'Bid Only' and gather information using a 0 per cent bid modifier – from there you can put together testing plans.

Don't forget to add Bing into your testing plans too. Remember that you tend to see different audiences between the two search engines, so don't presume that as Google does it then Bing will too. By knowing your audience it gives you an important insight into many parts of your marketing strategy, from your content to your online advertising.

A few points to keep in view

Three key things to remember when advertising on the search engines:

- *Optimize your ads*: your ads need to entice users to click on them if you are going to get traffic. Think carefully about your title and ad copy. Remember, you want targeted copy that will appeal to people who are *ready to buy* – so be specific. Generating clicks that don't convert *will cost you money*!

- *Converting clicks into customers*: once you get the clicks, you need to turn your new prospects into paying customers as often as you can. It is your *conversion rate* that will make or break your PPC campaign. Don't direct traffic from your ad back to your home page. Send it instead to a page directly related to the text of the ad they have just clicked on – a product page might work, but better still would be a specific *landing page* tailored to reinforce your PPC campaign. Remember, if you fail to convert your traffic into revenue, all your PPC campaign will do is haemorrhage cash.

- *Measure everything and test, test, test*: the best way to learn is to start small, track your campaign carefully and study the metrics (see the online-only Bonus Chapter 1, Measurement and Data, available at www.koganpage.com/understanding-digital-marketing). Try out different ad combinations, different landing pages, different keyword combinations and measure how the changes affect your CTR, your conversion rate, your cost per conversion and, ultimately, your bottom line.

Mastering the intricacies of PPC advertising could take a lifetime, but the basics are straightforward enough, and the best way to learn is to dive in and start using it. You will also find plenty of resources to help you, both in the search engines' advertising sections and in the online marketing community. A great place to start is the free online webinars in the Google Learn Classroom (https://www.google.co.uk/ads/experienced/webinars.html) and Bing's resources for advertisers (http://advertise.bingads.microsoft.com/en-us/how-to).

Top 10 tips for paid search marketing success

1 Define your goals and objectives before you start any paid search campaigns.

2 Target your search account to your website – create individual ad groups around products and services you have pages for.

3 Keep keywords in each ad group to a minimum and ensure they are all thematically relevant – ideally less than 25 keywords per ad group.

4 Write bespoke creative for each ad group and always run with three or four variations of messaging so that you can test which works most effectively for your business.

5 Think carefully about match types: don't put everything on the default broad-match option unless you know what you are doing.

6 Include as many negatives as possible and look to add these at an ad group level.

7 Decide carefully about whether to use in-house skills or an agency.

8 Focus always on the 'quality score' and the user experience. Badly setting up search hits your pocket very hard, and costs much more money than is necessary.

9 Keep a close eye on competitors and the search landscape – their messaging and keyword coverage give you an indication of what will work for you!

10 Optimize, optimize and optimize the account – this needs to be done regularly in order to get the best out of performance.

Steve Walker, head of SEO at STEAK, offers us his expert views on how search engines use behavioural data as a ranking factor.

Expert view

How search engines use behavioural data as a ranking factor
Contribution by Steve Walker, head of SEO at STEAK

Google use 200+ factors within their ranking algorithm, the majority of which are a closely guarded secret. Website content and quality of links have for a long time been seen as some of the most powerful metrics that Google use; however, there is evidence to suggest that behaviour signals – how searchers interact with Google's result page (SERP) and the interaction with the website once visited – are beginning to grow in significance within the ranking process.

Patents filed and awarded to Google have revealed how this data could be incorporated as a ranking factor:

The general assumption [...] is that searching users are often the best judges of relevance, so that if they select a particular search result, it is likely to be relevant, or at least more relevant than the presented alternatives.

Google Patent, 2014, https://www.google.com/patents/US8661029

▶

Alongside patents, numerous leading Google spokespeople have revealed how this kind of feedback can help to improve the quality of the results page. A specific example from a Google employee's testimonial at a Federal Trade Commission breaks this down in detail:

> The ranking itself is affected by the click data. If we discover that, for a particular query, hypothetically, 80 per cent of people click on result number 2 and only 10 per cent click on result number 1, after a while we figure that probably result 2 is the one people want. So we'll switch it.
>
> Google's former search quality chief, Udi Manber (quote shared by Danny Sullivan, co-founder of Search Engine Land)

Google's primary aim is to provide the best searching experience for its users; it is logical that this proprietary behaviour data would be used throughout this process – being used as a method of judging the quality of the other ranking factors in delivering the most relevant result, using 'real-time' data from the searchers themselves.

What do we mean by behavioural data?

Behavioural data is an umbrella term for a selection of metrics that are derived from the actions of the searcher, from how the searcher interacts with the listings on the results page through to the engagement once browsing the web page:

- *Search query volume*:
  - Definition: the volume of searches for a specific search term.
  - How it works: the volume of searches using a query in conjunction with a brand entity (eg Amazon, HSBC, Sony) gives Google an understanding of the relevancy between the brand and the search term in question. For example, if a large volume of people search for 'PC World Laptops' it is logical that people would view the company PC World as a relevant result for the singular term 'Laptops'.
- *Bounce rate/'pogo-sticking'*
  - Definition: the percentage of visitors to a particular website who navigate quickly back to the search engine results page after viewing the landing page.
  - How it works: if a searcher visits a page and then quickly returns to Google it is a good indication of that website being an unsatisfactory result and not answering the original searcher's intent.

- *Click-through rate (CTR)*
  - Definition: CTR is the number of clicks that your search listing receives divided by the number of times your listing is shown, expressed as a percentage (clicks ÷ impressions = CTR).
  - How it works: if a listing has an unusually high CTR for its ranking position it indicates that the website is a more attractive result than the higher-ranking websites, and potentially deserving to be more visible on the results page.
- *Dwell time/'long click'*
  - Definition: dwell time is the amount of time that a visitor spends on a page after clicking on its listing in a SERP, before coming back to search results.
  - How it works: the length of time a searcher interacts with the clicked website before returning to the search results is a clear signal of the quality of the website in question.

What proof is there?

In mid-2015 Rand Fishkin (founder of SEOMoz) recruited his Twitter followers to investigate the impact of behaviour signals on search results.

He requested that his followers search for the term 'best grilled steak', click on the first result and then return back to the results page as soon as the page has loaded – increasing the bounce rate of the first listing and creating signals that lead Google to believe the result was a low-quality result.

The second stage was to click on the fourth result but stay on the clicked page for a significant amount of time, without returning to the search results – increasing the dwell time of the clicked page and indicating to Google that this particular result answered the original search query the most effectively.

After 70 minutes and approximately 500 interactions, the result that was engineered to show positive engagement increased in ranking position from fourth to first place.

This is not to say that these were the only variables at play; however, within the limitations of an SEO experiment the above example provides a good indication into the likelihood that behavioural signals are used within the ranking algorithm.

▶

How can we improve behavioural signals?

It is important to mention that these kind of signals are extremely difficult to 'game' or artificially manipulate, Google uses advanced methods to detect programmatic interaction with their search results pages (ie through the use of scripts/bots to inflate click-through rates) and can quickly discount any effects.

Behavioural signals are a complex metric to influence, but there are tactics that can be implemented to improve the chances of seeing the benefits of this kind of ranking factor:

1 *Use brand awareness channels (display/social) to drive inbound searches*: through the use of awareness channels like display (eg Google Display Network) and paid social activity (Facebook/Twitter ads) it is possible to increase search referral traffic by 6 per cent on average (Wordstream Facebook ROI study). Increasing the volume of brand visitors to your website is beneficial on its own, aside from the potential SEO benefits based on increased brand plus target keyword searches.

   Alongside this, increasing the audience's familiarity of the brand also has a positive impact on CTR, in a similar way that RLSAs (remarketing lists for search ads) are able to increase paid CTR by targeting searchers who have already visited your website and are aware of your brand.

2 *Test the messaging within your search result listing*: it is possible to incrementally improve your search listing in a similar way you would A/B test with paid search ads to drive CTR increases. The page title and meta-description are the shop window of your website, they need to accurately describe the content of the page as well as encourage the searcher to click on the listing – through the use of emotive and eye-catching copy.

3 *Create content that answers the intent of the searcher*: this should go without saying but it is important that the focus of content creation is how you can fulfil the searcher's needs – it is not about creating content specifically for search engines.

   Categorizing target search queries into types of intent (navigational, transactional and informational) is a good way to ensure that your content achieves the searcher's goal. For example, if a searcher types the term '15-inch laptop 8gb ram i7 processor', then based on the level of query detail it is likely they are in the latter steps of the 'laptop' purchase journey and are looking to make a transaction.

What kind of result does the searcher actually want to see? A good result for this type of query would provide the searcher with numerous examples of this kind of product, displaying high-res images, specifications, the ability to shortlist products, clear information on costs, positive reviews, business accreditation etc.

If your content answers the searcher's query in the most effective way possible then the metrics shown above are likely to be created naturally with limited intervention required.

Integrating SEO and paid search

In a constantly changing market, using paid search unassisted or relying totally on the power of SEO will never fulfil the potential of a brand's online performance. Where SEO has always been effective is in its long-term viability as a low-cost acquisition model. PPC, on the other hand, offers instant gratification – the main reward of a successful integration of PPC and SEO is measured in conversions.

Use PPC to inform the viability of targeting terms for the SEO strategy. With Google continuing to encrypt referring search terms in ever greater numbers, there is no keyword-level tracking available to any analytics teams, therefore PPC data is becoming the only accurate way of testing keyword conversion rates. PPC conversion data will underpin all SEO keyword research.

PPC creative is also the best way of testing click-through rates. As standard best practice is to rotate three or four pieces of creative to increase the click-through rate, the best performing is a natural fit for SEO descriptions.

If a page has a higher-than-average bounce rate, this is an alert to Google that the page is not relevant for that search term and will not only see wasted paid-for clicks but a gradual downgrading of that page's authority. By monitoring analytics closely we can be sure to spot these issues and bring in the SEO team to improve on page factors and content.

Mobile search

Over the last few years, every year has been the 'year of mobile', but now mobile search is most definitely here and it is consuming more and more marketing spend – a report from the IAB in April 2016 shows that mobile accounted for the vast majority (78 per cent) of digital ad spend growth in 2015, increasing 60.3 per cent year on year to £2.63 billion – or 30.5 per cent of all digital advertising.

In late 2013, Google introduced cross-device conversions as part of the launch of Estimated Total Conversions. More and more purchasing journeys are taking place across multiple devices. According to Google, 82 per cent of smartphone users turn to their phone to influence a purchase decision while in a store.

For years, advertisers have understood that multiple devices are involved in a user's conversion cycle, and to have a closer understanding of the process is key to maximizing the potential for their online activity. The problem has been simply that previously marketers have not been able to align the data.

Now, when a user is signed in to their Google accounts across multiple devices (mobile, tablet, desktop, etc), Google can record the user journey to a point of conversion from clicks from each different device, and then use this data to provide an 'estimated total number of cross-device conversions'.

What this will do is give advertisers far more insight into the role of various devices in the conversion cycle and better data to which to optimize for accounts. The undoubted outcome will be an increase in mobile-device targeting, as advertisers are able to attribute better and understand mobile's involvement in the overall key business-performance metrics. One thing is for certain – the importance of mobile will continue to grow at astonishing rates:

> Search marketing has always been about serving the right ad to the right audience at the right time. Now, with today's searcher moving continuously across platforms – from mobile, to tablet, to desktop – it is also about serving the ad in the right format on the right device. Search is focused on responding to demand in a time-critical way, but the level of optimization required to do that successfully has massively increased. Mobile search is an increasingly competitive landscape, and one that is growing at a phenomenal rate – this year [2014] it looks like more than half of all mobile ad spend will come from paid search.
>
> Nick Hynes, co-founder and CEO, Somo

Black hat, the darker side of search

The SEO methods explored earlier in this chapter are methods that adhere to the search engine's own guidelines (or at least they did at the time of writing

– but guidelines can change, so it is important to keep up to date: check the links to the webmaster resources earlier in this chapter for the latest information). Generally referred to as 'white hat' SEO, these techniques are seen as legitimate optimization of a site to align it with the needs of the site visitor and simultaneously make the site content accessible and easy to index by the search engines.

But there is another side to SEO – an altogether darker and more sinister side, where less ethical practitioners attempt to exploit every trick and loophole they can find in order to 'game' the engines, increase their rankings and drive traffic to their sites. Dubbed 'black hat' SEO, search engine spamming or spamdexing (spamming the indexes) when discovered, offending sites are quickly banned from the search engine index.

But the black hat SEO is not worried by bans or penalties. For a black hat, banishment from the search engines comes with the territory. They are not interested in building quality sites with sustainable high rankings – they are looking for short-term gains from high traffic to ad-laden sites. By the time one batch of sites has been banned they have already moved on to the next. Black hatters typically have many sites running on many different domains across a variety of hosts, all exploiting loopholes in the system in order to artificially boost their rankings and generate advertising revenue.

Why should I care what colour hat these guys wear?

On one level, you shouldn't need to. The battle that is raging over artificially inflated rankings in the SERPs is between the black hatters and the search engines. It is up to the Yahoo!s, Googles and Microsofts of this world to wage that war.

Essentially, black hatters are simply taking the principles of SEO we discussed earlier in this chapter and pushing the boundaries to the extreme. Instead of a manageable selection of keywords for which they can create unique and engaging content, black hatters create lists of hundreds or thousands of keywords and stuff their pages full of keyword-rich bunkum created by automated content-generation tools. Instead of building links naturally, they use automated 'bots' to spam posts stuffed with links into blog comments, guest books, forums and wikis all over the web.

Black hats typically are not interested in you or your site – unless it is as a possible repository for link spam in your blog, guestbook, forum or wiki (and that can generally be avoided by implementing security features on your site that require human intervention to post). What is perhaps more significant is that by pushing their spammy sites up the SERPs they are artificially pushing down more legitimate sites like yours, making them less visible to searchers and potentially affecting your traffic and revenue.

Some common black hat SEO techniques

- *Keyword stuffing*: repeating keywords over and over again on a given web page. This is less successful now as search engine algorithms are better at distinguishing this gobbledegook from properly written content.

- *Cloaking*: a technique that uses code to show one search-engine-friendly page to the spider, and a completely different page to a human visitor. The engines hate this as it makes it impossible for them to gauge the quality of the content a user is seeing.

- *Invisible text*: essentially text that is the same colour as the background of the page – result, humans cannot see it, search engines can. This is like keyword stuffing – but with the cloaking element of showing different content to the search engine bot and the human visitor.

- *Doorway page*: these are highly optimized web pages whose sole purpose is to send traffic to other pages either through an automatic redirect or by simply being full of links.

- *Spam page*: a page with no meaningful content and that is full of ads from which the webmaster makes money if someone clicks on them.

- *Interlinking*: the practice of setting up multiple websites on a given topic and linking backwards and forwards between them purely in an attempt to increase their rankings in the search engines.

- *Buying and selling links to help boost search ranking*: buying and selling links purely to manipulate your search engine ranking is frowned upon by the search engines.

- *Buying expired domains*: buying up expired domains that contained high-ranking pages to try and garner some of the old site's inbound 'link-juice'.

This is just a small selection of the techniques that black hat SEOs use to boost their rankings and drive traffic. As a rule of thumb for your own site, if what you are doing *adds genuine value to the end user*, you generally have nothing to worry about. If, on the other hand, you are implementing something to artificially manipulate your search engine rankings, you could be venturing into grey – or even black hat – territory. If you value your domain's long-term reputation, be very careful.

When you come across these sites while browsing the web they can be irritating, and having to deal with spam in any medium is infuriating, but for the most part your business does not need to worry too much about the black hats who are doing their own thing to their own websites.

Bringing in the pros

While SEO and PPC campaigns can certainly be managed in-house, if you lack specialist search talent and want to fast-track traffic to your site, then bringing in a professional search marketing consultant can pay real dividends.

If you decide to bring in an external consultancy to help with your search marketing, do your homework and choose wisely. There are many excellent SEOs out there who will do a great job of promoting your business online, but equally there are unscrupulous companies looking to exploit the uninitiated. Not all SEO companies are created equal, and it is an unfortunate fact that some of them will stray into less than ethical territory to secure high rankings quickly... making them and their services look good in the short term.

The good news is that, having read this chapter, you are now armed with the knowledge you need to engage positively with your prospective search marketing partner, understand what they are telling you, and to discuss your SEO requirements with them in some detail.

Here are a few things to bear in mind when you engage with an SEO professional:

- Make sure you are dealing with a reputable company that has a strong track record to back up their claims.

- Ask to see case studies and get references from previous clients.

- Check their own site – has it been optimized? Does it adhere to search engine guidelines?

- Look and listen for any hint of the black hat techniques listed above. If there is any doubt about the ethics and integrity of the company, walk away. It is your domain they will be playing with, and it is not worth risking your reputation with the engines.

- Once you have engaged an SEO company, don't just leave them to it. You need to keep abreast of what your SEO company is doing on your behalf – after all, it is your site.

Universal search – more opportunities to rank

Universal search is a term coined by Google to describe a fundamental change in the way it presents its web search results. Billed by commentators as one of the most significant and radical developments in the history of the search industry, universal search (or blended search, as it is also known) takes results from Google's specialized (or vertical) search engines (Google News, Google Books, Google Local/Maps, Google Video, Google Image, Google Groups, etc) and slots them into standard web search results in order of relevance.

Nick Fettiplace, head of Earned Media, and Jonathan Verrall, associate SEO director from Jellyfish Digital Marketing Agency, have written us an exclusive article on Google News, including how to get your site into Google News and SEO recommendations. To read the article, go to: www.koganpage.com/understanding-digital-marketing.

According to a recent report by Searchmetrics in 2015, 79 per cent of all keywords return search results that integrate at least one Google universal search element; 55 per cent of search results for the keywords tested included video integration; 40 per cent, images; 16 per cent, shopping product listing ads (PLAs); 13 per cent, news stories; and 7 per cent, maps. Since the introduction of Google Shopping results in early 2013, the frequency of the element has increased tenfold.

As you would expect, other major search engines were not far behind, and both Yahoo! and Microsoft's Live Search introduced similar blended search results soon after Google. For users, this development is a huge boon. Instead of having to manage and navigate multiple specialized search tools, users can now enter their search query in one convenient location in order to find results across multiple platforms.

But what does all this mean for search marketers? Essentially, there are two ways of looking at it. On one level it is a potential threat, in that for any given keyword phrase your pages now have to compete with results for news, video, maps, discussion groups, images and a host of other sources in order to get those coveted top SERP rankings. On the other hand, if you produce the right sort of content and submit it to the relevant places, universal search offers additional opportunities to rank for your chosen keyword phrases (see Figure 4.3).

Figure 4.3   Universal search results page on Google.com for the search term Darth Vader

Shifting goalposts – search innovation and the quest for relevance

Search engines by their very nature are always innovating in their quest to deliver that optimum search experience to each and every user who types in a query. The pace of search innovation can be frustrating for search marketers, as it keeps 'shifting the goalposts'. Just when you think you've got this search thing 'sussed', along come the leading search engines with a development that changes things again.

Here's the thing... the search engines don't care a hoot about upsetting your finely honed SEO campaign. Remember the prime directive we discussed right at the start of this chapter? Search engines are striving to deliver the most relevant, valuable content to their users, improving their user experience and retaining or increasing their market share.

To that end, the leading search engines constantly 'tweak' their ranking algorithms, refining the way they assess relevance and authority based on content, links and other factors. This constant tinkering with the nuts and bolts of how search engines assess relevance has always been a challenge for search marketers, but more recent developments, aimed at delivering tailored search results to each individual user, have caused quite a stir in SEO circles.

Personalization: search results tailored to individual users

Back in 2007 Google started to roll out the personalization of search results for users who were signed in with a Google account. What it meant was that Google would start taking the search history of users into account when assessing the relevance of search results.

Let's say, for example, that you searched for 'Mustang' while signed in to your Google account, and you had recently been searching and clicking on results for car-related stuff. The search engine might reasonably assume you want information relating to the Ford Mustang car rather than, say, the Wikipedia page for the mustang horse.

Then, in late 2009, Google really shook things up by extending similar search personalization to all users, whether they had a Google account or not. The move sent the SEO world into turmoil, and instantly rendered as pretty much meaningless the coveted SEO goal of 'being number one in Google' for any given keyword phrase. Now, my number one search result could be different to your number one search result, which could be different to everyone else's number one search result.

Ultimately, search personalization served to move the focus of SEO away from a race to the once-coveted positions in the top of the SERPs, and shifted it back to where it really should have been all along: delivering great content that adds real value for users, and making sure that search engines are aware of that, and monitoring and measuring success based not on your position in the SERPs, but on the actual number of targeted visitors referred to your site by the search engines. That, after all, is what sustainable SEO is really all about: harnessing the power of search engines to help you deliver outstanding, relevant content to your target market.

Search gets social – integrating updates from online connections into search results

Back in 2009 Microsoft fired the first salvo in the battle to make search more social by announcing deals with both Twitter and Facebook to include real-time status updates in its Bing search results. Google followed suit by announcing a similar deal with Twitter for its own real-time search, and by introducing a feature it called 'Social Search' into its main web-search offering.

When a web user is signed in to their Google account and conducts a web search, Google now incorporates publicly available content created or recommended by a user's online friends and connections across Google's range of products and other publicly available web services.

That means that along with regular web results, users who are signed in will see relevant content that their online 'friends' have shared publicly on YouTube, Picasa, Flickr, Twitter, on their blog, in their Google Reader and in lots of other places online.

The rationale, of course, is that old search engine mantra of relevance. The web is becoming increasingly social, and people are more willing than ever to share information, opinions and experiences. We also trust the recommendations of people we 'know' online and, by incorporating content from our extended online network into search results, search engines are betting we will find those results to be more relevant, useful and personal.

What does social integration into search mean for search marketers?

On the surface, having recommendations from a search user's online social connections appear in the standard web SERPs may seem like bad news from a search marketer's perspective. It means that there is yet more content competing for those limited spaces on the first page of the SERPs for any given search term. Then again, if you are creating compelling, useful and... that word again... *relevant* content for your target audience, the stuff that is being recommended in those social search results could easily be yours.

Social search emphasizes the need to get out and engage with your customers in the social arena, to create useful, compelling content that is worth sharing, and to build enduring relationships with the people you want to do business with. The integration of a social element into search results is growing in importance, and while there are privacy concerns and other stumbling blocks that need to be overcome, ultimately the search engines' obsessive quest for relevance is turning search into a very personal experience.

budget to achieve 100 per cent impression share and positive ROI is being recorded).

Keep track of your impression share, overlap rate and outranking share. When you make big changes you should recheck performance and understand the impact.

Setting up bidding rules as well as your own CPC optimization is important. We find that Google's Enhanced CPC rules ensure that products are bid to conversion potential.

3 *Dimensions*

Use the 'dimensions' tab to run search query reports and look at device performance for optimization purposes. In the dimensions tab, segment by all levels including category, product, item ID, custom labels. The more information you have about performance at each level the more tailored you can be with your strategy. Day/hour parting and geographic bid multipliers are both key tools to increase efficiency and grow revenue.

Look in detail at device performance as mobile positioning is becoming increasingly important. Google have confirmed that more than half of UK searches now come from mobile devices and this is continuing to increase. Mobile search and shopping campaigns need to work together to make the most of this increased traffic. On mobile, Shopping Campaign ads now always appear above text ads, and work in a carousel fashion. On a desktop, eight Shopping Campaign ads can be shown at the same time, but on mobile, if you're not in position 1 or 2 on the carousel it could be fatal for a campaign. Make the right decision for mobile bid adjustments and results will improve.

And finally...

The evolution of paid search through Google Shopping is presenting more and more opportunities to run sophisticated campaigns that really drive profitability. Now RLSA has made it possible to retarget customers who did not buy in previous visits with rich and relevant product listing ads, brands are seeing a 10 per cent increase in conversions and a 35 per cent decrease in CPA.

With this increase in complexity and the huge growth potential, more brands than ever are turning to specialist digital agencies to help them clean up their merchant feed and optimize their shopping campaigns.

But whichever way brands choose to test, plan and execute their paid-for search advertising, the future is being shaped by Google's increasingly sophisticated ability to predict and direct customer behaviour.

Looking forward

Both the increasingly widespread adoption of high-speed internet access in the home, and the ever-increasing capability and market penetration of mobile digital devices, are opening up a slew of new digital media opportunities for marketers the world over. The rise of social networking sites, and the word-of-mouth and viral marketing opportunities that they offer (see Chapter 5), may in time dilute the prominence of SEO and paid search advertising in the digital marketing mix. Likewise, as ever-increasing numbers of web users develop a 'feel' for where they need to go to find the things that they want online, or access branded content directly on the move through dedicated smartphone applications, they are likely to rely less on search for certain things.

As the ways that we interact with the web change, though, search engines are developing to move beyond strings of text typed into little boxes. We reveal so much about ourselves through online search, and Google is increasingly using our data to become less reactive, less keyword driven, and instead to be able to anticipate our needs before we are even aware of them. Search is becoming smarter, more conversational, more context-aware.

While the significance of search may wane for a proportion of people and for certain applications over time, given its current level of importance for both internet users and digital marketers, the propensity of major search engines to innovate and adapt, and the fact that new people are going online and discovering the value of search engines every day, search looks certain to remain a cornerstone of digital marketing for some time to come.

CASE STUDY   STEAK and We Are Marmalade

Marmalade is the leading provider of motor insurance for young people in the UK; the company has pioneered the use of telematics technology within the car insurance vertical, giving them the ability to insure newly passed drivers at significantly lower premiums than regular insurers.

Marmalade began working with **STEAK** in February 2015. They were in the process of increasing investment into digital channels and required specialist consultancy to help them capture more of the online market.

Location

UK.

Challenge

We were given the following objectives:

- Gain insight into the learner-driver insurance-purchase journey.
- Grow organic traffic by 30 per cent.
- Achieve a top-five ranking for 'Learner Driver Insurance'.
- And, ultimately, increase online sales.

Marmalade faced a distinct selection of SEO challenges:

- Their website was not optimized for mobile users: this was prior to the separation of the mobile algorithm in April 2015; based on their young target audience the loss of mobile visibility would have had a significant impact on their sales.
- They had a high-risk link profile: Marmalade had created an affiliate network with a range of independent driving schools across the UK; unintentionally through the use of banners and exact-match anchor text they had also created a pattern of link manipulation – they were at significant risk of manual/algorithmic penalty.
- They still wanted to grow despite the unstable foundations: they had bold growth targets and wanted to see significant improvements in market share against aggregators and traditional providers.

Target audience

Young drivers.

Action

We followed the define, stabilize and grow framework:

- *Define*: we needed to understand customer search behaviour and map out their online journey. The existing marketing intelligence on young drivers was low – the demographic was not traditionally a priority for established insurers and, as a result, all of our research had to be undertaken in-house.
- *Stabilize*: we needed to provide technical consultancy on the mobile website prior to the separation of the mobile algorithm; we also needed to dedicate a

significant amount of time to mitigating the risky link profile through analysis and the creation of a removal strategy.

- *Grow*: the define stage indicated opportunity to expand upper funnel activity through creating a range of commercially focused pages. Alongside this, Marmalade needed to stay competitive against aggregators and traditional insurance providers who had also entered the market. We needed to devise a way of capturing the audience's attention and creating content that increased the website's authority.

Implementation

- *Define*:
  - To help Marmalade get a closer understanding of young drivers, we conducted our own research using proprietary website and CRM tracking data. Our insights uncovered interesting trends suggesting that young drivers were consulting someone else before purchasing. Our conclusions? While young drivers were the ones who needed insurance, the parents were the real decision makers. This insight helped inform the TOV that should be used across commercial pages: although Marmalade targets a young audience, the parents still 'sign-off' on the purchase and as a result they needed to be accounted for with specific messaging.
  - Our search-behaviour analysis highlighted a selection of commercial themes that the website in its original form didn't cater to. The search behaviour around the 'telematics' product was also different to how it was originally marketed, with the general public referring to it as being 'black box' technology.

- *Stabilize*:
  - In the run-up to April 2015 and 'mobile-ageddon' we worked closely with Marmalade's internal development team, outlining the requirements for the mobile website from an SEO point of view. The mobile website was launched at the beginning of April allowing for indexation before the algorithm update.
  - A detailed technical audit of the website was carried out, picking up on a range of areas that could provide incremental benefit. The addition of product schema to achieve rich snippets in SERPs – boosting CTR for 'Learner Driver Insurance' and consequently increasing Marmalade's ranking position to number two.
  - Due to a legacy of low-quality link building, STEAK needed to mitigate Marmalade's risk of receiving a penalty. We created a disavow strategy where links were submitted based on severity, in batches and by keyword group, allowing us to test the effects throughout the process.

- *Grow*:
    - Based on our search behaviour analysis we expanded on the current set of commercial pages on the website developing manufacturer pages (Citroen, Ford etc) for their 'Cars for young drivers' product, capitalizing on the demand for fuel and car products. We also separated out pages for the telematics and black box technology. In its original form one page was used to target both these terms; with such a high search volume we recognized that a bespoke section for 'telematics' technology was necessary.
    - To ensure we stayed ahead of competitors we needed to continually increase authority; to do this we developed a content strategy based on the target demographic's online habits and tastes.
    - An example of this in action is 'Carmalade' – Marmalade's guide to motoring festivals in 2015. An interactive resource hosted on the Marmalade content platform, its promotion was integrated with a competition to win tickets to each event; over 1,000 people shared the campaign. Not only was this a success from an SEO point of view (creating high levels of engagement signals), it also assisted in driving an increased readership of the Marmalade blog, thus assisting future content projects.

Results

- Organic visibility increased 95 per cent compared to the start of 2015.
- Organic traffic increased 70 per cent year on year, 64 per cent of which was non-brand.
- Number two in the search criteria for 'Learner Driver Insurance' – up from the pre-campaign position at number six.
- Number one position for 'Learner Insurance' – up from number six pre-campaign.
- Number six for 'Student Car Insurance' – up from number 38 pre-campaign.

Links to campaign

https://www.wearemarmalade.co.uk/blog/the-best-events-for-young-drivers-this-summer

About the creator (STEAK)

STEAK is an integrated performance marketing agency, focusing on results and tangible ROI.

Comment

A key lesson for the client was that strategy needed to be led by a deep understanding of the customer's search behaviour. They have also realized that significant gains can be made from making incremental optimizations, maximizing the current ranking power of the website without immediately having to turn to resource-intensive content/outreach campaigns to drive growth.

Through our close working relationship we have been able to create a strong understanding of the capabilities of SEO within the Marmalade team and also the strategic marketing considerations that need to be made for SEO activity to provide the best return possible.

Testimonial

They are so enthused, but the significant difference with these guys is that they deliver. Not only on time and within budget but also with great quality. The team at STEAK are truly outstanding and I hope to be working and making more successes with them for a long time to come.

Scott Robinson, digital marketing manager, We Are Marmalade

Understanding social media 05

OUR CHAPTER PLEDGE TO YOU

When you reach the end of this chapter you will have answers to the following questions:

- What does the term social media really mean?
- How is it changing the digital marketing landscape?
- Why should I get involved?
- How can I harness the power of social media to reach and engage with my target audience?
- How can consumer input help me to do business more effectively and refine my products and services?
- What are the social media rules of engagement?
- How can I use influencers in my social media marketing?

Join the conversation

Do you listen to your customers... really listen to them? Do you take their opinions, ideas and criticisms on board, and allow them to inform your business decisions? If you do, you are ahead of the game. Historically, marketers have focused on delivering a particular message, to a predefined target audience, with the aim of eliciting a specific response. Consumers were sometimes consulted in the process, of course – through market research, consumer surveys, focus groups and the like – but by and large the marketing tended to be 'show and tell' in nature, the consumer's role that of a passive recipient of information peddled by the marketer.

Now, thanks to the increasingly interactive nature of the internet, and a shift in the way that people are consuming media, all of that is changing.

Consumers are talking, just as they always have, only now they are talking online to more extensive groups of their peers. The conversations they are having seamlessly transcend geographical, temporal and cultural boundaries.

Marketing too is evolving rapidly to become more of a conversation than a lecture. Progressive marketers realize that to be heard in today's interactive world, they need to participate in that conversation – and, of course, if you want to get the most out of any conversation, you have to spend part of your time *listening*.

Through blogs, wikis, social bookmarking, online discussions, social networks, peer review sites and other online media, we have the potential to foster a much more productive and meaningful relationship with our customers, to gain powerful insight into their perceptions of our products, services and brand, and allow them to contribute and collaborate in our businesses in ways that were never possible before.

Understanding social media demands a paradigm shift for the marketer. We have to realize that our target audience is, in fact, no longer an audience at all. They are now active participants in a constantly evolving debate; as online marketers it is a debate in which we cannot afford to sit on the sidelines. In fact *Understanding Social Media* is now its own publication, sistering *Understanding Digital Marketing*... that's how important this channel really is.

What is social media?

Social media is the umbrella term for web-based software and services that allow users to come together online and exchange, discuss, communicate and participate in any form of social interaction. That interaction can encompass text, audio, images, video and other media, individually or in any combination. It can involve the generation of new content; the recommendation of and sharing of existing content; reviewing and rating products, services and brands; discussing the hot topics of the day; pursuing hobbies, interests and passions; sharing experience and expertise... in fact, almost anything that can be distributed and shared through digital channels is fair game.

A huge range of websites now leverage elements of social media to engage with their audience, and some, including a number of the highest-profile sites to emerge in recent years (the Facebooks, Twitters and Instagrams of this world), base their entire business model around the burgeoning popularity of online social media, user participation and user-generated content (UGC).

Social media is nothing new

One of the biggest misconceptions about social media is that it is a new phenomenon. Online social interaction has been around since the very beginning. In its crudest form social media predates the web by some two decades. Primitive dial-in bulletin board services (BBSs) and online communities such as Compuserve and Prodigy allowed users to post messages online for other members to read and respond to, UseNet newsgroups (early internet discussion groups) allowed like-minded participants to exchange views about all sorts of topics ranging from brain surgery to budgerigars, while e-mail discussion lists did the same. Internet relay chat (IRC) introduced real-time chat into the mix, and browser-based forums and chat rooms brought the discussion on to the web.

What has changed over recent years is the reach and penetration of these social media technologies, their adoption into the everyday lives of a mainstream audience, and the proliferation of user-generated content and peer-to-peer interaction that is resulting from it. In the past, online discussion was generally restricted to early adopters: technologists who felt comfortable interacting over the net, and who had the technical skills to fathom clunky, often unwieldy user interfaces to accomplish their goals. Today, though, anyone can participate through slick, well-designed browser-based user interfaces that adopt conventions that everyone is comfortable with. It's easy, it's convenient and it's incredibly powerful – not because of the technology, but because of how that technology nurtures the connections between people.

Time to get involved

Effective social media marketing is about leaving at home the sledgehammer approach to product promotion. Stop beating your prospects over the head with the cudgel of marketing hyperbole, and instead work to develop your skills in the subtler art of consumer engagement. Find out what people are interested in, what they are talking about, and then provide useful information, advice and content for them. Talk *to* them, not *at* them, and above all, *listen to them*. If you manage to do that effectively, then social media can have an incredibly positive impact on your organization's online profile (see Figure 5.1).

Just how deep you choose to steep yourself in the social media marketing game will depend a lot on your business, your customers, your goals and your overall digital marketing strategy. But there really is something out

Figure 5.1 Why it is important for your business to get involved in social media

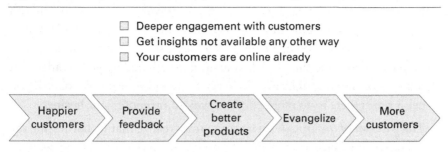

☐ Deeper engagement with customers
☐ Get insights not available any other way
☐ Your customers are online already

| Happier customers | Provide feedback | Create better products | Evangelize | More customers |

there for everyone. Here are just some of the potential benefits of engaging with your customers through online social channels:

- *Stay informed*: find out what your customers really think. Get invaluable insight into their perception of your products, services, brands, industry and more general topics of interest. Knowing your customers is the key to effective digital marketing – and engaging with them on a social platform can be incredibly revealing, without being intrusive.

- *Raise your profile*: by engaging proactively through social media you appear responsive, and can build your reputation as an authoritative and helpful player in your field of expertise.

- *Level the playing field*: focus groups, market research surveys and other offline methods of gauging consumer sentiment are expensive and can be well beyond the means of smaller businesses. Now, any organization can immerse itself in the social web to discover what consumers are talking about and how they feel, with little or no financial outlay.

- *Influence the influencers*: often the people who are most active in social media circles will be the element of your target market who can be classified as *influencers*. While small in number compared to the market as a whole, these influential individuals have already gained the trust and respect of their online peers, and fostering their good opinion can have a disproportionate impact on your broader online reputation (see later on in this chapter for a guide on how to work with influencers).

- *Nurture brand advocacy*: by engaging positively with people who already have a positive attitude to your brand, you can nurture passionate brand evangelists who will voluntarily advocate your organization through online social media. And your greatest brand advocates may well sit inside your business – encouraging your employees to actively participate through social media can exponentially expand your reach.

- *Pass it on*: one of the most powerful aspects of social media is its capacity for viral propagation. It is the online equivalent of word-of-mouth marketing, except that online the word can travel further, faster. Whether it is a video on YouTube, a high-profile news story about your company, a post on your blog that is picked up and distributed by your readers – if it hits the right note, suddenly it's everywhere, and your profile soars. If you get it right, there is no more effective way to promote your business.

- *The wisdom of the crowd*: smart companies realize that by harnessing the collective intelligence of online communities they can find answers to some of their most challenging business problems. Getting input from online communities using social media is affordable and effective. As well as helping to solve real business dilemmas it can also help you to make more informed research, design and development decisions, based on what customers actually want. Now there's a radical concept!

Different forms of social media

Social media websites come in a wide variety of 'flavours', which are all broadly based around the premise of personal interaction; creating, exchanging and sharing content; rating it and discussing its relative merits as a community. The content can be links to other websites, news articles or blog posts, photographs, audio, video, questions posed by other users… anything, in fact, that can be distributed in digital form.

Most social media websites do not fit neatly into a single category; they tend to mix a range of social components that transcend the discrete boundaries people try to define for them. Still, given our human propensity for filing things into nice, neat boxes, there are several generally accepted groupings into which most social media sites sit with relative comfort, based on their primary function. Those given below are a taster, and far from exhaustive. Start looking, and you will find plenty of social media sites/components out there that do not fall neatly into any of the categories we outline below, some that span multiple categories and others that defy categorization altogether. All of which demonstrates the dynamic, constantly evolving nature of the space. As the saying goes… we live in interesting times.

Social media submission sites

The first sites to allow users to tag and share content they liked were book-marking sites such as del.icio.us, or more recently Pinterest (www.pinterest.

com) which allow users to 'save' bookmarks to their favourite web resources (pages, audio, video... whatever), categorize them using tags (labels that help you to identify and filter the content you want later) and share them with their online friends. The concept is much the same as adding a page to your browser favourites, just taken to the next level.

Social bookmarking sites have declined in popularity and been largely superseded by social media submission sites, such as Digg (www.digg.com), Reddit (www.reddit.com) and StumbleUpon (www.stumbleupon.com). These sites are rather like social bookmarking sites, but instead of saving personal bookmarks for your own future reference, you actively submit links to content you 'like' for the online community to rate and rank. The more people who 'vote' for a particular content item, the higher up the rankings it rises. Submissions that get enough votes end up on the site's home page, which can drive significant traffic spikes to the site in question.

As well as the votes, of course, there also tends to be a lot of discussion and debate on these sites, which means they can offer tremendous insight into the way people think and react.

What's in it for marketers?

- *Find out what people are interested in*: you can use social media submission sites to gauge what type of content in your particular field people find compelling. Look at the content that is floating to the top. Ask yourself why it is so popular. What is appealing about it, and how can you draw on that to make your own content more compelling?

- *What's the buzz*: as well as what's 'hot' on the sites, there is a lot of discussion going on around popular content items. The more popular an entry gets, the more people see it and the more debate there is. Examine what people are saying – look at reviews, comments and discussions; find out what people like, what they don't like, and use that insight to inject that elusive 'buzz' quotient into your own content.

- *Amplify your exposure, traffic and online reputation*: having articles and other content ranking highly on these sites can give you a tremendous boost in traffic. However, they also give you the opportunity to raise your profile and perceived authority within your online community. By contributing constructively, submitting relevant and interesting content, and joining the debate surrounding on-topic content you can boost the community's overall perception of your brand – and by extension your power to influence others.

Forums and discussion sites

Online forums and discussion sites have been around since the early days of the internet. Broad, general discussion groups such as Yahoo Groups (http://groups.yahoo.com) and Google Groups (http://groups.google.com), where anyone can sign up and start their own online or e-mail discussion community on any topic under the sun are still popular, and you will find a tonne of other discussion sites focusing on general, industry-specific (vertical) and niche communities covering every topic imaginable.

What's in it for marketers?

- *Get closer to your customers*: checking out what consumers are talking about in forums is a great way to find out what makes them tick. The more you can learn about your customers, the better prepared you will be to engage with them in a meaningful way.

- *Raise your profile*: contribute to the discussion, offer help and advice, demonstrate your expertise. Soon people will start to respect and trust your contribution to the community – and that can do wonders for your online reputation and profile.

- *Nip bad things in the bud*: by participating in forums you will be able to spot potentially negative comments or conversations relating to your business or brand, and be proactive in resolving them before they escalate (more about this in the next chapter). What's more, if you are already participating as a valued member of the community, you may well find others jumping to your defence.

- *Targeted traffic*: traffic should not be your main reason for joining a discussion forum – blatant off-topic promotion, and linking to your own sites for the sake of it, is frowned upon, but most forums allow (even encourage) one or two links in your signature (a short snippet, usually a few lines, that is appended to the bottom of every post you submit to a forum). Make sure you follow the forum rules on this, but by including links in your signature you give other people on the forum a convenient way to find your site(s), and to discover more about you and your company. Many will click through for a closer look, particularly if you make regular, valuable and relevant contributions to the forum.

Media-sharing sites

Media-sharing sites are incredibly popular. Pinterest (www.pinterest.com), which lets people save and share images and videos grouped around topics (or 'pinboards'), has reached 176 million registered users since its launch in 2010. Sites such as Instagram (http://instagram.com) and Flickr (www.flickr.com) allow communities of members to upload, share, comment on and discuss their photographs; YouTube (www.youtube.com), Blip.tv (www.blip.tv) and Vimeo (www.vimeo.com) *et al* do the same for video content; and a host of other social media sites support alternative media types: Slideshare (www.slideshare.com), for example, is a site that allows people to upload, share and discuss their presentation slides with the world.

The sites typically allow you to make content publicly available, or restrict access to the people you specify, to send content to your 'friends' and even to 'embed' (seamlessly integrate) the content in your blog post or website for others to find it, distribute it and discuss it.

To match our ever-shortening attention spans, the current trend in media sharing is towards the micro. In January 2013, Twitter launched its Vine app (https://vine.co), which allows users to create, share and comment on six-second looping videos. Vine has proved popular, gaining 40 million users within eight months. Instagram responded in mid-2013 by expanding its service to support videos with a slightly more generous limit of 15 seconds. And going even further, messaging app Snapchat lets people send pictures and videos that self-destruct up to 10 seconds after being seen – the ultimate in disposable content!

What's in it for marketers?

- *Find out what turns your target market on*: by analysing the popularity of items on content submission sites, and reading the user comments, you can gain insight into your target market's likes and dislikes, and can incorporate that into your own content creation.

- *A ready-made vehicle for content distribution*: these sites are the ideal vehicle for rapid distribution of your own digital media content. In fact a whole microdiscipline of digital marketing has evolved around YouTube and viral video content. Hit the right buttons with your audience, and who knows, maybe your video clip could become the next 'The Man Your Man Could Smell Like' from Old Spice (http://bit.ly/UDMOldSpice) – with 52,687,295... and counting.

Reviews and ratings sites

Reviews and ratings sites do exactly what the name says: they allow users to review and rate companies, products, services, books, music, hotels, restaurants... anything they like. They can be stand-alone review sites, such as Epinions.com (www.epinions.com) or Yelp (www.yelp.com); or a review component added to a broader site, such as the product rating and review facilities on e-commerce sites such as Amazon (www.amazon.com).

You will also find specialist industry-specific review sites covering many vertical markets, like TripAdvisor (www.tripadvisor.com), which focuses on travel; or RateMyTeachers (www.ratemyteachers.com), which allows pupils and parents to rate and comment on their educators.

What's in it for marketers?

- *Advertising*: most review sites rely on advertising to generate revenue, and therefore offer advertising opportunities for businesses either directly or through advertising and affiliate networks.

- *Insight into what's good, and what's bad*: even if people are not rating your business directly, you can still get valuable information on these sites on what is working for consumers and what is not within your particular industry. If you run a hotel, for example, you can see what are people's main gripes, and what they particularly appreciate, then apply that knowledge to your own business.

- *Find out what people really think*: if consumers are posting reviews about your business, that sort of feedback is pure gold – reinforcing what you are doing well, and pointing out areas where you can improve. It's market research – for free.

- *Demonstrate good customer service*: by monitoring reviews and responding in a constructive way to negative feedback, you can show good customer service in a very visible way.

Social network sites

These are your archetypal social media sites – the Facebooks, LinkedIns and Google+. These are the sites that people automatically think about when you mention the words social networking. They are, to paraphrase Facebook's opening gambit: '*social utilities that connect you with the people around you*'. They basically let users build up a group (or several discrete groups in the case of Google+ Circles and Facebook Lists) of 'friends' with whom they can share things in all sorts of ways – from videos, to articles, games, groups and causes, to… well, if you haven't got one already, sign up for a profile of your own, and you'll soon get the idea.

Huge numbers of people use social networking sites, and those numbers are growing all the time as those people invite all of their friends and contacts to join them. Today Facebook heads the social networking pack with 1.59 billion active monthly users (as of 31 December 2015).

There have been signs of late that Facebook may be peaking. While it is still growing in developing markets, it is reaching saturation point in some developed markets such as the United States. A Pew Center report published in 2015 showed that while Facebook remains the most popular social media site among internet users, it was the only platform not to see significant growth among internet users since 2012. Today, 72 per cent of online adults use Facebook, a change that is not statistically significant from the 67 per cent who did so in 2012.

Other sites, such as Pinterest and Instagram (which is owned by Facebook), have experienced significant growth between 2012 and 2015. Today 31 per cent of online adults use Pinterest, up from 15 per cent in 2012. Likewise, 28 per cent of online adults use Instagram, a 15-point increase from the 13 per cent of internet users who did so in 2012.

Social network sites are popular because they offer users the ability to find and connect with people they already know in novel, convenient ways; to rekindle old acquaintances, and reinforce new ones. They make the process of communicating with a large network of people easy and painless. You post information to your profile and it is instantly available to those of your friends who are interested. You can broadcast information to all of your friends simultaneously, or choose who you want to share specific content with.

Mark Zuckerberg, Facebook's founder, summarized the company's mission thus: 'At Facebook we're pushing to make the world a more open place, and we do this by building things that help people use their real connections to share information more effectively.' That pretty much encapsulates the social networking phenomenon that is gripping the online world today.

What's in it for marketers?

- *Advertising*: social networks are increasingly opening up to paid advertising and offer flexible advertising options, usually based on the PPC model, for businesses looking to target their ads based on the profile information of users and/or particular actions. While the targeting angle is a compelling one, and social network audiences are large, it is important to remember that most users visit social network sites to *socialize*. They are not really in 'buying' mode, and the jury is still out on how effectively social network advertising converts. It is something to consider, certainly, if it's a good 'fit' for your business, and you have a clearly defined audience that is interested in your product or brand, but be cautious: consider the context in which your ads will be seen and seek to engage, entertain or inform rather than just sell – and track your results carefully.

- *Improve your online exposure/reputation*: social network sites usually allow organizations to set up their own profile or page. Members of the network can then become 'fans' or 'like' these pages. Your page is essentially a business hub within the network, and it can be a great way to build a community around your brand and monitor what consumers think about you, find out more about them, and to offer valuable content. Having a presence on these networks, keeping your content up-to-date, relevant and valuable to your audience, and responding positively to the feedback you receive is another great way to boost your online reputation.

- *Nurture social evangelists*: your social network can be a great place to attract brand advocates and to recruit and nurture brand evangelists. People on social networks love to share. Find the people who are passionate about your industry, your brand, your products – reward them with valuable information and content... then watch as they put all of their passion, zeal and social media acumen to work promoting your brand to the rest of their social network. And don't forget that your greatest brand evangelists may sit inside your organization!

Blogs

In the space of a very few years the widespread popularity and adoption of the blog (an acronym of weB LOG) as a medium of self-expression and communication have caused one of the most fundamental shifts in the history of modern media. Suddenly, anyone can be a publisher.

Barriers to entry have come crashing down, and free, easy-to-use blogging platforms have liberated millions of individuals, giving them access to a global audience. Setting up a blog can take as little as five minutes of your time on a free hosted service such as Blogger (www.blogger.com) or WordPress (www.wordpress.com), and setting up a blog on your own domain and hosting service is only marginally more complicated.

The blogosphere (the collective name applied to the global blogging community) is *the* home of internet buzz. If something is worth talking about online (and often even if it's not) it will be written about, commented upon and propagated through the blogosphere.

It is not just private individuals who are blogging, of course – the blog is becoming an important tool in the business marketing arsenal too, adding a personal element to the bland corporate facade, helping companies to reach out and make human connections in an increasingly human online world.

Bloggers read each others' posts, they comment on them, they link to each other prolifically, and the best of them have a massive following of avid and loyal readers. These readers go on to elaborate in their own blogs on what they have read, and spread the word through their own online social networks.

If you choose to do only one thing in the social media space, then get to know the popular blogs in your industry. Who are the people behind them, what are they writing about, what turns them on (and off), which topics generate the most comments? Prominent bloggers tend to be the biggest online influencers of them all – you need to be aware of them, build a relationship with them, and leverage that position where possible in order to help spread the word.

Never underestimate blogs. Their simplicity belies an unprecedented power to mould and influence online opinion. As a digital marketer, blogs and bloggers can be your salvation... or your damnation. Treat them with the respect they deserve.

What's in it for marketers?

- *Potentially massive exposure*: traditional press releases to your local media outlets are all very well, but get your story picked up and propagated by prominent bloggers and you will get more online exposure, traffic and inbound links (think SEO) than any traditional press release could ever hope to achieve (for more tips on getting online press releases picked up by bloggers, see Chapter 11: Understanding online PR).

- *Consumer engagement*: use your own corporate/business blog to add your voice to the blogosphere. Try not to use your blog as a vehicle for blatant product and brand promotion, but rather as a platform to offer your readers a personal insight into your company and brand. Sure, product announcements, and press-release-like posts are fine, but look to add value with genuinely useful content too. You could offer your opinions and insight into industry news and events, comment on and link to other blogs that are discussing relevant issues, or get your resident experts to post 'how-tos' on getting the most out of your products. Engage with the online community, and they will engage with you in turn. The more you give of yourself, the more you will get back.

Podcasts

Podcasts are, in many ways, just the rich media extension of the blogging concept. A podcast is simply a series of digital media files (audio or video) distributed over the internet. These can be accessed directly via a website or, more usually, are downloaded to a computer or synchronized to a digital media device for playback at the user's leisure. They tend to be organized as chronological 'shows', with new episodes released at regular intervals, much like the radio and television show formats that many of them emulate. Users can usually offer their feedback on particular episodes on the accompanying website or blog.

Whatever your area of interest you will find podcasts out there covering it; and podcast portals such as iPodder (www.ipodder.org) Podomatic (www.podomatic.com) and Apple's iTunes (www.apple.com/itunes) offer convenient hubs to find, sample and subscribe to podcasts of interest.

What's in it for marketers?

- *Listen and learn*: leading podcasters in your industry will very probably be talking about things that are relevant to you as a business and to your customers. Podcasters also tend to be social media enthusiasts – influencers who have their finger on the digital pulse of their audience. You can harness their understanding of the online community in your particular space by analysing their podcasts, and the comments and feedback from their audience, to feed into your own digital marketing efforts.

- *Do it yourself*: podcasting is easy to do – but can be difficult to do well. At its most basic, all you really need is a digital audio recorder (your computer and an attached headset will work fine), some editing software and a place to post your files once they are ready. Depending on your business, your audience and your goals (back to strategy again), podcasting may well offer you a valuable additional channel to reach your market. It could also help position you as a progressive digital player in your industry.

Microblogging

Microblogging has become popular with a mainstream audience (and hence with businesses, brands and the mainstream media) in a very short space of time. Its rapid rise in popularity is thanks in no small part to widespread adoption of the best known microblogging platform, Twitter, by well-known celebrities, and the voyeuristic compulsion of millions of fans to check out what their idols are doing 24/7.

Twitter is essentially a short-message broadcast service that lets people keep people up-to-date via short, public text posts of up to 140 characters long. Leading social networks, like Facebook and LinkedIn, also offer similar microblogging functionality within their 'walled garden' networks through the 'status updates' feature.

The true value of microblogging is not necessarily in the individual posts, it is in the collective aggregation of those mini-posts into more than the sum of their parts. When you receive frequent, short updates from the people you are connected to you begin to get a *feel* for them, to develop a better understanding of what they are all about, and to feel a stronger connection with them. Twitter can offer an immediate and surprisingly accurate barometer of public opinion on the web.

What's in it for marketers?

- *Your finger on the digital pulse*: as a marketer, microblogging platforms give you access to high-profile thought leaders in your industry. The most progressive among them are likely to use microblogging services to post snippets about what they are doing, how they are doing it, links to new online resources and thoughts on developments at the bleeding edge of the industry. By 'following' these thought leaders you can harness that valuable intelligence, and use it to inform your own marketing decisions.

- *Communicate with your customers*: why would you want to microblog to your customers? Well, some very high-profile companies do (including Dell, the *New York Times*, ITN News, the BBC, Southwest Airlines and British Airways, to name but a few), not to mention prominent politicians (Barack Obama, for example, was prominent on Twitter during the 2008 and 2012 presidential campaigns), and other high-profile public figures. In a world where e-mail has become increasingly noisy, offering a microblog feed provides beleaguered consumers with a convenient and alternative way to subscribe to your updates without adding yet another newsletter to their cluttered inbox.

- *Raise your online profile*: microblogging offers you yet another opportunity to get in front of your online audience and establish your expertise. Be forthcoming, answer questions, provide interesting snippets of news and advice, direct people to useful blog posts, articles and other resources… yours and other people's. Help people, learn about them, listen to them, and give your online reputation another boost.

- *Generate traffic*: Twitter thrives on sharing links to interesting content, so letting your followers know when you publish your latest blog post, white paper or video can help drive significant traffic to your website.

Wikis

Wikis are online collections of web pages that are literally open for anyone to create, edit, discuss, comment on and generally contribute to. They are perhaps the ultimate vehicle for mass collaboration, the most famous example, of course, being Wikipedia (www.wikipedia.org), the free online encyclopaedia.

At the time of writing (April 2016) Wikipedia reported that it has a staggering 5,136,637 English language articles in its database. There is a grand total, including all Wikipedias, of over 38 million articles in over 250 different languages. Despite criticisms from some quarters over the accuracy of some of its articles, and the perceived authority of the information it contains, according to independent web-tracking company Alexa (www.alexa.com), in April 2016 Wikipedia was ranked number six globally in terms of online traffic, more than 5,000 places above its commercial rival *Encyclopaedia Britannica*.

What's in it for marketers?

The concept of using wikis as a marketing tool is still a new phenomenon, and their value may not be as readily apparent as some other forms of social media. However, they are a powerful collaborative tool, and with collaboration between companies and their customers in the ascendancy, look out for increasing use of wikis by innovative organizations in the not too distant future:

- *Build a strong collaborative community of advocates around your brand*: wikis can be a great way to encourage constructive interaction and collaboration between people inside your organization and people outside it (your customers). Consumers begin to feel ownership and connection with a brand that encourages, facilitates and values their contribution. That ownership evolves into loyalty, then advocacy: powerful stuff from a marketing perspective, especially when you consider these contributors will often be online *influencers* who will go on to sing your praises on other social media sites.

- *Harness the wisdom of the crowd*: how much talent, knowledge and experience do you have inside your organization? Probably quite a lot – but it pales into insignificance when compared to the massive pool of talent, experience and expertise you can access online. Retired experts, up-and-coming whizz kids, talented amateurs, undiscovered geniuses... they are all out there. Wikis give you a simple, powerful and compelling way to draw on and capture some of that collective intelligence. Why not harness a wiki, for example, to help refine the design of your products, come up with your next great marketing campaign, define a more efficient business process, produce and/or augment product documentation, develop a comprehensive knowledge base – or anything else that might benefit from a collaborative approach.

What's next for social media sites?

New social media sites are constantly springing up and fading away, and keeping on top of this ever-changing environment can be daunting. While there are signs that Facebook may be peaking, a recent report released by the IAB UK states that Instagram is the fastest-growing social network with over 400 million users worldwide (as of September 2015). Kevin Systrom, founder of Instagram, said: 'When Instagram launched nearly five years ago, 400 million seemed like a distant dream. Our community has evolved to be even more global, with more than 75 per cent living outside of the United States.' Other social apps such as Snapchat are also gaining rapid popularity, particularly amongst teens and millennials. Brands are beginning to trial advertising through Snapchat, such as the pizza delivery company Domino's 'Dough to Door' campaign. Advertising results are currently difficult to measure, however, due to the lack of analytics tools on Snapchat.

As social media sites mature, there is growing pressure on them to demonstrate they can actually make money – particularly for those sites such as Facebook, LinkedIn and Twitter that are now public companies with shareholders. We are already seeing more of a push towards advertising, and Facebook – in April 2016 – updated its policy on branded content and released a new tool that makes collaboration on branded content easy, and gives marketers more visibility into and control over all of their efforts on Facebook.

Influencer marketing is the next big thing in social media as consumers look at fellow consumers to inform their purchasing decisions. We asked Stephanie Ryan from We Are Social to give us We Are Social's guide on influencer marketing.

Expert view
A guide to influencer marketing
Contribution by Stephanie Ryan, We Are Social

Very few things can drive a sale as effectively as a word-of-mouth recommendation. This age-old insight is more relevant than ever in a digital world where 95 per cent of millennials consult their peers when making a purchasing decision, according to research from SocialChorus.

So how do brands leverage this behaviour to make sales? Native advertising taps into the monumental power of word of mouth and places brands and products within organic content created by a trusted source, creating a more pleasurable experience for consumers and a more powerful marketing solution for brands. The success of native advertising is no surprise given that 70 per cent of consumers want to learn about a product through content rather than through traditional advertising (SocialChorus).

Nowhere is native advertising more dynamic than on social media, where the rise and rise of influencer marketing is giving brands a powerful new tool for reaching consumers. Making influencer marketing work for a brand is a multistep process, and it pays to do it properly. Here is everything you need to know.

What is an influencer?

An influencer can be defined as someone with an above-average ability to affect others with their thoughts and opinions. Their influence over potential consumers may span one or more areas, usually across multiple communication touch points. Quite simply, an influencer is someone who has built up enough credibility with a certain audience to be able to have an effect on what they spend their money on.

It is easy to get influencers confused with ambassadors and celebrities, but there are crucial differences. The relationship between an influencer and a brand is typically a mutually beneficial one that presents the opportunity to co-create unique content for an audience. An ambassador is someone (usually high profile) who is employed by the brand to publicly embody brand values and messages over a longer period of time. While an influencer will incorporate a brand or product into their content organically, an ambassador has the more tightly controlled role of acting as the voice of a company. Celebrity endorsements are different again and usually involve a famous individual accepting a hefty sum to appear in a brand campaign.

What makes someone an influencer?

To achieve big results for a brand, an influencer should be able to offer these three essential qualities:

- *Relevance*: for the right audience to be targeted, the influencer's area of interest or expertise needs to match the brand's. For example, a fitness influencer is a good fit for a sporting goods company.
- *Reach*: the influencer needs to have an established and extensive audience, preferably across multiple social platforms.
- *Engagement*: an influencer's high follower count means nothing if their audience is not engaged. Fans and followers should be actively liking, sharing and commenting on content.

How does working with influencers benefit brands?

Influencers allow brands to go further into a relationship with an audience than they could with traditional communications means. Working with the right influencer offers various benefits:

- A wider, more targeted and generally more engaged audience for content.
- New communities relevant to specific brand objectives.
- A passionate, forward-thinking audience.
- The ability to develop a two-way conversation, instead of simply talking at consumers.
- A long-term mutually beneficial relationship.
- Co-creation to produce unique content for the brand's community.

What do influencers do?

They're all bloggers, right? Not exactly. These days, influencers are creative publishers who can work across a number of platforms. Here are a few examples of the many forms they come in:

- *Bloggers*: individuals, groups or communities blogging online.
- *Vloggers*: individuals, groups of communities blogging via the medium of video, most often on YouTube.
- *Social media influencers*: may not have a blog, a vlog or a website, but are highly influential on one or more social platform. Think popular photographers on Instagram or prolific Tweeters.

▶

- *Brand advocates*: highly active fans of brands who are perceived as authorities by fellow fans.
- *Online niche communities*: for example, fan communities, parenting websites, blogging hubs.
- *Product review companies*: for example, a third-party platform through which word-of-mouth campaigns could be conducted.
- *Experts*: individuals who are widely respected as experts in their chosen fields. For example, sports medicine or veterinary care.

Objective and influencer criteria

Before working with any influencer, you need to ask yourself: 'Are they a good fit for my brand?' To figure this out, select which of these four objectives you are looking for. This will give you an idea of the criteria you need to look for in an influencer:

Table 5.1 Objective and influencer criteria

Your objective	Influencer criteria
Longevity	Loyalty
Brand awareness	Reach
Positive perception	Authenticity
Engagement	Creativity

Here is more of a breakdown of those influencer criteria:

- *Loyalty*: an influencer who will work with brands for the long term, not just the short term.
- *Reach*: a large audience across one or multiple channels.
- *Authenticity*: an influencer who is seen as authoritative and honest in the way they communicate with their audience.
- *Creativity*: someone who is perceived to be creative in their use of formats and media.

The different types of influencers

No two influencers are exactly the same, but there are certain types that pop up quite often. Here are a few common influencer profiles currently very popular with brands:

The media pro

This category applies to individuals who curate stories in the manner of a professional media organization. They will generally have a consistent editorial tone and go beyond reporting by capturing their own content. The media pro's reach, credibility and authenticity are usually quite high. The trade-off is usually low loyalty as consumers treat them like any other news source.

What interested brands need to know: These are the influencers who want more than just a story. They want to get under its skin.

Example: a kids' arts and crafts blog run by someone who carefully selects ideas and stories from around the web, testing out some ideas and sharing photos of the results.

The creator

These are the people innovating within their chosen discipline. They create their social content as a by-product of their day-to-day job or life. Due to the credibility they can possess amongst their peers, working with them can potentially provide interesting stories for other influencers in the field to share. Loyalty and reach are often mid-level with creators, but they more than make up for it with high creativity and authenticity.

What interested brands need to know: creators want to innovate storytelling and content. They want to provide followers with something unique and engaging.

Example: a group of three people who create bespoke textiles in their free time, sharing pictures of their creations, their process and other insights.

The passionista

The passionista writes or creates because they live it, or love it. They are deeply passionate about their subject matter and their content offers a very personal perspective on news and events. They will often have low reach due to their singular focus and desire to please themselves before their followers, but they do have very high loyalty and authenticity.

▶

What interested brands need to know: the passionista wants to be supplied with exciting stories that they can share and get involved with.

Example: a mummy blogger who covers her passion about healthy living for kids.

The aggregator

The self-elected news-breakers on the web, aggregators are professional publishers who rely on others for their content. They can be relied upon to be the first to pick up news stories and post with high frequency on a daily basis. While loyalty and creativity are typically low, reach can be significant.

What interested brands need to know: aggregators thrive on exclusive news that will raise their credibility and that they can post with minimal effort.

Example: an environmentalist news outlet that aggregates all the day's top stories about climate change and sustainability.

Choosing the right channels

In addition to deciding your brand objectives and working out which kind of influencer is a good fit for your brand, you also need to think about *where* they are influential. This determines what content they like to produce and ultimately the kind of content you will be able to co-create with them. Here are some thought-starters on the best channels for specific types of content:

- Blogs: long-form reviews and articles.
- Instagram: creative image-led posts.
- YouTube: episodic content such as tutorials and reviews.
- Twitter: conversation drivers and news exclusives.
- Pinterest: inspiration-led pieces.
- Facebook: reach.

Finding influencers

Here's the kind-of tricky part. You know what you are looking for in an influencer, but now you need to track them down. The multistep process for identifying and securing influencers is outlined below:

1 Scope: decide on your objectives, what you would like to do with the influencers and how many you would like to recruit.

2 Search: do some desk research to profile and validate any potential influencers.

3 Rank: rank candidates in line with key brand objectives.

4 Due diligence: ask yourself all the relevant questions. Is this person working with competitor organizations? Are they over 18 years old? Are they open to being approached by brands?

5 Select: secure a final list of influencers based on brand objectives and corresponding influencer criteria.

6 Outreach: get in touch using personalized sell-in copy and clear timings and deliverables so they know what is expected of them.

Reaching out

Once you have a list of the influencers you would like to work with, start planning your outreach. For best results, make sure you have a proper process in place. Here are the bases you will need to cover:

- *Check you've done your due diligence. Then check again.* Your selected influencers might look great on the surface, but you also need to do some background research to ensure they are a good fit. Ask yourself:
  - Is this person already working for a competitor brand?
  - Has this person explicitly stated online that they do not want to be contacted by brands?
  - Have they stated that they only do sponsored or paid work? (This is an important one if you don't have the budget to pay influencers.)
  - Has this influencer expressed any negativity towards your brand in the past?
  - Have they posted anything controversial, offensive or in poor taste in the past?
  - Is this person over the age of 18? (If they're not, you will need their parent or guardian to sign a consent form.)
  - Has this particular influencer been approached by your brand before?
- *Making the first move.* It is important to get off to a good start if you want to set up a positive and long-lasting relationship between your brand and an influencer. Make an excellent first impression with these tips:
  - Ensure your outreach e-mail is highly personalized for each influencer. Show that you understand and appreciate what the influencer does.

▶

- Be polite, but not too formal. Write as if you were chatting to them in real life and sign-off with your name, rather than the brand's name.
- Make sure you frame the opportunity as one that would be mutually beneficial, rather than as a favour they would be performing.
- Tell them what you are envisioning for the campaign, but also invite them to share their ideas too.
- If possible, suggest meeting in person to discuss the opportunity further.

How to work with influencers

You have outreached to your chosen influencers and they have accepted the opportunity to work with you. What next?

Managing the relationship

There are generally two ways you can work with an influencer: via a talent agency or directly. Working with an agency ensures better process and structured management, although it can result in lower value for budget as agencies tend to demand everything is paid and contracted for. Choosing to work directly with the influencer or their agent is often more cost-efficient, although it can occasionally entail a lack of process.

Scaling involvement

With your objectives in mind, work out what level of involvement you will invite your influencer to have:

- low involvement: simply sharing the story;
- medium involvement: being a part of the story;
- high involvement: helping to create the story.

This is also the right time to think about how your brand wants to use influencers in the long run. Here are three potential options:

- *One-offs*: the influencer is used for a one-hit campaign over a short time frame.
- *Stable of talent*: multiple influencers are recruited and provided with a set of feature templates and a clear brand storyline to create a suite of content with their own unique spin. They will then act as ongoing contributors, providing serialized content for your brand.
- *Ongoing contributors*: influencers are recruited on a long-term contract. They are given the flexibility to co-create with your brand on a regular basis.

Briefing influencers

The most important thing to remember when briefing your influencers is that you will need to give them a good degree of creative control. Make sure they are aware of the elements they need to include that are completely necessary – such as the inclusion of a product, or the use of a hashtag – but hand them the reins in terms of creative direction. Their fans follow them for a reason, and if you dilute their originality the content will be less successful.

A couple of final things

Ready to get started? Before leaping head-first into working with influencers, double check you have got all your bases covered:

Table 5.2 Dos and don'ts

Do	Don't
Choose a handful of good influencers to invest time in	Outreach to hundreds of influencers
Pick influencers who are a good fit for your brand	Simply choose influencers based on followers
Personalize outreach messages	Send out generic outreach e-mails
Ensure the parents of underage influencers have signed consent forms	Forget to do your due diligence
Be clear about mutual expectations	Forget to check in with influencers often
Ensure the campaign is a natural fit for the influencer	Suggest they post anything that is not a good fit for them
Make sure influencers are on the best channels for campaign objectives	Only look at traditional influencers
Give influencers creative control	Try and tell influencers exactly what to create or write

▶

Final checklist

- Have clear objectives before you approach an influencer.
- Choose influencers who are relevant to your brand. The biggest does not always mean the best.
- Be upfront and explicit about your expectations.
- Respect and understand your influencer's expectations.
- Give them helpful details on what they need to include in the content they create for you. For example: hashtags, @mentions, terms and conditions, or advertising disclosures.
- Be open to creating a long-term relationship.
- Trust your influencers and give them creative control.
- Strive to be authentic in everything you co-create.

Social media dashboards – all your updates in one place

The proliferation of social media platforms today can make it a pretty daunting task to keep track of what's going on between all of your different social media accounts. Luckily, it's easy to consolidate your various social media streams and updates in one convenient location using tools dubbed 'social media dashboards'.

Dashboard software takes a variety of forms, from desktop-based applications to web-based services and mobile applications that let you keep track of and update your accounts on the move. Tools such as HootSuite (www.hootsuite.com) and Tweetdeck (www.tweetdeck.com) have evolved quickly from straightforward Twitter clients into fully integrated social media dashboards that incorporate multiple social media accounts spanning different platforms. You will also find 'enterprise' class social CRM software, which essentially do the same thing.

Ultimately, these dashboards give you a convenient place to monitor all of your social media activity in one place, and the best of them offer built-in statistics and measurements, scheduled updates, keyword monitoring and more.

The rules of engagement

Social media, then, offers a wealth of opportunity for consumer engagement and building brand awareness, but in such an open and dynamic space that it is critical to consider carefully what you are doing.

The 'rules' of social media are really about applying a bit of common sense to what are essentially human relationships. The key thing to remember is that this is *social* media – people are going online to interact and exchange information and content with similar, like-minded people. They are unlikely to be interested in your latest sales pitch, and they are certainly not interested in promotional hype. They want interesting, fun, informative, quirky, addictive... whatever turns them on.

When it comes to social media, you are not just sending out a message, you are inviting a response, and what you get might not be quite what you are expecting. You need a plan to engage in social media marketing, but you also need to be flexible and respond to the community:

- *Draw on what you already know*: you already have a wealth of knowledge about your customers – who they are, what they like to do, where they hang out online. Okay, so one of the main reasons you are getting involved in social media is to get to know them a little better, but the point is that you are not going into this blind. Use that knowledge: apply what you already know about your customers, your business and your brand to your social media strategy. As you learn more, refine what you are doing accordingly.

- *Don't jump in unprepared*: have a clear plan before you start – know who you are trying to engage with and what you want to achieve. Define ways to gauge and measure your success, with frequent milestones to help keep you on track. But remember to be flexible, and modify your plan as necessary in response to community feedback.

- *Look, listen and learn*: before you engage in social media marketing, spend some time 'lurking' (hanging around without contributing). Familiarize yourself with the different types of social media sites that you plan to target. Go and use the sites, read the blogs... immerse yourself in the media. Look, listen and learn. Just like in real life, every online community is different.

- *Be open, honest and authentic*: nowhere is the term 'full disclosure' more appropriate than in social media. Don't go online pretending to be an independent punter extolling the virtues of your brand. You will get found out, and when you do your company will go 'viral' for all the wrong reasons. Never pretend to be someone or something you're not.

- *Be relevant, interesting and entertaining*: everything you do should add value to the community, as well as moving you towards your business goals. Be helpful, be constructive, be interesting and entertaining – join the conversation and offer valuable, authoritative and considered advice. Make a real effort to engage with the community on their terms, and you will usually find them more than happy to engage with you in return.

- *Don't push out a 'spammy' message*: don't join social media sites just to submit a tonne of links and push information about your own products, or flood the community with posts on why your company is the best thing since sliced bread. It smacks of spam, and adds nothing to the conversation. At best the community will ignore you; at worst, well, we're back to the negative viral effect again.

- *Respect 'rules'*: if the site you are frequenting has policies, guidelines and rules – read them and abide by them.

- *Respect people*: always be respectful to your fellow community members. That does not mean you always have to agree with them; healthy debate is good in any community. When you do disagree, though, always be polite and respectful of other people. They have as much right to their opinion as you do to yours. Don't make it personal.

- *Respond to feedback*: if users give you feedback, this is invaluable. Let them know that you appreciate it, that you are interested in what they have to say. Be responsive, and show them how you have used that feedback constructively.

We asked Anna-Marie Odubote from Social Chain, the UK's largest influencer network, to give us Social Chain's five commandments for social media marketing.

Expert view
Social Chain's five commandments
Contribution by Anna-Marie Odubote

1. Make me feel (either way)

Feelings are powerful, and it is important to harness this power to produce memorable marketing. You don't remember all of the compliments you've ever received, but you will always remember that time in school when everyone laughed at your bad haircut.

Don't be afraid to make people feel sad, negative or confused, and don't be afraid to be playful. The old adage about bad publicity rings true, and negative responses are forever harder to forget. An 'OMG these shoes are awful' is better than silence; the fact remains that people are still talking and thinking about the shoes – more so than they were before. It is a move towards an understanding of the product, and even if one person is to respond negatively, the subjectivity of taste dictates that their friend might disagree. This creates more room for debate, and further publicity for your campaign.

#Susanalbumparty

Susan Boyle's infamous album launch party hashtag is a prime example. In what appeared to be an embarrassing blunder, the genius hashtag hurled Susan Boyle back into the limelight. From the *Guardian* to *Forbes* to *OK* magazine to Capital FM, everyone around the world was talking about the singer and her supposed PR disaster. And, between the jokes, everyone knew that Susan Boyle was releasing her album, generating product awareness that stretched across the globe.

#DipPick

(That's DipPick with a P). Hostelworld wanted to generate a buzz around holidays, encouraging people to share their poolside selfies and pictures. But it was clear that the Hostelworld audience wouldn't retweet or engage with a branded hashtag like #hostelworld or a typical hashtag like #holidays. Branded hashtags in isolation are too dull to incite engagement, and hashtags like #holidays are too broad to even attempt measuring engagement. And so Hostelworld created the funny, taboo hashtag #DipPick, connecting the campaign. When you are able to poke fun at yourself and you are not afraid to look silly, people will proliferate your message without realizing that they are advertising on your behalf.

Now, about that harnessing. Once you appreciate the power of negative emotion, the way in which you implement it is up to you. When we talk about evoking a negative response, it is not about providing shoddy service and encouraging people to complain on Twitter. It is about using messaging to control the way in which people respond to your product; manipulating the way in which people engage with your brand.

This game will ruin your life

A campaign that Social Chain ran for an app called TippyTap is a good example of this strategy. The game was fairly rudimentary but addictive in

▶

nature, and we played on this fact; 42 of our UK-based Twitter pages simultaneously began warning people about downloading the frustrating, addictive game, as it would ruin their 'lives/university degrees/everything'. We didn't push any links to download when we created the conversation around the app, but with a potential reach of 4.3 million people, TippyTap received 100,000+ downloads in the first eight hours and 9,281 mentions in the first five hours, trending at number one on Twitter for two hours, and number one on the app store for two weeks. The game currently stands at over 2 million downloads.

Always: try to rouse an emotional response.

Never: underestimate the power of 'bad' publicity.

2. Riding relevance

It is on you to create topical, meaningful conversation. If people are watching a puddle in Newcastle, you need have an eye on that puddle in Newcastle too. And if you don't already know about #DrummondPuddleWatch, take a moment to look into it – you won't be disappointed. People remember the way that brands respond to the latest news, and if you hit the nail on the head, you can create content with traction way beyond the topic's initial life cycle. Be agile, and be on it.

Black and blue

When #TheDress broke, every brand and his dog jumped on the trend. From success stories like Behr Paint's response, to a weak attempt from Hellman's Mayonnaise, #TheDress was THE topic. In a thoughtful and intelligent move, the Salvation Army created a dramatic and powerful campaign highlighting the effects of domestic violence. With copy that read 'Why is it so hard to see black and blue?', strong imagery and smart messaging tied the trend to the theme, and created an unexpected, yet effective execution:

> Hellman's
> Tweet: We see #blueandyellow... of course. Bring out #TheDress
> Retweets: 3, Likes: 8
> Posted: 6.34 pm – 27 Feb 2015

3. No need to shout

Imagine going to see your favourite comedian perform live. You have spent your money on a couple of good seats, and you've been looking forward to the night for quite some time. You and your friend arrive and take your seats as the lights lower. The warm-up acts get the crowd going, and before long, the compere announces the headline act. Amidst claps and cheers, the comedian greets the audience and waits for the noise to settle. He opens the act with a few jokes that have you all in stitches, and you eagerly anticipate the rest of his show. The room quietens, and the comedian lifts the microphone to his mouth, before bellowing out 'BUY MY DVD'. Everyone is silent now. You hear a 'What?' from the rows behind you.

'BUY MY DVD', he repeats. 'BUY MY DVD, BUY MY DVD, BUY MY DVD.' He shows no sign of stopping, and now everyone is looking at each other with a mixture of confusion and annoyance. 'BUY MY DVD!' People begin to pick up their things and leave, muttering to each other and looking back towards the stage as they walk up the aisles. You and your friend soon do likewise. The comedian carries on shouting for another 90 minutes, before exiting the stage at his scheduled time. By this point, the only people left in the auditorium are an old man who has fallen asleep and a group of die-hard fans who believe that the performance is perhaps just a big, elaborate joke. At the end of the show, only the gaggle of fans sticks around to purchase the DVD.

Don't let your brand be the shouting comedian. If your content becomes pushy, dull and offers little to your followers, they will up and leave in the same way that you would leave the comedy show. Don't think that you can post bitty links and expect your followers to click them, or buy whatever you are selling. In the same way that you would make a cash investment for a show, people are investing in your brand when they follow you. They invest because they believe that you can provide content that will enrich their lives in some way; whether it is funny posts, interesting news or regular updates. Don't get complacent and let them down with boring, ill-thought-out messages.

Visuals can be incredibly helpful with creating that engaging content. Articles with images gain 94 per cent more views than those without; and posts with photographs on Facebook receive a 37 per cent higher level of engagement than those with just text. And it's a lot easier to sell products to a loyal and trusting audience.

Always: create content that is as engaging and interesting as it can be.

Never: get complacent and take your following for granted.

▶

4. Talk to your audience

The way you talk to your great auntie Barbara probably isn't the way you talk to your best friend, and the way you talk to your boss definitely isn't the same way you talk to your little brother (unless your little brother is your boss, in which case, as you were). Code switching is a vital facet of human interaction that allows us to relate on several levels, and yep, you guessed it, it just so happens to be vital on social media too. A 16-year-old girl is not going to engage with someone who speaks like her dad, in the same way that her dad would be lost if you asked him to decipher a string of emojis.

RT to save a life

The vernacular of social media is evolving at breakneck speed, with new terms introduced to the collective lexicon all the time. Think about how much slang evolves in small regions or towns. Now imagine that on a global scale, with kids from Surrey picking up on slang from Chicago, all because they follow the same Twitter account. It's not as overwhelming as it sounds – it's just a case of staying attentive and aware.

Tesco Mobile

When Tesco Mobile rolled out their #nojoke campaign, their irreverent tweets ticked all of the boxes. Funny, relevant and youthful content elevated their Twitter brand to cult status, garnering attention from fans and news outlets alike. From the #TMFollowChallenge to the on-trend colloquialisms, people couldn't quite believe that a company as big as Tesco could talk like them too. And in a world of stiff tweets about customer service, Tesco Mobile's tweets shone bright:

Profile: Felipe @JayFeliipe
Tweet: Immediate turn-off if a girl's mobile network is tesco mobile
Posted: 11.36 pm – 15 Oct 2013
Retweets: 594, Favourites: 187
Response: Tesco Mobile @tescomobile (16 October)
Tweet: @JayFeliipe Are you really in a position to be turning girls away?

Profile: Li Lou @LiyahSummers
Tweet: When you call someone and it goes through to their Tesco Mobile Voicemail... LOOOOOOOOOOOOOL
Posted: 4.47 am – 30 Jun 2013
Retweets: 1,466, Favourites: 408
Response: Tesco Mobile @tescomobile (16 October)

Tweet: @LiyahSummers When you realize your mates are ignoring you
LOOOOOOOOL #nojoke
Retweets: 11,287, Favourites: 7,111
Posted: 5.46 am – 30 June 2013

Taco Bell employs a similarly sassy social media strategy, featuring
everything from Mean Girl's quotes to tweeting the Illuminati. Their
success across the United States has been rampant, with funny tweets
racking up tens of thousands of likes and retweets:

Profile: MeanGirlsQuotes @MeanGirlsQuotes
Tweet: Karen: You wanna do something fun? You wanna go to
@TacoBell? Regina: I can't go to @TacoBell, I'm on an all carb diet!
#MeanGirls
Posted: 12 July 2012
Response: Taco Bell @TacoBell
Tweet: @MeanGirlsQuotes God, Karen you're so stupid.
Retweets: 653 Favourites: 352
Posted: 10.26 am – 12 July 2012

Always: think about exactly who it is you are talking to.
Never: assume that one size fits all when it comes to tone of voice.

5. Understanding platforms

The platforms we use and the way in which we use them have undergone
a monumental shift. From Myspace bulletins and Facebook pokes to
Snapchat selfies and Periscope feeds – with the exponential growth of our
technological capabilities comes an exponential surge in ways to advertise
across social media.

Facebook is no longer the one-stop shop for connecting – instead of
posting our sporadic thoughts and opinions through the platform, we use
Twitter. Instead of uploading silly selfies on Facebook we use Snapchat.
We can watch live content with people around the world through Periscope.
We can rose-tint our lives with Instagram. We can share funny videos
through Vine. And on Facebook? We do a diluted version of all of the
above, alongside ignoring friend requests from our grandma. But Facebook
is evolving to keep up with growing trends. Recognizing that people are
now using the platform to share video content, it has become deft with
video amplification, maintaining its place as a social media powerhouse.

▶

We now have more platforms than ever before, and this inherently changes the way in which we interact with them, even down to the lexis we employ, or the times of the day we post. It is all fairly self-explanatory – don't get left behind when it comes to new platforms. Learn what they are and how to use them, and don't expect a manual either. One of the joys of social media is learning through doing, and experiencing the platform in the same way as the user.

Always: bear in mind the differences in how we use each platform.

Never: ignore new platforms and their development.

Understanding   06
e-mail
marketing

OUR CHAPTER PLEDGE TO YOU

When you reach the end of this chapter you will have answers to the following questions:

- What is e-mail marketing and how can it benefit my business?
- How can e-mail marketing tools help me?
- How can I use technology to manage my customers?
- How can I write effective copy for my e-mail marketing campaign?
- What are the main design considerations when crafting an e-mail?
- How can I make sure my e-mail marketing campaign won't be seen as spam?
- How can I test a campaign's success?

E-mail – the power channel

E-mail marketing is one of the most powerful elements in your digital marketing toolbox. It lets you communicate easily with your customers on a personal level through a universally accepted digital medium. E-mail frequently outperforms other digital channels for return on investment (ROI) with studies consistently agreeing on a return of around $38 for every $1 spent (Direct Marketing Association (DMA); Campaign Monitor).

The most common way for a customer to be added to your e-mail list is through an initial purchase or enquiry, meaning that e-mail is not cold-acquisitions marking but retention of your most qualified prospects and loyal customers.

Due to its efficacy, e-mail has become a victim of its own success. More and more e-mail is sent every year, with the latest figures (2016) citing around 2 billion marketing messages sent each day. This leads to the scenario where the inbox is a battleground and companies must compete for attention. Some marketers think that sending more campaigns is the only lever to pull to increase response rates for e-mails, but of course this only compounds the problem. Starting an e-mail marketing programme means you are competing with a high frequency of communications from well-known and established brands.

So how do you send e-mail that is a sustainable part of your overall digital marketing strategy and continues to deliver outstanding ROI? As necessity is the mother of all invention, the problem for e-mail will also become its solution as marketers adopt more sophisticated methods using advanced big data solutions and algorithmic approaches in order to capture the gaze of the customer more regularly. In addition, taking advantage of the fact that e-mail is one of the most used apps on the smartphone means that mobile gives e-mail further reach to the connected consumer. Understanding mobile e-mail is pivotal and will separate batch marketers from those that receive the highest benefit from e-mail. In many ways the solution to e-mail cut-through will bring about a golden age of smarter e-mail that delivers value to both your customers and your business.

Get it right and customers will still open your e-mail

The truth is, many customers will welcome regular e-mail communications from your business. They will open an e-mail containing a newsletter or promotion from you, as long as they recognize your brand, they are expecting to receive communication from you, and are confident it will contain something of value to them. The key is to make these messages relevant and interesting for your chosen audience; fail in that, and unfortunately your message will be ignored or discarded, or worse still – marked as spam.

E-mail marketing can be a tricky field to navigate effectively. You have to simultaneously respect your customers' right to privacy, protect your brand and, ultimately, maintain your value proposition over time. It is very easy for your carefully cultivated e-mail prospects to unsubscribe from your mailing list, and once you've lost them, they are probably gone for good.

What exactly is e-mail marketing?

E-mail marketing is one of the best and ubiquitous methods of retention marketing. In its simplest form, it is an e-mail sent to a customer list that usually contains a sales pitch and a 'call to action'. This could be as simple as encouraging the customer to click on a hyperlink embedded in the e-mail. Some examples of e-mail marketing campaigns could include:

- a hotel promoting rooms in a destination that the customer has been browsing online;
- a recruitment company informing business clients about the latest candidates on their books;
- a gadget store offering a money-off code to be used online;
- an automotive brand updating its customers about a new model release.

The important aspect to remember is that these messages are to an audience that have some level of connection with your brand and should be treated differently from any cold campaigns you run through other channels.

You can use e-mail when you don't have anything specific to market, as a mechanism to maintain consumer engagement, strengthen brand perception and add credibility to your business. Examples might include:

- an accountancy firm keeping in touch with its clients by informing them about changes in tax legislation;
- a weekly newsletter from a public relations company that contains interesting snippets of industry news and web links to longer articles;
- a daily digest or breaking news alert from an online newspaper, including up-to-the minute social posts.

Because e-mail is an incredibly cost-efficient communications medium, it can be used to deliver both sales and general brand engagement.

E-mail marketing tools

When it comes to managing and sending your marketing e-mail, you probably will not want to rely on your standard desktop e-mail system to do the job. While it is a perfectly feasible approach for very small lists, as more people subscribe to your e-mail offering it will quickly become cumbersome and unmanageable.

What you need instead is one of the many custom e-mail marketing systems out there, commonly known as e-mail service providers (ESPs). These can either be software that you install on your local machine, software you run on your own server, or a software-as-a-service (SaaS) offering hosted by an online service provider. These systems let you manage your e-mail list, craft your design templates for your messages and, most importantly, help you to track your e-mail campaigns (see Figure 6.1).

Figure 6.1 E-mail marketing specialists like Benchmark Email (http://bit.ly/UDMBenchmark) offer scalable hosted e-mail solutions to help you manage every aspect of your e-mail marketing campaigns

Some of the functions that e-mail marketing tools can provide (and this is not an exhaustive list) include:

- Easy-to-use tools that let you create and work from e-mail templates without having to be a technical expert.

- Testing tools that allow you to check your message will make it past major spam filters.

- Tracking tools that show how many people have ignored, opened or responded to your e-mail.

- Personalization tools that let you modify the content dynamically to individuals or specific target profiles on your list.

- Customer data tools to help understand the performance across your whole database over time, not just a specific campaign.

Customer relationship management

It is no good using e-mail marketing tools if you don't know who you are sending your e-mails to. Customer relationship management (CRM) is a business concept that has been around since the 1990s. It is the art of keeping your customers happy and maintaining an ongoing personal relationship with them – and these days data is relied on more heavily to achieve this.

For retailers in the past, customer recognition used to be as simple as remembering a customer's name when they came into the store and – over time – getting to know their likes and dislikes in order to retain a personal connection. Now, with increased connectivity and personalization, even the smallest stores can operate online and enjoy worldwide reach. Geography and a physical location are no longer limitations for most businesses and as a result CRM has become a lot more sophisticated and machine driven. The best ESPs make the complex simple so that the marketer is not overburdened by an abundance of data and can still execute timely and effective e-mail campaigns to all customers.

For instance, if you keep a record of the products or services that a customer has bought from you in the past, what they have looked at on your website, how often they have contacted you – you can merge that data with the relevant demographic details, then, using CRM technology, you can track and anticipate what those customers are likely to be interested in. The result? Relevant marketing that is much more likely to convert.

When it comes to e-mail marketing, CRM can help you to segment your list, allowing you to focus on the customers most likely to respond. You can fine-tune your e-mail offering and align it with your customers' purchase history. The possibilities are virtually endless.

If your business already uses CRM systems for more traditional marketing, then you should be able to incorporate that data into your e-mail marketing strategy. Some CRM systems cater for e-mail campaigns as part of their feature set, while others integrate with your chosen e-mail marketing solution. Furthermore, most ESPs now understand that an e-mail strategy must start with data and so have built their software in line with this. Using real-time data will help e-mail marketers to get the best response rates, for example if you were an online travel agent, simply adding the live currency rates into an e-mail about booking holidays abroad can increase response rates by double and above. A big-data store accommodating CRM data too will allow for this in-the-moment content in an e-mail that changes when the customer opens it, not at the point of send.

We will talk about technology where appropriate as we progress through the chapter but, ultimately, e-mail marketing tools will only prove effective if you, as a digital marketer, have the appropriate data sources at your disposal and spend time developing the right e-mail strategy for your business.

Before you start

Before you begin planning your e-mail marketing campaign, there are a number of things you need to consider from practical and legal perspectives.

Building your e-mail list

As we mentioned earlier, people will not respond to seemingly random e-mail communications: they won't even open them. So before you can do any e-mail marketing you need to build up a list of customers and prospects who *want* to receive e-mail communications from your business. The best way to do that is to encourage them, whenever you get the chance, to opt in to receiving your e-mails.

Your website is the hub of your digital marketing world (see Chapter 3), and is a natural place to ask people to sign up for your opt-in mailing list. All you need to do is place a simple, prominent form on your site encouraging visitors to sign up for the latest updates, direct to their inbox. If they like your site and value your content, many will welcome the opportunity to hear from you by e-mail with regular news, special offers and occasional one-off promotions. There are many ways to increase sign-ups from your web channel and these include:

- static but clear calls to action at the top of the page;
- pop-up windows that can be easily closed if required;
- a prominent offer such as a percentage discount upon sign-up.

Use your extended web presence to encourage sign-ups, too. Embed a newsletter sign-up form on your brand's Facebook page, for example, and encourage sign-ups by linking to your sign-up page from the occasional Twitter update. You could also use your e-mails to encourage readers to introduce your newsletter to their friends, and perhaps even offer an incentive for them to do so. There are lots of ways you can harness broader digital marketing principles to help you build your list organically… get imaginative!

If you are in a hurry to build a list and send out a campaign quickly, another option is to rent an e-mail list from a specialist marketing company, but be careful. You need to make sure that the organization providing you with the list is a member of your country's Direct Marketing Association or similar, and that they tick all of the boxes in terms of their anti-spam and privacy policies. People on these lists should have opted in to receive e-mail offers from third-party companies or 'partners' – if they haven't, then any mail you send them is essentially spam, regardless of your impeccable intentions. You will also need to check that no one on your rented list has already unsubscribed from your own mailing lists. If they have you will need to remove them before you send out your campaign, though most ESPs will do this automatically. Like most things in life there are no shortcuts without sacrifice, and the response from any rented list will be lower than your organically grown qualified prospect and customer list. Not only that, but if large numbers of customers start marking your messages as spam, then it could affect the performance of your main list of treasured contacts as your sender reputation suffers. Largely this route is not therefore worth the risk.

Sometimes third parties offer direct-response campaigns where the customer understands that they are directly signing up to your list. For example, a competition on an affiliate's site where you offer a prize or product as a giveaway. Again, you would need to consider the response rates of someone who has only signed up to your communications in order for a chance at a prize of some sort. If they have shown no signals to purchase, you may have to work harder in order to persuade them to convert later down the line. Unless the third party or affiliate is very well aligned to your brand or product, it may well be worth taking the time to grow your own database.

Arguably the most common way to attract opt-in is when a customer completes some kind of transaction on your website, such as purchasing a product, downloading a white paper or requesting additional information. By making an e-mail address a mandatory component of the transaction, you can add to your e-mail list. Legalities vary here, but in many countries, including in the UK, it is fine to send marketing e-mails to people once they have completed a transaction with you, as long as you have given them the option to decline. This is referred to as a 'soft opt-in'. And remember, every marketing e-mail you send out must provide the recipient with a straightforward way to unsubscribe from your list – an opt-out, if you like.

Legal requirements

As an e-mail marketer you must always stay up-to-date with the law in your jurisdiction. Sending out unsolicited e-mail to random consumers will breach spam legislation in most Western countries. Anti-spam laws are there to enforce ethical e-mail marketing practices that respect customer data and privacy. Legitimate businesses will follow the laws, but spammers are hard to trace. They will typically use underhanded techniques to harvest e-mail addresses and send large volumes of unsolicited e-mails.

Back in late 2007 spam accounted for an astonishing 95 per cent of all e-mail traffic. Things have improved slightly since then, now the figure is estimated at more like 59 per cent of e-mail traffic. But this is still a ludicrously high volume of spammy e-mail.

According to Securelist, in the first quarter of 2015 the United States remained the biggest source of spam, sending 14.5 per cent of all unwanted mail. Russia was in second place with 7.27 per cent. Ukraine came third with 5.56 per cent of the world's spam. Vietnam (4.82 per cent), China (4.51 per cent) and Germany (4.39 per cent) followed the leaders of the rating. India brought up the rear in the Top 10 with 2.83 per cent of all spam distributed worldwide.

The practice continues because: 1) it costs very little to send a marketing e-mail to millions of people on a list; 2) even the tiniest conversion rate turns a profit for the spammer; and 3) most spam cannot be traced, and originates outside the relevant jurisdictions.

Spam is a constant threat to legitimate e-mail marketers in general. It is almost certainly against the law in the country you are operating from and, what's more, it annoys the very people you are hoping to connect with: your future customers. When you are just starting out, and don't have much of an opt-in list, it can be tempting to emulate spammy techniques like ignoring opt-outs. Don't do it!

Anti-spam legislation in the United States and Europe

US law

In the United States, the CAN-SPAM Act (Controlling the Assault of Non-Solicited Pornography and Marketing Act) came into effect on 1 January 2004. The Federal Trade Commission has a fact sheet, accessible at www.business.ftc.gov/documents/bus61-can-spam-act-compliance-guide-business, outlining legal requirements for businesses sending e-mails. The main points include:

- Don't use false or misleading header information.
- Don't use deceptive subject lines.
- Identify the message as an ad.

- Tell recipients where you are located.
- Tell recipients how to opt out of receiving future e-mail from you.
- Honour opt-out requests promptly.
- Monitor what others are doing on your behalf.

Apart from being fined up to US $16,000 for violating any of these terms, there are additional fines for using spammers' techniques, including automatically generating e-mail addresses or harvesting them from the web.

European law

The Privacy and Electronic Communications (EC Directive) Regulations 2003 is the overriding anti-spam legislation. You will find that individual countries will interpret the law in their own ways, and you need to take data protection legislation into account, too.

In the UK, you can download a fact sheet for marketers from the Information Commissioner's Office website at www.ico.org.uk. This clearly outlines, in Q&A form, what digital marketers can and cannot do with e-mail. As we have mentioned, having the recipient opt in to marketing messages is crucial (but don't forget the 'soft opt-in', which means that once you have collected contact details from someone who has bought a product or service from you, or expressed an interest, then you can go ahead and market to them as long as they have been given an easy way to opt out).

Logistical problems

Sometimes the mail just does not get through. There are a variety of reasons why your e-mails may not arrive in your customers' inboxes. They may have been inadvertently/incorrectly categorized as spam by the internet service provider (ISP), or filtered into a junk-mail folder by a web-based or desktop e-mail client. Spam filters are so aggressive these days that people may not see much spam in their inbox, but an overzealous spam filter can sometimes intercept legitimate mail too. For the customer this seems great, but it does mean that they can be missing out on potentially useful and informative e-mails – like your latest newsletter!

In e-mail marketers' jargon, when a legitimate e-mail is blocked by a spam filter it is called a 'false positive'. These false positives can be a real setback to your e-mail marketing endeavours. Even discovering that your opt-in marketing e-mail is being blocked can be a tricky proposition, and resolving the problem can be difficult, especially when you feel you have followed the rules to the letter.

Your best bet is to try to avoid the spam-trap problem from the beginning by making sure your e-mails don't look and read like spam. If your e-mail software has an option to test how well your message will fare with spam filters, use it, and change anything that it flags as potentially suspect. You should also make sure that all of your e-mail can be traced back to a valid IP address from a reputable host. If you do that, there is no real reason for your e-mails to be blocked.

An organization called the Spamhaus Project (www.spamhaus.org) works to track and block spammers. On their website there is information on why legitimate e-mails can sometimes be blacklisted, and what you can do to resolve the problem.

E-mail formats

Another reason your e-mails may not be seen is that you are sending them out in a format that your recipients' e-mail clients – the software or website used to read and reply to e-mails – doesn't recognize. This is not as much of a problem as it used to be, because the adoption of internet standards has improved significantly, and pretty much all of the e-mail clients today will seamlessly handle rich text or HTML e-mail, unless the user has specified otherwise.

When you send out your marketing e-mail, you can normally choose to send it in its most basic plain text form (with no formatting). You can be fairly certain that all of your prospects will be able to read it, but it is hardly the most aesthetically pleasing experience. One step up from plain text is rich text format, which allows you to format the text with font sizes, colours, bold and italics, and allows recipients to click on web links. This looks better than plain text, and can be very effective for simple informational newsletters.

The most sophisticated e-mails are built using HTML (the same code that developers use to build web pages). This essentially means that your e-mail can look exactly like a regular web page, complete with images, web links and all the rest. Images are not usually sent with the e-mail, but are usually pulled in from a webserver when the e-mail is viewed. It is this technique that allows dynamic and real-time elements to be presented in your e-mails. HTML e-mails can and should tie in with the look and feel of your website, providing a consistent look and great brand continuity when your prospects click through to your landing page. The most advanced e-mails change based on a customer's behaviour online and – vice versa – can affect what the customer sees next time they land on a web page.

For most e-mail marketers HTML is now the standard format for sending mail, but it is important to remember that many e-mail clients (and web-based e-mail such as Hotmail and Gmail fall into this category) automatically block external images for security reasons until recipients override the setting, either for an individual message or for all messages from a particular sender. It makes sense, therefore, to do two things: 1) make sure that your e-mail message works even without the images (ie ensure your value proposition and call to action are clearly outlined in the text); and 2) encourage your readers to automatically allow images from your address for future e-mails.

Generally you will not need to worry about sending different versions of your e-mails to different customers. An internet standard called MIME (Multipurpose Internet Mail Extensions) means that messages today go out in 'multipart' format. This means that your recipient's e-mail client will be able to view the message in the best way it can, and if a recipient has set their client to receive text-only e-mails, then that is what they will see.

More and more people are accessing their e-mail – including your e-mail marketing missive – on their smartphones while on the move. That presents a challenge for the e-mail marketer. Think about smaller display sizes; users may not see your entire subject line, for example, and small display size may affect the way that your carefully crafted e-mail looks. Think about mobile users when you are designing your message. Try to ensure it will work on a smaller display, keep your key content to the top right of the e-mail, and make sure it works in text-only form too.

With a small display you have less room to manoeuvre, so be sure to 'hook' the reader early with killer content.

Planning your campaign

As with any part of your digital marketing strategy, to get the most out of your e-mail you need to define who you are targeting, why, and what you want out of it. Do you want to generate more sales? Or are you looking to maintain a relationship with your customers by keeping them up-to-date with the business? It is important to be specific here, and to make sure that your e-mail marketing strategy feeds into your overall business goals.

Digital customer relationship management (CRM) can help you to segment your customers, and to target specific groups with tailored e-mail offerings if that makes sense. You can also deliver personalized content to them, and wherever possible you should endeavour to personalize all of your e-mail marketing as much as you can. At its most basic, this involves using your prospect's real name in your e-mail messages, but more sophisticated software will allow you to pull in specific dynamic content based on a particular customer profile. For example, an e-mail from an airline could highlight the number of frequent flyer points a customer has left to spend before they expire, or an online bookshop could recommend new books based on a customer's purchase history.

You should ask yourself what you are hoping to achieve for your business:

- Increase sales or bookings?
- Increase engagement with your brand?
- Increase brand recognition?

The more that a customer interacts with your message, the more you are likely to hit your objectives. Therefore, the main behavioural metrics to plan for and observe are:

- *Open rate*: this is the total number of opens, as a percentage of the segment you sent the mail to, regardless of how many individuals are opening.
- *Click-through rate*: this is the total number of links clicked in your e-mail, as a percentage of the segment you sent the mail to, regardless of how many individuals are clicking.
- *Unique open rate*: this is the total number of *subscribers* that open a message, as a percentage of the segment you sent the mail to. So if I open your e-mail twice, I contribute two points to your open rate but just one to your unique open rate.
- *Unique click-through rate*: as per the unique open rate, the unique click rate is the number of *individuals* who click at least one link in your message, as a percentage of the segment you sent the mail to. So if I click on two links in your e-mail on one day, and then a further two on another day or on another device, I contribute four points to your click-through rate but just one to your unique click-through rate.
- *Unsubscribe rate*: this is the number of subscribers who opt out of your message, as a percentage of the segment you sent the mail to.
- *Bounce rate*: this is the number of subscribers who did not receive your message, as a percentage of the segment you sent the mail to, because it was rejected by their mail server or undeliverable for another reason.

To really gain insight from both the click-through and open rates you should look to find a ratio between these two figures. If you divide the click-through rate by the opening rate, you will gain insight into the success of your campaign from the addressees who opened the e-mail. This indicates whether readers considered the content interesting or whether you need to look at ways to optimize it further. The key metric for all e-mail campaigns is the conversion rate that analyses the number of recipients who have carried out a specific action – eg purchase, download or registration – in relation to the broadcasted volume of e-mails.

Start with clear ideas of what you want these numbers to be and you will not go far wrong.

Focus on great content

Good e-mail design is important, and it makes a lot of sense to establish some brand continuity between your e-mail templates and your website design. Every aspect of your digital marketing campaign should, of course, work seamlessly together. But *always* remember that your e-mail content is paramount. Your template design should complement, rather than compete with, your e-mail content for your readers' attention.

In order to get a better click-through rate you can use visible text and graphic calls-to-action (CTA) throughout the message. Some people will react more quickly to imagery, others to text – so allowing them to click through from both makes sense. Furthermore, not all e-mail browsers download images automatically, so having a text link provides a possible CTA in that instance. Some brands also use what is known as a 'pre-header' at the top of the message, which should be a quick summary or a teaser of what to expect in the e-mail. Usually about 5 per cent of people click through on this, providing it is useful and engaging.

One of the most effective levers to create great e-mail content is sending content that is not only unique to the individual, but also adapts and changes in real time depending on:

- stock levels (for retail e-mails);
- the weather;
- the time of day;
- their browsing history;
- third-party information such as live currencies;
- availability for booking (say, tickets or hotel rooms or flights).

Brands that are able to use real-time data like this will see the best response to their e-mail content. Use your judgement, your knowledge of your business and your customers, and craft your message to suit. Test your content regularly, and tweak it to yield optimum results.

Above all, remember that crucial call to action.

When and how often?

You should think carefully about the frequency of the e-mails you send out to your list. Send mail too infrequently and you drop off your customers' radar, but send them too often and you start to irritate them. People don't want to be bombarded with marketing e-mails, even if they have opted in.

Sometimes it can be hard to predict how often you should send out marketing e-mails, and when, in fact, is the best day or time to send them. That's another reason why it is so vital to track and analyse every aspect of your e-mail campaign. Testing of both frequency and time of day is a highly worthwhile exercise. If you notice people suddenly starting to unsubscribe from your lists, ask yourself why. Are you sending out e-mails too often, or has a change in format prompted the exodus? Whatever it is, keep a close eye on your campaigns and the data they generate, and when things do go awry, try to rectify the problem as soon as you can. If you don't, you risk your e-mails being perceived as spam, and that can do more than just damage your e-mail campaign – it can have a serious impact on the broader online reputation of your business. Many businesses have fallen into the trap of relying on frequency to deliver better overall numbers (including number of sales, revenue, bookings, interactions, etc) and it stands to reason – the more e-mail you send, the more response you will receive. However, frequency will also affect the opt-out rate of your database and you may end up losing customers who would have been valuable. Proceed with caution and test as much as you can.

Lessons from your own inbox

You can learn a lot about what works and what doesn't in e-mail marketing by taking a closer look at your own inbox. Examine the array of newsletters and marketing e-mails you have signed up to receive. Do any of them jump out at you and scream 'read me'? Why?

What is it about a particular message that makes you want to open it? Are there any e-mails you have signed up for that you actively look forward to receiving? Are there some that you never open? What are your competitors doing? Do you think it works for them?

A good example of a great e-mail is the house-alert e-mail from Rightmove, an aggregated property site in the UK. They trigger e-mails based on your preferences for area, type of property and price range. The subject line is personalized and states the content of the e-mail '2 new properties added'. The content then goes on to show that these are relevant based on an area you have drawn on their online map (see Figure 6.2). If it were really smart, it would remove the properties that had sold before you even open the e-mail, so you only see available properties.

Figure 6.2 Rightmove trigger e-mail example

Hello Jess
2 new properties have been added that match your search.

Property for sale in London Road (Drawn Area) in the last 3 days

View all results on Rightmove >

Analyse the marketing e-mails in your own inbox, deconstruct them, and apply what you learn to your own e-mail marketing campaigns. As your e-mail campaigns evolve, you will naturally start to find what works best for you. After all, no one knows your business or your customers like you do.

E-mail design

When working on your e-mail design, think in terms of 'above the fold' – just like with a newspaper folded in half, the top of your e-mail should capture the recipient's attention immediately and encourage them to read on. Don't force them to scroll through pages of text before they reach your 'once-in-a-lifetime' never-to-be-missed offer. Get to the good stuff early, and leave less important stuff for lower on the page. Also remember that e-mail clients often show a short 'preview' of the message body below the subject line in the inbox. Use this: engage prospects with those first couple of lines and entice them to open your message. As mentioned earlier in the chapter, mobile should be a huge consideration as more than half of e-mails are now opened on smartphones.

Your design should reflect your corporate identity and branding, and should extend through to the landing page that the e-mail links back to. Consistency and continuity are key here, and a seamless experience between your e-mail and your website promotes trust and, crucially, improves conversion.

Use rich media judiciously

While it is possible today to embed all sorts of interactive content into HTML e-mail templates, you need to think very carefully about why you are doing it. Does it really add value and enhance your message? Will your e-mail still degrade gracefully and work for people who have rich media content disabled, or whose e-mail software cannot handle it? Would your rich media content be better employed on the landing page that your message sends people to, rather than in the body of the message itself?

Writing killer e-mail copy

While the design and look of your e-mail are important, copy is a great trigger for galvanizing people into action. Beneath the gloss and the sheen, you need to write compelling, engaging copy in order to get results.

First, it should be instantly obvious that the e-mail is from you. Use your company or brand name in the 'e-mail from' field – and make sure it matches the brand that the user signed up for. It is important that people recognize instantly that this is an e-mail they have opted in to – or they may inadvertently flag your legitimate message as spam (using the 'report as spam' button that is integrated into many e-mail clients today). That not only means that future messages from you will be relegated to that particular user's spam folder, but if it happens too often, may ultimately have repercussions for the deliverability of all your e-mail. Using your brand in the 'from' field also provides a branding opportunity, even if the recipient does not open the message.

Crafting the e-mail subject line is one of the most important steps in writing your e-mail. The subject is the one piece of creative copy that you know your prospect is going to see *before* clicking through to open your message. It is your one chance to engage and enthrall them and it can be a teaser or a direct explanation of what they can expect in the e-mail . Why should the prospect open your e-mail from a list of tens or potentially hundreds of messages landing in his or her inbox every day? Your subject line should answer that question.

Don't try to be too clever with your subject line – clever subjects can be ambiguous, and ambiguous e-mails rarely get read. Your subject needs to be descriptive, yet compelling, which can be a tricky combination to pull off, but if you manage it you will see your e-mail open rates soar.

For the main body of your content you need to ensure you are talking your customers' language. Always remember to keep your audience in mind, and write accordingly. Remember that people are busy, and e-mails need to get to the point relatively quickly to hold attention and interest. Make sure your value proposition and call to action are crystal clear, and that key elements of your message (including links back to your website) are easily scannable and stand out from the body of your copy. Usually when it comes to copy for e-mail, less really is more.

Keep the tone of your copy friendly and approachable, and tailor the language to your audience. Yes, this is a business communication medium, but formal corporate prose is the last thing people want landing in their inbox. Keep things light and conversational, engage with the reader on a personal level (address the individual, not the crowd). You may be sending to a list of thousands, but to the reader it is one-to-one.

Proofread everything at least twice... and then get someone else to read through it too. Read it in plain text and in its final HTML form. Make sure your content is accurate, not only in terms of spelling and punctuation, but also in terms of the detail.

E-mail delivery

Making sure your e-mails are delivered to the people on your list is another crucial element in your e-mail marketing. It is good practice to send out your e-mail to a few 'test' or 'seed' e-mail addresses of your own in order to make sure everything is arriving in the inbox as you expect it to before sending it out to your entire list.

Keeping your mailing list 'clean' is vital, and you should endeavour to honour unsubscribe requests as soon as they arrive. Many of these will be handled automatically by your e-mail service provider/e-mail software, but you should also monitor for unsubscribe requests through other channels (think other company e-mail addresses, social media, etc) and remove them manually where necessary.

If you find that mail to certain addresses on your list is bouncing regularly (ie messages are undeliverable), investigate why. If the address is dead, purge it from your list (but don't remove addresses immediately – e-mail downtime is a fact of life, and occurs more often than you might think). Most e-mail service providers allow you to specify a bounce limit beyond which they will automatically purge addresses from your active lists and move them to a separate bounce list. You can then view them and either delete them or reinstate them as part of your routine list of housekeeping.

If a lot of your mail starts to bounce it is worth checking to see if a particular ISP or webmail provider is blocking your e-mail. If it looks like that is happening, it is important to contact your e-mail service provider immediately to try to get the situation resolved.

When you send out your messages you should be prepared for a rush of incoming replies. Automated 'out of office' autoresponders and 'unsubscribe' requests will start to arrive as soon as your e-mail message hits people's inboxes, so don't be surprised to see them. This is probably the main reason you want to choose a dedicated (but monitored) e-mail address as the 'from' address for your campaigns.

Measuring your success

Beyond the basic metrics covered earlier in the chapter, what else can you analyse to shed light on how you progress and evolve future campaigns? You can use e-mail marketing tools to analyse:

- approximately how many people opened e-mails over time (called your 'open reach');
- when people typically opened your e-mail;
- what links people tended to click on and therefore what content contributes to the click-through rate;
- who never opens their e-mails;
- the types of e-mails with the best conversion rates;
- the types of e-mails that drive the highest revenue per subscriber;
- the tracking of e-mails that regularly bounce;
- how many people unsubscribed from your lists over time, known as your 'unsubscribe reach';
- which e-mail clients/providers (if any) blocked your messages;
- how frequently a series of e-mails is opened by a particular subscriber.

Running programmes

Programmes of e-mails can be used around specific events such as customer birthdays or welcome initiatives. A series of messages will be sent out in order around a particular moment in the customer life cycle. These are automated and triggered by customer behaviour.

Expert view
Welcome e-mails
Contribution by Gemma Walton, e-mail specialist, SmartFocus

Bienvenue, willkommen, bienvenido, välkommen, welcome – there are so many different ways of saying it, but welcome campaigns are an essential part of your e-mail marketing strategy.

In the past, e-mail marketing was simply sending as many e-mails to as many people as possible and just getting your message out there. However, more recently the focus has changed and it is now about sending relevant, personalized e-mails and creating a relationship with your audience.

The best way to start this relationship is by creating an effective welcome campaign. The welcome message that a member receives as confirmation they have signed up to receive your e-mails can often be their first interaction with you as a brand. This welcome message provides you with the ability to introduce yourself, as well as to ensure your members are aware of the benefits they can gain from receiving your e-mails.

Welcome campaigns often have one of the highest engagement rates of marketing e-mails that are sent out. Research by Return Path discovered that 'welcome messages were read 42 per cent more often than others'. With such high engagement rates it is important to ensure that your welcome campaign is as effective as possible.

So what makes a good welcome campaign? Obviously it will be dependent on the type of industry you operate in and the audience you are sending to. However, by following the formula below you can build brand loyalty and introduce your members to your e-mails:

1 *Confirmation*: the first stage of a welcome campaign is the initial confirmation of sign-up message. In this first message, you should thank the user for signing up to your e-mails. However, you should also provide them with a bit of information about you as a brand. This can help to personalize their experience with you, make a positive impression and help to create a relationship. I would also recommend setting the expectations of the type or amount of e-mails they will be receiving from you. This provides your members with a teaser and can persuade them to open and interact with your e-mails.

▶

2 *Information gathering*: the next stage of your welcome campaign is to find out some more information about the member. When they signed up for your e-mails you may have collected some information or maybe just their e-mail address. By focusing this next e-mail on them you can direct your recipients to a preference centre that will allow them to update their preferences and 'personalize their e-mails'. The more details you collect, the more you can segment your data and ensure that you are sending relevant e-mails, thus resulting in higher engagement rates. A good example of this can be seen in the welcome e-mails for Selfridges department store, who encourage their members to personalize their e-mails:

Welcome

Now a confirmed fashion insider, you'll be treated to our e-mails brimming with the best of Selfridges. From the latest designer arrivals to exclusive homewares and in-store events, personalize your e-mails today so we can keep you in the know about the things you love.

Personalize your e-mails here >

3 *Personalization*: the final stage of your welcome campaign is to use the information you have just collected from your members to send them relevant content. By sending a message such as this you are proving that you are taking into account the information they provided and that it is being used to benefit them. It will also encourage members to continue to provide you with information in the future.

Throughout all these messages you should ensure you have provided links to your other channels, specifically social channels. You may find that some members will be more likely to interact with you through these channels, so you need to ensure they are aware you are present on social and make it easy for them to interact by providing clear links.

By following these steps you can create an effective multiwave message welcome campaign and start to build a relationship with your customers.

Testing

To gauge the success of a potential e-mail campaign, you can also run A/B split tests with groups of subscribers. This simply means sending two (or more) versions of an e-mail that communicate the same message in different ways (using a different subject line, for example), and monitoring to see which one is more effective. Based on the results, you then send out the more effective version of the message to your entire list. This can be used for content, timing, format – anything for which you want to test the performance.

We asked Simon Bowker, Teradata eCircle's managing director for the UK and a leading practitioner of e-mail marketing, to provide a point of view and advice on measuring e-mail success.

Expert view

Analytics

Contribution by Simon Bowker, marketing automation expert at Oracle

The process of integrating the different strands of marketing analytics can be daunting. However, the good news is that the best e-mail service providers (ESPs) will be able to provide you with a 'plug and play' solution, which will join your e-mail and web analytics packages seamlessly.

Before making significant changes to your digital marketing strategy it is often worth considering an e-mail audit to assess exactly what stage you are at now, and to gain a better understanding of which parts need improving. Broadly speaking, this should cover six core areas: strategy, segmentation and personalization, layout and content, list growth, automation and efficiency, and analysis.

E-mail service providers' technology should give you direct access to critical information such as impressions, clicks, open rates and bounces. The best ESPs also have analytics capabilities so you can also drill down much deeper into your customers' behaviour to see click-through rates from specific sections of the e-mail, revenue and orders from a campaign, and conversation rates.

Information gathered from the analytics packages can then be fed back into your database and used to enhance future campaigns. For example, if you can identify customers who have clicked through from the campaign but have not purchased, you can then target these people with an automatic abandoned-basket campaign – reminding them to return to their purchase or offering them suitable alternatives. Results from abandoned-basket campaigns are typically very high, with 25 per cent open rates and clicks of 15 per cent.

The future of e-mail marketing

The days are long gone when companies did not need to personalize and they could still be successful. Personalization is the future for e-mail and is improving all the time. All marketing will become more connected so that it feels the same across every channel and every message.

In order to do this, companies will need to use the massive amount of data that is collected to build a single customer view and good understanding of all behaviours and moments, no matter how brief, where the customer interacts with your brand.

It is going to be very important for companies to get all their marketing channels integrated and offer content to customers through the device and in the manner that they prefer, instead of the other way around. The more integrated and connected a consumer is with a business, the more they will use their services and shop for their products and, ultimately, drive revenue. In the future, if a customer doesn't find a business or a retailer on their chosen device or content offered in the manner they want, they will run to the open arms of the competition. E-mail is a part of this landscape and must be triggered by action both in physical locations and online.

User-generated content and true e-mail dialogue between customers and businesses is also more focused than ever. With the increasingly available and affordable technology that can be easily integrated with existing systems, we expect to see adoption of user-generated content across the board from small to medium-sized enterprises up to multinational companies.

E-mail – a vital component of digital marketing

The real beauty of e-mail marketing is that it lets you deliver your message directly to an individual who actually wants to hear from you. Compare this to your website, which is necessarily more generic (to appeal to a broader audience) and needs to work harder to attract and retain a visitor's attention.

While e-mail marketing is just one of the many ways of connecting and maintaining a relationship with your customers, it is getting better all the time and, as marketers become more sophisticated, e-mail will continue to deliver a very high ROI.

CASE STUDY   The Entertainer

Aim

Helping The Entertainer to send smarter e-mails and smash revenue results through real-time personalization.

The Entertainer is the UK's largest high-street toy retailer, with 120 stores and the e-commerce site thetoyshop.com. The business has been operating for over 35 years and currently opens one new store per week, with their e-commerce site running since 1999.

Overview

The Entertainer required a single view of their customers. They needed to make the complex simple in order to interrogate their customer data from across all online channels, to understand who their customers are, how often they shop with them, what kind of products they liked and their lifetime value. This was all information that, previously, The Entertainer was unable to access.

The Entertainer decided on Message Cloud from SmartFocus, one seamless platform that allows companies to understand their customers and to connect in real time – whether by e-mail, mobile, web or social channels. The Entertainer now has a single customer view to power smarter e-mails tailored for specific personas. These drive contextualized, real-time messages relevant to each individual, which has hidden complexities as the consumer (the child) is not the buyer (the adult). Using advanced algorithms to address the complex buyer personas has enabled the company to achieve astounding increased results.

The challenge

The Entertainer has a variety of different customer groups and stocks many brands that are distinct and separate from each other. Historically, the company had been sending standard e-mails with no data attached other than a store number or customer postcode collected in-store. They were unable to recommend potential next purchases based on past or crowd behaviour, they could not send an e-mail campaign to their highest-spending customers or to abandoned baskets, and could not send e-mails recommending suitable offers by age and gender.

The solution

All transactional and marketing campaign programmes were migrated to The Message Cloud, allowing for 100 per cent personalized and fully responsive messages driven by customer behaviour. A single customer-view database was built, incorporating the tools needed to maximize all data to increase lifetime value and deliver real-time personalization for web and e-mail. Alongside the creation of this database, a new e-mail service solution was integrated to allow segmentation of e-mail addresses using attributes from the database. The recommendations engine now gathers data while the customer browses, interacts and orders from the website.

The Entertainer not only gained exposure to a larger audience but converted the highest possible number of consumers into lifetime customers. By improving communications to prospective, first-time and returning customers, they saw a significant ROI by offering live personalization.

The platform enabled The Entertainer to react to stock levels the second that an e-mail is opened. Sales are maximized because their e-mails always show products that are in stock to customers.

Results

Within one year The Entertainer has:

- 3x e-mail revenue;
- 2x open rates;
- massively increased conversion rates;
- 120 per cent increase in mobile sales;
- 60 per cent increase in returning shoppers;
- significantly increased average order value (AOV).

The Entertainer has *doubled open rates* across campaigns because they can now segment and personalize subject lines to different groups of customers.

Conversion rates have increased due to smarter e-mails. Seeing a moving countdown timer, for example, gives a sense of urgency to a customer for the ending of an event or promotion, telling them, for example, that they have four hours left until a sale ends – or how long it is until the Christmas delivery cut-off.

Repeat shoppers have increased *60 per cent year on year*. Previously only 14 per cent of their online customers made a repeat purchase.

Quote
Rob Wood, head of Online, The Entertainer:

> *There's so much noise for potential customers and e-mails are getting increasingly competitive. This means you only get one chance at your e-mail, so it needs to be smarter and work harder. The information you used*

to set up your e-mail two days ago might not be the best information when the e-mail is opened. And if you know customers are not going to look at every single one of your e-mails, you need to offer them the very best message when they do choose to interact with your brand.

We tripled our e-mail revenue last year compared to the year before, which is a brilliant result for us and something we are really happy with. We've used the same database – it's not like we have massively grown the database. All we have done is send better messages to the same people and got a better result from that.

Rob Mullen, CEO SmartFocus:

Customers rely on us to deliver business-critical, joined-up marketing campaigns that make a difference to their customers and to the growth of their business. Looking forward, we will continue to focus on the importance of contextualization of experiences and how brands can send relevant, real-time messages to their customer to strengthen consumer relationships.

The future

The next step for The Entertainer is to bring personalization and segmentation on to thetoyshop.com. This will allow the company to segment on past purchase history and browsing behaviour, and will enable a home page that reflects products and brands that customers have bought or looked at before. Customer behaviour on e-mail can influence customer content online and vice versa. This cross-channel approach is becoming the benchmark of personalization that customers are coming to expect.

About the creator

Special thanks to Charlotte Albrecht and the team at SmartFocus for their collaboration.

Understanding mobile marketing

07

OUR CHAPTER PLEDGE TO YOU

When you reach the end of this chapter you will have answers to the following questions:

- What is mobile marketing?
- What is the potential for mobile marketing?
- How do I go about setting up a mobile marketing campaign?
- What can mobile marketing do for my business?
- What are the top tips for building a successful mobile marketing campaign?
- What role do mobile apps play in an increasingly mobile marketing world?
- How significant are location-based apps and mobile gaming?
- What are the privacy issues surrounding mobile?

Mobile – market size and rate of growth

The Mobile Marketing Association defines mobile marketing in 2016 as the following:

> Mobile Marketing is a set of practices that enables organizations to communicate and engage with their audience in an interactive and relevant manner through any mobile device or network.

Over the past decade or so, mobile marketing has gone from being a fairly broad advertising term to referring to a rather specific type of marketing. Once used to describe any form of marketing that made use of a moving (mobile) medium (things such as moving billboards, roadshows and other transportable outdoor advertising), today it refers to a completely different form of advertising: reaching out to connect and interact with consumers through their mobile electronic device of choice.

As with other forms of online marketing, mobile marketing in its various guises has evolved rapidly in a relatively short space of time, fuelled by consumers with a hunger for anything that can help them to streamline their congested, hyperconnected lives. As lifestyles evolve to become ever more generic, global and portable, the lure of the 'always connected' mobile device gets ever stronger.

In the UK, mobile ad spend soared by 60.3 per cent to reach £2.627 billion in 2015, accounting for 30.5 per cent of all digital advertising, according to a study published by IAB and PwC in April 2016.

According to ZenithOptimedia's new Advertising Expenditure Forecasts, in 2018 mobile advertising will overtake desktop and account for 50.2 per cent of all internet advertising. ZenithOptimedia forecast that global mobile advertising expenditure will total US $114 billion in 2018. 'Growth of the global ad market is being driven by advances in technology, especially mobile,' says Steve King, ZenithOptimedia's CEO.

The growth in smartphone adoption and mobile media tablets is a major driver in the growth of mobile advertising budgets. In 2015, the International Telecommunications Union (ITU) estimated that there were 7.1 billion mobile subscriptions worldwide, equivalent to 96 per cent of the global human population. While the majority of handsets are so-called 'feature handsets' (non-smartphones), sales of smartphones overtook feature phones back in 2013, and are expected to continue to grow rapidly, particularly in developing countries. The ITU also reported that, in 2015, 69 per cent of the global population was covered by 3G mobile broadband, up from 45 per cent in 2011.

A Portio Research study in 2015 reported that worldwide a total of 8.3 trillion SMS messages were sent, which is almost 23 billion messages per day. According to figures from Ofcom, SMS message traffic peaked in 2011 and has been declining ever since, which Ofcom ascribes to 'increasing use of newer communication methods'.

Meanwhile, OTT (over-the-top) messaging traffic from apps such as WhatsApp, Facebook Messenger and Apple iMessage is growing exponentially. Portio expects cumulative OTT messaging traffic to exceed 100 trillion messages from 2013 to 2017. In early 2015, it was announced that WhatsApp had overtaken traditional SMS messaging. Data compiled by *The Economist* showed that 30 billion WhatsApp messages were being sent every day by the end of 2014, far more than the 23 billion SMS messages sent each day.

Another study, this time by Ovum, shows that by 2018 application to person (A2P) messaging traffic will reach 2.19 trillion messages. What is A2P messaging? It is simply automated messages from an application rather than a person. It is widely used in financial services, advertising, marketing, business administration, ticketing, television voting, etc. When your mobile operator sends a text to your phone to say your latest bill is available online, or your credit is running low... that is an A2P message.

But what does that mean in mobile marketing terms?

Despite all the hype surrounding mobile web access, search, apps, smartphones, tablets, location-based services and everything else – for the time being, at least, messaging is very much at the heart of the mobile marketing industry. But things change quickly, more so in mobile than perhaps any other branch of digital marketing, and marketers around the world would do well to prepare for a future dominated by mobile access to online information and services.

The steady rise of mobile has become *the* main event in the digital marketing arena over recent years. Mobile has, of course, been the 'next big thing' for what seems an eternity, but with the continued growth of smart-phone adoption (increasing by more than 30 per cent year on year), the convergence of mobile computing, improved connectivity and development of the cloud, mobile is finally rising to realize its potential.

Mobile internet adoption is increasing at a rate that is eight times that of the equivalent for desktops 10 years ago. More than half of all new internet connections now originate from mobile devices. We are in the midst of another fundamental shift in the way that people access digital information and services – when most marketers are still reeling after the last one.

Don't ring the death knell of desktop and laptop computers just yet, though; for many things (writing this book, for example) a 'proper' computer is still likely to be a better choice than a mobile device. But there is little doubt that the scope of their utility is diminishing, and as people get used to accomplishing more and more with the devices in their pockets, they will turn to their computers less and less.

And not only are consumers using mobile devices more frequently to connect to the internet, but they are increasingly using a variety of different devices and form factors, moving back and forth between smartphone and tablet.

As marketers, we need to adapt to this shift in communications technology and learn once more to engage with our audience through their current medium of choice, and optimize their experience, however they choose to connect.

'Show and sell' is dead, welcome to the world of 'utility and entertainment'

A great example of a brand embracing the 'utility and entertainment' aspect of mobile to maximum effect was the 'Axe Wake-Up Service', a campaign that ran in the mobile marketing capital of the world: Japan.

Research showed that 70 per cent of Japan's urban male youth (the brand's target market) used their mobile phones as alarm clocks. All Axe did was to use this generic consumer behaviour as a platform, and built a campaign around it (see Figure 7.1).

Figure 7.1 The Axe Wake-Up Service campaign – entertaining and useful... the essence of effective mobile marketing

Axe simply launched a service that allowed the consumer to visit Axe online, enter their mobile number and set a wake-up call time. A young, attractive woman would then make the wake-up call, even appearing by videophone if the customer desired. Naturally, the campaign reminded the customer to

spray on a little Axe to smell great. The brand took an existing consumer behaviour, and offered a useful and entertaining solution that built upon it in a fun and engaging way. The result: a runaway success!

So what can mobile marketing be used for?

The answer to that question could take up an entire book... and then some. Because mobile is essentially a new, exciting and convenient way for people to access online information and services, elements of your mobile marketing can be employed to achieve many of the same business goals as any other form of digital marketing. You can use mobile to:

- build awareness of your brand, product or service;
- foster and nurture conversations with your online community;
- gather valuable insight into consumer behaviour;
- take iterative customer engagement to the next level;
- harness the wisdom of the crowd;
- drive lead generation and new business;
- establish loyalty programmes, competitions and rewards;
- build a deeper and more personal brand experience;
- target your market more effectively based on demographics, geography and behaviour;
- retain more customers and reduce 'churn';
- listen and learn.

The list could go on and on... but you get the idea.

With massive uptake of internet-connected mobile devices accelerating all the time, marketers need to start taking mobile seriously as a fundamental component (if not the principal component) of their digital marketing strategy. The potential of mobile is profound – and the impact of mobile marketing is only going to grow.

Mobile: evolution on steroids

Innovation, and the very human desire for something newer and better, is driving the rapid evolution of the mobile device. We are never content with the status quo. Last month our all-singing-all-dancing smartphone was the bee's knees... but today, well, today we really *need* that shiny new tablet.

You know, the one that is so achingly cool we don't even need to turn it on to impress our friends. Next month a new version of our phone will hit the shelves – sleeker, brighter, faster... It's all happening so damned quickly.

When you break it down it is not really that different to the evolution of biological systems – it just happens much, much faster. Darwin's theory of the survival of the fittest still applies, but instead of waiting hundreds of thousands of years for new species to evolve, in the mobile ecosystem we have new mobile devices evolving in a matter of months.

Manufacturers introduce new features and form factors in their mobile devices all of the time in an attempt to capture and retain a share of this burgeoning new market. If those features resonate with people (are truly useful, fun or, ideally, both), then the positive selection pressure of people handing over hard-earned cash pushes the retention and enhancement of those features; if they don't, they die. Over time this leads to the iterative refinement and development (the evolution) of devices that are ideally suited to their particular niche in the digital ecosystem.

Full circle: from tablet to tablet

In the beginning there was the stone tablet: Flintstone marketing at its best. Today the tablets we have to play with are a bit more functional, and weigh substantially less. But are tablets here to stay, or are they a passing fad?

Tablets are interesting because they are not really portable in the way that your mobile phone is portable. It's still mobile – but it's not something people have with them 24/7 like their phones.

They are also not fully fledged computers in the more 'traditional' sense. You still will not find many people sitting down at their iPad to write a 10,000-word business report, or to create a complex financial spreadsheet.

Tablets sit somewhere in the middle ground. The bigger screens and intuitive touch interface mean that tablets excel as media consumption devices: watching online video, catching up with a TV show you've missed, accessing blogs, websites, social media, video-calling your gran, playing games and running apps are all quick, convenient and intuitive on a tablet. They are also fantastic for doing simple online tasks quickly: things like online banking, ordering a birthday gift for your mum on Amazon, subscribing to a new podcast, quickly checking your e-mail or discussing a TV show you're watching with your peers on Twitter.

For more complex tasks you will still typically boot up the laptop... but for convenience and instant gratification, if there's a tablet available, you'll reach for it every time. There is little doubt that tablets are here to stay, and with competition hotting up, the constant pressure to innovate will drive their continued evolution. Tablets will become more capable, and as more of us acquire the habit of using them we will do more things online with them – which of course means that as marketers we have to factor the rise of the tablet into our online strategy.

How big are tablets going to get?

No, we're not talking screen size… we're talking market size.

Various reports from industry behemoths such as Morgan Stanley and Cisco suggest that there could be potentially up to 75 billion internet-connected devices by 2020. To put that number into perspective, we passed the 10 billion device milestone in 2013, according to analyst firm ABI Research, and the number keeps growing apace.

Gerd Leonhard, from the aptly named Futures Agency in Switzerland, concludes: 'Tablet devices will become the way many of us will read magazines, books, newspapers and even attend live concerts – and kick off an era of mobile-augmented reality with content being bundled into mobile service contracts to be consumed on any mobile or tablet device.'

However the future of mobile marketing evolves, tablet devices are likely to play a significant role in that evolution. They span the divide between mobile phones and full-blown computers, are already the quintessential device for multimedia consumption and are getting more capable with each iteration. Tablets are here to stay.

Mobile user experience

As consumers increasingly interact with brands via a variety of different mobile devices, understanding the different requirements for mobile channels and making sure customers have a good experience, no matter how they choose to connect, will be critically important for marketers.

In Adobe's '2015 Mobile Consumer Survey' the company highlighted some key best practices and recommendations for mobile channels:

1 Treat mobile like it is more than a channel. Mobile is not just about creating experiences for smaller screen sizes. Given that some consumers will continue to shop at bricks-and-mortar stores while others would be perfectly happy with a mobile-only institution, it is important that your mobile strategy compliments the entire customer journey. Picture mobile as a way to improve customer experience overall, and your company is more likely to improve overall conversion.

2 Design mobile experiences with ease of use in mind. With limited screen space and the occasional interruptions consumers experience while engaging

in their mobile devices, marketers need to cut to the chase and make content easily accessible. Consider emerging technologies that eliminate the need for customers to search back and forth, such as 'shoppable hotspots', which quickly give mobile users the content they want in one click.

3 Use metrics to measure mobile app and web success. To measure mobile success, you must manage it first. When developing and managing apps, mobile teams must understand how often consumers download and launch their app, what paths they take, and if their interactions drive monetization. To get the most out of your mobile channels, consider using metrics for user acquisition, engagement, conversion and retention in order to help you measure ROI.

4 Target and personalize by audience segment. Your brand is the common denominator between your customers – beyond that, each customer is uniquely different and expects a unique experience based on their level of engagement and interests. To keep them captivated, consider using A/B testing, optimization and location-based targeting to create relevant, personalized experiences wherever they go.

The rise and rise of mobile advertising

It has been a while coming but in 2016 we could finally say that this was the year of the mobile. Thanks to the innovation of the likes of Steve Jobs, bringing fresh thinking to smartphone design, the mobile phone is now so versatile that many people couldn't live without it.

Wherever you are – watching TV at home, travelling to or from work, or just out and about – mobile devices are becoming the method of choice for connecting to the internet. Just think how often you reach for your phone to play games when you are travelling, to check your social networks for updates, or pick up your e-mails.

So, for advertisers why is mobile media so powerful?

A smartphone is the owner's mini personal computer, always with them and always connected. It allows them to send and receive e-mail, instant messages, surf the web, find out the weather, play games, watch TV, even make phone calls and text too! Built in GPS means they will never get lost and can always find a local restaurant, petrol station or ATM. Whether it is looking for a bite to eat or how to repair a puncture, there is always an app for that. Used in the right way this is hugely powerful for advertisers. Mobile advertising allows advertisers to target people on the move or at home and capture them when they are most receptive.

In a nutshell, advertising to consumers via their mobile device is the future and brands that are quick to learn how to use this highly innovative medium will be the ones to win the mind share of the public.

In 2011, for the first time, standardized key metrics for measuring advertisements were established for the mobile interactive industry. Developed in a joint effort by the Interactive Advertising Bureau (IAB) and the Mobile Marketing Association (MMA), and with the assistance of the Media Rating Council (MRC), the 'Mobile Web Advertising Measurement Guidelines' provide a framework to govern how ad impressions are counted on the mobile web.

In 2016, the IAB, MMA and MRC announced updates to the guidelines for counting mobile web and mobile in-app served ad impressions. This important update eliminates 'count on decision' as an option for reporting served impression counts. MRC staff have been communicating the need for this change with measurement vendors ever since the initial release of the guidelines, and doing so now helps ensure that counting occurs only after an ad is actually delivered to a mobile app or browser.

The measurement guidelines for mobile applications and mobile web advertising will help marketers to assess accurately the delivery of ads within mobile websites and apps, and offer a clear way to count ad impressions, assuring them that their advertising messages are reaching mobile consumers.

More than anything, the guidelines demonstrate the mobile industry's commitment to its marketing partners to create a transparent and consistent business environment for buying and selling ads, to establish actionable guidelines that work across a complex industry, and to encourage the continued growth of mobile advertising.

These kinds of developments are encouraging. We still have a long way to go but there are exciting times ahead for everyone involved in the mobile advertising industry today.

CASE STUDY   Periscopix and Oasis – mobile conversions increased 255 per cent year on year

Oasis is a global British fashion brand that pioneers print design, and lives and breathes design. Periscopix have been running their PPC accounts for two and a half years and, over this time, they have seen customer mobile behaviour significantly change.

In the ever-fierce world of fashion, they set their sights on new ways to increase the conversion volume, without breaking the bank.

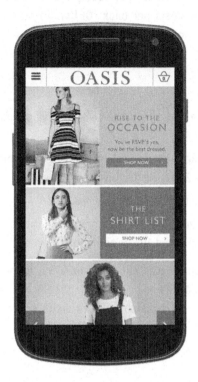

The challenge

Mobile has been a key growth area across the industry, with Google reporting that mobile queries surpassed desktop searches for the very first time over Christmas 2014.

Periscopix were keen to capitalize on this spike in mobile use in a cost-effective way, and so they worked with Oasis to set an objective to define the campaign: 1) increase conversion volumes across mobile; 2) without increasing overall cost per acquisition (CPA).

Action

Traditionally, poorer performance is seen across mobile, with lower conversion rates and consequently higher CPAs. The temptation is therefore to apply negative bid adjustments across accounts. However, Oasis's customer mobile behaviour is ever-changing, and Periscopix needed to make sure that the account was ready to respond to this. This was done by ensuring that the account had: 1) mobile-specific ad copy with relevant unique selling propositions (USPs) and calls to action (CTAs); 2) mobile-appropriate bid adjustments for each area of the account.

As mobile grows in importance for the account and the business, the next step was to extend the reach, where previously the desktop campaigns had been restricted due to rising costs per click (CPCs). To do this Periscopix set up a campaign that focuses on mobile traffic only, targeting all potential customers at any time of day.

Results

- 36 per cent increase in the percentage of clicks coming from a mobile device year on year (YOY).
- The majority of traffic (41 per cent) now comes from mobile, with 34 per cent from tablet and only 25 per cent from desktop.
- 45 per cent increase in mobile conversions YOY.
- Whilst there have been increases in conversion rate across the board, mobile conversion rates increased 10 per cent more than desktop.

Best of all, all of the above was accomplished in a cost-effective way! Despite pushing areas where mobile had been working really well, mobile CPCs remained at 84 per cent cheaper than desktop. Conversions are increasing whilst CPA is steadily decreasing:

FIGURE 7.2

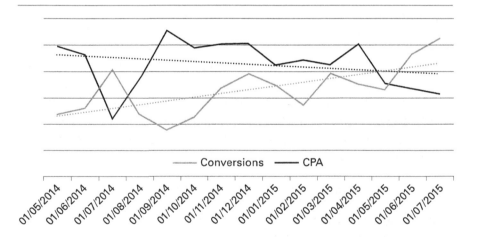

In the first full month of the mobile campaign, Periscopix saw the following results:

- At top level:
    - 198 per cent increase in mobile traffic with a 255 per cent increase in conversions YOY; mobile revenue increased by 263 per cent as a result.

- The campaign itself:
  - The campaign has a CPC one-third of the account average, with CPA following trend.
  - Black Friday alone saw a 400 per cent increase in conversions through the same keywords on mobile YOY.

FIGURE 7.3

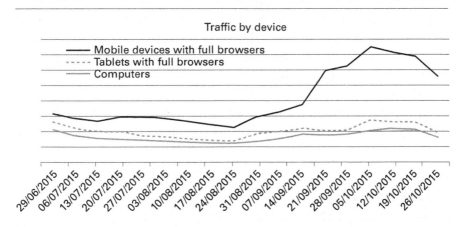

Traffic by device

- Mobile devices with full browsers
- Tablets with full browsers
- Computers

29/06/2015 06/07/2015 13/07/2015 20/07/2015 27/07/2015 03/08/2015 10/08/2015 17/08/2015 24/08/2015 31/08/2015 07/09/2015 14/09/2015 21/09/2015 28/09/2015 05/10/2015 12/10/2015 19/10/2015 26/10/2015

Links to campaign

https://www.oasis-stores.com/
http://www.periscopix.co.uk/

About the creator

Periscopix, a Merkle company, runs massively effective online advertising campaigns for some of the world's biggest brands.

Location, location, location

The fact that your mobile *always* knows where you are can be a bit disconcerting, but there is no denying that it is also an incredibly useful feature. Using maps on your mobile device always comes in handy to quickly find out where you are, how to get to where you want to be, locate a nearby Thai restaurant that your friends recommended, or find the nearest cinema showing the film you want to see.

But what about taking the utility of knowing *where* people are, and using it to help them make the most of what is available around them, discover cool new locations, locate friends who happen to be nearby or avail themselves of the latest offers from local businesses? Welcome to the world of location-aware applications and location-based services. These apps use your mobile's built-in GPS or triangulate your position based on data from the mobile phone masts that your device is connected to, and use that data (with your permission, hopefully) to do all sorts of clever things.

The real opportunity with location-aware applications from a marketing perspective is that they offer businesses with bricks-and-mortar premises the opportunity to deliver real-time information, offers and incentives to people *who are physically in the area*. Location information is something that marketers can leverage to make the information they provide to prospects more *useful and relevant* than ever... and that will always drive higher conversion rates.

Remon Pepers from Targetoo gives us his expert view on location-based advertising and how to set up a successful location-based marketing campaign.

Expert view

Location-based advertising and how to set up a successful location-based marketing campaign
Contribution by Remon Pepers, Targetoo

Mobile advertising continues to show rapid growth acceleration and has become an unmissable part of any marketing strategy. Smartphones have become essential personal devices that people carry with them almost everywhere. Smartphones can tell a lot about their user through what apps they have installed and display certain user behaviour. Through location-based mobile advertising, unique opportunities to reach out to consumers wherever they are, and the ability to display tailored experiences, become possible.

Imagine you are about to open a new retail store and you want to create awareness of your brand in the local vicinity. You could include special offers tailored to consumers who are approaching the store location, and could even change your creative message and offer based on the weather. Location-based advertising is effective when combined with out-of-home (OOH) advertising. You could supplement your OOH advertising (in tube stations and on billboards at bus stops, for example) with location-based advertising, so that when users come out of the tube station they get a notification on their phone and are reminded of the OOH ad they just saw. Increasing the amount of touch points you have with your audience contributes to higher brand awareness and engagement.

Location-based advertising is also a very valuable way to collect data and build user profiles. If you are advertising nationwide you may start noticing different peak hours of performance in different cities, or when some locations simply outperform others. Alongside location data, a lot more information can become available such as user demographics, interests and device information.

So how exactly do you acquire data and determine someone's location?

There are several instruments to determine a location, some more effective than others:

- GPS: currently the best way to determine a user's location. Required to be switched on and shared by the user.
- Wi-Fi: when a user logs in to Wi-Fi at a shop or restaurant.
- Antenna triangulation (carrier): less accurate than GPS and Wi-Fi, but still an effective way to know what area/city the user is in.
- IP address: the least accurate of the four and rarely used for targeting on a very granular level.

So what does it take to set up a successful location-based advertising campaign?

One of the key ingredients to a successful location-based campaign is *reach*. You want to be able to reach as many users as possible on the locations that are relevant to you. In order to get reach – especially on a hyperlocal scale – you need to gain access to as many apps and mobile websites as possible that share location data. This means that the more apps you have, the higher the likelihood of a user utilizing one of these apps and the better your ability to target users. Along with reach, having a tailored message depending on the person who sees it becomes more and more important.

Conclusion

Location-based mobile advertising offers advertisers the capability to reach out to relevant audiences with a relevant message, resulting in increasing brand awareness and engagement. It also provides advertisers with a better understanding of these audiences so that they can improve and evolve their marketing strategy around it.

Check-ins checking out?

The first location-based applications, like FourSquare (www.foursquare.com), Gowalla and Facebook Places, relied on users making a conscious decision that required action: they needed to physically 'check in' at locations using software on their mobile device.

Over time, check-in profiles built up. Users were awarded points, badges and 'mayorships' as their 'status' grew and they checked in to locations regularly. All of this, of course, was designed to reward repeated use of the service, encouraging people to 'check in' wherever they went, and ultimately establish a habit that would endure beyond initial experimentation with the 'shiny new toy' of location-based social media.

Ultimately, though, the act of checking in has proved to be one of the biggest challenges facing location-based models, because there is no intrinsic value to the process for users. Facebook, after acquiring Gowalla in 2011, has since retired Places and relegated location sharing to a status update tag. While FourSquare continues with the check-in model for now, it is trying to combat user fatigue by making the check-in process simpler.

Instead of requiring people to manually check in to receive relevant information and promotions, marketers can now use mobile-phone technology to automatically detect when someone is nearby and send messages to them, provided they have agreed to receive them, of course!

Mobile gaming

Mobile gaming has been described as the wide-open battleground of the entertainment industry. While the likes of Facebook and Zynga dominate social games, and big publishers such as Xbox, Sony and Nintendo rule console games, the global smartphone games market is still patently up for grabs.

Mobile games are huge because mobile devices are... well, mobile! You have your mobile with you 24/7. Sitting in a doctor's waiting room with time to kill? Waiting for the bus home from work? Waiting in line at the supermarket checkout? What are you going to do? Almost invariably, if you have one, you'll whip out your smartphone.

Some people will update their social media status, some will check their e-mail, others might read their favourite blog, and even check in using their location-based service of choice to check out local offers. But many will fire up the latest and greatest mobile game.

There are millions of mobile games spanning the gamut of mobile devices and mobile platforms. And where there are games, there is an audience, and where there is an audience there are opportunities to promote. Brands are already delivering promotional messages *within* mobile games and even *sponsoring entire games* in order to drive consumer engagement.

With potentially billions of users in the mobile market, mobile gaming could well grow to become the single largest gaming market of them all. Smartphone games have been growing fast since 2007, when the iPhone was introduced, and tablet games followed suit with the introduction of the iPad in early 2010. Mobile games are now the fastest-growing segment of the video games market. According to PwC, mobile gaming's share of revenue will grow from 10 per cent in 2008 to 17 per cent in 2017.

Successes like that of Rovio's now legendary Angry Birds, which has been downloaded more than 200 million times, mean that mobile game companies can attract tens of millions of dollars in investment capital.

The games market today is dominated by consoles, with mobile games accounting for a relatively small but rapidly expanding slice of the pie. Few doubt that the growth will continue, as emerging digital markets in Asia embrace the smartphone revolution, and mobile devices become the primary connectivity and entertainment device of choice for a massive chunk of the human population.

But it's not all a bed of roses in mobile gaming. Established mobile game developers such as Digital Chocolate have warned that a glut of games being released on major smartphone platforms means that game developers will find it very hard to make money. They point out that, in many cases, average revenue per game does not even cover development costs. A rash of poor games can ruin the market for everyone, making it more difficult for consumers to find what is 'good' and generally tainting the gaming experience on mobile platforms for everyone. At the time of writing (April 2016) there were 530,868 active games in the App Store, with 'games' being the most popular app category, taking up 23 per cent, followed by 'business' in second (10 per cent) and 'education' in third (9 per cent).

But it's not just about the numbers, either. Savvy mobile marketers need to remain neutral in their assessment of the market and, of course, platform agnostic. The winning platform for your business is not necessarily the one with the most apps, it is the one that retains and engages the attention of your particular target market.

Mobile applications

Mobile applications are quite a simple concept. They are just pieces of software that are pre-installed on your mobile phone or are available to download from the internet. They are nothing new. There have been mobile applications available for multiple handsets for years now – ranging from games to currency conversion tools to more complicated applications allowing you to broadcast live video and audio from your phone.

As technology advances rapidly we are moving from a push model to one of pull. People no longer want shoved down their throats information they don't really need. Today's consumers want to be in control; they decide what they want, when they want it and how they want it delivered – and the result is modern mobile apps.

App stores and the explosion of mobile applications has been little short of revolutionary. 'I've never seen anything like this in my career in software', was how Apple founder and CEO Steve Jobs described the initial success of the iPhone App Store – and once again it seems Mr Jobs was right on the money.

Every major media outlet in the world has run pieces on the success of the App Store. The phrase 'there's an app for that' peppers headlines and conversations around the world. The *New York Times* heralded the revolution in mobile applications as a 'new gold rush'.

There are more than 1.5 million applications in the App Store as of June 2015 (and counting) – with hundreds of thousands more available across Android, Blackberry, WebOS, Windows 8, Symbian and myriad alternative operating systems in the market. In mid-2015, Apple announced that more than 100 billion apps had been downloaded from their App Store since its launch in 2008.

The subsequent launch of a variety of tablet devices has generated yet more app-related hyperbole, and with the launch of Chinese-made sub-US $100 handsets running Google's Android operating system, and a serious push from Amazon and all of the major smartphone manufacturers, we live in interesting times for mobile marketers.

The hard reality is that there is a significant number of different application platforms available to brands, agencies and marketers. Choosing the right platform, talking to the right audience, and breaking through the noise generated by the sheer volume of applications released on a daily basis is an incredible challenge. At the time of writing the previous edition of this book (2014), Apple's App Store and Google Play were neck and neck. As of January

2015, Google Play has more apps than Apple's App Store. The latest numbers come from appFigures, an analytics service that monitors data from the thousands of apps that use its platform. The report noted that all three app stores it looked at – Android, iOS and Amazon's Appstore – saw a large amount of growth, but Google saw significantly more than the other two; appFigures doesn't speculate about the reason behind these changes in growth but there are likely a few factors at work. Android still has an overall larger marketshare than iOS globally, so it makes sense that more developers would be attracted to the platform. Google also makes it much easier for developers to create new apps and doesn't put Android developers through the same lengthy approval process as Apple.

Over the last few years, we have seen apps released by nearly every brand on the planet. Users like branded apps. Research by Admob, one of the biggest mobile advertising networks in the world, found that 70 per cent of iPhone users surveyed had downloaded a branded app.

Some of the download figures for branded applications are enormous. Barclaycard released a Waterslide app, which tied in with a successful UK television ad campaign, and which was downloaded more than 9.5 million times. Lighter manufacturer Zippo was one of the first companies to release an app – a simple interface that allows you to 'flick' a lighter on your screen and produce a flame. That simplicity has been rewarded with more than 6 million downloads. Audi's A4 Driving Challenge, where players take a new Audi A4 round a track, has topped 4 million downloads.

The difficulty for brands and developers is how to measure the success of these applications (see the 'measurement' section later in the chapter). Download numbers are a possible metric, but they don't tell the whole story. Engagement is key.

Research by New York-based app analysis company Pinch Media has shown that only 20 per cent of users return to a free application after one day. After 30 days, fewer than 5 per cent are engaging with the app.

Top tips for building a successful app

- Plan, plan, plan: scope the app well in advance.
- Do your research.
- Understand the business model around the app (free/paid).
- What problem is it addressing?
- How will the app be marketed? Who are the target profile/demographic?
- How will you measure success (not just downloads)?

- Focus on design, user interface (UI) and user experience (UX) – the best, most popular applications are simple, effective and look good (see Chapter 14 for more information on optimizing user experience).

- Think about content – are you building an entertainment app that will amuse people for 30 seconds before being deleted? Or are you building a utility that people will use on an ongoing basis?

- Think about the device – problems occur when brands try to shoehorn existing content on to a mobile device. Instead of thinking about the limitations presented by screen size – think instead about the options in terms of the device you are targeting.

What insights does mobile analytics deliver when measuring mobile marketing?

Mobile KPIs

We look at KPIs for general web-based analytics in bonus online-only Chapter 1 (Measurement and data, available at: www.koganpage.com/understanding-digital-marketing), and the basic premise with mobile is exactly the same... a KPI gives an instant snapshot of how your campaign is doing. As with other elements of your digital marketing, measurement and analysis of your mobile metrics are invaluable. They allow you to instantly gauge how well your mobile strategy is working, and to adapt it to deliver better results.

Some examples of popular KPIs for mobile campaigns might include:

- total downloads;
- total app users;
- new users;
- frequency and duration of visit;
- bounce rates;
- segmentation by device type;
- CTRs.

Successful digital marketing is all about iterative refinement – constant tweaking based on interpretation of real data to deliver more effective marketing creative that drives conversion. It is exactly the same with mobile campaigns. By using real data, and the insight it provides, we can focus our efforts (and our finite marketing budget) where they will yield maximum results.

Some of the variables to watch in your mobile campaigns might include:

- User segmentation: it is important to understand which users are interacting with your campaign and taking the actions you want. Are there trends or patterns based on the users' country, device type, platform or other variables?

- Timing: look at the timing of your campaigns in different regions. Do some times yield better returns than others? Understand what times of day are likely to deliver higher conversion rates with your particular audience.

- Advertising channel: based on your analytics you can identify which advertising channels deliver the best results across your mobile portfolio, and reinvest your budget accordingly. The key here is to ensure an independent and viable comparison across all your mobile advertising channels.

According to research carried out by specialist UK-based mobile analytics company Bango, 83 per cent of brands do not use mobile-specific analytic tools, and 27 per cent of brands failed to implement any sort of analytics for their mobile campaigns – that's throwing away a massive opportunity to improve the ROI that they see from their mobile spend.

We know from the statistics presented at the beginning of this chapter that mobile marketing is growing fast, yet the Bango survey shows that brands are missing a beat when it comes to utilizing real data to enhance the performance of their mobile campaigns. Accurate and comprehensive data, and effective reporting, help to keep campaigns focused, deliver enhanced ROI, and ultimately drive brands to achieve more success with their mobile marketing campaigns.

Mobile privacy

If the holy grail of mobile marketing is accurate and effective measurement, then its arch-nemesis must surely be privacy. Privacy concerns are rife across the web, but are more prevalent than ever when you are talking about a device that most of us carry around with us all day, every day: a device that knows exactly where we are, when and for how long.

How much data do consumers *really* want to share with marketers anyway? From a marketer's perspective the more data we have about a prospect, the more effectively we can deliver useful, relevant, timely information to them exactly when and where they need it. That all sounds great for the consumer too… and it is, as far as it goes. That old chestnut 'when advertising becomes useful it ceases to be perceived as advertising' was never truer than when someone's mobile phone helps them to find a local Italian restaurant that six of their friends recommended over the last few months.

There are plenty of 'win–win' examples like that. Essentially that is what mobile marketing at its best is all about. But things are intensely competitive in the mobile arena, and there is a line in the ever-shifting sands of the digital marketing landscape, beyond which mobile marketing becomes intrusive rather than informed. Defining exactly where that line is – that's the tricky bit.

Most responsible marketers realize that sending mobile advertising without the relevant permission or consent causes more harm than good. The mobile equivalent of e-mail spam is only going to turn consumers off in an era when you really need to be engaging in a productive and enduring relationship with them.

For mobile marketing to work, consumers need to have confidence that their privacy will be protected. If they don't, it doesn't really matter how well crafted, imaginative or cool your next mobile campaign is. Without consumer consent and buy-in it is really not going anywhere. Successful mobile marketing needs to be *permission based*, it needs to be *relevant and useful* (or entertaining) and it needs to be part of a broader mobile engagement strategy that extends beyond the initial 'blip' of campaign-based marketing.

As with many other areas of digital marketing, the legal framework in which we operate has struggled to keep pace with innovation and change. The law is playing catch-up as it tries to deal with issues such as unsolicited mobile advertising, behavioural targeting, and the use of personal identification and location-based information without the user's explicit consent.

Many mobile telecommunications regulations across the developed world are woefully outdated, particularly when it comes to unsolicited commercial communications. The result is a flood of fast-tracked legislation and regulation aimed at assuaging consumers' fears that governments around the world are not taking their privacy seriously. The danger, of course, is that rapid-fire reactive legislation is often poorly thought out and ends up stifling innovation and simultaneously disrupting the user experience, which is bad for marketers and even worse for consumers.

What impact all of this legislation and regulation will have on the evolution of mobile marketing remains to be seen, but when the dust settles, if user privacy concerns have been allayed, at least somewhat, then that's good news for mobile marketers. While regulation and legislation by their very nature give us more hoops to jump through, ultimately it has to be better than the anarchy that would otherwise prevail. If unscrupulous marketers are allowed to fuel consumer paranoia about privacy, then people will simply stop engaging with *any* form of mobile advertising, no matter the source. That would be bad news for everyone.

There are undoubtedly some very serious consumer protection issues that marketers need to be aware of as mobile takes off. Some of the key legal elements that mobile marketers should carefully consider include disclosure, privacy and consent, as set out below.

Disclosure

Marketers should clearly disclose the terms of any offer. With the growth of mobile applications, the spotlight is being centred on how transparently mobile marketers disclose the terms of things such as in-app purchases. The limited space on mobile screens can present challenges when it comes to full disclosure, but marketers need to find creative ways to make sure that consumers see material terms before they part with their money.

Privacy

Mobile companies are increasingly coming under fire for not adequately disclosing their mobile data-collection practices to consumers. As we have already discussed, there is a huge push around the world to bring legislation up to date in the mobile privacy arena. Now is the time for marketers to put their house in order in terms of mobile privacy. Keep an eye on legal developments in your jurisdiction/those of your customers, and pay attention to how new mobile privacy proposals may ultimately affect your mobile strategy now and into the future.

Consent

Consent or permission is another key area, and one that is likely to become more critical as mobile commerce and payments take off. Issues such as how to ensure that the person making a mobile transaction is, in fact, authorized to do so will be at the forefront.

Many companies using mobile as a direct communications channel to their customers have been caught out for failing to get consent before sending promotional text messages. In some cases settlements reached into the millions. Make sure you get a consumer's permission before contacting them on their mobile.

Mobile data

As with privacy, a lot of interest is now being paid to our behaviours and the data trail that we are leaving behind on a daily basis from all our activity on mobile devices. According to the Ericsson Mobility Report published in February 2016, global mobile data traffic grew 65 per cent between Q4 2014 and Q4 2015. Other highlights include that social networking is second only to video for driving mobile traffic growth. Over the next six years, total social networking traffic will be around 12 times that of the previous six years. The report also detailed results from a study where time-to-content delays followed by an additional pause in video playout leads to a jump in mobile users' stress levels. Conversely, a delay-free experience triggers a positive emotional response and increases brand engagement for mobile operators.

Futurists (now there's a job title we'd love...) are also predicting that new 'open' environments will lead to a new generation of mobile devices with even more sensors capturing ever-increasing streams of data about our movements in the physical world – including things such as temperature, noise, location and even smell!

Add sensor data to user data, voice data and other data sources and it is easy to see how that data could be used to build a picture of individual behaviour that is scarily close to the mark. It poses some tough questions. How will all this potentially valuable and personal data be filtered? Who is going to own it? Where is it going to be stored? How is it going to be secured?

Further exploration

We have only really scratched the surface, and looked at a high-level snapshot of the mobile marketing landscape. Getting into the detail would go far beyond the scope of this volume. The years ahead promise to deliver more innovation, change and rapid development in the mobile space.

Mobile marketing is finally coming of age. With the gradual introduction of sophisticated new technologies, marketers are beginning to track results and manage mobile metrics in ways similar to those used for the web. Some critics argue that the medium is still not reaching its full potential: of course it's not... even in terms of digital marketing it is still a baby, but it's growing up fast. In this chapter we hope we have shared some of the boundless scope and potential that make mobile marketing so exciting. Mobile is already a significant layer in the digital marketing mix, and over time will grow in importance as more people turn to their mobile devices for the information, answers, products and services they need every day. Whether mobile marketing is a good fit for your business is up to you to decide... but the potential of mobile is certainly worth exploring.

Some other areas of mobile that fall beyond the scope of this chapter, but may be worth a quick 'Google' include:

- SMS and short-code mobile marketing;
- mobile payments;
- mobile commerce;
- QR codes;
- augmented reality;
- mobile mapping;
- mobile banking;
- mobile health.

Building a multichannel marketing strategy

As mobile increasingly becomes the preferred method for connecting with the internet, savvy marketers who ready themselves for the new multichannel world can take advantage of opportunities to get closer to their customers than ever before.

The intimate nature of mobile – always close and always on – can provide a wealth of data about our habits and movements, perhaps more than some of us realize or would want! And with consumers increasingly willing to purchase through their smartphones and tablets, there are already signs that smart companies can reap success through targeted marketing campaigns.

Mothercare is using mobile, for example, to provide relevant promotions by pinpointing a customer's location, sending details of their nearest store and identifying special offers available to them. It is also building longer-term relationships with new customers through its mobile app, which provides week-by-week advice to pregnant mums.

TUI Travel has also seen success with its MyThomson mobile app, which provides information and planning tools to support holiday-makers, from the moment they book their travel to the end of their holiday, and allows them to share their experience through social networks. MyThomson became the most popular travel app on the Apple App Store shortly after launch and had over 180,000 downloads within a few months of release.

Mobile is a unique channel, with differing needs for different device-form factors and connections. It can no longer be thought of as an add-on to a marketing strategy but needs to be integrated fully into the overall marketing mix. People expect a positive experience no matter what device they are using – nothing kills a mobile web experience like a pesky pop-up!

The year of the mobile is finally here. Make sure you're ready!

CASE STUDY   FCB Chicago and Illinois Council Against Handgun Violence – *Unforgotten*

Summary

Every year 30,000 victims die from gun violence in the United States. People have become numb to it. How do you overcome their apathy and compel them to get involved? You turn apathy into action by bringing back the victims to tell their stories.

Introducing *Unforgotten* – an installation/exhibit that featured lifelike statues of gun-violence victims in their actual clothes. A mobile app identified the name tag on each statue, activating a video of a life that was lost but not forgotten. The app connected you to a website where you could read and share more stories of victims. Most importantly, the app also enabled you to immediately take action by volunteering and by signing a petition for change. The entire experience was documented with an online film.

The exhibit simply could not be ignored, overlooked or forgotten. It was an emotional way to humanize the tragedy, an unforgettable way to connect people with the victims, and a compelling way to get people involved.

Unforgotten did what all the headlines and news couldn't – it stopped people in their tracks, moved them deeply and motivated them to take action to keep guns out of the wrong hands. With over 100 million earned impressions, the Illinois Council Against Handgun Violence achieved unprecedented awareness and engagement. Due to the success, in 2016 the exhibit began touring and impacting communities beyond the launch location.

Location

United States.

The challenge

Every year the US public is bombarded on our news streams with thousands of stories about gun violence. With so many stories, people had become numb, making it difficult for organizations like the Illinois Council Against Handgun Violence to make a significant impact.

We needed a way to make people feel this senseless loss of life. Up close, personal and face-to-face. The *Unforgotten* exhibit did that by humanizing the tragedy and connecting people with the victims in a way that simply could not be ignored.

Target audience

The general public.

Action

Unforgotten launched with a haunting outdoor exhibit featuring lifelike statues of gun-violence victims in their actual clothes. The families of victims, community leaders, passers-by and the press attended the event. The exhibit appeared at the announced location, and also popped-up guerilla style at various places around the city. This all led to our PR effort, with news of the travelling exhibit spreading and interest in future locations growing.

The lifelike statues of gun-violence victims worked to draw people in. Once they got close, they saw the name tag on each statue that worked with a mobile app, activating a video of the victim's story.

A mobile app used augmented reality to visually identify the name tag, activating a video of a life that was lost but not forgotten. A Wi-Fi hotspot on the premises let exhibit visitors immediately download the app. Viewers were also invited to share the video and visit the *Unforgotten* website. Once on the site, you could learn more about gun violence, sign our petition and share additional stories.

Exhibit visitors were encouraged to wear name tags in memory of the victims, post pictures at #unforgotten, and change their Facebook profile picture to represent a victim. Every one of our calls-to-action was another way to keep our victims unforgotten.

We also documented the event with an online video so that the rest of the world could virtually experience the exhibit. It was released online and shared by viewers who chose to 'unforget' the victims of gun violence. Those visiting the *Unforgotten* website were also invited to view and share the video. The video features poignant family interviews and emotional reactions to the statues. The video humanizes the tragedy and gives the gun-violence issue a new and original voice. It ends with clickable links to view the website and sign a petition for change.

Results

The campaign goal was to remember victims of gun violence, while raising awareness of this important and politically charged topic in the United States, specifically in Illinois where the campaign originated. We launched in April – when research indicates that shootings start to escalate because of warmer weather – by bringing attention to the issue in a new and original way. Knowing that news about gun violence would become more prevalent during this time, we believed we could rally people to sign a petition encouraging the government to enact more common-sense laws to get guns out of the wrong hands.

Links to campaign

https://www.youtube.com/watch?v=dvKxuwn02Zs

About the creator

FCB is the oldest and newest advertising agency in Chicago. Founded in 1873 as Lord & Thomas, and reintroduced as Foote, Cone and Belding, we create big transformative ideas that drive change.

Comment from creator

The statues are really powerful, but the app allows the experience to cross through into the digital realm, giving people the tools and motivation to share the victims' stories, their own stories and also sign the petition.

Jordan Sparrow, art director at FCB Chicago

Content marketing and native advertising

08

OUR CHAPTER PLEDGE TO YOU

When you reach the end of this chapter you will have answers to the following questions:

- Why do I need to create content for digital marketing success?
- How does content strategy influence my entire digital strategy?
- How is content used by PR, social and search teams?
- What do I need to think about when creating digital content?
- How can I share the digital content I am creating?
- How do I calculate ROI and set KPIs for my content?
- What is *native* and why is this important to my strategy?
- What content themes work for native?

Why content? – An overview

You cannot talk about digital marketing without simultaneously talking about content. Today we live in a digital landscape where content is everywhere. You are nothing online if you do not create content. Content in its myriad different forms is the currency that digital marketers use to engage, interact and influence their customers. Content is one of the few marketing channels that allows marketers to contact their potential customers along all phases of the customer cycle, during research, purchase and review.

Content works. In this chapter we show you why content works, how it works and how it sits within an overall digital marketing strategy. We show you how content can be used to make your brand innovative, win new customers and influence your target audience. We also demonstrate how content can work for any brand, big or small, and how to come up with the ideas that can really invigorate your content marketing. Ultimately we show you that the size and scale of digital mean that content is now at the heart of everything you do online. It increasingly powers search, social, PR and paid-for advertising, too. As digital marketers, it means that we have to take content seriously; you can get away with not being the best at creating it yourself personally, but you do need to know where to find the best content, how to formulate strategy and how to use that content to build engagement.

The growth of content marketing in the digital age

Content marketing is not new: it has been around for over a century in many different guises. John Deere, the tractor maker, created and published its own magazine, *The Furrow*, as far back as 1895. In 1900 Michelin, the tyre manufacturer, began producing a maintenance guide filled with travel and accommodation recommendations for French motorists; in 1966 Nike published and promoted a 19-page booklet entitled *Jogging*, practically inventing the sport of running in the United States – and selling a lot of their trainers to boot (excuse the pun) in the process. Content marketing worked. The distribution method for this content in the pre-digital age was direct mail. Content, in the form of ideas, product information and reviews, was what many mail-order customers wanted to read. In the days before Google, consumers needed information in order to make their purchases. Millions of these purchases were based on branded content that they read via direct-mail marketing material.

Content marketing works and will always work because it offers value to a potential customer; it fills their immediate requirement for information; it engages them and it does not use coercive methods to 'sell' to them. Done right, it is a very powerful brand-building and business-building tool.

Content marketing worked then, and in the digital age it works just as well, if not better. So why the increase in content?

There are a number of reasons why content marketing has seen a resurgence in digital marketing circles in recent years. One of the overriding reasons behind the growth of digital content marketing is because 'now they can'. The barriers to entry for a business or brand to become a publisher are effectively nil. The start-up cost of becoming a publisher – creating content for your blog and/or social media profiles – is next to nothing. Self-publishing platforms such as Wordpress make it easy – and free – to set up. The biggest investment is time. In the digital age all brands can, with ease, become publishers. Not for them the costly printing and distribution process of days gone by.

Content marketing is also growing because, as mentioned above, it works – no matter what the size of your business. Content is a strategy being adopted by leading brands such as P&G, Coca-Cola and Amex, as well as by smaller businesses and even one-person entities. Coca-Cola – one of the biggest brands on the planet and with colossal marketing budgets – has put content at the core of its 'Content 2020' advertising strategy mission:

> All advertisers need a lot more content so that they can keep the engagement with consumers fresh and relevant, because of the 24/7 connectivity. If you're going to be successful around the world, you have to have fat and fertile ideas at the core.

But for every Coca-Cola investing in content there is a small business capitalizing on it too. And this opportunity exists for your business right now. Why do this? Essentially because it is cost-effective: just 11 per cent of small businesses surveyed in the United States for BusinessBolts.com spend more than $500 per month on content marketing.

Search

One of the biggest reasons for digital marketers to embrace content comes down to Google. When you dominate the digital landscape as heavily as you do when you are Google – where you have entire industries basing their businesses around what you do – any change is going to be noticed. But the Google Panda (2011), Penguin (2012) and Hummingbird (2013) algorithm updates, of which there have been several tweaks and updates in the intervening years since, entwined search engine optimization (SEO) with content like never before. We will not go into too much detail about the updates here, as these are covered in Chapter 4. But, essentially, Google is looking to give value in search results for sites with better content. Google guidelines recommend that sites should: 'Create a useful, information-rich site, and write pages that clearly and accurately describe your content.'

This has led to the entire SEO industry embracing content in a way that they never did before. Most SEOs pre-Panda paid lip-service to content. They knew they needed it, but didn't value it. They paid for dirt-cheap, poor-quality content, often sourced by non-native writers; or, worse still, spun one article into 1,000 other versions that made no sense at all, but did the job for their link-building needs. This no longer works. Google identifies the quality of the content and has downgraded, or de-indexed, the really poor websites that host the spun content, essentially making redundant these ways of working for SEOs worldwide. Today, search teams value good content and are increasingly updating and revising their business models to become more content-focused.

'We don't have massive paid search budgets, and rely a lot on good SEO, and our content is what helps us rank,' says Graham Charlton, editor-in-chief of Econsultancy.com: 'Simply by smart use of anchor text, good internal linking and quality and shareable content we can rank very highly for some competitive terms.'

CASE STUDY   B&Q

Overview

The creative approach of generating unique, engaging content, combined with the 'hotspot' image creative, ensured that B&Q's campaign offered truly engaging content to consumers in a premium publisher environment.

The challenge

B&Q Autumn/Winter Decor – A/W Decor is a product-led brand campaign that focuses on getting people to do up their rooms, so everything from paint to sofas. The challenge was in getting people to engage with content and ads in the environment they are already in, without driving them to the B&Q site. The campaign brief was designed as a pure branding campaign, with sales performance a secondary consideration.

Target audience

Aimed at an ABC1+ demographic interested in home decor and lifestyle.

Action

The Adyoulike Native Story was recommended as the best Adyoulike product for meeting engagement KPIs. Adyoulike created bespoke editorial for both the 'Into the Country' living room and 'Prelude' bedroom A/W collection.

Alongside bespoke editorial, written by the Adyoulike content team, Adyoulike also created an image 'hotspot' for both areas. This involved taking a B&Q image asset and adding image links direct to check-out pages for particular B&Q

products. All of this was accessible via the Native Story, distributed into native content environments across publishers.

Delivered on a cost per thousand (CPM) the campaign created engagement, delivered in-depth information not possible with standard display and created measurable dwell time and social activity.

Results

The campaign performed well over its month-long run, as the figures below show:

- Headline impressions: 1,926,375.
- Average CTR to Native Story: 0.68 per cent.
- Total sponsored page visits: 21,510.
- Average dwell time on Native Story: 9 minutes 27 seconds.
- Social media shares: 40.
- Earned media Native Story visits: 8,371 (28.06 per cent earned media visits).
- Direct visits to the B&Q website from story (3.05 per cent CTR) CTR to B&Q site: 401.
- Number of direct sales generated: 132.

Campaign KPIs of engagement were met. This is evident by a high article-swell-time of 9 minutes 27 seconds, 40 social shares and 28 per cent of all Native Story visits coming from earned media visits.

These engagement rates for a brand campaign simply cannot be compared to other media where dwell times, engagements and depth of content cannot be achieved.

Three keys to success

1 Delivering interesting content titles and creative within a native environment was key to the success of this campaign.

2 The unique image 'hotspot' solution increased engagement rates, social shares and direct traffic sales to the B&Q website.

3 Campaign headlines distributed across premium publisher environments 'in-feed' to maximize visibility and engagement.

About the creator

Our special thanks to Dale Lovell and the team at Adyoulike.

Expert view

How to use content marketing to tap commercial opportunities in organic search

Contribution by Rob Welsby, director of search and insight at Further

> *'Content marketing probably won't help you acquire customers,' an article in the Guardian declared confidently in late 2015. 'It might raise brand awareness but content rarely appeals enough to turn consumers into customers.'*
>
> (See: http://www.theguardian.com/media-network/2015/oct/16/ content-marketing-brands-acquire-customers)

The piece highlighted research for the Customer Acquisition Barometer (CAB), a trend survey of 1,072 people, which found that only 10 per cent were prepared to give personal information to a *familiar* brand in exchange for some kind of content, and only 9 per cent would do the same for brands they did not know.

The conclusion?

Traditional marketing tools like coupons, competitions and freebies are much more reliable ways of acquiring customers than content marketing.

But content marketing is all about subtlety and influence. It is far more complex in its actions and interactions with consumers across multiple channels than a simple, binary and direct relationship that equals: 'I'll give you this (money, data) if you give me that (content).'

If you want an example of how content market can fuel commercial opportunities, look no further than organic search. Get content marketing right and search engines like Google and Bing will reward a brand with better keyword rankings and greater online visibility. That means more traffic clicking through to your site and more opportunity to convert those clicks into customers.

Why Google loves good content – and what good looks like

Google is notoriously secretive about its 200+ factor algorithm that determines the order of search results. The algorithm's purpose is simple enough: deliver the best possible answer to someone's search query. But what makes one answer better than another? The short answer: Google's assessment of a website's content.

Part of the assessment is technical. What content can the Googlebot crawl and index? What can it find on a site? Following technical best practice for search engine optimization is vital. But the other element of the assessment is qualitative. What does this content mean? How might it be relevant to the original search query? In Google's first decade of operation, that meant keyword matching: marrying the characters typed into a search bar with characters on a webpage. In Google's second decade, we have seen the advent of semantic search – the attempt to go beyond character matching and towards interpretation of what a string of words mean in a sentence. Indeed, in what context has that string of characters been used? The Googlebot is learning to read – and it is looking for quality.

However, type the query 'what makes a high-quality web page' into Google and you will get a bewildering 400 million results. There are top tips, research papers and plenty of opinions – some more qualified than others. Helpfully, in November 2015 Google published the 160-page guide that it gives to its team of search quality evaluators. These 'human raters', as they are more commonly known, are asked to score the quality of different websites. Their conclusions do not directly affect search results, but they give Google an indication of how well its algorithm is satisfying human needs in delivering the highest-quality search results. The human raters' conclusions feed into the Googlebot's machine-learning about what weight to give the different factors in the algorithm – helping to determine the defining characteristics of high-quality search results. So what are the human raters looking for?

Again, there are multiple factors to consider. But digital content marketers need to think of the top four at least:

1 The quality, clarity and quantity of main content (MC): content that tells the visitor what the page is about and relates to its primary purpose.

2 The quality of supplementary content (SC): content that complements the main content by adding an extra layer of supporting information. This helps to build a positive user experience of the page and site.

3 The level of expertise, authoritativeness and trustworthiness (EAT) of the page and the website: will the user believe the page/site as a credible source of information?

4 The reputation of the website: evidence of awards, citations and references from credible sources that support the third factor and demonstrate this is an authoritative and trustworthy site.

Together, those four factors give a clear indication of what Google will reward with high rankings in search results: clear, easy-to-use, authoritative, trustworthy web pages with deep, interesting and useful information. In effect, Google is looking for good on-site content marketing.

From keywords to transactions: defining commercial opportunities in two steps

Consumers don't just use one query when they are interested in a given topic. They are driven by multiple motives – and those motives change the format of the query. Sometimes they are looking for information: the 'how', 'what' and 'when' factual questions about the topic. Sometimes they are looking for comparisons, so their queries are around 'best *x, y, z*' or 'reviews of'. Sometimes they are just looking to transact, so they are searching for a specific product name or use phrases like 'cheap *x, y, z…*' or '*x, y, z* deals…' For example, on any given day the global searches around iPhone6 will vary from 'when was the iPhone6 launched?' to 'iPhone6 reviews 2016' to 'iPhone6 deals' and variants of all three. So which query would a smartphone vendor want to rank highly for in search results? Primarily transactional queries as they are directly related to the bottom line of the business. Second, the comparative queries that suggest someone is at the research phase of the sales funnel.

But what of the informational queries? While not as directly sales-related as the other two types of query, here are people interested in the topic and looking for something. We don't know yet if they might want to buy. But surely it is worth getting them to our website to find out what their next step might be – and nudge them to take that one step closer to the online cart? As soon as they have clicked to the site, the first seed of brand awareness has been sown at the start of the user purchase journey. In other words, there is good reason to think broadly about what people are searching for online and how that might be relevant to your brand.

But your website isn't Wikipedia. You haven't gone into business to offer an encyclopaedic answer to every possible search query. You want to focus: 1) where there is a close transactional intent; and 2) where there is a significant number of people searching around that topic each month – in the expectation that some, at least, will be interested enough in what you tell them that they buy either now or in the future.

Step 1

The first step is to take the range of keywords relevant to your business and categorize them. What is the topic? What is the search volume? Google's AdWords Keyword Planner will give you data. Think about the intent behind the search – is it informational, comparative or transactional? Is this keyword of growing, declining or stable interest? Google Trends will help you here. Are there seasonal or predictable market variations relating to this topic? Use your own market knowledge. The recommended outcome is to build a spreadsheet that organizes your keywords as topic categories and by volume.

Step 2

Now you need to look where you currently rank for the highest volume terms in each relevant category. Assuming that the top three search results will get over 50 per cent of the available clicks from users, how far off are you from the top of page one?

Now look at who ranks ahead of you for those high-volume queries. If the answer is Wikipedia and a host of news media sites, the odds are stacked against your brand reaching the top of page one. Think about the human raters' guide: are you a more authoritative news source on a general topic than CNN or the BBC? Best move on to the next set of categorized topics on your list.

The result of these first two steps is an understanding of the topics you should target because they are: 1) relevant to you; 2) have strong search volume; and 3) you have a realistic chance of improving your search rankings.

The data you have gathered through this process will tell you where you can reasonably expect to rank for different terms – and the incremental traffic to your site that you are likely to generate by ranking more highly. What you need to do now is think about what content you need on your site in order to move your rankings.

Content gap analysis

You've got the topics, you've understood the type of queries that are driving volume of search traffic. You've read and digested all 160 pages of Google's Search Quality Evaluator Guidelines and know what best-practice

▶

principles are being applied to content quality in relation to organic search. Now you need to do one other thing. You need to assess the competition. You need to look at the quality of your competitors' content when it comes to the topic categories you have decided to target. What ground have they covered – and how well have they covered it? Have they left a gap in information and expertise that you can fill? Can you do a better job of answering a search query with your content than them? Be systematic – and be honest with yourself. Oh, and check out what their content looks like on a smartphone and tablet, not just your desktop machine; Google is rewarding sites that are mobile-friendly.

Most likely what you will find is that some of your on-site content needs a modest tweak, some needs to be updated and upgraded considerably, some will need to be created from scratch. But now you will be able to prioritize on-site content work by what the data is telling you about the extent of the commercial opportunity to drive incremental traffic.

Defying the conventional wisdom

So congratulations! With relatively little effort you have become that rarest of beast: a marketer who can draw a link between content creation and its potential commercial value. It may not be the binary equation 'content + consumer = cash' that the *Guardian* was talking about. But it is using content marketing as a data-informed tool to optimize performance of organic search as an acquisition channel.

What is your next move? Well, how do you apply what you have learned about search intent, search volume and the topical opportunity to paid search?...

Do

- Think about the intent behind searches – is someone looking for information, to make a comparison, or to transact?
- Use the Google AdWords Keyword Planner to understand the kind of search-traffic volume associated with different phrases.
- Use Google Trends to assess how search interest in a topic changes over time.
- Group and prioritize keywords by topics and search volume.
- Look at the 'content gap' that you could exploit for high-volume topics.

Don't

- Just repeat what is already out there – create better, more relevant content that is aligned to what people are searching for.
- Forget to look at who ranks for the highest relevant search terms – in order to assess what are your realistic chances of reaching the top of page one.
- Try to do everything – prioritize on where you have the best chances of increasing search traffic.
- Overlook trying to incrementally improve what is already there as well as creating content from scratch.
- Forget to monitor your results by tracking performance in Google Analytics.

Social

Social media has also played a key part in the growth of content marketing. Social media sites such as Facebook, Twitter, LinkedIn, Pinterest and Instagram, as well as Google+ and YouTube, are where the majority of on-line users spend their time. This is typically the first place they go to online – and the last place they check out of before bed. Invariably on these sites it is content that they are consuming: shared links to videos and editorial by their friends and contacts. Many people like to follow their favourite brands online too. All brands, big and small, know they need to engage with their customers via social media. But how do you engage with your customers without content?

The answer is you can't. There are only so many times you can send customers to your website home page or tweet another discount code. That's not engagement, that's old-style marketing. And it doesn't work with social media. In order to succeed with social media, brands have to have something worthwhile to offer. Interruptions to the user experience are seldom rewarded. At best they are ignored and are therefore irrelevant; at worst they can really damage your brand... enter content and a coherent content strategy.

'Good content is social currency, without it a brand has nothing to share,' says Omar Kattan, chief strategy office for Dubai-based content marketing agency Sandstorm Digital. 'Effective content in a social setting is content that is based around the brand's story. It must also fulfil the brand's overarching business objectives and help drive customers down the leads funnel to induce a purchase, sign-up or enquiry. Successful brands manage to place their customers at the heart of this story so that they are able to relate it to their lives and will therefore be in a better position to buy.'

What skills do you need to be a good content marketer?

Digital marketers are asked to do a lot. Not only are digital marketers expected to be up-to-date with everything new that comes along in digital, they are then expected to be able to plan and manage a myriad different number of campaigns to accompany these new innovations too. And increasingly they need to be able to come up with content. It's a tough ask. As with all marketers, in order to be a good content marketer you need to have a combination of great organizational skills, meticulous attention to detail, creativity and analytical acumen.

Essentially you need to be creative enough to develop great ideas, have the wherewithal to be able to create that content, and then you also need to be able to carry out analysis on what works, dive into the stats and use technology to analyse results. Content marketers in many respects need to be left-brain obsessives who love to live and breathe data and, on the other side, creative right-brainers with a journalist's nose for an interesting story.

Content strategy

Why do I need a content strategy?

Content strategy is the planning and development of how you intend to attract and engage with your chosen audience via content. It is vitally important for any success when it comes to your content marketing. Plan first, create content later.

If you don't put a proper content strategy in place, the likelihood is that your content initiatives will fizzle out. It is hard to evangelize to others within an organization – and create buy-in – without a conceptualized content strategy in place. There is a lot to think about at this stage of your content development.

It is easy to be overwhelmed when tasked with creating a coherent content strategy for your business. For success it is important that you break everything down to basics. Start at the beginning and think about what you want to say, who you want to speak to and what you want to achieve from the outcome. Think like a publisher, but back up your thoughts with real digital-marketing data. Create a strategy that focuses on customer and business needs.

Remember that content marketing is one of the few marketing channels that can work along the entire customer journey – so you need a strategy that speaks to your customers at all points along this cycle. This is where data analysis comes in. This is where a content marketer's ability to digest data and look at trends combines with creativity to formulate an overall content strategy. Before creating your content strategy you need to look at all the data. Look at your site's analytics. What pages convert best into sales? What, if any, existing content is shared and visited? Look at your social media pages and do the same. If you can, create a social listening report, analysing what your target audience likes to talk about online. Look at Google trends to research what people are searching for online. Look at what your competitors are doing or have done for success. Then, most of all, think about what your business objectives might be.

When planning your content strategy you should ask yourself these questions:

- Who do I want to target?
- Is there a specific topic or niche where we want to excel?
- What do I want those I target to associate with our brand?
- What information are my customers looking for?
- What type of content do my customers look for?
- How can I keep existing customers happy?
- How can I attract new customers?
- What do we like/dislike about competitors' content strategy?
- Is there anything I do not want to highlight about our brand?
- What overall business objective do I want to achieve from my content marketing?

Write a content strategy document

Once you have your content strategy firmly identified it is important that you create a content strategy document. This doesn't need to be a mammoth

90-page blueprint; in fact it should be no more than one or two sides of A4 paper. If you can condense your content strategy to this core, it will have more chance of success and more people within your organization will understand it.

This content strategy document is a simple, but extremely effective content mandate that outlines what, why and how you will go about creating content. Include what KPIs you may want to achieve from your content strategy. But you do not need to overcomplicate this document with details around tone of voice, style guides, and dos and don'ts. These are details that can be covered in additional documents.

At this stage it is probably worth noting that this document should be fluid. Your content strategy will undoubtedly change over time. Reviewing your strategy and updating your content strategy document will help ensure that you consistently deliver the content that your customer base is looking for and the results you want to achieve. The first piece of content you create as part of your content marketing initiative should be your content strategy document.

Where does content strategy fit into your marketing: who owns it?

It is important to understand where content fits within your organization. This is a crucial question within large organizations with different departments. Ownership of the content process is key. In the past, content often sat somewhere uncomfortably between web development, SEO, social and PR teams. It was the neglected and ignored ugly duckling that no one wanted to think about. Those tasked with ownership of the content process failed to fully understand it, or grasp its overall importance.

This has now finally changed, but there are many misconceptions about who 'owns' the content process. Is content strategy the responsibility of your SEO team? Or perhaps your social media team? Or maybe your PR or corporate communications team? All of these marketing departments should have input into the process. But your content strategy should come from the top. It needs to holistically cover all of your marketing channels. Your content strategy is not an advertising campaign, a search, social or PR strategy. It is more than that. Given the importance that content plays within all of your marketing channels, content strategy is increasingly becoming the preserve of dedicated content marketers who fully understand the content production process and how content can be used for overall digital marketing success.

The significance of content to your digital marketing strategy means that you cannot shoehorn content into a specific channel, with an 'and we'll do a bit of content on the side' kind of approach, and hope for any sort of overall success. If you do this you are not 'thinking like a publisher' and giving your customers what they want – you are simply feeding the search and social media beast. And if you work like that you will not create anything original that adds value to a customer buying cycle.

Let's review the various channels in more detail:

- *Search strategy*: content is now at the heart of any search engine optimization strategy. Search engines love unique, quality content that enhances the user experience. Keywords, link building and content gap analysis are important elements of search and are welcome add-ons to your content strategy; but your content strategy should be far more than just a list of keywords, meta-data rewrites, link-building initiatives and landing pages.

- *Social strategy*: content is the lifeblood of any brand's social platform. Whether a business to business (B2B) approach on LinkedIn and Google+, a consumer angle on Facebook and Twitter, or something that incorporates all social platforms, content is what drives brand engagement. But the content needs to appeal to the right people, as well as the right platform. Social strategy will inevitably feed into your overall content strategy, but it should not rule it. You need a content strategy in place in order to succeed with social media; but you don't necessarily need a social media strategy to succeed with content marketing. Your content marketing strategy should come first, followed by a social strategy that makes it easy for your audience to share the content you are creating.

- *PR strategy*: content marketing is not PR in 'new clothes', likewise content strategy is not identical to your PR strategy. They should share fundamental similarities, such as brand message and voice, but they differ somewhat, often, with their target audience. For example, some PR and corporate communications strategies are targeted towards journalists and government, rather than the consumers they may want to target with content. Relying on your PR strategy to become your content strategy is not always feasible or advisable.

What content should I be creating?

There are many different types of content that you can create. The content you create will depend largely on your brand, your target audience, resources and your budget. But as mentioned earlier in this chapter – content can work whether you are a mega-brand such as Coca-Cola, or a one-person business entity.

Types of content

Irrespective of your budget, create content that your customers will like and then amplify the reach of that content.

Here is a quick overview of the type of content you may want to think about creating:

- *News and blog content*: this form of content is easy to create and should represent a first tick on your list of content marketing to-dos. It is relatively quick and easy content for almost any brand to create and host on their own website. Covering news that is specific to your industry, or writing tip-style consumer-facing blog posts, preferably published each day, works for a number of reasons. First, you are ensuring your site looks up-to-date: your customers don't want to click on your blog and see that the last post was made eight months ago. Second, search engines like regularly updated, content-rich websites; it signals to them that the site is being looked after and is of relevance to potential searchers. Third, publishing short-form content on your own blog on a regular basis gives you something to promote – and engage – with your customers on social media channels. Just as newspapers and magazines may also carry in-depth features and interviews, they also carry lots of news in brief (NIB) that they know their readers find of interest.

- *Features, guides and interviews*: longer-form content published to your company blog works in the exact same way as the above shorter-form blog content. You do not need to publish this content on a daily basis, and what you create may be as a result of customer service issues that you would like to address, keyword ranking reports, or a change in focus of your overall business strategy. Interviews with key members of a company, for example, can work well to highlight business strengths and 'tell the story' behind a company. In addition to publishing this content on your own company blog, one of the benefits of longer-form content is that, when it is really good, it can be used for outreach and amplification purposes too, more of which we come to later in this chapter.

- *White papers*: either working internally on your own private data and analysis or via specialist data and research companies, a great way to create content that your customers may want is to create a white paper. A white paper that identifies major issues within your business sector – and offers your overall company opinion on how to solve it – not only positions your brand as a thought leader that knows its stuff, it can also be used to generate business leads too. How? Create the white paper as a downloadable PDF and then ensure that anyone who wants to download it has to fill out their contact details. This gives you a new database of contacts that are pre-vetted to be interested in your product or services (because they downloaded a very specific white paper), which you can call upon to build up your business.

- *e-books*: in a similar way to the white paper above, extending that idea and creating a relevant e-book that is of relevance to your customer base can work extremely well too. Again, this will establish your brand as a thought leader and it can be an even more successful way to generate new business leads too. And, thanks to digital publishing advances and the growing popularity of e-readers, creating and publishing an e-book is an extremely easy way to go about distributing content. It is an increasingly popular content-marketing tactic.

- *Infographics*: a graphical representation of data, infographics are useful at illustrating reams of data that can often be confusing to write down in detail. They are used extensively online by digital marketers. Why? They are highly shareable, that's why. Whether a B2B business illustration or a more tongue-in-cheek-style infographic such as 'The Cost of Being Batman' (MoneySuperMarket.com), the premise is the same: infographics gain a lot of social shares, drive traffic and generate inbound links.

- *Video*: video content is increasingly important for digital marketing success. Big consumer-facing brands often opt for humour – Compare the Market/Meerkat, or extreme events such as Red Bull – with the aim of creating a viral hit, as video content works for all brands. Company overview-style videos offer a great introduction to your company for potential customers; Q&As on common customer queries or industry issues, delivered in a concise manner do not only aid the customer cycle – giving customers what they want – they can also be used to promote your brand digitally too.

- *Photographs*: with the increasing popularity of platforms such as Instagram and Pinterest, more digital marketers are turning their attention to the creation of photographic content. This could be publishing photos of a latest product line; photographs of customers using their products; or something a little bit different.

Go online to www.koganpage.com/understanding-digital-marketing to read an article by Jeff Ortegon, creative director at Undertone, for a guide on designing impactful and effective content ads.

How much content should you create?

There is no set rule on how much content to create. This will differ depending on your objectives, industry and available resource. But as a general rule, the more content you create, the better – provided that it is good. Provided that it is planned and based on an overall content strategy. If your resources are tight, putting some available budget into content is better than doing nothing at all. Test what works, optimize – and plan.

Content production

How to brainstorm ideas

As illustrated in this chapter, content marketing relies heavily on ideas. Digital technology now means that we have at our disposal distribution tools that marketers a generation before could only have dreamed of. There are few barriers to distributing your content – provided you plan effectively. Today, invariably the success or failure of a digital marketing campaign comes down to the idea behind it. So you need to come up with ideas – and lots of them.

Many marketers fear making mistakes – or are too scared to share their ideas in case they are ridiculed by colleagues. But if you don't share your ideas, who else is going to? How else are you going to hit upon success? Coming up with ideas consistently can be tough. This is where brainstorming comes in.

> 'No idea is so outlandish that it should not be considered with a searching but at the same time steady eye.'
>
> Winston Churchill

We could go on about the various techniques that different groups and organizations use to generate ideas, but the best advice we can give is – just think about it. Clear your to-do list and give yourself some time to really think about what your customers want and what your business objectives are. Look at all the data and insights at your disposal and then don't be afraid to roll up your sleeves, shout out ideas and see what comes from it all. Remember, there are no bad ideas, just less relevant ones!

Creating a content calendar

After you have written your content strategy overview document, after deciding on what type of content is right for your business and after brainstorming ideas, it is a good idea to plan out your content schedule via a content calendar. An organized calendar will save you time by having a structured time frame to stick to, which eliminates time-wasting activities.

Here are a few tips on creating a content calendar:

- *Seasonality*: think about the key seasons and trends in your business and what content you want to create in the run-up to and during these times of year.
- *Topics*: for each month, pick strong themes that can break down into subcategories. Think about events that you could write about that take place in any given month.
- *Timing*: break down your calendar month by month, then week by week, then day by day. This will increase the structure and regularity to your work.
- *Share*: share your content calendar with your team of content creators, both internal and external, as well as all of your other marketing channels. If you can give your SEO, social, PR and display teams insights into what content you are going to be creating in the future you will have a better chance of achieving a more integrated digital marketing strategy.

Objections to content

'We can't create content ourselves.'
Answer: outsource content production.

The demands on digital marketers are increasing all the time. Analysis of big data, new marketing channels to manage and the 24/7 nature of online mean that few marketers have time to actually create the content that their brand needs for digital success. And, in most cases, they are often not skilled enough to create the specialist content that their brand deserves.

The likelihood, then, is that you have to outsource some or perhaps all of your content production. This could save you time and money. You have a few options here when it comes to outsourcing content:

- *Freelancers*: you can go through the laborious process of recruiting a freelancer to work on your content. Many organizations operate in this way. The bonus is that you can build up a relationship with a dedicated content creator who ideally comes to understand your content objectives. The downside, however, is that individual freelancers typically have more than one client, which means constantly changing deadlines and periods when they are unavailable (not to mention they do occasionally go on holiday and get ill too). Also, when it comes to scaling-up your content needs, few individual freelancers can cope with volume content requirements on a regular basis. Managing their deadlines, proofing their work and providing feedback all come down to you. The process can work well, but provided you invest the time to recruit and nurture the right person.

- *Cloud-based content platforms*: there are a growing number of collaborative platforms that service the content requirement needs of brands and their agencies. These platforms are effectively online marketplaces that connect those who need content, with those who can create it. They recruit content creators and take a small percentage of your content fee. They are relatively simple to use and can help you to scale your content production easily. But note that in many instances the content creators on specific platforms are of differing levels of quality. Again, your strategy and managing and proofing the content sent to you are your own responsibility.

- *Recruit a content agency*: as we have set out throughout this chapter, content marketing is increasingly becoming a separate function to your other digital marketing channels. Specialist content agencies are springing up to aid brands in their content marketing needs. The benefits of recruiting a specialist content agency is that you can use their expertise and services to develop your own content strategy, to create a content calendar for your business and to ensure that you are receiving quality content to deadline. You also have someone to brainstorm ideas with to ensure your content is good, and someone to help you champion the cause for content within your organization. The negative side is that some, if not most, of these content-marketing agencies work on a retainer model, which can significantly add to your overall digital marketing costs.

Whatever option you take will have the same immediate issues when it comes to outsourcing content. Before outsourcing your content production there are a few things to think about in order to make the process easier for everyone involved. The most important stage of outsourcing your content creation is the initial briefing process. To really get the benefit from outsourcing you need to be able to communicate what you want to achieve. Again, this illustrates just how important the initial content strategy document can be. It can feel a little bit slow to start off with, but once you are armed with this document you can share it with your content providers and really hit the ground running with the type of content you want to see.

'There are too many compliance issues and sign-off processes for our business to create content.'
Answer: put a plan in place that makes content possible.

One of the objections that come up time and time again when you talk content to certain brands is compliance. For many heavily regulated industries such as financial services and the health sectors there are a myriad different compliance processes that need to be adhered to. This can make content creation a challenge, but it is not impossible. In many of these industries you will find people who use the compliance process as the excuse they need to avoid creating content. Don't let them win. The case for relevant content within these sectors is, if anything, stronger than for other sectors; consumers are looking for valuable content that they know they can trust.

In order to create this relevant content it is important to ensure that all legal regulatory compliance issues surrounding the content you create is met. Create a dos and don'ts list of what content you should and shouldn't create.

Work with your compliance departments to ensure that a workable process is established and a sustainable relationship put in place between content producer, marketers, brand head of digital and compliance teams, while also working towards established KPIs. Given the importance – and the continued importance – that content is likely to play in future digital marketing campaigns, it is best to embrace content now rather than rush to it at a later date.

'There is nowhere on our website to publish content and we have no development resource.'
Answer: setting up a blog on your own website is easy.

This is a common objection raised by those looking into content for the first time. It is, understandably, often a more pressing concern among smaller businesses, where their developer resource is limited. The truth of the matter is that publishing content onto your own website is very easy to set up. Services such as Wordpress allow you to set up a blog on your own site easily – and for free. There is some resource required in making your blog look and feel like part of your overall website, but this should not take up too much of your team's time to get done. Alternatively, there are thousands of specialist Wordpress theme designers who can do the work for you for a one-off fee: it should not cost more than US $400. Once set up, you are good to begin publishing content at will.

There are also plenty of other ways to get set up, too. Many content services can provide XML feeds directly into your site, for example, which only require a minimal amount of technical input. Again, given the value that content brings to your digital marketing, the amount of investment and time it takes to set up your site to publish content is certainly worth the effort.

Promoting your content

Creating content is just one part of the content marketing process. Once you have created that content, you've got to market it. As already mentioned, content is the currency with which brands engage with their customers online. A natural distribution channel for any content that you create should be social media. We also recommend that all of the content you create is as shareable as possible (social-sharing buttons on your own website content pages, for example) and, when relevant, is published under Google+ Authorship too. But again, much of this will be covered in the 'Search' chapter of this book (see Chapter 4).

These are great strategies to amplify the reach of the content you are creating. But in addition to these practices, let's look in a little more detail about some other ways you can go about promoting your content.

Blogger outreach

Bloggers are a key conduit to speaking to your customer base online. Blogger outreach is an incredibly effective way to raise your brand profile, increase your brand reputation and share the unique content that you are creating and publishing. Bloggers tend to have a disproportionate level of influence among their specific online communities; they have highly relevant and large social media followings and work well to promote highly relevant content within their communities. There are, of course, particular ways in which you should go about conducting blogger outreach, much of which will already be covered within this book in the chapters on online PR and reputation management (Chapter 11) and the search pages (Chapter 4).

Essentially you are looking to build a relationship with bloggers through content. This may mean encouraging them to promote your own branded content that you have created and that is specific to their particular niche. For example, car brand Fiat, looking to promote the Fiat 500, created a humorous 'Motherhood Rap' video (available at: http://www.youtube.com/watch?v=eNVde5HPhYo). The video spoke to mums and was an instant hit with the mummy blogging community when promoted via blogger outreach. The mummy bloggers loved the video, shared the content socially and embedded the video into articles they were writing. The result was a huge viral success; the latest YouTube count reveals 4.2 million views and over 19,000 likes. The video was promoted and shared throughout the mummy blogging community and gained additional coverage on automotive, trade and national news titles. Blogger outreach was the channel used to distribute and share the content, but again it was the content itself that was key to the campaign's overall success.

Bloggers are very particular, so wherever possible you should look to involve them in the creative process. It is an increasingly common tactic for bloggers to be involved in the content-creation process as well as the distribution of that content. This can be as basic as working with them on a specific blog post that is of interest to their readership, asking them to film themselves reviewing a product, or perhaps hosting a content-led competition on their website. Remember that bloggers are publishers; they know what content works best for their communities, and if as a brand you can work with them to create content that works for that community then they are only too happy to get involved.

Native advertising

One of the biggest digital marketing trends of recent years, native advertising is a new, exciting online advertising medium that has content at its core. Even if you are unfamiliar with the term, you almost certainly would have interacted with a native ad. Facebook-sponsored posts, Twitter-promoted tweets, BuzzFeed-branded articles, publisher-sponsored posts and content recommendation units: these are all forms of native advertising.

You cannot talk native without talking about content. Native advertising is transforming the digital marketing landscape. Given the proliferation of content marketing, it is natural that new content-based advertising models have developed. The figures around native advertising growth are astounding.

Data released by Adyoulike in December 2015, Europe's leading native advertising platform and network, showed how the value of native advertising worldwide is expected to almost double from US $30.9 billion in 2015 to $59.35 billion in 2018 (published on their blog in January 2016: https://blog.adyoulike.com/uk-native-advertising-revenue-increases-300-in-2015).

Expert view

Contribution by Clare O'Brien, senior industry programmes manager at IAB UK, 2016

Digital media is fundamentally an access, not distribution, medium, and so audiences will naturally only engage with content that resonates because it is relevant, useful or meaningful. For instance, it may need to be entertaining (a diverting short-form documentary video, perhaps) or purely utilitarian (a recipe, maybe) to capture the attention of individuals who are tuned in to doing something specific at any given time.

To claim the attention of their audiences advertisers need to produce the kind of content people want – *where and when* they want it. Audiences are fragmented across dozens of media platforms (themselves often sharing content and audiences) and getting the right content to the right audience at the right time is the function of programmatic advertising. Study after study demonstrates that CTRs are substantially improved with this form of content-based digital advertising over traditional banner campaigns – some claiming upwards of 30 per cent higher CTRs. In most respects, the development of native and content-based advertising marks one of the most important evolutionary steps in digital advertising.

Quoting from AdYouLike's blog post:

The data was the first time that native advertising growth has been charted globally. In North America, the native advertising market is expected to soar from $11.49 billion in 2015 to $22.56 billion in 2018, while Western Europe is expected to see growth over the same period from $7.09 billion to $13.91 billion. Other markets like Asia-Pacific and Latin America are set to see equally impressive expansion.

(Posted December 2015: https://blog.adyoulike.com/native-advertising-set-to-double-by-2018)

Figure 8.1

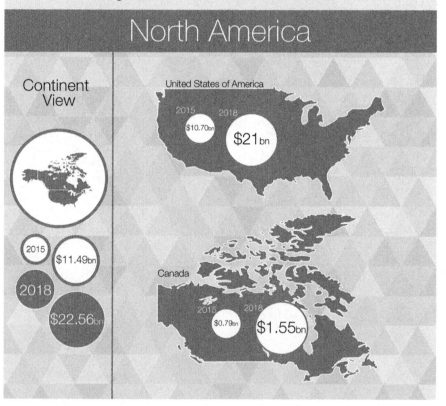

'Native Advertising is eating the World'

Adyoulike
Native Advertising™

Native Advertising spending by regions and countries 2015-2018

Native Advertising spend is expected to double in the next three years, rising from $30.9 billion in 2015 to $59.35 billion in 2018.

North America

Continent View

2015
$11.49bn

2018
$22.56bn

United States of America

2015
$10.70bn
2018
$21bn

Canada

2015
$0.79bn
2018
$1.55bn

Figure continues overleaf

Figure 8.1 *continued*

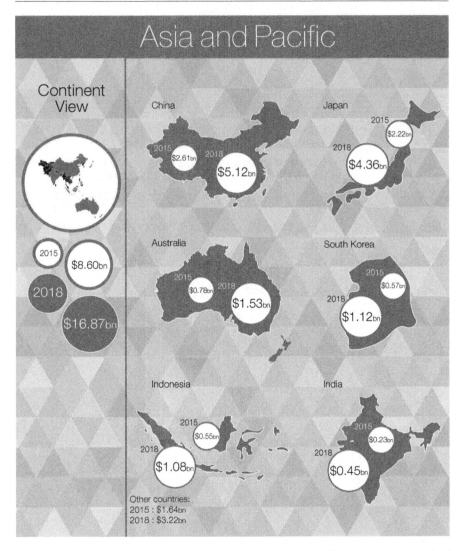

Figure continues overleaf

Figure 8.1 *continued*

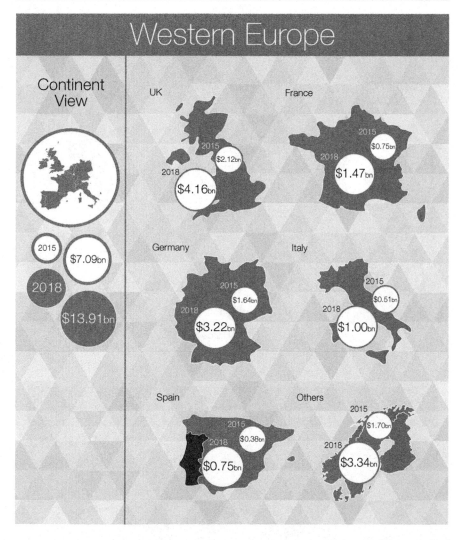

Figure continues overleaf

Figure 8.1 *continued*

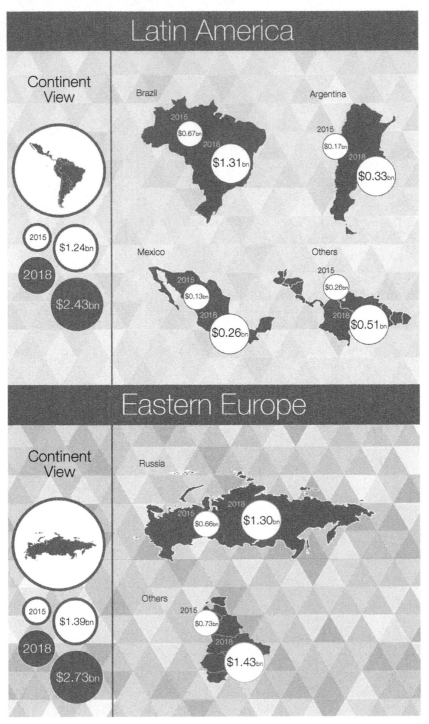

Figure continues overleaf

Figure 8.1 *continued*

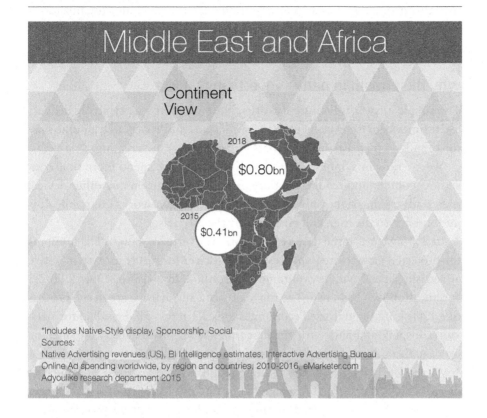

What native means is that the right-branded content, distributed to the right audience, can now offer rewards to advertisers that far outweigh anything they can hope to achieve with more traditional forms of advertising alone. This is native advertising, and why it is so exciting.

What is native advertising?

Native adverts are contextually relevant posts that combine paid, owned and earned media into a clearly labelled branded message that is user-initiated. Native placements sit seamlessly into the overall design of the host site so that they look like part of the site, rather than any external element to it.

Native advertising offers brands the opportunity to speak to, interact and engage with customers at the places where they congregate online – all in a native environment; the content is what drives the interaction between consumer and brand. Crucially, given the growth in mobile, native advertising works across desktop, tablet or mobile device.

Native campaigns are clearly labelled as 'sponsored', 'promoted' or simply 'advertising'. This is a legal requirement, of course, and organizations such as the IAB, in the United States and Europe, are working with regulators on more concrete guidelines for running native ads.

Why the growth in native advertising?

The simple answer is because it works. Native advertising typically delivers 5–20 times better engagement than banner ads and it acts as a unique way for brands to increase the reach of the content they are creating.

We are now in a 'mobile-first' digital age when we spend more time consuming content and reading on our smartphones than on any other device; native advertising is the only advertising medium that works on mobile. It is unobtrusive to the user, and effective for the advertiser.

In 2016 we are at the dawn of the native advertising boom. The numbers for projected growth are impressive. A key driver for future growth in native advertising spend will be programmatic trading. In 2015 the OpenRTB 2.3 specification was launched. The move now means that we are in the process of establishing standardized economies of scale across all digital ad formats: video, display and native for the first time. What this means is the opening up of native advertising to large swathes of new ad revenue.

As the US IAB's Real-Time Bidding (RTB) Project clarified at launch in 2015: 'This is one of the most significant updates to OpenRTB as it allows for native ads to be targeted, optimized, and transacted on programmatically, reducing workload on publishers and advertisers alike' (http://www. iabuk.net/blog/programmatic-native-advertising-what-openrtb-23-means-for-digital).

Just some of the companies offering native campaigns globally – in different guises – include Outbrain, Taboola, Nativo and Adyoulike; while publishing groups such as BuzzFeed, AOL, Atlantic Media and more also have native offerings. Many more publishers and dynamic ad-tech companies are likely to be working native in the future.

Native advertising is here to stay.

The future of online content

In a November 2013 interview with *Adweek*, WPP CEO Sir Martin Sorrell explained how digital now accounts for 35 per cent of all WPP business worldwide. When asked about what he would do if he was starting a new business today, he said:

> You'd be more focused on media investment and data investment management and digital. The company would be much more balanced. In other words, it wouldn't be classic advertising-agency led. It would be much more neutral. You would be much more respectful of people in the media business. You'd be dabbling in content. Same approach in a way as now, but different focus.

While all of what he said is interesting, the fact that Sorrell specifically mentions content is significant. The head of the largest advertising group in the world believes that content is the future. As we have outlined throughout this chapter, we believe it is too. Content overlaps, aids and is part of everything you do in digital marketing. It is increasingly what your digital marketing strategy and launch campaigns will rely on for success.

If the first 15 or so years of digital were defined by technology, uptake and the creation of new marketing channels, the next 15 years may well be characterized by what we do with all of this technological stuff. How do digital marketers utilize all the tools at their disposal in order to win new audience and reach out to their customers?

Increasingly, digital technology will be used to do what humans have always enjoyed: tell and share stories. Some of these stories will be shared and created by brand marketers. There will be more technological advances in the years ahead, but these will increasingly be focused on content – and what it can do for the content that brands are creating and looking to share.

Keeping an eye on various content trends can be time-consuming, so we asked Brad Nickel, content marketing manager at Adbeat, to give us his expertise. After analysing hundreds of pieces of content across various networks, he has pinpointed nine specific content themes that just plain work. These are themes that some of the biggest publishers, brands and advertisers use to drive millions of dollars' worth of traffic to their content, boost their audience and increase their bottom line.

The best part – many of these themes are 100 per cent evergreen. This means you can leverage them in articles for weeks, months or maybe even years at a time to bring in new readers.

Expert view

Nine evergreen content themes that work for native advertising
Contribution by Brad Nickel, content marketing manager, Adbeat

1. Information content themes: education

Informational content aims to educate the reader about a new or unheard of concept relative to their lives. This could be an article about 'the future of innovation in technology, business and city infrastructure', for example. These longer, more dense, paid editorial articles are an amazing way for big brands to build awareness and get new ideas and internal developments out in public.

Another great example is a recent article about 'the potential dangers of artificial sweeteners'. This article touches on a topic that does not permeate the news or current culture. You might still achieve decent results with a similar article titled 'Is Sugar Safe?', but most people already know that sugar is considered to be unhealthy. However, most people do not know that a 'harmless' diet cola might not be so harmless after all. This is a piece of information that pretty much anyone who drinks diet cola or dumps packets of sweeteners in their coffee would be interested in.

The type of content that challenges common ideas is the type of content that gets attention. Another excellent example is the 'tool' from Prudential Insurance that shows people how much it will cost to live in their dream retirement location.

Interactive content, or information presented in a visual format (like an infographic), is an amazing way not just to get people clicking on your paid content, but get people *sharing* your paid content.

Now, all of this begs the question: how do you find the right topic for this type of content? Well, a lot of it comes down to just doing basic research:

- Keyword research will help you to discover the organic searches leading readers to your site.

- Read recent news stories and blog posts about a specific concept related to your product or service. BuzzSumo (buzzsumo.com) offers a great tool for uncovering this info.

- Use topics in popular culture to ideate your content.

Additional tools you can use to discover conversations taking place online include Google Trends, Trends by Twitter and Google Correlate.

2. Pleasure to your eyes: interesting visual media

There is nothing like a few funny cat pictures to brighten your day. People love visual media and they especially love visual media that makes them laugh.

You can promote funny content even if your business is 'serious'. Providing value can be as simple as giving readers a way to escape the pressures of everyday life. Light, fun articles and slideshows are a great way to do this.

There is a reason why more and more viral sites such as Buzzfeed continue to see success: people *love* it and (contrary to popular belief) get *value* out of it.

Examples could include a slideshow of beautiful pictures, or funny work cartoons that bring a bit of humour to the daily grind. This stuff works not because it is mindless fluff. It works because we like people who make us smile and bring pleasure to our day... and we will often trust and give money to these people, too!

3. Simple and effective: how to/tips and tricks

According to Google, more than 100 million hours of how-to content have been watched in the United States so far this year (as of 5 April 2016). Therefore, some of the most effective pieces of sponsored content give step-by-step instructions or tips and tricks. People want to know they can improve their lives!

How-to articles might be the easiest pieces of content to crank out. You just put together an article based on something you already know. It doesn't need to be anything complex. For example, if you sell car parts, you can simply write an article or record a video on how to fix a flat tyre or remove nasty odours from your car. Simple, easy and effective.

4. Engage them: quizzes and surveys

- Which Spice Girl are you?
- Which Justin Bieber song describes your personality?
- What type of selfie are you?
- Which 'Game of Thrones' character are you?
- Which celebrity should you spend Valentine's Day with?

▶

Anyone on Facebook has probably seen friends sharing their quiz results in their news feed. Viral quiz sites have blown up over the past couple of years. But don't worry if personality- or celebrity-related quizzes are not relevant to your business.

Many advertisers are seeing amazing results with quizzes that provide real value beyond just entertainment. Surveys and quizzes are another great form of interactive content. People are less likely to bounce – that is, leave a website after the initial click-through – when you give them something to do. This makes each dollar you spend on native advertising that much more profitable.

5. The online review: product recommendations

Another trusty tool is the online review, which Moz revealed has a huge (67 per cent) influence over consumer decisions. Just like when a friend recommends a service, movie or new genre of music, these can be fairly effective at providing authentic information – even if from a stranger on the internet. (Note, however: not all online reviews are created equally.)

Many of the new FinTech companies like Wealthfront (investments based on computer algorithms) and FundRise (investment crowdfunding platform) use product reviews/recommendations from trusted third-party sources to promote their brand.

Analysis paralysis is a real problem. There are just too many product choices. Your target audience will appreciate a good recommendation. Go on and give it to them.

6. Go back in time: nostalgia

We've all been there. A bad day at work… a break-up with the love of our life… that project due tomorrow that we haven't even started yet (and it's 1 am).

During turbulent times in our professional or personal lives, we yearn to be teleported back to the days when life was simple. We think back to biking around the neighbourhood with our best friends, playing our favourite video games and having someone else to worry about our problems.

Those feelings of complete comfort and zero responsibility are intoxicating. That's why nostalgia is such a powerful emotion. It causes people to turn inward, and start to actually feel that comfort and happiness. You can tap into this amazing emotion by reminding people of their youth. Especially when it comes down to classic TV shows, our favourite childhood toys and the sports teams we grew up watching.

7. Money, money, money

Everyone has, at least, some stress about money. For some of us, it is on our minds *all the time*. According to a recent study, 62 per cent of Americans report losing sleep over money problems.

Not to mention that our society celebrates the rich and famous. We look at these people with shock ('They spent $50,000 on WHAT?') and awe ('Wow, I'd love to get paid $20 million to swing a golf club!').

So it is no wonder that articles about money and net worth are some of the most commonly seen pieces of sponsored content, from the world's highest-paid athletes on Forbes.com, to everyone's dream of kicking back on the beach and making millions by trading on the stock market.

Oh, money. It's a love/hate relationship. But people certainly love to click and read about it.

8. Make them wonder: curiosity and intrigue

A lot of curiosity-based content gets a bad rap because it's just clickbait.

Now, clickbait headlines have become somewhat of a joke inside marketing offices, but clickbait is a real issue. People are sick and tired of it, and Facebook started cracking down on clickbait articles, even changing their algorithm so this content would be shown less in the Newsfeed. However, if you're careful and actually include payoff you promise in the headline in the content of the article, you'll be golden.

Most curiosity content is based around strange or bizarre content that people are not used to seeing every day. People love that type of content because: 1) it's interesting; and 2) it gives them something to talk about!

It could be hybrid animal breeds you never knew existed (yes, these are real); or strange places, or an article on '15 real death-row requests that will send a chill down your spine'. Sometimes we forget that the world is a strange place. And strange equals interesting. Point out the all the weird stuff going on in our world and you'll soon find yourself with more eyeballs on your content. But remember: make sure to stay far, far away from posting anything that resembles clickbait.

▶

9. TV, film and radio personalities

It's funny – few people will admit to reading Hollywood news. Yet, the supermarket is filled to the brim with celebrity tabloids, there is no lack of shows like *Entertainment Tonight* or *Extra* and some of the most popular native articles are related to Hollywood celebrities. Psychologists believe there is a biological and hierarchical reason why people are so concerned with the personal lives of celebrities: http://www.livescience.com/18649-oscar-psychology-celebrity-worship.html.

Historically, humans lived in smaller groups. It was important to know what high-status people (think of them as 'stone age celebrities') in your group were doing. Why? Because their decisions probably impacted your life.

Now we're in the 21st century and knowing who Ashton Kutcher (someone considered high-status) is dating has zero impact on your life. Yet, our brains are still programmed to find it relevant.

The key (in this author's opinion) is to make the content as tasteful as possible. There are too many articles out there about celebrity weight-gain, 'you-won't-believe-what-she-wore-at-the-Oscars' and other negative celebrity gossip. Give people what they want without being degrading to others.

Don't think celebrities are relevant to your market? Your readers might not be interested in Kim Kardashian's fashion *faux pas*, but they might be interested in hearing what Gordon Ramsay's latest dish is if you run a recipe site. The key to avoiding any backlash from readers is to keep it clean, positive and tasteful.

Conclusion

It might seem like some of these themes won't apply to every business. Trust me that they do. Almost any business can use any of these nine themes in their content amplification strategy. Sometimes you will have to be a bit more creative. Sometimes you will have to think outside the box. Maybe you will contemplate using a theme you don't really feel comfortable with. But is it worth the risk? I'd say yes.

Our thanks to Sarah Gavin at Outbrain for her contribution, below: brands partnering with more traditional publishers to create custom experiences is becoming a greater part of the media ecosystem.

Expert view

Should you incorporate native partnerships into your brand publishing strategy?
Contribution by Sarah Gavin, Outbrain

Let's look at the pros and cons of incorporating native advertising partnerships into your brand publishing strategy:

Pros	Cons
It's a heck of a lot more effective than display ads when it comes to engagement.	Custom creative with a hand-picked media partner can be tough to scale. It's important to navigate this question with your media partners to find the opportunities to maximize effectiveness – from creating serialized programmes to deploying retargeting or recommended media platforms.
Publishers are true experts at engaging audiences with content. What they don't build for you themselves, you can learn how to do just by partnering with them.	
Done right, people will actually *remember* your native experience. Take Netflix's multimedia article on women inmates for the *New York Times*, for example (http://paidpost. nytimes.com/netflix/women-inmates-separate-but-not-equal. html).	If your media partner is the one hosting the content, they also get the benefit of collecting all the data. Not you.
	If you're partnered with an incongruent publisher or misguided creative execution *The Atlantic* can tell you all about it.
Once a user engages with your native ad experience, you can retarget them with relevant display ads that have a much better chance at effectiveness.	

Technology, content and creativity converge in native advertising

The really exciting thing about content and native advertising for any emerging marketer is the fact that – for the very first time in the history of digital marketing – technology, content and creativity are all at a converging point.

▶

> The technology that many predicted would kill creativity and commoditize marketing down to 'painting by numbers' and big data solutions has emerged as the engine room of future creativity in advertising. The convergence of technology, creativity and data now means that what can and cannot be done is largely only limited by our imaginations.
>
> Native advertising continues to push the creative boundaries. Brands continue to invest in original digital ideas; agencies are investing heavily in creative solutions to facilitate the growth. Publishers are becoming ever more creative in the solutions they offer advertisers. It is set to transform advertising as we know it.
>
> It is happening already. Content has a very bright future ahead of it. In the beginning there was the word; today we are just at the beginning.

About the contributors – closing thanks

Our main contributor to the expertise in this content chapter (again!) was Dale Lovell, chief digital officer at Adyoulike, Europe's leading native advertising technology platform.

Based in London, Dale has worked in journalism, digital publishing, content strategy and creative content marketing for over 15 years. In 2015 he was listed as a BIMA Hot 100, alongside Adyoulike UK MD Francis Turner, in recognition as a digital leader striving to push the industry forward. He sits on the IAB UK's Content and Native Council and is a regular commentator in the digital press in the UK.

Additional thanks to Sarah Gavin, Outbrain, Brad Nickel at Adbeat and, last but not least, Rob Welsby of Further.

Understanding   09
programmatic

OUR CHAPTER PLEDGE TO YOU

When you reach the end of this chapter you will have answers to the following questions:

- What is programmatic ad buying?
- Who is involved in the programmatic ecosystem?
- What are the challenges with programmatic media?
- What is the future of programmatic advertising?

I've worked in media since 1984. In my first week I encountered a service called Cognotel – a very primitive service using phone lines to send textual information from one subscriber's office to another.

I remember how long it took to construct a logo or icon from coloured pixels. Similar technologies took place in France (Minitel) and in the United States (Prodigy) – technologies that would be short-lived but stood shakily on the shoulders of Samuel Morse, Alexander Graham Bell and other visionaries from the past.

Even then (1984) we toyed with the idea of sending ads but it was just too much like hard work. It was another 13 years (1997) before I finally did place an ad on a website that was the same distribution technology as our earlier friend Cognotel but used a new protocol called HTTP – an acronym that instructed the zeroes and ones to be directed to a server connected to this thing called the world wide web. And the rest is history!

By 1997, particularly in the United States, there was already an embryonic but thriving marketplace for online advertising. Hotwired first published banner ads in 1994. This involved a simple discussion between a website publisher and an advertiser (AT&T). This was really easy – one transaction, one CPM and an agreed budget or period of time. Everyone was happy.

But as we all know, the number of websites and places to advertise went through the roof – how on earth were media agencies and advertisers expected to cope with the sheer volume of opportunities?

The more parties an advertiser had to deal with, the more expensive it was to manage, but (as always) the market responded and opportunities developed:

- more data led to better targeting;
- automation led to scale and lower cost;
- reduced overheads were achieved through the centralization of inventory.

Networks sprang up to simplify the process further – Tremor Media and the AOL networks, for example. Advertisers liked this because they could buy at scale; and publishers liked this because they could sell at scale.

However, there soon emerged grave concerns over a lack of transparency and a lack of precision. Plus publishers still had lots more inventory to sell too. What was needed was something even more efficient and, ultimately, something faster! Something a bit more like 'search' where you could bid for inventory.

The exchanges (Google, Yahoo) added scale but the advertiser needed better technology to manage multiple exchanges and audiences. Say hello to programmatic – intelligent software to acquire and manage digital advertising in the same way that global financial markets trade and swap equities and other asset classes at the speed of light. However, programmatic focuses on the audiences rather than the sites and empowers advertisers like never before. Oh, and by the way... it's huge (see Figure 9.1).

Emarketer predicts that 83 per cent of all display advertising in the United States will be programmatic by 2017. That's as big as the search market.

Myself and the team behind the creation of *Understanding Digital Marketing* are proud to have collaborated with AppNexus, the global technology company whose platform optimizes programmatic advertising, to collaborate on this chapter. Note: AppNexus has recently coined the term 'programmable media' as the next evolution in programmatic.

Figure 9.1 Global programmatic spend (US $billion)

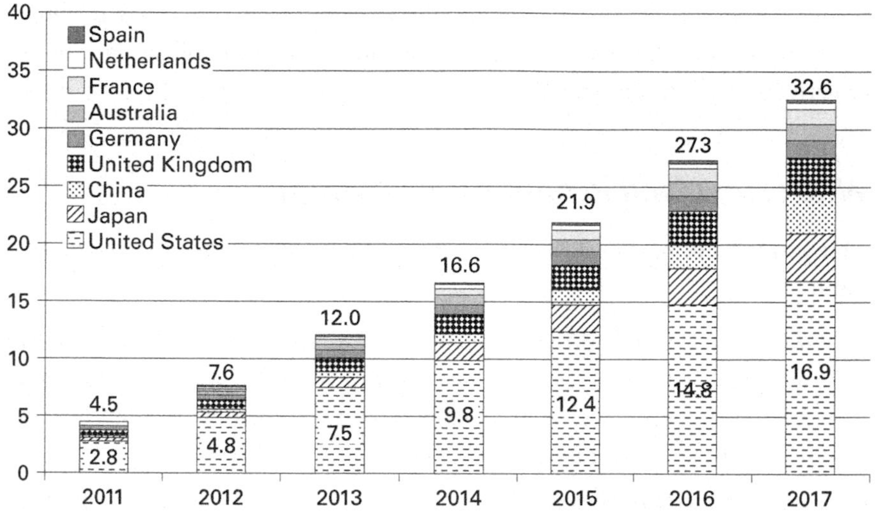

Legend:
- Spain
- Netherlands
- France
- Australia
- Germany
- United Kingdom
- China
- Japan
- United States

Values by year:
- 2011: 4.5 (2.8)
- 2012: 7.6 (4.8)
- 2013: 12.0 (7.5)
- 2014: 16.6 (9.8)
- 2015: 21.9 (12.4)
- 2016: 27.3 (14.8)
- 2017: 32.6 (16.9)

SOURCE: Business Wire (2015)

What is programmatic ad buying?

Programmatic ad buying is the automated process by which digital advertising inventory is auctioned off – often, though not always, in real time. When an end user opens a mobile app or clicks on a webpage, this action triggers a series of events lasting roughly half a second (sometimes less) in which multiple advertisers bid to serve an ad to that end user. It is a process wholly unique to digital marketing.

In traditional offline advertising, a company creates an ad campaign and then purchases advertising slots using different kinds of media: on television, in magazines and newspapers, and on roadside billboards. With online advertising, the same thing happens, but the logistics behind media planning, or selecting where and when you will run your ads, are different.

That's because the internet is a much more fractured, individualized medium. There are far more websites run by far more organizations than there are TV networks and shows, and the interaction between consumer and media event has been narrowed down to a single person viewing a single web page or using a single mobile app. Think about that dynamic versus a single newspaper being printed once a day and read by thousands, or a single TV ad aired to a large population.

Another big difference between programmatic and traditional advertising is this: with programmatic, you have the ability to tag consumers via a browser's cookie file or by their mobile device IDs, a process that allows advertisers and other parties to segment consumers and collect data on ad effectiveness on an individual level.

Who is involved in online advertising?

Many different parties interact in the online advertising ecosystem (see Figure 9.2):

- *Publishers (sellers)* provide inventory, or the space where ads are displayed. This may be a website or a mobile app. For example, www.nytimes.com, www.cnn.com, and www.imdb.com are all publishers who sell ad space to buyers.

- *Advertisers or marketers (buyers)* purchase inventory from sellers in order to display advertisements to consumers. Microsoft, Amazon and Target are all examples of advertisers (though each of these companies also operates as a digital publisher in its own right).

- *Ad networks* serve as brokers between groups of publishers and groups of advertisers. Networks traditionally aggregate publishers and advertisers and also handle remnant inventory, but they can have a wide variety of business models and clients.

- *Consumers* are the target customers for advertisements. They are the ones opening a mobile app or clicking on a web page.

- *Data providers* provide information useful for targeting. This can be contextual information about the website or web page where the ad is displayed (for example, you wouldn't want to display a vacation ad next to a newspaper article about a plane crash), behavioural data about users, viewability data that determines whether ad units were likely to have been seen by a set of human eyes, or other kinds of data.

- *Data management platforms (DMPs)* are centralized systems for gathering first-party data, integrating with third-party data, and applying this data to one's advertising strategy. A DMP may offer the following features: estimating the likely reach for a user segment; measuring the lift from using data; acting as a financial clearing house between data buyers and sellers; and assisting publishers in monetizing data on their users. DMPs most commonly work with user data but may also work with contextual data, or other types of data.

- *Demand-side platforms (DSPs)* enable advertising clients to buy digital media on many different selling networks, exchanges and platforms through a single interface.

- *Supply-side platforms (SSPs)* allow publishers to access demand from many possible networks, exchanges and platforms through a single interface.

- *Rich-media vendors* create, serve and manage rich-media advertising. Rich media refers generally to advertisements with audio, video or other interactive elements.

- Publishers, advertisers and networks interact through unified ad trafficking systems called *ad exchanges*. An ad exchange allows advertisers and publishers to use the same technological platform, services and methods, and 'speak the same language' in order to exchange data, set prices and, ultimately, serve an ad.

What is an ad serving?

Ultimately, the objective behind programmatic buying is to serve the right ad, to the right audience, at the right time. So what does it mean to serve an ad?

Ad serving is the process of: 1) determining which advertisement goes in which ad slot on a given publisher's web page or mobile app; and 2) delivering (or 'serving') the advertisement. The computer or group of computers responsible for this is called an ad server. Major publishers, networks and advertisers sometimes have their own ad servers. Most large ad servers also can:

- choose the ad that will most benefit the advertiser or the publisher, and that meets each party's criteria;

- record how many ads were served and on what pages or screens;

- record performance data, for example, whether the ad was clicked on, when the viewer stopped playing a video ad, or if the ad can be tied to a purchase or some other action;

- funnel performance data back into the matching process;

- capture and make available user data, which is information about a consumer (user), including browser habits and demographic data.

An ad server can be a publisher's ad server, where the publisher decides who gets the impression, or an advertiser's ad server, where the advertiser decides which creative goes in the slot they have been assigned. Or it can be an intermediary ad server that attempts to maximize the benefit to both sides.

Figure 9.2 Programmatic buying ecosystems

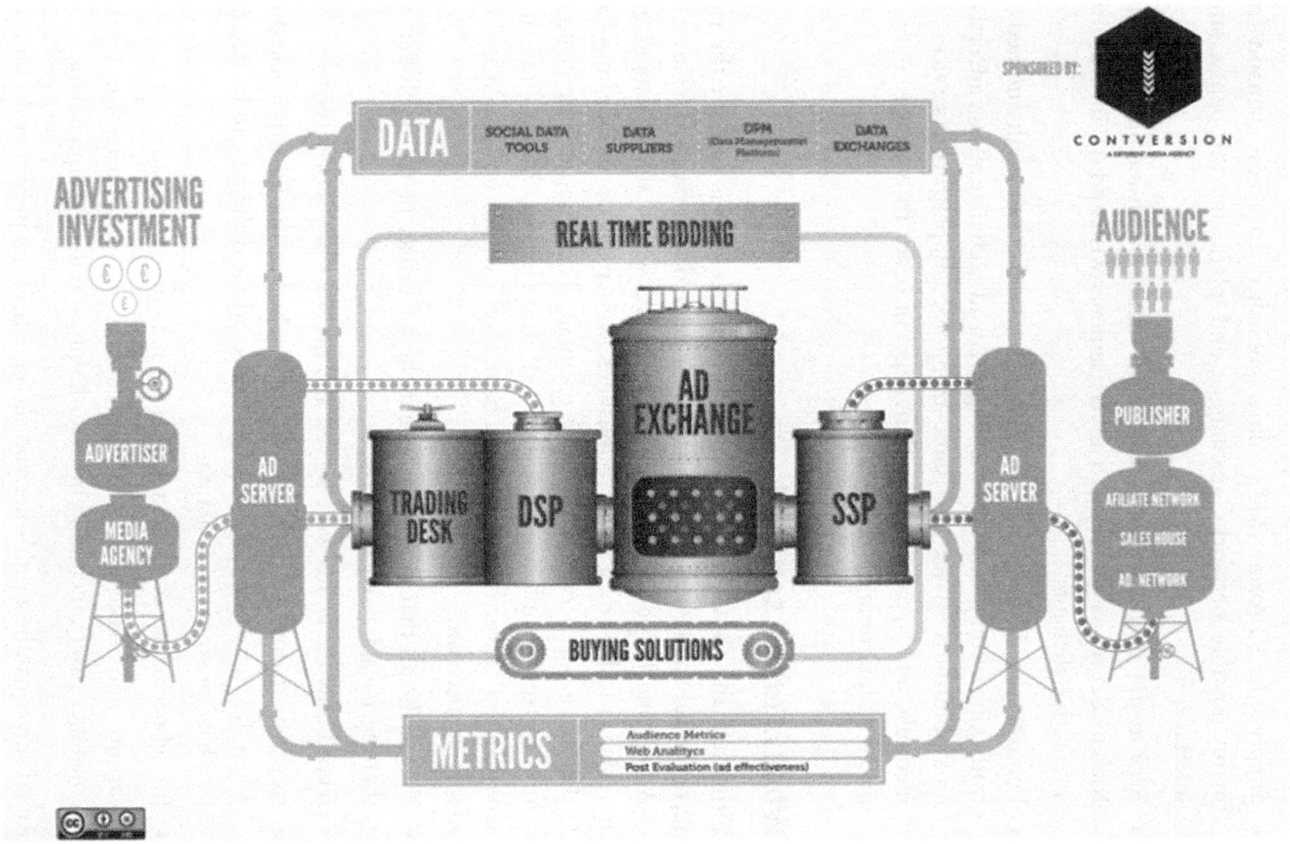

SOURCE: IAB, Spain, 2014

What do digital marketers need to know about programmatic buying?

Imagine if you had to pay a fee to view content from your favourite websites or use your favourite mobile apps. Thankfully, due to programmatic advertising, you don't have to. Programmatic buying simply refers to buying ad inventory through automated means, as opposed to more manual buys where advertisers are in contact with a sales team, or other 'offline' mechanism. Advertisers want to be able to target their products to the right viewers. Publishers, in turn, want to better monetize their sites or apps. Successful monetization gives publishers the option of offering users free content, rather than charging them for it by using a pay wall.

To better understand how this type of transaction between the publisher and advertiser occurs, you will need to know about the different ways in which inventory is bought for display advertising, and each of the various pricing models that exist.

How advertisers acquire publisher inventory

There are three different ways through which sellers and buyers meet to transact on media: RTB auction, deals/packages and direct.

RTB

Real-time bidding (RTB) is an open-marketplace programmatic auction where ad inventory is sold and bought on a per impression basis through a bidding system that occurs in the milliseconds before a web page is loaded by a user. When people talk about 'programmatic advertising' they often mean RTB.

An RTB auction is more effective for an advertiser than a static auction because, unlike having to pay a fixed rate for each impression in that bucket, the advertiser can value each opportunity to buy an ad impression in real time, allowing for accepting or rejecting each ad impression in the campaign.

Deals/packages

Deals and packages constitute a bid-based marketplace based on relationships between specific publishers and advertisers.

Typically, to initiate the purchase and sale of deals and packages, a publisher invites an advertiser to bid on its inventory, and it enables the advertiser to gain first access on specific ad inventory before it is made available to other buyers in an open auction.

Open-auction deal bids compete with RTB bids. Private auction deals are sometimes prioritized over the RTB marketplace. Packages are pre-made deals that buyers can browse, making offerings more visible and accessible to the marketplace. Packages can also be a great jumping-off point for private deal negotiations. This marketplace generally gives the advertiser access to high-quality, brand-safe inventory.

Direct

In a direct marketplace, advertisers are buying impressions in bulk at a fixed CPM rate instead of going through a real-time bidding auction. This model provides the advertiser with a guarantee, or a reservation, on the ad inventory. Advertisers and agencies will often pay premium prices to access this type of inventory, as it allows them to target specific audiences based on geography, browser, etc, and the advertiser gets certainty of campaign volumes. Direct buying works well for advertisers who want better control over the placements of their ads. Direct buying also gives them the flexibility to employ rich-media formats such as page takeovers on a home page, where no other ad is shown.

Pricing models for the sale of online ads

There are a few main ways of pricing media: CPM, CPA, CPC and sponsorship. Generally, the price of an impression is determined by what buyers are willing to pay in real time, as well as the quality of the product. This type of buying means that ads can be targeted to specific user groups or segments, and budgets can be managed in real time.

Note to reader

It is important to note that RTB operates on a second-price auction model. This means that the highest bidder wins the auction but pays $0.01 more than the second-highest bid. Second-price auctions allow a more accurate valuation of the item up for auction.

CPM

Cost per mille (CPM) is when the price is based on 1,000 impressions. This is good for publishers as they will still get paid for every impression and risk nothing on ad performance.

For buyers, a $1 CPM price means that if their ad is shown 1,000 times, they pay $1. For sellers, a $1 CPM price means that they will receive $1 for every 1,000 ads they display.

vCPM

Viewable cost per 1,000 impressions (vCPM) means that an advertiser only pays when an ad is shown on screen for one second or longer for display ads, and two seconds or longer for video ads.

CPC

Cost per click (CPC) is the average amount that is charged for a click on an ad. Unlike CPM, CPC is a performance-based metric. This means that a publisher only gets paid once a user clicks on an ad, regardless of how many impressions were served before the click actually occurred.

If an ad receives two clicks, one that costs $0.20 and one that costs $0.40, the average CPC will be $0.30.

CPA

Cost per action/acquisition (CPA) is best for an advertiser as they only pay the publisher when it results in a sale, or a conversion against their campaign goal. If $100 is spent on a campaign, and as a result gets 10 acquisitions, this would mean a CPA of $10.

Sponsorship

Sponsorship is when the advertiser accepts a lump sum from the publisher in exchange for displaying their ad for a specified amount of time.

The ads are purchased on a CPD or cost-per-day basis, and the cost would be for a percentage of all the views over the duration of a campaign. There isn't any additional charge for 'clicks', and there is no limit to how many 'impressions' the ad receives over that time frame.

Deeper dive

Programmatic buying allows marketers to bring sophisticated, data-driven decision processes to their advertising campaigns. Unlike broadcast and out-of-home advertising, digital ads can be customizable, and accountable to factors such as viewability and conversion measurement. By applying auction dynamics, both publishers and advertisers are able to achieve mutually compatible objectives in a transparent and well-functioning market.

Here are some of the key definitions that govern programmatic buying:

- *Network*: for buyers, a network represents their account as a whole. At the network level, buyers can decide who is eligible to sell to them and what level of inventory audit they require. They can also create lists of domains and apps for efficient whitelist or blacklist targeting in line items, put in place a cap on how much they are willing to spend per day on third-party inventory, and more.

- *Insertion order*: an insertion order represents a financial agreement between a buyer and a publisher that specifies what objective a buyer would like to execute. The insertion order contains information such as the total budget a buyer allocates to a publisher for a period of time, or which third-party verification a buyer utilizes.

- *Line item*: the line item under an insertion order represents the agreed-upon strategies the buyer sets out. It contains information that the buyer specifies, such as how much money the buyer has allocated towards an offering, or which kind of targeting the buyer needs.

- *Creative*: a creative is an actual ad, hosted either by a first-party or third-party ad server. Creatives belong to a specific advertiser and come in different formats, including:

  - Banner ads: text or image ads that appear above or alongside content.

  - Expandable ads: ads that can be enlarged beyond their initial dimensions, often by user interactions such as scrolling down the page or mousing over the ad.

  - Pop ads: ads that display in a secondary browser window. Pop-up ads display in front of the initial browser window, while pop-under ads display behind it.

  - Video ads: video ads may play before, during or after the main video content. A special video ad unit – outstream video – is embedded within the body of an article, mostly set to auto-play when the reader reaches the part of the page that contains the ad. The sound is usually not activated unless the reader hovers over the ads with their mouse. Outstream video does not require video content; it can be served against a banner unit.

– Mobile ads: mobile ads may be in-app ads or web ads that are optimized for display on mobile devices.

• *Segment pixel*: a segment pixel is placed on web pages to collect data about users, such as pages they visit, actions they take, or qualities such as gender, location and purchase history. When a segment pixel fires, the user is added to a segment, which can later be targeted to attempt to reach the user again (this, in turn, is called 'retargeting').

Segment pixels belong either to the entire network or to a specific advertiser. Network-level segments are available for targeting in all line items under all advertisers. Advertiser-level segments are available for targeting only in line items under that specific advertiser.

• *Conversion pixel*: a conversion pixel is placed on a web page to track user actions in response to an advertiser's creatives, such as registering at a site or making a purchase. When a conversion pixel fires, an exchange determines if the conversion (the registration, the purchase, etc) can be 'attributed', or tied to the user clicking on or viewing one of the advertiser's creatives previously (conversion attribution).

A particular buyer can have many different conversion pixels. The buyer associates each conversion pixel to many line items (examples include tracking payment or performance goals on a CPA basis, or valuing impressions based on CPA optimization data).

• *Third-party creative pixel*: a third-party creative pixel is used to trigger a third-party action when a creative is served.

A buyer can have third-party pixels at the network, advertiser or creative levels. Defining these pixels at the network and advertiser levels lets a buyer save time by applying pixels to creatives across the network or advertiser rather than one by one, and helps them to avoid the repeat auditing of creatives.

• *Click tracker*: a click tracker is used to track clicks associated with creatives. This is done by attaching the tracker as a 'piggyback pixel' on the externally hosted creative.

Expert view

An industry expert summary on programmatic

Contribution by Jon Walsh, a veteran of online display media

'Programmatic' falls into either programmatic direct or RTB.

'Programmatic direct' (also known as automated guaranteed/premium programmatic) allows advertisers to buy guaranteed space on desired publishers directly (eg an advertiser wants to ensure their campaign is viewed 1 million times over the course of a certain month on WSJ.com, on a certain section, using a particular creative format).

This type of programmatic gives assurances and guarantees to both the premium publisher and the advertiser. The basic benefits are a reduction in overhead for the publisher and a simplification for the advertiser/agency in the booking process.

The majority of programmatic, however, currently exists within the real-time bidding (RTB) infrastructure, so many people often confuse 'RTB' as 'programmatic' – technically speaking RTB is an element of programmatic.

RTB is the process by which ad impressions are bought and sold on an impression by impression basis – all transacted in milliseconds. To achieve this the industry has evolved a distinct infrastructure – supply-side platforms (SSPs) for publishers and demand-side platforms (DSPs) for advertisers and agencies.

SSP's job is to deliver the highest revenue-generating ad for the publisher for every single available impression, thereby lifting the overall yield. It should also incentivize publishers to continue to curate a valuable audience to attract the highest bids and maximize their revenues. DSP's job is to purchase and deliver the ad for the advertiser at the lowest possible price whilst still securing the desired impression.

In order to maximize value for publishers and cut out maximum wastage for the advertiser, data needs to be introduced to the mix; this is where RTB really offers value. It helps provide assurances to the advertiser, knowing they are reaching the right audience.

Data either comes from the advertiser – allowing companies to retarget consumers who have already interacted with their business in order drive the consumer down the marketing funnel – or from third-party data owners.

Third-party data is data that is segmented into a wide variety of 'buckets' (that can overlap), such as demographical information or psychographic information or income levels.

Data can also derive to 'in-market' information, which shows that a consumer has recently researched buying a particular product or service – this allows a relevant advertiser to swoop in and close the sale for their brand. This can also be referred to as 'who is' – in other words, 'who is in the market for a hoover right now'.

Data requires cookies to store information, which can then be used by advertisers – without cookies the whole value of the RTB ecosystem is massively reduced.

Advertisers seeking greater control... and assurances

It should be no surprise that, as the market for programmatic grows and develops, marketers and advertisers expect greater transparency and assurances. There have been countless horror stories of unfortunate ad placements where the advertiser's message unwittingly appears beside a story that makes the advertiser appear insensitive, sloppy or, even worse, opportunistic.

The atrocious advertising following the Boston Marathon bombings is an example. I have decided to leave out the name of the advertiser in question here as I don't want to have them included in this book. Just do a quick search for 'bad ad placements' and you can find a whole load more.

Advertisers have other concerns too – the level of ad fraud, misuse of data and the level of transparency available to them. The programmatic sector of the business and the stakeholders that comprise this space have had to address these concerns in a whole manner of ways. Later on in this chapter we will hear from one of the world leaders in the programmatic industry, Brian O'Kelley, founder of AppNexus, who discusses some of these critical factors.

I was recently intrigued by a live Q&A session that took place in London. Organized by the wonderful people at Altair Media, the session featured advertisers from three leading brands: B&Q, Reckitt Benckiser and Virgin Active. Altair Media wanted to shed light on the approaches of leading brands and the challenges they are overcoming in a new and rapidly evolving marketplace.

The contrast between the views making the trade press and the views of brands beginning to understand the programmatic marketplace became apparent during the live Q&A session. Rather than focusing on fraudulent impressions and viewable impression rates the focus was on cost-efficiency, making it work for brand advertisers and understanding the differences between the many technology providers that all say they are the solution to all of your needs.

The programmatic buying marketplace has seen a significant rise in demand from advertisers around the world over the past few years. A new forecast by IPG Mediabrands-owned Magna Global has estimated that the market will be worth US $37 billion by 2019. This growth and the explosion of suppliers and stakeholders have caused the market to become more complex and the advertisers, who are funding the whole market, to start to question, audit and explore their options.

After all, programmatic is fuelled by data and now that clients are starting to understand the value of their own data many are bringing the programmatic buying in-house.

Now back to the opinions of the brand marketers from the Q&A session I recently attended:

- *Reckitt Benckiser*: Sameer Amin says: 'We are taking ownership but approaching programmatic cautiously. When we see the efficiencies and cost savings we will then look to bring in-house.'

- *B&Q*: Steve Warrington says: 'Our approach is still in its infancy but we intend to invest in this area so we can take more ownership. Ultimately the aim is to have enough control so that we can be both using and driving the data, going beyond the standard optimizations and making the most of what programmatic has to offer.'

- *Virgin Active*: Anne Tulloch says: 'I bought through an agency as well as managing an in-house trading desk. An always-on approach with campaign up-weights, I also have a thorough approach to ensure each partner is tested fairly and have time to build data pools, monitoring success through KPIs of views as well as channel stacking. This is the start of the journey.'

Brands... the broad view

Anne Tulloch at Virgin Active has been incorporating programmatic media buying into marketing plans since 2014. 'I see programmatic as a cost-effective opportunity for reaching audiences at the right place, right time with the right message,' she says. 'I think the market is still in its infancy in terms of what can be bought but there should be no limit to this type of media buying. As other media channels become digitally enabled the market should have a consolidated view across all activity. In particular, I would expect the auction process that has worked so well for search to be equally applicable for display advertising.'

B&Q is also embracing the opportunity to maximize the use of data. Steve Warrington describes how 'this use of data allows B&Q to place highly relevant timely ads in front of customers'.

Reckitt Benckiser takes a cautious view. Sameer Amin says: 'There is a clear opportunity here but it is always important to be aware of buzzwords and fads. Our aim is to understand the model and where it adds value for us. We may only need to use certain aspects for optimum impact for our brands. This involves a "test and learn" approach, which means working in partnership with agencies and media owners.'

David Harvey at Altair Media agrees that: 'Understanding the programmatic model is obviously important and that understanding will be gained through robust testing and developing partnerships with each stakeholder in the programmatic chain. Those partnerships must be developed through mutual trust to ensure fads and short-term gains do not prevail over long-term structures and success.' He continues: 'Programmatic offers us huge potential to deliver personalized messages and the next 12 months should see an improvement in transparency, trust and education across the industry.'

Challenges for marketers

Any new methodology brings challenges for the people adopting it. Sameer Amin says: 'The first challenge is explaining the benefits to other stakeholders internally in the business. You may find that people are so used to brand and TV that you have to invest some time to "sell" the benefits across the business.'

Steve Warrington at B&Q agrees: 'People are used to putting an advert or product in front of someone. We need to explain that this is about meeting customer needs so that they understand the benefits over traditional advertising.'

Once the campaign is up and running, measurement becomes the key focus for most marketers. Tracking the impact of programmatic is crucial to its ongoing success. 'Agencies need to provide clarity so we can retain control and properly direct the strategy. Otherwise there is a danger of this being a black box,' says Steve Warrington.

This search for transparency is also a concern for Sameer Amin at Reckitt Benckiser: 'All suppliers will tell you that they are the best. We need data to demonstrate the impact on sales.'

Measurement of programmatic buying is a huge focus for all of the stakeholders. Digital is the most data rich and accountable media channel, so it is natural for measurement to be the focus for programmatic.

Anne Tulloch is concerned that the focus for programmatic is based on direct response metrics and believes an opportunity is being missed: 'It is important to recognize that programmatic is one of many channels in the marketing mix and therefore rather than success being based on last-click metrics a broader attribution approach needs to be taken. There is also no reason why programmatic buying cannot deliver against brand metrics, especially with the introduction of larger formats.'

David Harvey from Altair Media agrees: 'It is an important point that highlights how programmatic has evolved within a direct-response ecosystem that has focused on delivering to a specific conversion point. Optimizing programmatic media to brand metrics will be an important challenge for every stakeholder involved.'

Challenges for the industry

Ensuring the brand is in safe environments is a key concern, as is the worry of ad fraud. Sameer Amin says: 'You might be buying 10 billion impressions and there are no absolute guarantees from ad-safe technology.'

Measurable and viewable impressions is another challenge, as Steve Warrington at B&Q says: 'The ads need to be seen.' Anne Tulloch adds: 'What does visible actually mean to a brand? There is no point buying the leader board at the top of the page, as with banner blindness it may be "viewed" but not actually seen. Being further down the page may have a bigger impact.'

Transparency is vital to the uptake and success of programmatic buying. Anne continues: 'Having transparency on costs, such as ad serving, is important, as there are margins and vested interests to consider. Trading in-house gives that transparency and also the transparency of where the ad actually appeared.' Sameer Amin at Reckitt Benckiser says: 'The agency or media owner model needs to reflect the shared risk by providing shared reward. Put simply, they shouldn't make money if we are not.'

Sameer Amin also sees consistency of technology as a big challenge: 'Integration and capability are important, conflicting tech will mean the inventory sources are cut, eg ad sever needs to connect with YouTube, etc.'

'Transparency will improve as advertisers ask more questions of programmatic stakeholders,' says David Harvey at Altair Media. 'But I think in the next 12–18 months it will be the fraudulent activity that will begin to be the focus. Although the percentage of fraudulent impressions are small it is a multi-billion-dollar global industry, so the sums of money are vast. Therefore, it will get picked up by international law enforcement. Due to its sheer scale it will become a much hotter topic this year.'

Roles and responsibilities of the industry players

Steve Warrington says: 'The agency is there for education and outlining a strategy, including a framework of what needs to be done on a day-to-day basis. We view their role as helping make sure things are correctly stitched together.'

Anne Tulloch agrees: 'We always ask the agency what they think, as it is their area of expertise. We rely on them to challenge and ask the right questions.' And at Reckitt Benckiser: 'The agency role is to review and challenge. Agencies will need to work harder to justify fees and commission. We expect the agency to sense-check what we are doing is right.'

Steve Warrington at B&Q goes on to say: 'We expect them to be impartial and neutral to help us understand what is possible. We don't want them to be tied to just one tech provider or one media buying provider that will dictate what we do. We are seeking a supportive and collaborative approach to get the best bang for our buck and ensure there is no black box.'

Sameer Amin at Reckitt Benckiser adds: 'We need to be smart enough to realize that everyone has an agenda. As a client, we need to use more data and be scientific in our approach. We have an opportunity to have more control over how the buy works, but with that comes a responsibility.'

In summary

The views of B&Q, Reckitt Benckiser and Virgin Active have reinforced known challenges, such as transparency across the programmatic supply chain and brand safety. They have also raised interesting points such as how programmatic buying can be used to deliver brand metrics, and the integration between the different technology providers.

The market still has a long way to go before it answers these challenges, in fact you could argue that the market is not even listening to the brands that hold the budgets. Our hope is that the transparency across the industry will improve, but we have already seen further consolidation across the programmatic supply chain with global groups purchasing agencies and DSPs to add to their own stack. Will this consolidation help the transparency issue or is it simply just narrowing the options for advertisers?

Are ad fraud and brand safety really being taken seriously? It is estimated by an ANA and White Ops 60-day study that US $6.3 billion was lost due to ad fraud in 2015. There has not been much coverage of whether the fraudsters are being brought to justice for fraud on such a large scale.

But it is not all negative. The next 18 months have the potential to define the programmatic industry. Therefore, we need to balance our predictions for programmatic between the challenges and the opportunities.

Expert view

Altair Media's predictions for programmatic buying in 2016 and beyond:

- *Starting positively*: advertisers will be sourcing independent views on the programmatic supply chain as they take more in-house. This will act as a catalyst in driving more transparency across the market as marketing and procurement teams question the buying process.

- *A little negative*: over the next 18 months the focus on ad fraud will cause law-enforcement agencies around the world to take an interest in the issue. This will be driven by the volume of money involved and also the fact that many of the major suppliers are publicly owned and shareholders should be calling on the legal systems to crack down on the fraudsters bringing the industry into disrepute.

- *But staying positive*: the market will make inroads into servicing brand advertisers and fast-moving consumer goods (FMCG) marketers by adapting to delivering to less direct metrics such as propensity to buy and market share. This will also be helped by the integration of working data management platforms (DPMs) that will be able to monitor brand metrics and correlate to programmatic investment. So, no more mention of big data, but utilized data.

- *And finishing on a positive note*: an increase in the use of programmatic artificial intelligence to influence paid-search bidding strategies and that will inform e-mail marketing and wider CRM activities. Again, the catalyst for this change will be the take-up of DMPs and the utilization of a wider range of data points.

In summary, programmatic media buying is still in the relative early stages of its life and is being increasingly explored by brands and agencies. As the channel evolves it has the potential to fundamentally change the digital market and the relationship between brands and advertisers.

Developing the channel to work across both brand and direct-response campaigns will be crucial to the channel's expansion. This will be helped by the progression of measurement and attribution systems that will allow marketers to show the power of the channel in comparison to more traditional approaches. The next 18 months will prove to be an important year for programmatic media buying and, as Anne Tulloch says: 'We need to be there as it matures.'

Q&A with Brian O'Kelley, co-founder and CEO of AppNexus

Background

As co-founder and CEO of AppNexus, and chairman of the company's board of directors, Brian has more than a decade of leadership experience in the online advertising sector, including his tenure as chief technology officer (CTO) of Right Media (later sold to Yahoo! in 2007), where he led the creation and commercialization of multiple real-time bidding technologies, including the invention of the world's first online advertising exchange – the engine that powers and optimizes the real-time purchase and placement of digital advertising. Brian is an inventor of patents that enable AppNexus's technology to power innovative trading solutions and marketplaces for internet advertising. He has been an active investor in and early-stage advisor to such start-ups as Invite Media (acquired by Google in 2010), MediaMath, Dstillery and Solve Media. Brian is also a regular contributor to Forbes on technology-related topics and, among other honours, he has been named in

Crain's 40 Under 40, Adweek 50 and Silicon Alley 100 lists, and was recognized as an E&Y Entrepreneur of the Year in the New York region in 2012. Brian holds a BSE in computer science from Princeton University, where he is an active alumnus. He lives in New York City with his wife and daughter.

Q&A interview

Why is there a need to introduce programmatic to marketers?

In a recent study, Magna Global and Cowen & Company identified programmatic as the fastest-growing portion of digital advertising, which is *itself* the fastest-growing portion of global advertising. Simply put, all marketers need to develop fluency in programmatic, as it is the present and future of digital advertising. Moreover, as digital channels subsume what we traditionally think of as non-digital media, programmatic will assume greater meaning and importance. Aside from this pragmatic consideration, programmatic offers the unprecedented ability to target the right consumers with the right message at the right time, and to do so with accountability and measurement.

What problems were solved by introducing programmatic?

Programmatic solves multiple challenges. First, it automates what was otherwise a labour-intensive and costly process behind digital advertising. That is important because advertising pays for much of the great content that consumers have come to value in a free and open internet – from journalism and reference information, to games and social networks. If publishers and app developers cannot monetize this content, the internet will become smaller and fall behind pay walls. Programmatic makes digital advertising work at scale, and that has tremendous social utility.

Second, programmatic allows marketers to leverage data. At its heart, advertising is about delivering the right message, to the right person, in the right time and place. Programmatic is uniquely designed to fulfil that mission.

How can programmatic build trust among marketers? Is it helping to stamp out online advertising fraud?

Like all other marketplaces, the programmatic exchange should introduce practices and standards that ensure inventory quality. In general, the more direct the relationship between advertiser and publisher (meaning, the fewer intermediaries involved in the auction), the more marketers can enjoy confidence in their campaigns. Major platforms are taking steps to compress the supply chain, and that practice contributes greatly to quality. Ad tech platforms also have a responsibility to invest in data science and pre-bid detection protocols, and to be fully transparent about how they guard against low-quality inventory, invalid non-human traffic and bad actors.

Can marketers feel safe with programmatic – is there a risk their ads will appear on sites that are outside their control?
Increasingly, the handful of major platforms that serve both advertisers and publishers are able to provide a range of options that enable advertisers to maintain control. For instance, advertisers can 'whitelist' select domains against which their campaigns will serve ads. Likewise, reputable ad exchanges already have stringent processes in place to prohibit domains that serve objectionable material. The very fact that programmatic advertising is automated does not remove human judgement from the equation. On the contrary, programmatic should *enable*, *inform* and *enhance* human control over data and campaign decisioning.

Is adblocking a real threat to marketers? What is AppNexus doing about adblocking?
Adblocking is in many respects a natural reaction on the part of consumers to some of the negative aspects and excesses of programmatic advertising, particularly those practices that degrade user experience. When publishers load pages with too many ad units, or when advertisers deploy too many third-party verification services, end users pay the price in the form of longer load times and greater data usage (for which they pay dearly in the form of monthly surcharges to their mobile carriers).

AppNexus is taking a proactive stance on all of these issues. We have one of the industry's only 'viewability marketplaces', meaning, a marketplace in which advertisers pay only for viewable inventory; this arrangement delivers greater monetization to publishers, as marketers will pay more for quality units, and encourages publishers to eliminate low-value, low-viewability units on their page. Moreover, by eliminating arbitrage (or, multistep reselling and repackaging of inventory by networks) on our platform, we have compressed the supply chain, thereby reducing latency. Finally, we have a rigorous audit process that pre-screens creatives. Pilot studies show that consumers are willing to

▶

turn off blockers when they are presented with the value proposition of digital advertising. If we protect that value proposition by improving user experience, we will strengthen the social contract between publishers, advertisers and consumers – a social contract that we at AppNexus call the 'virtuous circle'.

Does AppNexus believe that programmatic will work across all media, including print?

Already, we have seen 'radio' and 'television' collide with digital. Streaming services like Pandora, Spotify, Netflix and Hulu have challenged the boundaries that traditionally divided different media. And, as one would expect, programmatic advertising is now available where it would recently have seemed inapplicable. It is hard to say where this begins and ends. A better way to frame the question might be: 'Does AppNexus believe that the lines between digital and non-digital media are quickly blurring?' The answer to that question is a resounding 'yes', and that necessarily means that programmatic advertising is a highly adaptable concept. If marketers are empowered to make data-driven decisions across screens, media and channels, the entire marketing ecosystem will benefit.

Should marketers deal directly with AppNexus or through their agency?

We try to provide as much choice and optionality as possible, as there is seldom a one-size-fits-all solution. Some marketers outsource functions to agency partners or marketing service providers, particularly when those third parties offer centres of excellence around creative, data science or campaign management. Others already have sophisticated capabilities in-house and work directly with AppNexus. Alternatively, some marketers build a hybrid model between the two. We believe in offering flexible and customizable solutions for our customers.

The future of programmatic advertising

As digital channels collide and merge with – and even subsume – other media, it is possible, if not likely, that programmatic buying will carry over to traditional marketing and advertising formats.

For example, if billboards are increasingly digital rather than static, why not run a real-time decisioning and ad-serving process against out-of-home advertising? As the lines between 'broadcast' and 'digital' become more blurred – particularly with the advent of in-home streaming devices and multichannel distribution arrangements – advertisers may find it possible to pinpoint their campaigns to specific viewers and listeners, rather than broader subsets. In short, programmatic buying is a highly extensible technology with wide-ranging applications.

Other changes are in store, as well. After all, programmatic advertising is only about 10 years old. While it has radically transformed digital marketing, it still poses technological challenges that require substantial redress. Such challenges include:

- *Supply chain inefficiency*: often, too many intermediaries are involved in the process of serving an ad; too much intermediation, in turn, creates latency and takes a large bite out of the ad dollar, as fees are paid at each step along the way. By the time advertisers and publishers pay for buy-side and sell-side ad servers, DSPs and SSPs, rich-media vendors and DMPs, as little as $0.50 may reach the publisher. This state of affairs is unsustainable in the long term. The future portends a more streamlined supply chain, lower technology fees and a more seamless delivery route.

- *Viewability*: for marketers, viewability is also a persistent concern. In an effort to compensate for diminished monetization – a phenomenon related to supply chain inefficiencies described above – some publishers drop ad units to the extreme top, bottom, left and right of their pages. End users are highly unlikely to bring these units into frame. Naturally, marketers want to know if they are paying for ad units that are actually seen by actual sets of human eyes (as opposed to bot traffic). The technology is already in place to measure viewability and to enable transactions based solely on *viewed* impressions. Marketers should anticipate a day in the not-too-distant future when all programmatic can be transacted only on viewable units.

- *Data*: marketers have traditionally been locked into using 'black box' algorithms provided by their ad-tech partners. This arrangement offers little visibility into auction logic and provides few assurances against data leakage. The next generation of demand-side platforms will necessarily allow marketers to apply their own, proprietary algorithms to campaigns and stream campaign data in real time. For those marketers who do not have in-house data science teams, third-party vendors may at some point license customized algorithms and decision trees to meet their campaign goals. The industry's use of data today is foundational, but expect it to grow in sophistication and nuance.

- *Privacy*: marketers naturally want hard data to inform their decisions. Consumers naturally want to ensure that their privacy is protected and respected. This issue is complicated, given that national and state jurisdictions define personally identifiable information (PII) differently. Through various self-regulatory organizations, the industry is working to achieve balance. In order to maintain the mutuality of interest that joins consumers, marketers and publishers in a 'virtuous circle', such balance is critical.

- *Programmability*: marketers increasingly demand more variability and programmability in their campaigns. In the future, it will not suffice simply to determine whether to deliver a creative to an individual at a specific time. More and more, marketers will want options as to *what* creative they serve, and across what particular channel (ie video or banner ad, e-mail, SMS, television or radio).

A changing business model

As the industry addresses some of these challenges, it is also undergoing a fundamental shift in how its business is modelled. Today, programmatic advertising is overly complicated and in many ways inefficient. If it seems that there are too many three-letter acronyms and categories to remember (SSPs, DSPs, DMPs, sell-side servers, buy-side servers) – and too many marketplace categories (RTB, PMPs, automated guaranteed, deals) to master – that's because there are!

Industry experts anticipate that as more 'point solution' companies – meaning, companies that can only perform one or two functions on either the sell side or buy side – are absorbed by larger players, much of this complexity will fade away. In the end analysis, the surviving platforms will perform the classic functions of a digital marketplace by powering trade, providing credit and clearing, ensuring quality and transparency, and offering reporting and analytics.

If this transformation takes place, advertisers and publishers will no longer need to sew together an inefficient patchwork of point solutions. They will have the option of using one platform to execute sales, serve ads and track monetization and performance. The result will be not only simplicity but, equally important, less friction and latency, coupled with greater efficiency.

For advertisers and publishers alike, consolidation may herald a welcome change – commoditization. Not only does complexity open the door to arbitrage, inefficiency, latency and fraud, it also takes an enormous bite out of advertising dollars. Simply put, more actors in the middle mean less power behind spend.

As the model shifts from stitched-together point solutions to single platforms, services that used to take a significant cut – whether from ad serving, data integration, reporting, viewability, etc – will become commoditized and even standard.

Why should advertisers pay extra for viewability reporting if they are using a single platform? Why should publishers pay extra for managing waterfalls if the single platform they use can manage allocation and yield across multiple marketplaces (eg RTB, deals, automated guaranteed)? Why should anyone carve out extra budget for a single-channel video vendor when a single platform can power exchanges across formats (video, audio, display) and devices (mobile, desktop, tablet)?

One of the great frustrations with ad tech is that it can chip away at a dollar more quickly than the tax man. That reality is about to change, and companies that cannot adapt to this era of commoditization will be left behind.

All about video 10

Introduction

Unless you have been hiding under a rock, you will know that video marketing has become a mainstay in the arsenal of the digital marketer. Not just on YouTube or Vimeo but, permeating throughout the whole customer experience and engagement strategies, video has brought a grown-up sense of quality branding and interaction to the brand/customer relationship.

Here our good friend Iolo Jones, one of the world's leading experts in the video world, collaborates with Stephen Woodgate of Microsoft, to bring you avid readers a chapter that is brand new to this fourth edition of *Understanding Digital Marketing*.

Lights, camera, action...

Video goes mainstream

Iolo Jones

Once upon a time, creating a film or video was an expensive operation requiring a team of producers and technicians. As a result, video only played a peripheral role in the marketing mix, especially outside very large organizations.

Meanwhile, operating a TV channel was the realm of media moguls with millions, if not billions, in the bank and the idea that a brand could operate their own channel was beyond consideration.

Now, of course, this has all changed. Thanks to the advent of cheaper technologies, including the internet and cloud-based platforms, anyone can have a shot at becoming a media mogul or including video as a core tool in the marketing mix of their organization.

But whilst any company or body can have a website or a social media profile, that does not necessarily translate into success in terms of exposure, marketing or revenue. This chapter looks at the techniques, tools and skills required to deploy a successful video marketing campaign.

Video has always been an engaging medium and is now a mainstream part of the marketing mix. It is increasingly being used in brand communications. One of the major reasons for this is that distribution of video is now both cheap and easy.

Gone are the days when you needed to duplicate VHS tapes or DVDs and then mail or hand them out in their hundreds or thousands. (The cost of producing video has also declined as the tools of the trade become much more accessible and cheaper, and increasing numbers of people become proficient in using them.)

But, just as with every other part of the marketing mix, when developing a video marketing strategy you need to think about content and context as well as technology and distribution. Just as you would not be advised to produce an ad and place it in just one publication or use a Facebook page as your website, you need to be able to distribute your video content to multiple outlets, platforms, apps and online systems and maintain your branding and the user experience across all of them.

The technical bits

Even if you are not technically orientated, some understanding of the technology underlying the field can be useful, so here goes...

Before doing anything else, you have to compress the video so that the video files or a live feed is small enough to be transmitted over the internet. Although the availability of superfast broadband is gradually becoming a reality, it should be remembered that in many developing countries, and in rural areas of many developed countries, ubiquitous fast broadband remains some way off. There is also the additional complication of data caps, which means that if your video stream is too large the user could be charged to watch it, resulting in the viewer actually paying to watch your content. So, video compression is important.

Today it is usual to compress a video or video stream into multiple data rates that will adapt to suit the bandwidth available to the viewer – someone watching on a mobile phone over 3G may get a stream at 500Kbps, whilst a viewer on Wi-Fi and a home fibre connection may watch at 7Mbps or greater. What is important here is the data rate, not the resolution – 1080p, the standard for TV HD, just defines the size of the screen and not how much data is being presented. Obviously, the higher the data rate, the better the quality but also the greater the cost.

Once the video is compressed it then needs to be served to the viewer. Unlike TV broadcasts where everyone watches the same signal, the vast majority of internet TV video is unicast, meaning that every viewer gets their own stream. The advantage of this is that the end user can have much more control over their stream – theoretically, for example, you can customize the stream for every viewer, eg showing different ads to viewers in different locations. The downside is that this uses massive amounts of bandwidth, all of which can cost to be delivered. Content delivery networks (CDNs) were developed in response to the need to massively scale unicast delivery. Companies such as Limelight, Akamai, Verizon and Level 3 built massive networks that would scale to meet demand (services such as YouTube that are 'free' to use subsidize the cost by using their own networks and generating ad revenue).

Finally, when the stream arrives at the user's device it has to be decoded and presented in a player or app. These days this could be on a PC or Mac, a smartphone, tablet or a smart TV. Of course, video streams can also be delivered into lifts and taxis, for example, or on to large billboards and seats at sporting events, and each of these has its own technical challenges (ie think how difficult it is to make a call from a major sporting event). Buffering has long been the enemy of effective online video delivery and this is where a good CDN plays its part.

There are other technical considerations: a lot of the time you will be happy if your content is distributed and copied, but in certain instances you may need to protect it from copying and piracy using encryption or digital rights management (DRM).

It is also worth being aware of the difference between live streams and on-demand video. Live streams demand specialist equipment and, usually, the use of a CDN is not an option. However, on-demand videos can be treated similarly to other internet content, the only difference being that the files have to be prepared so that they start to play video before the whole file has downloaded. Its ability to do this is a key reason why the MP4 file format has become the dominant video streaming at the expense of other file types such as MOV.

Some statistics on video marketing

The consumption of video over the internet may have been slow to start off, but it has developed into a flood; Netflix alone is now estimated to account for more than one-third of all bandwidth consumption on the internet (http://variety.com/2015/digital/news/netflix-bandwidth-usage-internet-traffic-1201507187/). The adoption of large-screen smartphones and other internet-connected devices is pushing digital video consumption rates through the roof.

Online video now accounts for 50 per cent of all mobile traffic and in 2015 online video accounted for 64 per cent of all consumer internet traffic, and this number is expected to rise to 69 per cent by 2017 and 79 per cent by 2018; 78 per cent of people watch videos online every week and 55 per cent of people watch videos every day (https://marketinginsidergroup.com/content-marketing/9818/).

Advertisers are naturally keen to go to where their audience is and, as a result, there has been a commensurate increase on expenditure in online video advertising, with $5 billion spent in the United States alone in 2015 (http://uk.businessinsider.com/social-media-advertising-spending-growth-2014-9?r=US&IR=T).

A major trend is the move towards watching video on ever smaller screens. The tablet share of video starts declined 7 per cent year over year, while the smartphone share is up 33 per cent; 46 per cent of all video plays in Q4 2015 were on mobile devices like tablets and smartphones (http://www.ooyala.com/videomind/blog/paid-media-ad-spend-climbing-5-2016-mobile-catches-tv). The smartphone has essentially replaced the tablet as the mobile video-viewing device of choice, its rise aided by the adoption of larger-screen smartphones (http://www.slideshare.net/adobe/adobe-digital-index-q3-digital-video-report).

The role of video advertising

Of course, video is now widely used within advertising campaigns, so let's briefly look at this sector.

Whereas the US $5 billion value of the market is impressive, this is still some way behind the $55 billion TV advertising market, but is growing much more rapidly. However, much of the potential growth has been hampered by the difficulties in matching advertisers with suitable video publishing opportunities. Existing TV broadcaster sites and portals like YouTube and Facebook account for the vast majority of this advertising spend, with Twitter recently announcing in 2016 that it had purchased NFL rights for $100 million in order to try to get in on this lucrative model (https://nflcommunications.com/Pages/National-Football-League-and-Twitter-Announce-Streaming-Partnership-for-Thursday-Night-Football.aspx).

The choices you have in buying media space for video adverts are mainly:

- Programmatic buying through an online platform or marketplace such as DoubleClick Ad Exchange (owned by Google).
- Buying directly from a major portal such as YouTube or Facebook.
- Buying direct from a variety of targeted sites offering 'native' ad serving.

Each of these has its advantages, but the direct buying probably has the most opportunities for impact.

Product placement is again a traditional technique largely used by film producers. The cars, watches, computers and even retail and food outlets you see in the movies often are not there by chance – they have paid for the placement. Now marketeers are increasingly placing their products with vloggers who can both endorse and promote their product to their audience. There is some controversy over the transparency of such arrangements and both voluntary and regulatory codes are being introduced.

Promoted distribution – services such as LinkedIn – have introduced the ability to promote content and this is likely to become another technique for the paid distribution of programming. Basically this guarantees you more eyeballs for your video on rapidly updating social portals.

Content investment versus media investment

Of course, paying for distribution of content takes budget and this budget could equally be spent on content production. In traditional TV advertising the cost of producing commercials has been eclipsed by the cost of the media buy. However, online the correlation is more difficult to assess and this is a value judgement you will need to make in planning your campaign.

Programmatic versus placement

Automatically playing your adverts into video content relevant to your audience may seem sensible, but the majority of programmatic buying is done on a behavioural basis. It is enough for a viewer to search for a lawnmower and then they will be shown lawnmower commercials. For mass-market campaigns this automation has its benefits in terms of reach and, to some degree, emulates how television advertising has long operated – the majority of TV advertising being purchased based on delivering audience units in television viewer ratings (TVRs), not necessarily in placing ads against relevant content.

If you are selling lawnmowers this may be the sensible approach to the market, but if your budget is more limited, or your audience is narrower, it may be worth being more flexible and searching out specific web channels and apps that will better complement your industry or context.

When to use video in marketing

Video marketing is yet another tool within the overall marketing mix and begs the question 'when should I use video?' But before looking at the context perhaps the first question to ask is 'why should I use video?'

If a picture is worth a thousand words, a video can have impact well beyond this. Think of how you react to each medium: words can inform, communicate details and even persuade; pictures leave an impression, whilst moving images can elicit emotion and make an impression that is unique. Video is therefore an essential tool in brand building. It is also a great tool for explaining – the number of 'how to' channels is not surprising given the clarity that video can bring to training and education.

However, although video can be a strong medium to put your message across, it can be difficult to get right. In a survey of marketing professionals (https://www.vidyard.com/ascend-2-the-benchmarks-for-video-marketing-victory/), the top five barriers to successful video marketing were said to be:

- lack of effective strategy (44 per cent);
- inadequate video budget (41 per cent);
- lack of compelling content (40 per cent);
- lack of production resources (39 per cent);
- lack of performance metrics (30 per cent).

Let's look at how you can get around each of the above with a well-thought-through plan for implementing video marketing within your organization.

YouTube is not a video marketing strategy

YouTube has become synonymous with online video, but although the site has an important role in your online video marketing, presuming that YouTube is the answer to a video marketing strategy may be a bad idea for many reasons, including:

- YouTube may be the largest online site for video, but there are other increasingly important outlets, including Facebook, Instagram and Twitter.

- You cannot fully control how your content appears – competitor adverts may overlay your own video even on your own website if you use a YouTube embed.

- On YouTube itself it is likely that competitor videos will appear recommended alongside your content, even if you manage your own channel.

- The terms for using YouTube are well defined by Google and you should get your legal advisers to review the YouTube terms and conditions.

We have seen companies spend six-figure sums on producing content for YouTube campaigns and then achieve only a few hundred views per video. YouTube these days is a very crowded place and standing out is difficult.

Of course, this does not mean that YouTube does not have a very valuable role to play in your video marketing strategy, but it needs to be balanced and used in combination with other opportunities.

Expert view
Video marketing
Contribution by Steven Woodgate, Microsoft

Embracing the new digital era

Digital is more significant than the Industrial Revolution. Just think about that very concept for a moment. And the biggest thing about that statement: we just don't know it yet.

Pragmatically, the digital economy will supersede all earlier 'revolutions' in its wealth creation. Obviously, change of this magnitude understandably causes uncertainty and insecurity.

How can digital be more significant than the transition to new manufacturing processes? From the 1760s to some time between 1820 and 1840 there was a big transformation of how we saw the world, how we operated – the world changed. We went from hand-production methods – where you would get dirt and oil under your fingernails – to machines. Not the machines you see now, but huge machines. We saw new chemical manufacturing and iron-production processes, improved efficiency of water power, the increasing use of steam power and the development of machine tools.

The Industrial Revolution marked a major turning point in history. Almost every aspect of life was influenced in some way. Average income increased and there was unprecedented sustained growth in population; the concept of 'standard of living' was introduced. It was the first time that technological innovation really kicked in for the masses – and industrialization increased wealth for all.

However, during this time there was intellectual and artistic hostility towards industrialization development. The Romantics stressed the importance of 'nature' in art and language, in contrast to these 'monstrous' machines and factories.

The Luddites – a group of 19th-century English textile workers – protested against these newly developed labour-economizing technologies as machines threatened to replace workers. The technological advancements ultimately jeopardized their role and they were replaced by less-skilled, low-wage labourers, leaving them without work.

There were people who went around smashing the very machines that were going to make them a living. They didn't want to embrace machines or, more probably, the uncertain future. They didn't want to embrace technology, or what we see as better ways of doing things. But what was interesting was that the people who were scared of the technology started to embrace it. They built things. They made things better. More importantly, they started to make money.

Come to the present day: where does YouTube fit into this scenario? It is a platform allowing anyone armed with a smartphone and poor Wi-Fi connection to become a millionaire and an overnight sensation. We are now in an era formed by a digital revolution, which has transformed information into an easily accessible commodity by the way of wearables and screens as small as pennies. Collecting any sort of information has become virtually effortless.

▶

'Gen C' is a powerful new force. One we didn't see coming. And certainly one that has made all marketers sit up to take notice. The YouTubers are the people who are redefining and re-establishing the rules of media consumption and scrapping our existing rulebooks of making money.

Gen C is used to describe people who care ever-so-deeply about creation, curation, connection and community. 'YouTubers' are now building community influence in society – 65 per cent are under 35, but they nevertheless span generations.

Love them or loathe them, they are becoming marketers' new best friends forever, or BFFs.

Connection

Empowered by the consumerization of technology, all Gen C need is a smartphone and some Wi-Fi and – bang – a 'YouTuber' is born. It is remarkably easy. Well, it looks it. These YouTubers, or indeed 'influencers', have built a global fan base on their YouTube channels, with audiences bigger than they know what to do with. As YouTube has grown – in 2016, 800 million people visit the streaming site each month, and 72 hours of video are uploaded every minute – kids who once messed around with poor video cameras and slow internet connections are now older, wiser and are taking on the entertainment industry. They have embraced the machines that threatened to end workforces.

Gen C seek out authentic content that they can consume across all online platforms and all screens, whenever and wherever they want. One of the reasons why these Gen C are somewhat precious, is because they are most incredibly difficult to reach with 'traditional' media – whatever 'traditional' means nowadays.

However, one thing that is certain is that we haven't seen the full extent of the Digital Revolution in our lifetime just yet.

The main values that really drove the Industrial Revolution – self-interest and entrepreneurial spirit – are making a surge in YouTubers. In an age of posting Facebook pictures of cats, and tweeting inane things about Kim Kardashian, we are in a 'self-interest world' and there are many who are trying to capitalize on making money from telling everyone about their lives, ie vloggers.

Back to the Industrial Revolution: many industrial advances were made that resulted in huge increase in personal wealth. These advancements greatly benefited society, as well as many youngsters who could only dream of earning such money.

Understanding the Industrial Revolution

With the advent of new technologies, mass-produced goods could be created and sold more cheaply and quickly than ever before, inciting a surge of production and consumption. With the explosion of manufacturing and trade, the rich who owned businesses got even richer. Middle-class factory owners who were very successful were able to move into the upper class. The tremendous new wealth created by industrialization allowed the upper class to build huge mansions, collect fine art and erect museums and libraries. The privileged social group had always enjoyed prosperity, but now they achieved a new realm of luxury and extravagance.

As a group, the middle class saw enormous benefits from the Industrial Revolution. The growth of new businesses and factories created thousands of new jobs. The middle class itself grew in size as occupations such as merchants, shopkeepers and accountants allowed the working class to lift themselves into a higher social stratum. As these workers earned more, they were able to take advantage of newly affordable luxuries such as furniture and fine clothing, giving themselves a comfortable life. They were also able to educate their children, so that their social standing would be maintained or even rise with the next generation.

For the poor and working-class people, their lives changed but did not necessarily improve. For centuries before the Industrial Revolution, the lower classes had earned their living through jobs in agriculture; now they worked in factories. Because factory work was usually easier than working in the fields, women and children joined the workforce in huge numbers. Wages, though, were very low, and even with an entire family working, it was hard to earn a decent living. Furthermore, the working conditions were often filthy, dangerous – or both. At the very least, the work was repetitive and menial in nature. As families needing jobs sought work in factories, they swarmed into cities, and the cities became overcrowded and rife with disease. Children who worked all day did not go to school, and so did not receive an education or advance themselves.

The Industrial Revolution had a lasting impact on all people, but not all classes benefited equally. Those who could take advantage of the better jobs or professions, or those who were lucky enough to be business owners, were able to enjoy comfort, privilege and leisure in many ways. Those who were uneducated and limited to unskilled labour often remained stuck at the bottom of the economic pile. Their working and living conditions lacked any comfort or safety, and their lives were often miserable, or at best, dreary and dead-end.

▶

It sounds depressing, but this is why the Digital Revolution is more significant than the Industrial Revolution. It is creating a space and a generation that is focused on doing good – armed with a smartphone and Wi-Fi they are able to achieve anything. Similar to the Industrial Revolution, however, the digital advance is due to the presence of an entrepreneurial class that believes in progress, technology and hard work.

The Digital Revolution

Think about the world we are in now. There has literally never been a better time to add value; there has never been a better time to share knowledge and views with the world. Innovation is at full throttle. Young professionals are making their mark in almost every industry. We are inspired to challenge, create new processes and develop new 'things'.

However, as with those who opposed the Industrial Revolution, so there has been some hostility towards digital. The primary reason that people feel insecure is because the impact and consequence of the digital economy are difficult to predict or envisage. It is not commonly known what this new digital economy actually looks likes, as we are still in the early days. People can't see it – they don't know what is in store. Most people don't understand how technology may affect them personally. Traditional institutions that society has historically relied upon to help us with such change – schools, politics, religion – are now struggling to keep pace with these developments.

However, we are no longer seeing the smashing of machines, but an uplift in inspiration, innovation and ideation. Not only are these Gen C youngsters connected and collaborative – they are also brilliant and bizarre.

YouTubers will start to become the mainstay. From interviews with the president to involvement in political debates, they have become increasingly more involved in the political landscape, bringing the younger generations with them.

Gen C is becoming more actively involved in important societal issues: ranging from politics to referendums to good causes. Propaganda is a source of heavy influence in every important debate or advertising campaign, but as technology progresses, propaganda is forced to evolve with it. Television commercials, digital signs and banners, graphics and social media campaigns have become increasingly prevalent across many walks of life, their presence dominating every form of media. This is persuading brands and marketers to place responsibility on one of the most prominent platforms to get their message out: YouTube.

Yet one thing is for certain: the future is utterly predictable.

Yes, predictable. We are going to see how digital will change things in the future. How digital and the next waves of generations will crack certain issues and work out how life can be made easier. We are now actually throwing the steering wheels out of our cars, and letting a new wave of advancement guide us. Following YouTube, we are seeing the rise of individuals on Instagram and Snapchat. Technology is enabling amazing things to happen – and as marketers it has never been as important to us as it is now, and to our consumers.

Over the next five years to 2021, 2 billion of the world's population will be considered as 'middle class'. That is incredible. More people will have connected devices and the 'internet of things' will actually be integrated into everything.

However, one of the issues we now face is that the industry uses terms like: programmatic buys, big data, automated trading desks, real-time bidding, clickbots, etc. Similar to industrialization, we are being dazzled by overcomplex jargon.

With this, we are essentially driving efficiency over effectiveness – exactly what those who went through the Industrial Revolution thought. We are under threat of missing the bigger picture. And, yes, technology can drive great efficiencies, but how can it deliver great effectiveness?

The younger generations will grow up with this fantastic infrastructure of digital that will change the course of the future and how we see the world. If you thought we have come a long way, we haven't even touched the surface.

The essentials of a video marketing campaign

Essentially, there are five elements to consider when launching an online video campaign:

- context;
- ideas and content;
- production;
- management and distribution;
- metrics.

Context

Deciding when to use video is perhaps the toughest call. Here are some pointers.

According to research amongst marketers, brand building is the most popular reason for using internet video, with 52 per cent of marketing managers selecting this as their main reason for adopting the medium; 45 per cent use it for lead generation and 42 per cent for online engagement (http://www.insidecxm.com/video-marketing-next-big-thing-digital-marketing-2015/).

According to a survey, the most effective types of video used (http://www.reelseo.com/top-video-marketing-advice-2015/) are:

- customer testimonials (52 per cent);
- demonstration videos (51 per cent);
- explainer/tutorial videos (51 per cent);
- thought-leader interviews (36 per cent);
- project reviews and case studies (26 per cent);
- webinars (20 per cent);
- vlogs (15 per cent).

Of course, these will change from context to context and from sector to sector. Videos can be highly effective in increasing conversion rates for e-commerce, for example.

Ideas and content

Coming up with a good idea can be the toughest task for any marketing campaign, and so it goes for a video marketing initiative. The general rule is to keep it simple and relevant, particularly if budget is an issue.

Every business and every brand should have a voice, and a video is a great way of shouting out to the world. Ideas don't have to be clever, they just need to be sound and in context. Try asking: what is my audience interested in? How do I inform, educate and/or entertain them (see: http://www.bbc.co.uk/historyofthebbc/research/culture/reith-1)?

Moreover, online video comes in all shapes and sizes, so it is important to consider the format of your campaign as well. Often you can use the same content in different ways, and it is important that your idea works across these formats.

Imagine a sports event where you can post a howler as a Vine movie, distributed on Twitter and Facebook for wider reach, then post a short edited film on YouTube, Tudou and Daily Motion. The extended highlights go on your website and mobile app whilst the full coverage, live and on demand, is syndicated to national broadcasters and web services around the world.

A major sporting event might be exceptional, but variations on this approach can be followed for everything from product launches to press conferences. And, as with all marketing activity, you can mix in your own ideas, voice and creative concepts.

Long versus short

In an interesting study it was found that the optimal length for video engagement was 81 seconds on Facebook, but 890 seconds on YouTube (http://www.reelseo.com/length-youtube-video/). There may be some cause and effect at work here, since it has taken a decade for YouTube to establish itself as a long-form medium, and Facebook is much more recent in its adoption of video.

Nevertheless, most studies show that viewers actually gravitate towards long-form video online: one study found that 95 per cent of all video content on publisher websites was under five minutes in length (Ooyala, 2016), but the same study found that of the most popular videos the average length was 24 minutes.

Choose your format

Here is a more detailed view of some of the formats you can produce as part of your video marketing campaign.

Channels

The reduction in costs and availability of management tools makes it easier than ever to launch and run your own TV channel. However, it should be remembered that TV channels change their programming every day, and to retain engagement with your audience you will need to produce or acquire fresh content on a regular basis. Also, channels no longer belong on one distribution outlet, so you may need to manage your channel across your own website, YouTube and a series of apps.

Producing channels from existing investments, eg sponsorships

If your organization is already investing in content-friendly areas then why not leverage this? Anything from charity work to sports sponsorship can make interesting and engaging viewing.

Instructional or product videos

One of the most common forms of online videos is that explaining a product or service on a company's web and mobile pages. At its most basic level, this can be simply produced using screencams.

B-roll, video news releases and support material

Once upon a time there used to be thousands of producers of video and TV. Now there are millions and they all need content to produce their videos, from news organizations to vloggers. You can make available general shots and views of your industry (make sure the sign with the company name appears in shot!) and distribute these freely.

Produced videos

Of course, the vast majority of content will be in the form of finished videos, often produced professionally and with high production values. Produced videos can adopt genres such as animation, drama, documentary or news, which will inform their format. Indeed, selecting such a format can be fundamental to the success of a production. The manufacturer of watches or soft drinks might select a documentary on extreme sports, whereas a pharma company may choose an interview with a panel of experts. We will look at this in more detail later on in this chapter.

Live feeds

The world moves fast in the internet era and producing live feeds provides a sense of occasion. Again, the subject can be anything from a new product launch to a world-record attempt. However, producing and streaming live events takes a very different approach to making on-demand videos and, again, you will find a guide below.

Webinars

Webinars are an instructional form of live streaming, with a presenter talking at a certain time about a relevant subject. Viewers can be invited to join in and the sessions are often interactive, with a presentation followed by questions and answers. You can also archive the production for later viewing.

Serials

Posting regularly updated content can help build audiences over a period of time and help the virality of the content.

Vlogging and livecasting

Perhaps there is no phenomenon more unique to the world of internet TV than the rise of vloggers. A smartphone and a camera are seemingly enough to become a global megastar, courted by leading brands. But, of course, it is not as easy as this. For every successful vlogger there are literally a million wannabes. The reality is that only a few hundred individuals outside larger media organizations make a living through this medium, but those who do find success are increasingly influential.

The majority of successful vloggers focus on narrow subject areas and, in narrow marketplaces, the size of an audience is hardly important. Rather, it is the quality of the viewers that counts. There has been a rise in companies such as Maker Studios (now part of Disney) who specialize in aggregating and marketing many vlogging sites.

Self-casting

A recent development has been the introduction of self-casting services such as Periscope and Meerkat, enabling users to go live from their mobile to the world wherever they are. At the time of writing this functionality is also being adopted by larger players such as YouTube.

Ultra short form

There is a tradition of ultra short-form content on the internet, starting with animated gifs. This content works on the premise that users have a very short attention span. Of course, it is difficult to communicate anything substantive in an 8- or 15-second video, but services such as Vine and Instagram's Boomerang have seen massive adoption for unique and quirky content – the video equivalent of a tweet.

Production

The production process for an online video in 2016 is little different to that followed by movie producers in the 1930s (or, indeed, TV and film producers today) – it may only be the resources that are different.

There are three key stages to the development of content:

1 *Pre-production*: this is the scripting and planning of the production – working out what resources you need, when and at what cost. You may produce a script, a storyboard, a schedule and a budget. You may need to undertake casting to find your talent, or negotiate with agents if you are working with celebrities. You will need to find one or more locations to film your magnum opus and you may need permission to film, not only from the location owner, but often from the local authorities such as councils. You may need an editor, an edit suite, a special-effects company, animators and graphic designers. Of course, you will need equipment for filming and the right mix of crew and front-of-camera talent to turn your idea into a reality. The great director John Boorman once succinctly described this process as 'money into light'.

2 *Production*: once you have completed the pre-production comes the actual work of filming your video. Of course, it would be as easy as thinking of something to say, switching on the camera on your laptop and pressing a button, but the reality is that it is often going to take a lot more than that. And what you are trying to do will inevitably cost more and take more time than you expect, so make sure you have a contingency for everything.

3 *Post-production*: ah, but the hard work is not over yet. Whether you are selecting a 15-second clip for Instagram or undertaking a full edit with special effects and an original music score, the magic only happens when you pull together your final production.

All of the above may seem daunting – after all, there is a reason why the TV and video production industry is full of very talented individuals who are as expert at producing video as you are at promoting your organization. Hiring a producer and a director to look after the business and creative sides of your production respectively may save you a lot of sleepless nights.

Once you have completed your production you then need to consider how to manage your content and this is dealt with in the distribution section below.

Going live

Producing live events is very different from producing on-demand video. Of course, you go through the pre-production stage where you plan and schedule and budget. But then things change:

- Getting the signal out: the first thing to consider is that you will need to get a signal from the venue or location where the live event is happening to the internet. The expensive way to do this is to push out a broadcast signal via microwave or satellite; the cheap way is to use the venue's existing internet connection. If you go down the latter route you will need to make sure that you have at least 2Mbps upstream uncontended, or not shared with other users, for a reliable feed.

- Managing the event: a live event does not allow for second takes, so it is essential to ensure that you know what you are doing, that you have a director looking after proceedings and good communications on the ground so that staff can talk to each other.

- Scaling the feed: for live events attracting an audience of more than a couple of hundred, a CDN is essential to scale the stream to reach thousands or even hundreds of thousands. The CDN should also be able to look after converting the feed so that it works on various devices and platforms.

It is worth pointing out at this stage that most corporate networks were not built to accept incoming streaming media at any scale and this may curtail your ambitions to livecast the CEO's last speech – there are times when, for technical reasons, on-demand trumps live.

There are services, such as that from Globelynx, which provide a turnkey going live solution for live streams, comprising a camera/lighting box with a web connection directly to a CDN.

Management and distribution

Many organizations believe that video distribution begins and ends with YouTube. However, as important as the ubiquitous Google service is, Twitter and Facebook, and even Instagram in certain instances, are also important for building an audience. But perhaps most important of all is the ability to build your own channel and destination whilst maintaining the ability to control distribution across a wide range of outlets.

It is worth thinking in terms of 'video everywhere' when planning your distribution strategy. Figure 10.1 shows just some of the outlets that you can consider.

Platforms and tools for video marketing

As with most marketing disciplines, technology underpins video marketing and there are a number of options to consider on how to tackle the technical aspects of the discipline. Organizations can build an in-house team, use third-party platforms or integrate shareware to manage their campaigns, or employ an agency or production company specializing in this area.

So, which is right for you? Well, of course, it depends. With a small budget you will probably end up doing everything yourself. You can use your laptop or mobile for filming; tools that are already to hand such as Microsoft PowerPoint for animation and graphics; and the shareware Camstudio for

Figure 10.1 Video distribution outlets

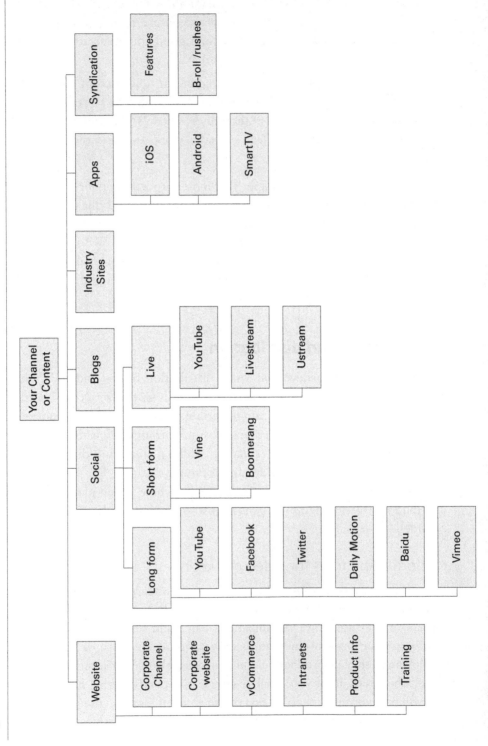

grabbing screens. There are lots of very cheap desktop editing packages available and you can manually manage the upload of content. Don't forget to factor in the investment in time that all of this will take, particularly if you are on a steep learning curve. Sometimes doing it yourself can be a false economy.

Your web developer is likely to have some experience in using services such as YouTube, Vimeo or JW Player to integrate video into websites on a basic level so that the video can be integrated and distributed once produced.

If you are more sophisticated you may use suites of tools from companies such as Adobe, Avid or Apple for production – if you bring in outside professionals (or indeed employ your own) they are likely to use similar tools. You can also consider investing in video platforms from companies such as Brightcove, Kaltura, Ooyala and VidZapper, which enable you to manage your video across your own web and mobile properties as well as other properties, portals and social sites.

If you have a serious budget then you can farm out your video marketing and video management to the increasing number of agencies and production companies specializing in this area.

The importance of meta-data

The importance of meta-data in your distribution cannot be overstated – think of it as 'video SEO'. Despite fantastic advancement in image and voice recognition, a programme that can 'see' video content remains a distant reality, so the best way to ensure that your content can be contextualized and indexed by web search engines (including your own) is to use effective meta-data.

Essentially, meta-data is information about data and is a way of describing the content of a video (see: http://www.videouniversity.com/articles/metadata-for-video/). This may be as simple as a meaningful title, or as complex as a full transcript:

- title;
- short description;
- keywords and tags;
- long description;
- transcript or closed captions.

Meta-data comes in two formats: encapsulated and associated. Encapsulated meta-data is included in the actual video file and is generally accessible to players, readers and bots by 'reading' the file. Most encapsulated meta-data tends to be technical in nature. However, it can be difficult to author without specialist tools and is often overlooked. The most basic thing to do is to give your video file a meaningful name such as '<The event> on <this date> on <this subject> for <our company>.mp4'.

Associated meta-data is a separate file that provides information about a video file. It is sometimes called a 'sidecar'. This may be very detailed and contain information about cast, producers, directors, rights positions, audio tracks, etc. It is usually held in an XML format, which is machine-readable by search bots and search engines, or can be set according to a predefined schema such as MRSS. Video feeds can also be defined using schemas such as MRSS so that multiple videos can be associated and made available to third-party services, including search engines.

If you want to optimize your chance of being discovered, we would recommend optimizing both sets of meta-data above.

Analytics and metrics

After spending budget, resources and effort on planning, producing, managing and distributing your videos you will want to see a return on your investment. You will therefore need to measure and analyse the feedback and metrics from your video marketing campaigns.

One fundamental thing that should be understood is how differently TV or video metrics and internet metrics work. Traditionally (and still today in some of the largest TV markets such as New York City, unbelievably), TV is measured by a sample of residents keeping paper diaries on what they watch. In other markets such as the UK, slightly more sophisticated monitoring is implemented using 'black boxes' operated by organizations such as BARB and Nielsen. Audiences are measured in terms of television viewer ratings (TVRs) (see: https://en.wikipedia.org/wiki/Television_Viewer_Rating), which are calculated by 'reach x time spent'. However, measuring impressions across multiple media outlets (and using this to justify their reach) has proven to be a nightmare for broadcasters.

The internet, of course, is measured by impressions, based on unique viewers visiting a web page. This has resulted in very different approaches to the presentation of video online. Services such as YouTube, which come from an internet heritage, have traditionally supported and encouraged clicking. Online TV services follow the lead of their broadcast parents by encouraging linear viewing, with the maximum opportunity to show lucrative online ads.

So, the internet tends to reward clicking and activity whereas TV rewards passive viewing, or in other words, TV is 'lean back' and the internet is 'lean forward'. Most video platforms come with their own metrics and consequently the measurement of video delivery can be very different to that of serving websites or apps.

Before measuring anything, it is therefore important to consider what metrics are important to you. Here are some key metrics:

- Views: the total number of views across all videos.

- Unique videos: the total number of different videos viewed.

- Unique viewers: individual viewers usually identified by their IP address.

- Completion rates per video: this can help measure the engagement of a video.

- Sessions: the number of times a viewer accesses the channel or app in a given period.

- Viewing time: the total amount of videos watched by all viewers in duration.

- Average time per viewer: the average time a viewer spends watching video.

- Average videos per viewer: the average number of videos viewed by viewers.

- Average session per viewer: the average number of times a viewer accesses the channel or app over a given period.

- Average time per session: the average length of time each viewer spends in an individual visit.

- Average videos per session: the average number of videos viewed per session.

For advertising or call-to-action videos the number of click-throughs or engagements might be important.

It should be noted that for all its vicissitudes, the measurement of online video is at present far more accurate than that of traditional television, where small representative samples of an audience are used to represent the full cohort. However, the result is that TV tends to oversample compared to internet metrics.

Gathering information from third parties

Most of the leading video portals provide both dashboards and application programming interfaces (APIs) to enable you to see how your videos are performing on their services. Unfortunately, at the time of writing no easy way exists to track your video across the multitude of distribution outlets on the internet. This is certain to be addressed in the near future, but in the meantime you will need to use a bespoke or manual solution.

Future development in video marketing

So, what comes next?

Video marketing has come from nowhere in under a decade to claim a meaningful part of many organizations' marketing budgets. Online video is commanding much higher revenues than online display advertising and is therefore seen as a priority for major sites and apps such as mainstream newspapers. One thing is for certain, more and more video and TV will be consumed on internet-connected devices, including an increasing proportion on smartphones. The evolution from the shackles of web- and television-based models is likely to continue and new, original formats will appear, particularly in areas such as advertorial and sponsored content and vCommerce.

Distribution will continue to fragment with more and more opportunities to use video arising. It is likely that larger companies will employ agencies specializing in video marketing, or their existing agencies will evolve to make this a more core part of the service they offer to clients.

Better tools will appear to produce, manage and particularly to measure the return on investment for video marketing campaigns. New formats will appear and formats such as sponsored productions are likely to become more commonplace. There will be a move to 'me TV', away from prescribed content delivery, where the user is in control of their own content mix.

Above all, the best way of predicting the future is to invent it, so the next stage in development is down to you and your video marketing campaigns.

Expert view

Inside perspective on the future of video marketing
Contribution by Kerry Gaffney, MOFILM

Where next with video?

That video is an important part of any digital marketer's toolkit, and will remain to be so, is a simple forecast that can be made with some confidence. A far more difficult matter to predict with such ease is what video in the future, even the next year or two, will look like; how it will be distributed, via what platforms, existing or new; and how people will watch or experience it.

Let's start with the simple notion that video will continue to be important because it is an effective tool for supporting most marketing objectives. When done well, it is particularly adept at raising brand awareness and message recall, but it can also drive intent and build customer loyalty. In 2015, a study by Nielsen revealed that a short view of an online video ad, a view of even less than one second, still improved ad recall, brand awareness and consideration to buy. This lift increased in line with the period of time that a film was viewed. Several studies have also concluded that online video is more effective than television commercials when comparing their effectiveness for message and brand recall.

Video is also important because it is clear that it is something that internet users enjoy sharing, creating and engaging with. While TV viewing figures are in decline, viewing figures on platforms like Facebook, Instagram, Snapchat, Vine and YouTube continue to grow at pace.

Then we come to the not so simple: what will video look like? When thinking about the 'what next' for video, it is easy to get overexcited by technology and the endless possibilities it brings. Today most video storytelling is linear, and is experienced through flat, two-dimensional screens. But what will it become once virtual-reality headsets are in every home? Or when 360-degree cameras, which negate the need to be a skilled editor, are just as cheap as a smartphone? Facebook and YouTube already enable users to upload 360-degree films. It is the lack of good-quality hardware at a good price that is currently holding people back from creating and sharing video in this format. That will change.

By 2021, will deciding to watch a video mean putting on a headset and completely immersing yourself in an alternate world? Will watching a film become more akin to a video-game experience, in which a viewer can explore the entire world? Will we expect to be able to create our own stories – a new take on the choose-your-own-ending books from our childhoods?

Could video become an intrinsic part of our everyday world through the next generation of wearables, augmenting our day-to-day reality? Or is this all hype and, after a brief flurry of experimentation, will video creation and consumption carry on as normal?

While there will be video content that pushes the boundaries of technology and storytelling there will still be a need for more pragmatic

▶

and prosaic video content. Consider, for a moment, how far we have come in the past decade or so since YouTube launched, and yet how little has also changed. In 2005, video meant an old-fashioned hardware format for watching films at home and most marketers only thought in 30-second blocks – a time length that has been dictated by the networks selling space between programmes since the advent of television advertising itself. It was not an uncommon phenomenon then, or unfortunately now, for brands to use YouTube as a new place to put their TV commercials and little else. Not much thought was given to how the needs of someone viewing a video online might differ to someone watching TV.

In the former's case, they are most likely either seeking content or are following a recommendation from someone they trust. When watching TV, adverts could be regarded as a tax you pay to get cheaper access to the content you actually want. Although it is possible to create TV commercials that people enjoy watching and will seek out to watch again.

The different needs of the users of each of the current platforms, and whether they are a passive or an engaged audience, have already played a role within the evolution of video and will continue to do so. The various strengths and limitations of each platform will also, undoubtedly, continue to have an impact.

For example, we have already seen the rise of vertical, or portrait, video driven by the use of smartphones and platforms such as Snapchat. There are also indications that vertical videos elicit more engagement from viewers. Snapchat claims that vertical videos have a view completion rate that is nine times that of 'normal' films. While that may upset the film purists who prefer to shoot and view in the more traditional landscape, it is a user utility decision that should be recognized and taken into consideration when creating video for that platform.

Certainly it does not seem to be impacting the growth of Snapchat. Launched in 2011 it enables users to communicate through photos and short videos that disappear within 24 hours of being posted. Despite this time limitation, at the time of writing it has already reached over 7 million video views per day – not far behind one of the current major players in the video market, Facebook. Facebook began making improvements to its own video offering early in 2015. Before then few people uploaded video directly to the platform, usually sharing links from YouTube instead. By November 2015 it claimed it had hit over 8 billion views per day. YouTube, the platform that revolutionized online video when it launched in 2005, took five years achieve 2 billion daily views.

The growth of video as the preferred format through which internet users seek to be entertained, to be educated and to communicate is certain to continue. Less than half the world's population currently has internet access, and there are a variety of programmes to help the rest get online as quickly and cheaply as possible.

The interesting part of what's next for video is how those users will adopt, adapt and advance with the new video technologies that are now here.

Augmented and virtual reality: want to read more?

Alex Gibson is a senior lecturer in marketing at Dublin Institute of Technology, Ireland. He has recently been researching the application of augmented reality and virtual reality technologies for marketers. To read an exclusive article on augmented reality and virtual reality in digital marketing go to: www.koganpage.com/understanding-digital-marketing.

Video marketing tips

- Video is no longer a one-off production, but should be an ongoing part of your marketing mix.
- Think about what role video can play in your marketing mix and develop a plan accordingly.
- Develop a strategy that goes beyond YouTube – there are many other ways of reaching your audience.
- Focus on what your audience wants to see – inform, educate and/or entertain.
- Leverage existing investments such as sponsorships to create engaging content.
- If your budget is challenged then you can use available tools such as a mobile phone, PowerPoint and Camstudio to create content.
- Live video can create a sense of occasion, but is very different from producing on-demand content.

- There are many other formats to consider, from webinars and vlogging to launching your own channel.
- Video advertising can be effective, but consider placing your ads directly with sites that reach your audience.
- Use technology to make the implementation of campaigns easier.
- Implement granular metrics to track the effectiveness of your distribution.
- Measure engagement by how much of a video is viewed by length – a simple percentage figure can tell you a lot about the effectiveness of your content.

Our thanks to Iolo Jones who was the lead collaborator and writer of this chapter. For the past decade, Iolo has been the CEO of TV Everywhere and the chairperson of rights management software company Rights Tracker. For many years he also sat on the course board for leading film and TV college Ravensbourne. He runs a popular industry blog at http://www.iptvtimes.net.

CASE STUDY   Unilever Cornetto

How do you increase product awareness when you know your teenage audience is not watching TV and therefore not seeing your TV ads? Answer: by creating engaging content that truly entertains them, grabs their imagination and inspires them to share.

Location

UK, Mexico, Turkey, Indonesia, Russia, Thailand, Spain, Portugal, Greece, Philippines, South Africa, India, Italy, Netherlands, Germany.

Challenge

Cornetto wanted to raise awareness of its ice cream among love-struck teens. The content needed to resonate and create active engagement in multiple markets and languages.

Target audience

Love-struck teens.

Action

Cornetto has always stood for love, but as our Cupids would say: 'What the world really loves is not a lover but a love story.'

In 2012, MOFILM directors shot films in the United States, UK, Hong Kong and Turkey. Each film was 5–10 minutes in length and all shared a strong central structure. Localized versions were distributed via YouTube by the in-market Cornetto teams and were warmly received.

Year two was all about sharing the love. Seven different directors shot seven love stories in seven countries. This time the films featured celebrities and popular music. Each film was also recut into a music video and distributed online through celebrity influencer networks.

In 2015, Cupidity went to the next level with the film *Two Sides*. MOFILM worked with A Taste of Space, which specializes in creating immersive experiences in both the online and offline worlds.

The film told one story from two perspectives that the viewer could switch between in real time. It also incorporated 3D sound, so that viewers really felt they were inside the character's heads, experiencing all the highs and lows as they plucked up the courage to ask each other out, and escape the dreaded 'friend zone'.

Two Sides launched as the first interactive video viewable across mobile devices without the need for an app – so teens could experience both perspectives of the film anytime, anywhere. Tailor-made assets inspired by the film promoted further engagement across Snapchat, Facebook and Vine.

Cupidity then went beyond the screen with an immersive theatre production aimed exclusively at teens; breaking down the fourth wall to put them in the action as it unfolded. The ground-breaking show took place in the world's first pop-up binaural cinema and, like the online film, it used 3D sound and allowed the audience to switch perspectives in real time.

During each show, the screen fell away to reveal the *Two Sides* world – transporting viewers from a cinematic experience into a live one, achieving a depth of engagement that is only possible with a live immersive experience.

Results

- Year one saw Cupidity become the fifth most shared piece of branded content in 2013.

- The entire campaign has received over 480 million views so far and has achieved a view-through rate of 45 per cent, well above YouTube average.
- Brand awareness and ad recall are also above industry averages.
- The unique *Two Sides* theatre experience created 85,000 real-life impressions and 70 per cent positive sentiment.
- Cornetto Cupidity has received a Cannes Lions, D&AD Pencil and two Lovie awards.

Links to campaign

http://bit.ly/MOFILMCupidity
www.cornettotwosides.com

About the creator

MOFILM's people-powered marketing approach enables strategists and film-makers to produce innovative ideas in a timely and cost-effective manner, while show-casing their talents to a wider audience.

It connects brands to its community of film-makers and creatives to produce more authentic content and get it seen by millions around the world. It has over 8,000 active film-makers from all over the world who have created over 25,000 videos for over 100 of the world's biggest brands, including PlayStation, Airbnb, Netflix, Coca-Cola and Unilever.

Quote

Technology coupled with a strong insight played a crucial role in helping us to reach the YouTube generation. The first instalment of Cupidity 2015, Two Sides, *is one of the first films produced using binaural technology. This takes 3D sound to a new level to provide a wholly unique directional-sound experience. Using POV-camera work,* Two Sides *also allows viewers to switch viewpoints throughout the film, swapping between the two lead characters to enhance the sensation of being transported into the story.*

Kerry Gaffney, MOFILM

Figure 10.2 Cornetto Two Sides advert

Understanding online PR   11

Nothing has changed, but everything has changed

The phrase '*nothing has changed but everything has changed*' could have been written for the world of PR. The basics of good PR have not changed for years – it is all about being noticed, being picked up by the media, and about presenting a great story, to the right people, at the right time (with the hope that they include why you are a part of it too).

But, in the same way that everything else has '*gone digital*' (whether it is music or books, or even newspapers), the digital environment is also dramatically changing things. When it comes to PR it is changing things in two interesting and occasionally paradoxical ways. First, PR messages today are fighting against a tide of ever-increasing levels of information. Imagine all the information that was ever created from the dawn of time itself to 2003 (if you want to be specific, that is five *exabytes*' worth – or five quintillion bytes' worth – of data). Well, according to Google CEO Eric Schmidt, this amount of information is now created every two days (see http://techcrunch.com/2010/08/04/schmidt-data).

While your average Joe Bloggs will not come close to being exposed to a fraction of these information sources, people are nevertheless being exposed to around 5,000 'branded messages' per day thanks to the huge growth in media consumption that the likes of Google, Facebook and Twitter have enabled through our smartphones and portable devices. And this means that gaining PR cut-through has never been harder.

According to ZenithOptimedia (June 2015), we all now spend around 490 minutes (nearly eight hours) of our day with some kind of media, but it is online media that has really changed the rules. Between 2010 and 2015 consumption through newspapers fell 31 per cent, while consumption of magazines was down too, by 23 per cent. Taking its place has been the internet – usage is up 105 per cent in the same period, and if you are still unconvinced about the power of digital, just think about the following statistics for a minute: in the same calendar year (between April and November 2015) the number of daily video views on Facebook *doubled*. A 2014 Ofcom report found that Facebook is now the default social media website for almost all adults who are online (96 per cent), and while Twitter's new user sign-ups slowed in the year 2013–14, as of 2015 there are still 288 million active monthly users. In Britain various stats estimate that there are around 9.5 million Twitter users – most of whom (25 per cent) are in the 25–34 age range.

The paradox with online, however, is the second key change. For while the amount of pure data is rising all the time, thanks to the tools that are creating this, the right story now actually has *greater* power to smash through all this background noise, and reverberate faster, and reach more people than has ever been possible before. News now breaks in 140 characters or less. The engagement of the Duke of Cambridge and Catherine Middleton was announced by Clarence House on Twitter, while in 2013 the *Guardian* announced that social media is now outstripping news wires as the fastest and quickest way for traders to source investor news. Today, there might be lots of competing news, but if you can create a piece of trending content, your messages can potentially reach millions, and in record time.

CASE STUDY   internet = speed

In the summer of 2014 there was one online trend that surpassed all others – the *Ice Bucket Challenge*. Within days the web was awash with videos of everyone from Tom Cruise to Bill Gates pouring buckets of ice-cold water over their heads, and with the ability to nominate other friends to do it too, it only added to the viral effect. Although the craze didn't come from an orchestrated PR campaign, it soon became associated with raising money for ALS – amyotrophic lateral sclerosis, a form of motor neurone disease (and in the UK to raise money for the Motor Neurone Disease Association), after golfer Charles Kennedy was nominated to take part in it and decided that the money raised by his challenge should go to ALS because his cousin suffered from the disease. When he then nominated his cousin's wife to soak herself and urge others to take it on too, the campaign suddenly took off.

From 1 June to 17 August, TechCrunch calculated that around 28 million people had joined the challenge, and 2.4 million videos of people doing it had been shared on Facebook (see http://techcrunch.com/2014/09/03/the-ice-bucket-challenge-by-the-numbers).

ALS.org normally receives around 8,000 visits per day, but for these heady summer months it shot up to an average of 630,000 visits – up 7,775 per cent. Some 11 per cent of these clicked through to make a donation, pledging ALS US $70.2 million compared with the $2.5 million it raised during the same period the year before.

But even before this craze broke, PR execs were realizing the power and speed of the internet. In March 2014 Cancer Research launched the #NoMakeUpSelfie campaign featuring the likes of Holly Willoughby and Michelle Heaton without make-up on, and this saw more than £8 million donated in just six days (see the *Guardian*'s 2013 report: http://www.theguardian.com/society/2014/mar/25/no-makeup-selfies-cancer-charity).

Although critics have called such events 'narcissism mixed with altruism', the awareness brought to some charities has been huge. However, just as easily as a campaign can take off, it can also suffer from backlash too – especially if inauthenticity is detected. Macmillan Cancer Support was criticized after it used the Ice Bucket Challenge to raise money for its own cause. As the challenge's popularity grew, Macmillan asked people to donate £3 'by sending ICE to 70550 (the Motor Neurone Disease Association can also be donated to by texting ICED55 £5 – or any amount – to 70070)'. It reportedly raised £250,000 but some thought it had jumped on the ALS bandwagon and then overshadowed it in the process.

What is online PR?

If PR is about creating reach, simplistically, online PR is about occupying this new and expanding digital space.

Online is powerful because it is where people go to in order to find the majority of their information, and it is also the place where they confirm whether a firm they are interested in is recognized by others. This peer-approval mentality is seen by interest in sites such as TripAdvisor and Checkatrade – where reputations are made or lost by how others perceive the organizations they have been in contact with. In short, if digital is the natural destination of many audiences today, digital is where you need to be.

Later in this chapter, we examine where online PR differs to traditional PR – but for the time being it is worth recognizing the elements about online PR that still obey the same rules as traditional PR.

PR essentials that still resonate in 2016

1 *It's all about the story*: whether it is online or offline, journalists want to hear about the 'story'. Storytelling is the big buzz phrase of the moment because it is a way of conceptualizing what your company is about, why it might be different, and why it is worth others hearing about it. Having a story also gives you the opportunity to frame all of your future communications, and do it consistently over time. If you cannot define your 'story' then you cannot define your business. Journalists need to 'get' what it is about you very quickly otherwise they will move on. As Jamie Holtum, former European brand manager for Heinz Tomato Ketchup, and now senior brand consultant at Butterfly London, says: 'All stories need a character, a conflict and a plot. BrewDog is one of my favourite companies at the moment [and winner of the CrowdCube Coolest Brand of the Year, 2015] – and everything it does is around the story of it being a disruptor brand, doing things differently, challenging existing brewers head on. All its messages stem from this storyline.'

2 *It's all about the 'what's new, now'*: successful PR is about using your overarching story to answer the '*So what?*' question that journalists will ask in different and exciting ways, and repeatedly over time. Maybe you are supporting a new charity, have a celebrity customer story, are growing like mad, have hit record sales, are expanding into new offices, or have even won local or national awards. Journalists are always reserved about simply promoting a company for its own sake – there needs to be a reason for them talking about you. One of the most popular techniques still is commissioned research, which creates a story you have ownership of. CV Library – the UK's largest recruitment website – consistently achieves journalist-friendly stories because it is able to mine its own data,

everything from 'Handwriting will be extinct in the next 25 years' to 'top interview horror stories revealed' (including how one candidate forgot their false teeth).

3 *It's all about knowing your audience*: successfully promoting yourself is really about resonating and creating an affinity with the people you wish to engage with – at both a business and personal level. Frame your story right, and it will identify a ready-made audience (and outlet) that will trust you, and talk about you amongst their own friends and acquaintances. It will also give you a reason to talk to the journalists who act as intermediaries in the relationship. These are the people who recognize that a good story is just as good for them as it is for their audience.

4 *It's all about timeliness*: like most things in life, good PR is about good timing. Journalists are copy hungry but time poor, but if you can fill a hole they will be much more receptive to your ideas further down the line. This means being organized and being happy to take a call whenever they might need to call you and not the other way around. Proactive firms will pre-empt relevant planned events – like the Budget – to have their viewpoint on it ready from whatever perspective they think the publication will want. Tim Martin, the boss of the Wetherspoon pub chain, is well known for his views on beer duty and the minimum wage, and always prepares a response to any announcements that cover these. Journalists can rely on him in the heat of having to file a story. His views are often e-mailed to journalists within minutes, not hours, of any announcements – journalists cannot afford for responses to be hours later. Those who sit back will miss the boat on getting their names out there.

5 *It's all about opinion*: a good media profile relies on you being the provider of pithy opinion. No one likes people who sit on the fence. Explosive opinion is rocket fuel for journalists because it creates debate and interaction. You need to be known by journalists you want to appeal to, and the best way to do this is to have a particular view on x or y that can be called on at a moment's notice. Remember, you cannot always rely on journalists picking up on the stories you may want to feed them – they have their own agendas. So, as well as being available and timely, those serious about their PR profile need to strike up relations with key publications, websites and/or editors, so that these key writers get a sense of who you are, and what makes you tick. You should aim to try to call or e-mail at least one journalist every week. They will be more receptive than you might think. They are under pressure to find new angles, and keep copy fresh. You might just be able to help them.

So how does online PR differ?

At first glance, there might not seem to be much difference between online and offline PR – both activities are still all about targeting gatekeepers to include you or your company's activities in their output.

But, online is different in a number of key respects. 'Traditional PR largely comprises media liaison, with the majority of content coming in the form of press releases and articles,' says Mark Houlding, CEO and founder of Rostrum PR. 'Here, keeping up consistent conversations with journalists is key. On the digital side of public relations, it is *content* that is king. While press releases and articles are still important, you have to think differently about how they are being placed – which means how they are going to appear on a website.'

Starting from scratch, this means that the writing rules for attracting the eye of journalists, and what needs to be included for publishing, do actually change. Here are the key points you will need to consider:

- *SEO*: recognize it, but don't overdo it. Those who purely occupy the online world will talk about one thing, and one thing only – SEO, or *search engine optimization*. This is the practice of trying to predict what people will search for on search engines, so that your content – which contains those words – rises higher up the results list. Writing content that includes frequently searched-for keywords or phrases relevant to a wide variety of search queries tends to increase traffic and raise content higher, as does updating content regularly so that search engines' crawler technology is kept busy. But, while this might be good for your own self-managed social media pages (such as Facebook pages or your Twitter/ LinkedIn accounts), overusing when trying to appeal to online titles should carry a health warning. Online publications tag their own content to maximize hits to *their* site – so don't come into conflict with this. By all means research good keywords, but if you overpepper them into your pitch material to journalists, your copy will come across as clunky and unnatural. Think content first.

- *Score your work out of 10*: to help decide where it goes. There is a tendency online to fire it off to all and sundry in the hope someone picks it up. This scattergun approach has meant that online has gained a reputation as being the place where all the unwanted print material goes. However, this is gradually changing. Content needs to be to a higher standard, so it is best to be aware of this. 'Lots of poor-quality content used to go online, but there has been a pulling back of this,' says Tara

Burns, divisional director at PR agency Man Bites Dog. 'It is no longer possible to view online content as secondary. Editors are looking for quality now, so give it to them.' One PR chief says he scores work out of 10 to determine whether it goes to everyone or not. Anything 5–10 (1 being top) is deemed suitable for wider coverage. Anything close to 1 needs proper targeting, and even exclusivity. You must be realistic in your scoring too – don't rate it 'great', if it really is only 'good'. For some outlets, like *Marketing Week* or the online forum Mumsnet, they will only run stories if they know it is exclusive to them.

- *Create appropriate content (and more of it)*: content is very much the theme in this chapter, but amongst the online community it needs even greater importance, and greater variety. Online you can no longer expect the same content to be appropriate for all. Readers expect the initial article they read to be the teaser for more. So, you need to provide links that will give readers the choice to come back to your website for more, and follow-up content (such as infographics, video, white papers, blogs, podcasts). Online publications prefer to keep people on their own website, but they accept that curiosity will draw people away.

- *Keep your sentences (even) shorter*: offline you have the room to say more, but when it comes to online, readers are looking at things on smaller screens (even Apple's latest iPhone launch reverted back to the smaller 4-inch screen size). This means that sentence construction has be aware of the smaller space readers have to look at your content. The *Gunning Fog Index* is a useful tool that measures the complexity of sentences – including looking for words with three or more syllables – to produce a mathematical formula for readability. *The Times* has a score of around 10, while the *Mirror* has a score of around 2. The ideal is for 5–7 because that means it is easy to read, and follow.

- *Mirror your audience (even more)*: if the site you want to target writes in a youthful and upbeat way, you need to make your own copy youthful and upbeat too. The editorial gatekeepers will not want to spend lots of time rewriting your words to suit their own tone of voice. Content that gets through the door is that which most closely mirrors the website. It is vital to remember that websites can often be very different to even the offline title that is part of the same stable. For instance, Mail Online – which is celebrity heavy, and photo-driven – is very different to the conservative content of the newspaper it supports.

CASE STUDY   It's all about credibility

Company

Arcadis.

Campaign

'Sustainable Cities Index'.

Background

In 2015, Dutch design consultancy Arcadis wanted to build its UK and global profile to put it firmly into the conversation around the sustainability of major worldwide cities – the area it consults in. As well as create coverage, it also wanted the PR to generate new business.

What Arcadis did

Andy Rowlands, head of corporate communications at Arcadis, explains how it tackled this brief: 'We knew the issue of cities growing rapidly was one that had both mainstream and industry-specific interest. We also knew there were lots of other city rankings, and therefore there would be a *'So what?'* effect. However, because most indexes only measure one element on their own [such as housing costs or population growth] we decided to create an index out of three different measures – city performance against 'planet', 'people' and 'profit' – with measures including carbon footprint, work–life balance and economic performance.'

Fifty cities were chosen – including Frankfurt, London, Rome, Tokyo, Dubai, San Francisco – and they were ranked at an overall level, while cities' individual positions could be seen according to which of the three specific measures they were compared to.

Credibility, credibility, credibility

'At first we only planned to rank 10 cities,' says Rowlands. 'But it quickly became clear the only way we would get media buy-in was to make it bigger. We also made sure the process for ranking cities was as credible and robust as it could be. There are lots of bloggers and a wider community of people who pore over these sorts of reports, so ours had to stack up to scrutiny. So we asked an academic, Dr Eugenie Birch, Nussdorf professor of urban research, to peer review it and write the foreword to the overall report we produced.'

Targeting and content

To make the research as 'findable' as possible, Arcadis created as much content as possible: its own microsite to showcase the research – including an infographic and video that people could watch to see the main findings – plus links to download the full report, or share it with others. It also used LinkedIn and its own Twitter feed. Dr Eugenie Birch tweeted the report to her own network of top thinkers in their field, further widening the reach, and giving it credibility at the same time. Journalists were approached across online, blogs and print, and a PR agency (Man Bites Dog) was appointed to write specific stories about each of the cities, which could be used to send more personalized city hooks to journalists in different parts of the world.

Results

Having a wide spread of content for people to interact with really paid off. Thanks to 480 separate pieces of coverage in the likes of *China Daily,* the *Telegraph, Fast Company, Bloomberg, The Wall Street Journal* and the *Guardian* (the last was the single-largest generator of links to Arcadis's website), the video was viewed 24,000 times (12x the target); there were 62,000 unique microsite clicks (the target was 1,500); the report was downloaded 12,000 times (17x target), and there were 187,000 LinkedIn impressions (and 637 views on LinkedIn), with 1,000 Twitter mentions. 'Best of all,' says Rowlands, 'analysis of leads tells us we have secured £20 million of new business alone, plus more in the pipeline.' This is a remarkable return on investment of £120,000 – which includes everything – the video, the research, the microsite and PR.

Take-homes

'If I was to put it down to one thing, I would say having great online content and making it findable,' says Rowlands. 'You have to give journalists a reason to answer the questions: "What's new?" and "Why now?"'

The campaign was so successful that it won CorpComm's 'Best International Campaign' award, and *Marketing* magazine's 'Best use of Thought Leadership' award. Arcadis intends to create a 100 cities index during 2016.

The rules of engagement

The gatekeepers of digital outlets are still – by and large – traditional journalists, which means you should approach them in the same way as you would approach any offline publication. Here are some good rules of engagement you should follow:

DO...

- *Your homework*: there is more to PR that just appealing to a journalist's sense of curiosity. You need to know what already works for them, which means researching what they need and seeing what they have covered in the past. Too many journalists complain that people pitching to them have not even read their publication. This is the first step you need to take to understand what type of story (and which piece of content – be it a blog, white paper, video or infographic) might appeal to their site. Helpfully, lots of news sites have a box that trends their most popular stories – either those read, or those shared. So, try to come up with something that ticks this box. Maybe a website has a regular slot that you can fill for them.

- *Think of what they need, not what you want them to say*: even better than providing outlets with relevant content is being able to provide them with something they haven't got. Often people think this means giving a story exclusively to them, but that is not always the case. 'A trend I'm really seeing at the moment is "co-creation",' says Tara Burns, divisional director at PR agency Man Bites Dog. 'This is where those seeking press coverage proactively invite publishers to, for example, insert their own questions into planned research that is taking place. This way the outlet feels they have got something unique to them, which they have been able to control too.'

DON'T...

- *Ask them if they got that press release you sent*: nothing infuriates journalists more than being constantly rung up, or e-mailed, and being asked if they received your press release. They will have done, because you didn't receive a bounce-back. If they like it, they will be in touch with you. Remember, just because they didn't bite this time, it doesn't mean they won't, but allow them to make that decision. Having said this, most PRs know that appropriate follow-ups can often generate coverage – journalists have bursting inboxes and so a well-placed call, smartly worded, is sometimes a good solution.

- *Be lazy*: even though journalists might guess you have sent the same release out to lots of different people, they like to feel that you are talking just to them. So, don't cut and paste the same e-mail, using clunky mail-merge tricks, because they will be spotted every time. Personalize e-mails to journalists or bloggers by saying just how much you think your story might be relevant to them and their readers. And don't, whatever you do, paste your entire e-mail list into your 'cc' column. If journalists can see you have sent it to all their rivals they are less likely to pick up your story.

- *Lose hope*: if journalists are anything, they are opportunists, and prefer going to people quickly, when they suddenly have a need. So, if your release did not produce a response two months ago, don't lose hope. It might not have been the right time. Suddenly though, it can be the right time, and good journalists will file things away for when they have a need for them. Know this, and make sure you can respond quickly, even if you thought the moment had passed.

CASE STUDY   Legal & General, 'Deadline to Breadline' campaign

Who

Legal & General.

What

'Deadline to Breadline' campaign.

What it entailed

Legal & General, the FTSE 100 insurance firm, wanted to dispel the myth that if householders suffered a sudden and significant drop in income, they would be able to stay above the breadline for a significant period of time before relying on government support. To do this, it partnered with PR agency Rostrum to promote the *real* 'Deadline to the Breadline' (or *'D2B'*). The aim of the PR was to increase awareness of the benefits of protection insurance, to show people how long they could really maintain their lifestyle if they lost their income. A second aim was to increase Legal & General's standing as the leading brand in the protection market. Digital media was tasked with making the story pervasive, reaching as many people as possible to deliver a personal – and deliberately scary – message.

What Legal & General did

Rostrum commissioned the Centre for Economics and Business Research (CEBR) to establish a thrice-yearly index of the D2B, which aimed to highlight the tangible dangers of not preparing for unforeseen events. It then targeted an extensive catalogue of opinion formers from both print and digital publications.

How they did it

A survey of more than 5,000 people (weighted to represent the UK adult population) provided a detailed picture of the public's income, savings and other financial support. This data, combined with a bespoke economic model created in collaboration with the CEBR, gave the D2B figure for the average UK family: just 26 days. This figure was at the heart of the PR strategy as it revealed the gap between perception and reality. Prior to the calculation, people believed they would last almost three times as long (72 days) before becoming reliant on friends, family and the state for financial support. In addition to producing a 31-page *Deadline to the Breadline* report, a one-page infographic (a first for Legal & General) was designed, which highlighted the key findings at a glance. An online calculator was also created that allowed people to determine their own D2B figure.

Results

The *Deadline to the Breadline* report achieved 21 press mentions in a single month, and by the time this third report was published, momentum had expanded to nearly 80 mentions in just one week. Press coverage was achieved in five national newspapers, while there were 19 broadcast events and 17 mentions on regional radio stations. On the social media side, Rostrum created a social editorial calendar for the *Deadline* series, to include scheduled tweets to promote each edition as well as including *Deadline to the Breadline* in L&G's ongoing #moneyhangout series of Facebook video debates between L&G spokespeople and key national and trade media. Highlights included a four-minute TV interview with Legal & General's corporate affairs director, John Godfrey, about the findings on Sky News – with an estimated reach of 4.5 million viewers – and national radio coverage with BBC Radio 4. After the wave of publicity that followed, Barclays Bank was so taken with the idea that it began using L&G's D2B calculator tool with its own customers in its Woolwich Mortgage Advisor branches.

Going it alone?

With the speed of communication seemingly increasing all the time, and many online marketing tools and reporting analytics available for free, perhaps the biggest question facing those wanting to do their own PR is whether or not they can actually do it themselves (rather than appointing a dedicated PR agency).

With a clear strategy in place and a team with enough time to dedicate to social media, there is no reason why a business cannot manage their own channels. However, consistency is key when it comes to social networks – if a business posts three tweets each day, for example, its followers will notice if this is not kept up over an extended period of time. Audiences become used to a certain level of activity, and will fail to interact if the channels are not up to their usual standards.

When it comes to targeting online publications the approach that firms must take will depend on whether the target is a traditional media outlet that has moved online, such as newspapers or trade magazines, or part of the new generation of influential bloggers and content creators. Whilst businesses can be hesitant towards the latter, if pitched well and to an individual who is certain to benefit the campaign you can reap the rewards of a successful in-house strategy.

However, it is worth understanding that expert consultancies exist to build a consistent, engaging strategy from the start, that is visual and crosses a number of different conversation topics. Businesses can often fall into the trap of too much self-promotion on social media. For those who do want to go it alone, though – here is some good information you cannot be without:

- *Sign up to journalist databases*: a good database of the most up-to-date trade, national and freelance journalists is essential if you want to properly target who receives your content. There are a number of services that businesses can buy into – from the likes of Gorkana (www.gorkana. com) that provides databases, to distribution and monitoring services; as well as Response Source (www.responsesource.com) that provides the same, as well as training and forward planning tools. Both enable businesses to take free trials of their services.

- *Download measurement tools*: Google Analytics helps businesses to see the popularity of blog posts and social network referrals, while tools like Google Tag Manager will track the number of social shares that come directly from your site. The latter eliminates trying to work out if shares come from other sites, or from sponsored ads, and allows you to know where to best place social sharing buttons. Other tools include Quintly – a tool that lets you benchmark and optimize your social media performance, including comparing your own numbers against those of your competitors. Kehole.co allows users to track how many people are using your hashtag, along with the number of retweets, likes and impressions that your campaign is generating. It will also track who the most influential people are in terms of engaging with your keywords.

- *Create 'hero' content that you can measure*: the beauty of online is that it is infinitely easier to measure – including metrics like how long people spend on your website per click, how many times they come back, how many times they view content or download it. This means that 'testing' what works can be a very personal and rewarding project. It is also where the insights gained can be used to tweak future PR in the future. As well as testing which stories go down well, a good tip is to create so-called *'hero content'* – good first-instance content that can be tested to see what other content is needed after that. This reflects the fact that content creation and then the measurement of it (which used to have a long time-lag) are moving closer together. Now, it is likely that a campaign will be altered as it goes along, based on real-time insight of what is working and what is not.

... Don't forget you can never fully control your PR – and online it is even more the case

The phrase 'there's no such thing as bad publicity' (often attributed to American showman Phineas T Barnum, the flamboyant circus owner) cannot be more wrong in today's digital age. Nowadays, a wrong foot can become national news within minutes, and if there is one thing you can be sure of, it's that loyalties in journalism are short-lived. If content is all about the story – and you are at the centre of it – then any previous good work buttering up the press will not count for anything.

CASE STUDY   VW

You only have to turn to the recent example of the emissions scandal surrounding Volkswagen, which first broke on 18 September 2015, to see how hard-won consumer trust can evaporate quickly. In a 2015 interview with the *Financial Times*, Professor Erik Gordon at the Ross School of Business, University of Michigan, stated: 'The mismanagement of the crisis will be a classic case study in business schools around the world.' Nearly everything VW could have done wrong, it did.

To begin with, the news was not even communicated by VW itself. Engineers admitted to the US Environmental Protection Agency (EPA) that 480,000 cars had been fitted with an illegal device that understated emissions of nitrogen oxides in official tests. When this was made public by the regulator, VW did make swift announcements saying that it had 'screwed up' and that the boss was 'endlessly sorry' – but while the first rule of crisis PR is to accept you have made a mistake, and say sorry, resigning CEO Martin Winterkorn disastrously said he was 'not aware of any wrongdoing on my part' – a statement that saw the press turn against a man who had previously been praised for his openness around difficult areas.

To make matters worse, in November the regulator said it had uncovered another cheat device – this time in Audi and Porsche vehicles (brands that VW also owns). This time its response was more combative, saying in a press release the same day that 'Volkswagen AG wishes to emphasize that no software has been installed in the three-litre V6 diesel power units to alter emissions characteristics in a forbidden manner.' However, the next day, it was forced to admit that 800,000 cars had understated their carbon dioxide levels and it was setting aside €2 billion to deal with the problem. Sales for VW fell 25 per cent in November – compared to the same period in 2014. Its share price also tumbled.

Don't think it can't happen to you

You may think it is not possible for your business to suffer loss of trust on an epic scale, but if there is one thing the internet is littered with, it is the diminished reputations of firms that have all experienced the ire of the Twittersphere and other online communities.

Godstone Farm – the Surrey-based animal petting centre – was still making the news in 2014 when the parents of a girl who contracted E-coli from a visit in 2009 won a share of an estimated £1 million in an out-of-court settlement.

To its credit, the farm has worked with the press and had always said it was sorry for the 'pain and suffering' of children who caught the bacterium, but this and other examples prove that PR works both ways: if you are courting press attention, you need to be able to respond when things are not going quite to plan.

Respond quickly – and you can nip things in the bud

It is for this reason that any PR strategies must involve careful thought about what happens when you cannot always control the agenda as you hoped you could.

The key to responding to Twitter taunts, or social media attacks in general, is to react as quickly as possible, which means regularly using online tools (see below) that scan social media sites for mentions of you.

Firms such as Virgin and Argos are current masters at responding to social media 'complaints' – but doing so in a way that actually makes them funny. By doing so, they often defuse the situation, and turn what was an initial complaint into a PR opportunity for themselves in its own right. Take what happened in 2014, for example, when Argos noticed this tweet:

Profile: Immy 'BADMAN' Bugti @BadManBugti
Tweet: YO wen u getting da ps4 tings in moss side? Ain't waitin no more.
Plus da Asian guy whu works dere got bare attitude #wasteman
Posted: 7.24 am – 8 March 2014
Retweets: 522 Favourites: 150

Rather than ignore it, or act in an overly corporate way, it responded with some enviable 'street' flair – by writing the following: '@BadManBugti: 'Safe badman, we gettin sum more PS4 tings in wivin da next week y'get me. Soz bout da attitude, probz avin a bad day yo.'

The reward for its efforts was a piece on Daily Mail Online, praising Argos's response, and even the goodwill of 'Badman' himself, who then retweeted: '@ArgosHelpers: 'respect. Sick guy'.

Virgin Trains is also responding to online incidents with similar panache. Its Twitter monitoring began in 2009, and today its staff are kept extremely busy. In 2014 information service Commute London found that Virgin Trains received 257,254 tweets in a single year. At first, Virgin tended to ignore abusive tweets, but now its staff are given freedom to use humour to redress potentially tricky situations.

One of the most talked-about social media interactions Virgin recently had was so-called 'Poo-Gate'. Commuter Adam Greenwood was using the toilet on a Virgin train when, to his horror, he discovered there was no loo paper. He tweeted his predicament while still sat in the cubicle, and within minutes Virgin had seen it and tweeted back – 'Which coach Adam?', where-upon the train manager was then able to send supplies to him. The story was picked up around the world, and Virgin estimates that 300 million items were written or shared online about the episode. Not a bad result considering this could have turned into a bad reputational issue.

Tools that enable you to see who is talking about you online include free service Social Mention, which gives you an RSS feed of your mentions, and can even give you a 'brand strength' score; Mention – which is a newer tool that replaced Google Alerts; Topsy – a search engine that lets you monitor brand mentions across the web; and Hootsuite, which helps you to keep on top of chatter in real time on social media platforms such as Facebook, Twitter and LinkedIn.

Your PR checklist for when your reputation is under threat

Anyone with a smartphone and a Twitter account can now become a 'citizen journalist', but thankfully many of the rules for dealing with reputational issues are the same as in traditional brand-boosting PR:

- *Comment*: businesses should always offer a comment to a story. Staying silent will only serve to aggravate the audience. Customers, stakeholders and journalists will all be demanding a response across a variety of channels.

- *Comment quickly*: in the digital landscape, stories can stay at the front of an audience's mind for a longer period of time because topics can stay trending. As such, the more delayed the reaction from the business, the more in demand it will be. Sometimes, something as simple as directing people to a response message on your website will work more effectively than having a silent strategy.

- *Comment with pathos*: if you have caused upset, or pain, or distress, then acknowledge it, and say sorry, and say sorry with good grace. Above all, sound like you mean it.

- *Comment next by offering solutions*: after addressing any upset, the next thing that people will demand is answers, or solutions to the problem. Even if you feel that the issue is a storm in a teacup, swallow your pride and decide on a plan of action that will satisfy the malcontents. Some pain now should see you weather the storm. Remember, online spats can quickly blow over – often because people will actually move on to the next thing. But don't take this for granted. It will blow over faster if you act with integrity.

Expert view

Steve Barrett, editorial director, PRWeek Global; editor-in-chief, PRWeek US:

Digital and social media have fundamentally changed all forms of communications and marketing. Brands, companies and organizations are now using a compelling mix of paid, earned, shared and owned media (PESO) to tell their stories and engage their stakeholders. The days of having one narrative for your staff, one for investors and one for customers are long gone. Communications is no longer a one-way broadcast process – it is an interactive conversation that will take place whether or not companies and brands choose to take part. Transparency and authenticity have to be the watchwords for today's communicators, and they are engaging a slew of new influencers alongside mainstream media and direct communication in order to get their messages across.

John Starr, managing director, Clareville Communications:

Digital is much more than being able to make people connect to you with one move of the mouse. The call to action that all PR needs to have has never been greater than in the digital space. Whatever you write, you have to enable the reader to navigate to you. The only way you can do this is to make things engaging, and worthwhile for people to give up their time. In this sense, the rules haven't changed at all, but a point a lot of people forget is this: just because it's online, it doesn't mean you can drop the quality. It's quality content that will always be king.

▶

Jamie Holtum, former European brand manager for Heinz Tomato Ketchup, now senior brand consultant at Butterfly London:

People are driven by emotion, so it is vital that your brand story evokes this. All your communications need the same ingredients if you are to be consistent about who you are and what you stand for. You need a hero; you need conflict that you are somehow able to resolve; and you need a plot. A great story poorly told is no story at all. So, don't think channel, think story first. A brand without a story is just a brand concept. The key is that your story needs to be the same, no matter what your channel is.

Mark Houlding, CEO and founder of Rostrum PR:

Businesses will have a goal in mind at the start of any campaign as to who they want to engage, and why, whether that is a FTSE 100 firm wanting to target more women at a senior level, or a baby-care brand wanting to engage with more stay-at-home dads. But this is where social media plays a key part. By tracking an audience from the beginning to the end of a campaign, there are tools available to see the change in demographics of a business's followers on Twitter, for example, and therefore judge whether the campaign was a success. Engaging key influencers in the target sector will also prove fruitful. By utilizing external spokespeople to promote a business's message, not only does it make the message more credible, it takes this message to the target audience at the click of a button.

Graham Goodkind, chairman and founder, Frank PR:

For the last few years, my main message has been the same. We tend to get way too wrapped up in the execution side of PR. If I had £1 for every time a client has asked for a Twitter, Facebook or social media idea I'd be rich. To me, though, it's not about the mechanic or the channel: it's all about the idea. That's what we should be thinking about from the off. Start with a blank sheet of paper and try to come up with a great idea. For a few minutes, forget about how or where you're going to do it. Focus on conjuring up that nugget of brilliance that is going to make something eminently shareable and then the rest will come naturally. You'll be able to apply it to the channel you need after that. But not before.

Andy Rowlands, head of corporate communications at Arcadis:

Online is all about being 'findable'. For one of our big campaigns [see case study] we had LinkedIn, Twitter and our corporate website. However, we've come to realize that as well as enabling people to find you, you also have to measure the return. Online is great for this, but it is often forgotten. In our Sustainable Cities campaign we built a dedicated portal so people could find us, but what we later realized is that we were not able to measure where they had got to us from (ie which channel). For our next campaign, we are going to take people direct to our corporate website – which serves another benefit too – it lets people see our services straight away. The portal didn't show people this quite so much, and created another step that people had to make before they got to our main website.

Understanding performance marketing 12

OUR CHAPTER PLEDGE TO YOU

When you reach the end of this chapter you will have answers to the following questions:

- What is a strategic partnership and how does it work?
- Would a strategic partnership suit my business?
- How do I go about setting up a strategic partnership?
- What is performance marketing and how does it work?
- What can performance marketing do for my business?

Recognizing opportunities for strategic partnership

In the context of digital marketing, 'strategic partnerships' are defined by an agreement between two (or more) parties where the desired outcome is a win–win for all concerned. Ideally a strategic partnership should be about synergy: all parties should come out of the relationship with more than any of them could have achieved alone.

One way to visualize a strategic partnership is in a bricks-and-mortar 'retail' context: brands rent space in high-traffic department stores in order to sell their products or services to customers who visit that store. The store brings in the traffic, the supplier sells their wares, the customer gets more choice... everyone wins.

Almost exactly the same process occurs online. A website that attracts large volumes of traffic will form long-term partnerships with suppliers to rent space in sections of their website; at the same time, online retailers or brands are looking for additional online 'venues' to peddle their wares. When they come together in the right circumstances you have all the ingredients for a mutually beneficial strategic partnership. Of course the 64-million-dollar question in all of this is agreeing the balance of risk.

Online strategic partnerships usually go something like this

A large portal (website) with 1 million visitors per day sells inventory (space) on its site to a travel company to advertise its products and special offers. In that instance, the burden of risk is entirely with the travel company – they are paying to advertise on the portal's website in the hope of attracting new customers. But wait a minute, isn't that just a form of online advertising?

Yes, except that, in order to mitigate some of the risk, the travel company may negotiate with the portal to lower the cost of rental in exchange for certain incentives. The incentive could be exclusive products or offers for the site's users (increasing the perceived value of the portal site, helping them to attract and retain a bigger audience).

With a tangible mutual benefit on the table, there is a good chance that the portal site will be temped to reduce the required advertising spend in return for:

- special offers – possibly around exclusivity;
- a revenue share of business accruing from the campaign, which can be tracked using page tags and analytics software;
- a long-term deal that can guarantee portal owners a healthy ROI.

Because portal owners now have a vested interest they will also support the partnership with some editorial and PR.

Hold on, isn't this just sponsorship? The burden of risk is still almost completely with the brand. While there may certainly be some value in the 'exclusivity' element of the deal it still doesn't feel balanced, because on the basis of no 'business being transacted' the only real loser is the merchant – in our case the travel company. In the case of a long-term deal that does not bode well for them.

A strategic partnership should be clearly balanced on both sides with risk being shared throughout. Just because the website has millions of users and is able to command money for advertising on their site does not mean they are going to be worse off by adopting a revenue-share model, rather than one that consists of upfront cash. This fact may not be the model actively sold by website owners around the world... but nonetheless, it is true!

Surely the aim of the site owner should be to maintain and grow traffic to their site by ensuring the content is of good quality and relevant in order to offer their audience something of value. In that respect, they are like good old-fashioned media. How, then, does it suit users if the site offers a series of exclusive offers backed by marketers and, ultimately, paid for by the highest bidder? In a word, it doesn't. However, it is a practice that has been rife among websites that, understandably, have been focused on using every trick in the book to maximize their revenue on the site, often enticing marketers with the formula of advertising masquerading as editorial (or special offers) in an effort to bolster advertising opportunity.

Tips on entering into strategic partnerships

Our advice to marketers seeking strategic partnerships with high-traffic websites is as follows:

- Do not enter into long-term arrangements without fully testing the site first. This is the real beauty of digital marketing – the ability to test before you invest.

- If you do decide to go for a long-term deal, make sure this is going to be of ongoing interest to the end users. Vary the content, change your offers regularly, use seasonality or other features to mix things up. You don't want to end up with the same message, day in, day out – except, of course, when it works!

- Talk to the site's other strategic partners – find out how long deals have been in place and how they value the association. Ask them how they go about tracking performance etc. If possible, find out which strategic partnerships they no longer run on the site, and what happened. Marketers can be quite guarded with this kind of information, so you may not get it – but if you can overcome their reticence the information can be invaluable.

- Agree how performance will be measured from day one, and ensure your advertising and promotional messages are fully 'tagged' to track all necessary data – remember it's not about clicks, its about actual conversions.

- Be prepared to disclose profit margins; seek to build a close, transparent relationship with the site, a relationship where both parties fully understand the commercial realities and the mutual benefit involved. A little bit of patience and commitment upfront will certainly help to establish realistic expectations.

What is performance marketing?

Performance marketing is an increasingly popular channel for brands within the digital marketing mix. In previous editions of the book I referred to this area as 'affiliate marketing', but like all things digital the term has steadily evolved – it is a relatively new term applied to an already established branch of digital marketing previously called 'affiliate marketing', and the industry has rebranded itself to ensure that it delivers in name what it delivers in practice.

Performance marketing, unlike other digital disciplines, is not a single medium or method of marketing. It is a way of utilizing any and all digital channels to market a brand's products or services, but where the brand only pays for the results achieved.

This may sound quite vague at this point but the workings of performance marketing will become clearer as we progress through the chapter.

Definition

Sources such as Wikipedia do not have a decisive definition for performance marketing (such is the recency of the term's adoption). It does have a definition for performance-based advertising though, which provides us with a good starting point: 'Performance-based advertising is a form of advertising in which the purchaser pays only when there are measurable results' (see: http://en.wikipedia.org/wiki/Performance-based_advertising).

Combine this with a definition of affiliate marketing and you start to get a flavour of what performance marketing is trying to achieve:

> Affiliate marketing is a type of performance-based marketing in which a business rewards one or more affiliates for each visitor or customer brought by the affiliate's own marketing efforts. The industry has four core players: the merchant (also known as 'retailer' or 'brand'); the network (that contains offers for the affiliate to choose from and also takes care of the payments); the publisher (also known as 'the affiliate'); and the customer' (see: http://en.wikipedia.org/wiki/Affiliate_marketing).

By combining these two definitions, we can create our own definition for performance marketing:

> Performance marketing is a type of performance-based advertising in which a business rewards one or more of its partners for carrying out some form of advertising or promotion of the business's products or services, which results in a customer taking an action. The action is prescribed by the business, allowing them to ensure their advertising spend is delivering actual, measurable results.

History

Performance marketing has been around since the dawn of the internet. Okay, not quite but very close. The first performance marketing programme (affiliate marketing, back then) was launched in 1994 by PC Flowers & Gifts. To put that into context, that is just three years after the invention of the web and a full two years before Larry Page came up with the idea for Google!

Early performance marketing programmes were very simple in their objectives and payment metrics. Partners (affiliates) were predominantly paid on a cost-per-click model (CPC), being paid a small amount for each prospective customer who clicked through to a brand's website.

However, these metrics quickly evolved to the cost-per-acquisition (CPA) model we know today, where brands pay partners a commission or revenue share for each sale completed by a referred customer. The first major brand to launch a CPA-based programme was Amazon, who launched their Amazon Associates programme in 1996, which is still going strong today.

Today's performance marketing programmes couldn't look more different from those of their early predecessors. While they continue to run on the same principle of paying for a prescribed action, the 'actions' are far more numerous and complex. It is not uncommon to find an individual brand's performance marketing programme paying for multiple actions. These could range from something as simple as a click to something as complex as a social media share or a positive review.

Introducing the players

So how does it work? In order to understand this, you need to understand the different players in the game and how they interact. There are four main categories of participants in performance marketing programmes and we will review them individually.

Brands/advertisers

Performance marketing is used by a wide variety of businesses. Due to the diverse mix of active publishers (covered below), any business looking to promote its products or services can find a route to market. Typical advertisers could include retail brands, travel companies, financial institutions and even dating websites. What all of the advertisers who use performance marketing share is an understanding of the value that the channel can bring and the reduction in risk that it can offer.

Publishers

Publishers are the websites that actually run the advertising on behalf of the advertisers and that receive a commission once a consumer completes the required action. Performance-based publishers come in all shapes and sizes. In fact, some of your favourite websites are likely to include an element of performance-based advertising.

Performance publishers could include price comparison websites, cash-back websites, websites promoting vouchers and discounts, review sites, blogs, paid search specialists... you name it, they could all be performance-based.

As you can see from the list above, publishers working with elements of performance encompass almost all areas of digital. This is the primary reason why performance marketing is defined by how brands pay their publishers rather than the actual type of activity undertaken. Normally, performance-based publishers concentrate on mechanisms to help consumers make a decision to complete an action, such as a sale, as they will only be remunerated once the action is undertaken.

Networks and tracking providers

While there is a distinct difference between networks and tracking providers, it is important they are defined together as they share many similarities.

A network is essentially the middleman. Networks operate the tracking systems that allow advertisers to track consumer actions and assign commissions to the relevant publisher. On the one hand, advertisers sign up to the network for a period (usually no less than 12 months) and the network provides advice on how those advertisers should be running their performance marketing activities. On the other hand, publishers voluntarily sign up to the network to gain access to the list of advertisers and voluntarily work with their brands. The network provides the tracking, billing and payment facilities as well as advice to both parties.

Tracking providers also provide tracking, billing and payment facilities but, generally, not the advice. More often than not, tracking providers license their systems for advertisers to use themselves, essentially software provision. It is up to the advertisers to implement their own performance strategies, find their own publishers and manage their own performance marketing activity.

Typically, advertisers who want a small or controlled performance marketing programme or who have the expertise to run a full programme in-house will use a tracking provider. The vast majority of advertisers will use a network, as they receive the advice they need and can dedicate less internal resource to their performance marketing programmes.

Agencies

Media agencies may or may not be involved in the process, depending on what they have been contracted to do for a particular client. Traditionally, media agencies have concentrated on other areas of digital, leaving the performance marketing activities to the advertisers to run themselves, or advising advertisers to contract specialist performance agencies to work alongside them. However, recent trends have seen many of the top media agencies setting up internal performance marketing teams to provide a full-service offering to their clients.

So how does it work?

For simplicity, Figure 12.1 shows a 'do it yourself' performance arrangement, where the web merchant is running their own performance programme. Things can get a little more complicated when a performance network acts as an intermediary between merchant and consumer, but the basic premise remains the same.

In its simplest form, performance marketing works something like this: advertisers work with networks or tracking providers to track consumer activity resulting from promotion by publishers.

Figure 12.1 How basic performance marketing works

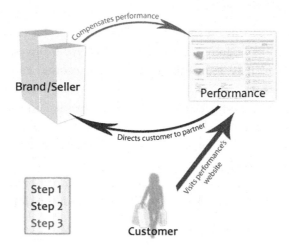

Looking at this process in a little more detail helps to make things clearer:

- *Advertisers work with networks or tracking providers*: as a first step, advertisers will need to set up their performance marketing programme. We will go into this in more detail later in the chapter, but for now let's define this as advertisers needing to provide a network with the commercials, creative and brand messages needed to engage with consumers.

- *Tracking customer activity*: as part of the set-up, advertisers will need to integrate a small piece of tracking code on to their website(s). This code tells the network or tracking provider when an action has been performed by the consumer as a result of promotion by publishers.

Once the set-up is complete, publishers are able to join the programme and gain access to all of the promotional collateral for a particular advertiser. They then use that collateral to promote the advertiser to their user bases. The network or tracking provider tracks the use of the collateral and the consumer engagement and action, recording commissions against the individual publisher accounts when consumers complete the necessary actions.

Why brands should use performance marketing as part of the marketing mix

In this section, we focus on why brands should use performance marketing if they are not already doing so. We review the benefits, investigate a few of the considerations that brands should take into account, and get some tips on what to look for.

On the face of it, performance marketing seems like a no-brainer and is something all brands should get involved with. In the main, this is true. However, there are a few important questions that brands need to answer before jumping in with both feet.

But first we will look at the benefits that brands can enjoy should they get their performance marketing plans right and develop a successful programme.

Benefits

The benefits of performance marketing are too numerous to mention so I have selected five that should resonate with the vast majority of advertisers. Rather than focus on the creative, marketing-related benefits, I have selected very business-centric benefits, which will aid many marketing managers to sell the concept of performance marketing into pretty much any department in their respective companies.

In this section, the assumption is that the advertiser has contracted a network to help with their performance marketing activity. I have made this assumption as this is how the vast majority of brands currently work in the space. There has been a shift in recent years for larger, more experienced companies to migrate their programmes to a tracking provider and manage their publisher relationships in-house. However, this is not the norm just yet.

The five selected benefits of performance marketing are as follows:

Reduced risk
Possibly the primary benefit of performance marketing is the reduced risk that advertisers can enjoy when it comes to budget expenditure. Many other marketing channels require upfront commitment with the promise of success. Performance marketing, on the other hand, requires the promise of budget commitment once success has been achieved. This is a very important distinction as it is the cornerstone of the performance marketing industry.

With advertisers paying commissions once a customer has completed a desired action, brands can rest assured that their marketing budget is being used to maximum efficiency. If customers don't complete the actions, the advertisers don't pay anything, making performance marketing possibly the least risky marketing method available. This is also the reason why performance marketing is a very effective method of advertising for small or niche brands, who may not have substantial marketing budgets. With smaller budgets, advertisers need to ensure that every penny is being used to maximum effect. Protecting the pennies and ensuring they are only paid out for a valuable customer interaction makes sense, not just for the smaller brands but for larger brands too.

It is for this reason that you will find most household brand names running performance marketing programmes.

Test and learn

As we have already discussed, brands can enjoy a significant reduction in expenditure risk when using performance marketing to promote their businesses. This allows them to be more imaginative with their performance marketing activities.

I have often referred to performance marketing as a sandbox, much like the ones you play in as a child. Here, brands can build things up, add to them if they are working, tear them down if not – and all the while be safe in the knowledge that they are not overreaching on the expenditure. After all, they only pay when things work and consumers interact.

Advertisers are therefore able to seek out and implement ways of promoting their products that are far less established than they would otherwise like. They can test new ideas, new marketing messages and ways of interacting with customers without risking some of that precious marketing budget on something that doesn't work.

If some of these new ideas work well then they are able to integrate them into their other marketing channels with confidence, allowing them to continually improve all marketing channels through the use of performance marketing.

Access to innovation

For advertisers who choose to run their performance marketing activities through a network, they gain the added benefit of having a partner who is continually adding to their pool of publishers. Any network worth their salt will have their finger on the pulse of the digital marketing ecosystem and be searching out cutting-edge publishers to broaden their offering.

Brands benefit from this in two ways. First, they can test any new, untried marketing methods in a low-risk environment. Marketing budgets are often set once per year and it can be very difficult to fence off funds for trying new things, especially when you don't know what those new things are or how much return you will see from them. Using performance marketing to try new areas of digital marketing allows brand owners to guarantee a return on their marketing investment, making it much easier to secure budget through the channel.

Second, they can be sure that their network or agency (provided they have picked the right one) will be actively seeking out the next big thing, meaning brands don't have to. Being in a position to make use of the latest trends in digital without having to invest significant manpower is very appealing and commercially sensible. In-house marketing teams are very often time poor and don't have the resources to continually keep abreast of industry progress. Having a trusted partner who can do this for you ensures that marketing teams can focus in the right areas.

'Free' brand exposure

By paying on consumer action, brands can push the payment point further down the purchase funnel. However, in order for publishers to entice consumers to interact with a brand's advertising, they still need to promote that brand and ensure that consumers are exposed to the brand message.

As with any form of advertising, not all consumers are going to relate to the message or interact in the way the brand wants, at least not immediately. However, there may still be value in these consumers, maybe just not right now. Many brands spend a huge amount of budget on branding activity (display, offline etc). In the performance channel, unlike many other channels, the exposure that a brand gets prior to a consumer interacting with it is essentially free, as there is no cost for a consumer who doesn't interact in the way the brand has prescribed.

This important by-product of the way that publishers are remunerated in the performance industry is a major reason why the industry is gaining traction with advertisers of all sizes.

Significant reach

We have already looked at the variety of publishers in the market and how they come from all areas of digital. This creates a significant opportunity for brands as they are in a position to leverage any type of digital promotion through one programme of activity.

Most networks have thousands of publishers on their network all looking to promote the right brands or offers to consumers. This offers brands immense reach in a very short space of time if they can offer publishers what they need.

For most advertisers, contacting and contracting this volume of publishers themselves would be impossible. However, through the use of a network, advertisers have access to a ready-made directory of possible partners.

If you are an advertiser who has an international presence, a partnership with the right network could be very lucrative as the network could provide both local and cross-border publisher opportunities much quicker than you could identify them yourself.

Considerations

As with anything in business, there are considerations that need to be taken into account before jumping in with both feet. Performance marketing works well for most brands in most industries. However, individual companies will have their own objectives, constraints and budgets and a full review should be conducted to ensure that performance marketing is the right fit.

Here we look at five of the most common considerations that advertisers should take into account before beginning their performance marketing programmes:

Cost

Cost is the obvious starting point and is often the most difficult element of performance marketing for advertisers to get their heads around. Unlike other areas of marketing, it is very easy to calculate the cost of an individual consumer interaction but very difficult to calculate the cost of the performance programme as a whole.

This is because, while brands get to set their own commission levels and negotiate their network fees, there is no intelligent way to predict the volume of consumer interactions they are likely to achieve. Get the publisher commercials and marketing message wrong and there will be no cost as there is no consumer interaction. Get them right and you could have thousands of interactions, each with an associated cost.

It is for this reason that most brands don't account for performance marketing costs from their marketing budgets. Rather, they account for it as a cost of sale. In this way they can factor the cost into each consumer engagement to ensure that each one is profitable, while leaving their marketing budget free for other areas of promotion.

So, brands need to consider what they can afford to pay for each consumer interaction in order to retain profitability, factor in cash-flow considerations and ensure that, should they succeed with their performance marketing activities, they have the funds to pay their publishers promptly and maintain a healthy margin.

Competition

Once brands have calculated their costs and can ensure profitability, they will be in a position to benchmark themselves against their competition. The first consideration when evaluating the competition is investigating whether any competitors are even active in the space. In the absence of competition, advertisers need to determine whether their competitors are absent for good reason and performance marketing may not be effective or, hopefully, if there is an opportunity to be first to market. This latter is a distinct possibility, as performance marketing is only now making it into the mainstream marketing press and so is still a relatively unknown area of digital.

A more likely scenario is that multiple competitors will be active in the space and it is against these other performance programmes that advertisers will need to benchmark themselves. It is tempting for advertisers to compare themselves based on non-performance metrics but it is important to compare the performance programmes based on their specific merits.

Advertisers should initially look at the commissions offered by their competitors, as this is where publishers will naturally focus once a programme is live. If the market rates are significantly higher than expected, advertisers should think carefully about whether they have other unique selling points that will entice publishers to their programmes. It is possible to be successful in the performance space while paying low commissions, but many other factors need to be in place to achieve this.

Once commissions have been evaluated, advertisers should then look at the collateral supplied to publishers by their competitors. This is often an area of opportunity and, with some careful thought, advertisers can quickly identify areas here where publishers are missing some key consumer messages.

As long as advertisers are able to identify a unique message that they can provide to publishers, and can compete on commercials, there is a very strong opportunity for a successful performance marketing programme.

Resource and expertise

Performance marketing is not a hands-off route to market. In fact, it is one of the most relationship-heavy, hands-on marketing methods.

Brands should take an objective view on just how much resource is available internally to look after the performance marketing channel. If advertisers have an agency running their digital campaigns, this evaluation is even more important, as adding a new channel may incur significant costs.

Should the resource be available, attention should then be turned to the level of expertise that resource has. This will impact on the level of service needed from a network or aid in deciding whether the use of a tracking provider is a viable option.

If there is a high level of performance marketing expertise within the team, advertisers may be able to negotiate lower rates with networks if the advertiser is able to assume more of the workload. Conversely, if advertisers need to rely heavily on their network for knowledge and education, more network hours will be required.

Having a solid understanding of the skills at an advertiser's disposal is crucial in ensuring that the performance marketing programme is correctly supported as, without the correct resource, few programmes achieve the success they could otherwise have enjoyed.

However, if the right balance is struck between internal resource, network expertise and sufficient account management time, even the most inexperienced marketing teams can run very effective performance marketing programmes.

Service level requirements

Once a thorough review of available resource and expertise has been conducted, advertisers will have a clear picture of the type of support they are going to need from their network or tracking provider.

The challenge is in matching their support requirements to vendors to find the right fit. Tracking providers are less of a concern as, generally, advertisers only opt for a pure-play tracking provider if they have substantial internal resource and experience.

When negotiating with networks around account management time, the level of service required should be very clearly outlined in order to ensure advertisers are not left short. Networks should act as an extension of an advertiser's marketing team and aid in achieving the goals of the business. In order to do this effectively, advertisers need to ensure that their networks are providing sufficient account management resource to manage any aspect of the performance marketing programme that the advertiser is not able to service themselves.

Delivery capabilities

You wouldn't hire a member of staff for an important position if they didn't have the required experience. The same rules apply to running a performance marketing programme. When selecting a network or tracking provider, it is crucial that whomever is selected can demonstrate experience in delivering positive results for clients in the same or similar industries.

This is particularly important when considering which network to work with, as there are so many options available. Depending on which industry an advertiser is active in, it is highly recommended that advertisers review at least three networks to ensure that the correct fit is achieved. Some networks specialize in particular industries, such as finance, and pride themselves on industry-specific areas such as compliance. Other networks may focus more on the retail sector and have better publisher tools, allowing for a more creative performance programme. Whatever the requirements, finding the right partner, with a proven track record in delivering results, is an important part of the set-up process.

Additionally, in recent years there has been an explosion of advertisers who either have international operations or ship their products internationally and so are looking to attract overseas consumers. If an advertiser's business has an element of cross-border activity then it is imperative that they select a partner or partners who can deliver in each geographic area.

Depending on where business is being conducted, advertisers may be able to identify a single partner who can provide international coverage through a single platform. However, brands should also consider market share and local knowledge when reviewing whether performance marketing will work in all territories. The performance marketing industry is an established area of digital in most developed markets. However, as the industry is relatively new, small markets tend not to be as advanced and may require a different strategy to deliver results.

During the review process, brands should look at the basics, such as whether a platform can handle local currencies and languages, as well as the more detailed market situation in order to determine what their performance marketing plans should be.

Many advertisers use different platforms in each market to leverage the local knowledge of their partners. While this approach creates a slightly steeper learning curve, as advertisers need to learn different systems, it can lead to bigger returns as a result of working with specialists in each market.

10 questions every brand should ask

While by no means a definitive list of questions, we hope the questions listed below – a basic cheat-sheet for any advertiser who is looking to begin a performance marketing programme – will help to answer some of the important questions that brands need to consider:

1 Do I have the time/resource to manage a time-intensive method of marketing?

2 Are any of my competitors using performance marketing?

3 Are their performance marketing programmes successful?

4 What can I offer that is different from what is already in the market?

5 What level of commission can I afford to pay and is it competitive?

6 Do I know how to run a performance marketing programme or do I need help?

7 Who are the providers I should be speaking to (networks/service providers)?

8 Is there a standout specialist for my industry?

9 What markets do I want to be active in?

10 Should I use a single partner or local specialists?

How to get the most out of your performance marketing activities

Once the decision has been taken to start a performance marketing programme and a network or tracking provider has been selected, the next stage of the process is to set up the actual programme.

This is a crucial part of the process, as the effort put in here will have a direct impact on the initial success of the programme. It is imperative that the programme is set up correctly from day one in order to help publishers to gain confidence in a brand's commitment to the channel. First impressions count!

How to set up a performance marketing programme

There are three main elements to the set-up of a performance marketing programme: the commercial structure, the technical implementation and the marketing collateral. The elements are interlinked yet each play different roles in the running of a performance marketing programme. In this section we will look at each one individually and then put them together to show the final implementation.

The commercial structure

The commercial structure of a performance marketing programme is possibly the most important element to consider. The commercials will determine how appealing the final programme is to publishers and provide a base for comparison against competing programmes.

Before setting up the commercials, advertisers will need to have decided on the user action that is desired. For the purposes of this section, we will assume that the advertiser is a retailer and that the user action is a completed sale of a product.

In the retail world, publishers are usually paid a commission in the form of a percentage of purchase price. The exact amount of commission will vary per transaction but the percentage will remain constant. How much an individual advertiser will be able to pay publishers is determined very much by their margins. However, once a commission has been decided on it is strongly advisable to get your network's opinion on whether it will appeal to publishers. Networks have access to far more data than any individual advertiser, and can much more easily benchmark a proposed commission structure against competing programmes.

Once the commissions have been decided on, the next important decision to be made surrounds reporting. Each network or tracking provider has their own unique reporting capabilities. Additionally, depending on a client's needs, they will each have more or less complex custom reporting available. Deciding on the level of visibility needed at this stage is crucial, as many reporting requirements result in changes to the technical implementation needed later. By missing off a critical piece of data at this stage, advertisers will create more work for themselves later when they try to make changes to their technical implementations. While changing structure is generally a straightforward exercise, it is much simpler to get the requirements right up front.

Once the commissions and reporting requirements are set, the network can set up the commissions within their platform and pass the commercial and reporting requirements to their implementations teams who will translate these into a technical requirements brief.

The technical implementation

The technical implementation will be led by the commercial structure and reporting requirements. However, a basic implementation will take the form of having to implement a small amount of tracking code into the advertiser website. In the case of our retail example, it is likely this code will need to be included on the sale confirmation in order to track completed sales.

The implementation of tracking code is usually done by a webmaster or development team so it is tempting for the marketing team to want to take a back seat until the work is complete. It is highly recommended for the marketing teams to gain at least a basic understanding of what is being implemented as this will ensure they are well aware of what consumer activities are being tracked and, ultimately, what they are paying for.

For advertisers with multiple digital channels, it may be worthwhile at this stage to discuss more complex features such as container tags and analytics integration to ensure that the performance marketing programme is integrated into the marketing mix from the start.

Once the technical implementation has been completed on the advertiser side, the network or tracking provider will complete a round of tests and should provide the advertiser with example reporting to ensure that what has been implemented is as the advertiser would expect.

Additional items such as product feeds will also be discussed in order to ensure that publishers have access to up-to-date product and pricing information once the programme goes live.

The marketing collateral

This element of the set-up can be completed while the technical implementation is under way, as it should rely heavily on any technical expertise. This element is very much sales and marketing related but with a slight twist. Unlike selling a product to a consumer, the sales collateral and marketing material needed for a performance marketing programme needs to sell the advertiser's virtues twice.

First, items like a programme description, a clear explanation of the commission structure and advertiser company stability and so on are needed in order to sell the performance programme to publishers. This is a crucial first step as, unless the marketing collateral entices publishers to join the programme and promote the products, the programme will never get off of the ground.

Second, assuming advertisers grab the attention of publishers, the advertiser needs to provide publishers with the marketing messages that appeal to consumers. It is important that advertisers remember that publishers are not experts in the advertiser's industry nor do they know the advertiser's business. Any information that can be provided to publishers to help them sell the advertiser's products or services should be shared. Additional items that will be required at this stage will include sets of banner creatives, textlink suggestions and high-performing keywords that publishers can target.

Once all three of these elements have been completed, an advertiser should be in a position to launch their performance marketing programme with confidence. They will be sure that, once sales start coming in, they are paying the right amount, have the right visibility and are providing the right collateral to continually help their publishers drive more business for them.

Programme set-up checklist

Here is a brief set-up checklist that will help ensure that an advertiser has all of their bases covered:

- Are commissions set at a level where each sale is profitable?
- Do I need to pay different commissions for different products and have these been set up?
- Have the reporting requirements been defined?
- Do these match with the advertiser's internal business reporting?
- Has the tracking been implemented to track the data the advertiser needs?
- Has the tracking been implemented at the right point in the purchase journey to track the right consumer action?
- Has the advertiser provided enough creative collateral for publishers to use?
- Has the advertiser provided live product information?
- Is the programme description strong enough? Will it entice publishers to join the programme?
- Has the advertiser provided enough information for publishers to promote the business to consumers with confidence?

If the answer to all of the above questions is 'yes' then the chance of success will be high.

Setting goals and KPIs

Now that we have a performance marketing programme set up, the next stage is ensuring that the results of the activity are in line both with company objectives and industry benchmarks. With this in mind, it is now time to set some goals and begin to monitor important KPIs. In the first few months of a performance marketing programme, the KPIs are unlikely to be record-breaking sales numbers.

Rather, initial focus should be put on publisher recruitment and traffic generation through the performance channel. Unlike some other channels that allow for instant results, performance marketing requires more of a patient start as publishers learn about the programme, analyse the benefits in comparison to other programmes in the market and ultimately begin promoting the products or services to consumers. Depending on the time of year and the level of competition, this may take a little while.

During this initial recruitment period, your network's experience is vital. They should be able to furnish you with a list of their top publishers and provide regular updates on progress on getting them on board. Getting publishers up and running is the most important aspect at this early stage.

Once publishers do start joining the programme, though, the focus needs to change to activation as it is very common for publishers to join programmes to plan for a future promotion, resulting in a long list of inactive publishers. A rough guideline should be 20–25 per cent activation rate, and if an advertiser is achieving this, they can count themselves successful. Again, the network should be helping here but this is the time for brands to really get hands on with their performance programmes and begin building relationships with their publishers.

At this point the goal should be publisher activation and the KPI should be traffic generated to the site (let's not worry about conversion just yet… remember that the branding element is free).

After four to six weeks, assuming all has gone according to plan, brands can start to look at conversions and optimization of publishers. This is the time where brands should be looking at providing their network with quarterly targets (set in conjunction with the network to ensure they are achievable). Targets should include a number of metrics. Conversions will naturally be the most important but traffic, impressions, number of new publishers recruited, conversion rate per publisher, etc should all form part of the monitored KPIs for the programme. After all, they are all valuable elements and all of these stats need to grow for the programme to continue to add value.

As business needs change, so should the goals and KPIs of a performance marketing programme. The best programmes continuously evolve to keep in line with the wider business strategy. The key is to communicate with both the network and publishers and really bring them into the decision-making process. Some of the industry's best performance marketers are not great at marketing. They are, however, fantastic at communication.

Top five tips to publisher success

Information is best when you hear it directly from the source, so here I have asked Oliver Jones, partnerships director at Yieldify (www.yieldify.com) for his top five tips on how to get the best from your publisher partners:

1 *Use the resources available to you.* Get to know your account manager and key contacts within the network you have chosen. Remember that they have won your business and are there to help. If you are starting a programme from scratch and don't have much experience of the industry, ask your account manager for advice on promotions, communicating to publishers, setting and achieving your objectives and any extras the network may be able to offer you. There might be resources for them to build you banners or creatives and set up links and automated reports. Use their expertise to find the intelligent insights behind your stats and results.

2 *Set clear goals and objectives for your programme with KPIs to measure your achievements* throughout each month. This will help you to spot any issues, correct them quickly and prevent any hiccups from happening again. Whether it be acquisition of customers, sales, e-mail database growth, lead generation or increased registrations, organization and planning in advance really are the keys to success. Create a promotional calendar to run alongside your set objectives. You can give this to your publishers to plan ahead. Doing this will establish a steady return from your programme.

3 *Make sure you set a competitive and appropriate commercial performance model that caters to the different publishers you may want to work with.* A tiered commission structure is a great way to incentivize publishers to promote your company. Paying higher rates to the publishers that drive more business to your site will motivate them to promote your company more and put more resource into working with you.

4 *Keep an open mind.* The industry as a whole is growing constantly, with many new and exciting publishers entering the space, many with different technologies available to help achieve your own set of objectives. Be sure to explore the market and keep your finger on the pulse. From traditional voucher code and cash-back publishers to on-site retargeters and basket abandonment partners, they can all help you to grow your business in different ways. Be open to testing each solution to find out which works best with your business model. The performance commercial model

allows you to do this with minimal risk as you are only paying commissions on performance.

5 *Build strong relationships and stay in touch with your key publishers.* Regularly talk to your top partners and arrange face-to-face meetings to review performance. A little effort goes a long way – and remember that this is a team game where you, your network and your publishers are working towards the same goals.

Embracing innovation

In this chapter, we have repeatedly mentioned the variety of publishers who are active in the performance marketing industry. This is of massive benefit to advertisers but can also come with some challenges. Most notably, how do advertisers evaluate such a diverse mix of publisher opportunities and identify the right ones for their business?

The first step is for advertisers to come to terms with the fact that there are likely to be times when they simply don't understand the publisher's proposition. That's okay. It is also the start of a potential opportunity. If a way of promotion crops up that an advertiser has never heard of, then it stands to reason they are not currently using it.

However, before diving into the detail of individual publisher opportunities, it is crucial that brands understand how each publisher works and the impact that their activity will have on other marketing channels.

Often, new publisher ideas slot in seamlessly alongside existing activity. Additionally, new innovative technologies can actually improve the performance of other channels. In a small number of cases, performance publishers can actually replace the performance of another channel.

All of these are good things but brands need to understand the impact of these activities to ensure that they are planning ahead effectively.

How performance marketing can enhance other marketing channels

Let's look at two examples of how performance marketing can improve the results or coverage that a brand gets from another channel. Take paid search as an example. Most brands will bid on their brand terms and other highly searchable, high-converting terms that will drive consumers to their website. More often than not, this activity is not conducted through the performance channel, with advertisers either using specialist paid search agencies or conducting the activity themselves.

However, if a brand also discounts some of its products or offers voucher codes to loyal customers, it is doubtful they will be bidding on discount terms, eg brand + voucher code. This is because deal-savvy consumers generally prefer to find discounts through specialist discount websites. Research has shown that consumers don't believe they will get the best discount directly from the brand.

So if an advertiser is not bidding on these discount terms, they are losing traffic by not being visible. In steps the performance marketing publisher. Most of the large discount code sites also offer additional paid search services, specializing in the brand + discount code space. In exchange for a strong discount offer, they will also normally conduct paid search activity on these terms for free (or at least as part of the agreed exposure and commission package). In this way, the advertiser can increase the exposure they get through paid search, provide consumers with the user experience they want and not increase their costs, as it is all still paid on a CPA.

Now let's take a channel that is not distinctly marketing, SEO. SEO is often viewed by brands as a free channel, as consumers visit their site from natural search results that do not incur a cost. So, depending on the strength of the SEO work, a brand will attract a certain number of customers each month. Then, depending on a few other factors, a certain percentage of those customers will convert, providing a conversion rate for the site. Usually, conversion rates are between 1 per cent and 10 per cent, depending on the site and the advertiser industry.

So how can performance marketing help?

Well, there are publishers out there who specialize in conversion optimization rather than new traffic generation. Take the guys at SaleCycle (basket abandonment remarketing) or Yieldify (onsite retargeting). Their technologies are designed to maximize the return from each individual customer by using technology to intelligently communicate relevant product offers to consumers before they move off to a competitor.

By improving the number of conversions from existing traffic, the advertiser's conversion rate improves, making SEO (or any other channel) more effective. Yes, there is a cost involved in using a performance marketing publisher to achieve increased conversions, and some of those conversions would have happened naturally anyway. However, the increase in conversion far outweighs the cannibalization of any existing conversions.

These are just two examples of how performance marketing can be employed to great effect when looking at existing traffic and conversion maximization.

Summary

- The performance marketing industry is growing faster than any other form of advertising and brands should seriously consider entering into a performance programme if they haven't already.
- The industry offers numerous benefits at very low risk and, with the variety of publishers in the market, brands can keep at the forefront of digital without investing large amounts of resource.
- Other marketing channels can benefit from the integration of performance publishers and overall conversions can be improved very quickly.
- While performance marketing may not be as well-known as other areas of digital, it can offer significant gains if implemented correctly.

Common pitfalls of performance marketing

Everyone makes mistakes. New entrants into performance marketing are no different and, as with anything digital, what works for one company may not work for another so there is bound to be a bit of trial and error involved in establishing your performance marketing programme. However, there are a few common pitfalls, which we will hopefully help you to avoid:

- *Focusing on actions rather than costs* – or 'Bambi syndrome' as some in the performance industry like to call it. This sometimes happens when a new entrant into the market realizes the true power of performance marketing. They see the number of sales rocketing, but forget to stay focused on the bottom line. It is not uncommon for a new programme to offer huge commissions to get off the ground by attracting top affiliate partners, but at some point commission rates will need to come down or the campaign will run at a loss.
- *The 'our message is timeless' effect*: you've worked hard, your launch content is outstanding, your creative elements are top-notch and affiliate partners flock to your campaign. Success! But don't sit back. The hard work is only just beginning. You will need to keep the various elements of your campaign fresh to keep affiliates interested and recruit new partners. A common mistake is for companies to take their eye off the ball when their collateral is working for them. By the time they realize performance is slipping, it's too late to come up with

▶

something new and their hard-won partners have moved on to the new 'best' merchant in the space.

- *If I brand it, they will come*: being a big brand does not guarantee success in the performance market. In fact, being a huge brand – the biggest brand – doesn't guarantee success. Your brand strength will help you to be recognized by affiliate partners, but don't get lulled into relying on your brand equity. Affiliates will not feel obliged to promote you – they will assess your offer on its merits, and will only choose to partner with you if your offer stacks up.

CASE STUDY   Slendertone and Optimus

Slendertone is a world leader in providing products that improve muscle tone and body shape. Optimus generated 122 per cent growth in affiliate revenue across five European markets.

Location

Europe.

Objectives

- To achieve significant growth in chosen EU markets.
- To support offline media activity with integrated online brand exposure.
- To improve the sustainability and profitability of affiliate activity.
- To successfully launch the Spanish affiliate programme.

Target audience

Fitness consumers in European markets.

Action

- The Slendertone product range is an educational sell requiring the brand website to supply content in local languages in order to maximize sales and conversion rates.
- To support Slendertone's approach, Optimus delivered country-specific affiliate programmes that supported the clients' local offline marketing calendar, which included TV campaigns.

- Cost of sale is key, so to maintain minimum cost of sale in the affiliate channel Optimus maximized volumes, whilst taking an aggressive approach to the fixed costs associated with each country programme. This was achieved in each market by ensuring that key volume-driving publishers were in place to support the scheduled advertising with onsite and newsletter exposure. This is in addition to a year-round promotional and code-based schedule designed to highlight seasonally relevant products and encourage publisher engagement with the programme.

Results

- The combined growth of the EU programmes delivered a staggering 121.8 per cent in sales versus the previous year (January to May 2014 versus 2015).
- Every country is in double-digit growth with Spain being the latest successful country extension in the EU programme.
- Key figures include:
  - Ireland: 56 per cent;
  - Germany: 204 per cent;
  - France: 112 per cent.

Link to campaign

www.slendertone.com

About the creator

Optimus is a digital agency specializing in online retail marketing. With offices in Devon and London, they work both nationally and internationally with the single purpose of driving online growth and sales for their e-commerce clients (www.optimus-pm.com).

Quote

Michaela Ewen, e-commerce manager (Germany), Slendertone:

Optimus has shown a good knowledge of European (EU) affiliate markets and has worked as a team with our country managers to ensure that all potential opportunities have been pursued to grow revenues. The nature of the Slendertone product makes it less simple to deliver localized communications on an ongoing basis. Optimus has risen to the challenge and helped to deliver big growth in the online channel through their multilingual expert EU account team.

Bonus online-only chapter

Going global – internationalization: cross border digital marketing

One of the key drivers for business growth is the opening of new, often international, markets. As businesses move into new regions the challenges of new languages and cultures can be a major barrier to success.

I was privileged to work with Greig Holbrook from Oban Digital and Roy Graff from Digital Jungle on this chapter.

To read this chapter, please go online to:

www.koganpage.com/understanding-digital-marketing

Understanding the IoT   13

OUR CHAPTER PLEDGE TO YOU

In this chapter you will discover answers to the following questions:

- What is the IoT?
- What do digital marketers need to know about the IoT?
- What user experience (UX) considerations do I need to be aware of in the IoT?
- What are the issues and concerns surrounding the IoT?
- What is the future of the IoT?

The internet of things

At the time of writing, the internet of things (IoT) is the biggest and most anticipated digital trend of the last year. According to Cisco approximately 50 billion devices will be connected to the internet by 2020, turning IoT into a reality. Experts from A T Kearney predict that the IoT will have a US \$3.5 trillion impact on the global economy within the next five years. Connected devices cover nearly every aspect of day-to-day life, including home energy systems, domestic appliances, security devices, entertainment products, interactive wearables and fitness products... the list goes on and on.

In 2016 John Lewis's flagship store on Oxford Street, London launched an IoT department – a smart home showroom, displaying a range of household products and kitchen appliances connected to the IoT. The 1,000-square-foot space opened in April after the retail giant reported an 81 per cent rise in sales of smart home products in the past year. The designated space aims to 'demystify the concept of the smart home', according to John Lewis's IT director, Paul Coby. The department is divided into four zones: kitchen, entertainment, sleep and home monitoring.

Current mainstream IoT products include Hive from British Gas, which allows you to control your heating remotely through a mobile app, and the recently unveiled Samsung The Family Hub™ refrigerator, with a Wi-Fi-enabled touchscreen that lets you manage your groceries, connect with your family and entertain like never before. The price point for these products (particularly smart refrigerators) is still high; however, as technology develops and price points become lower and more accessible, soon all of our fridges will be able to tell us when we are running low on milk – or, better yet, order it for us!

So what does this mean for digital marketers? The IoT opens even more digital channels for digital marketers to utilize and analyse. More channels mean more data and being able to analyse more consumer behaviour. Smart devices are able to track and gather user data, and send it back to the brand and/or manufacturer. The brand will then be able to use that data to create personalized marketing strategies similar to using advanced CRM.

The need for omni-channel and cross-channel personalization not only becomes possible but an essential part of marketing in the IoT, making the customer's journey seamless and integrated at every touch point.

James Bailey, a UX consultant with a passion for user-centred design, gives us his expert view on digital marketing and understanding the people in the IoT.

Expert view
Understanding the people in the IoT
Contribution by James Bailey, user experience consultant

The technological foundations for the IoT are being laid now. In the coming years we will see a great many companies, products and services being launched, and then disappearing without a trace. They will fail because they don't understand the point of the IoT: that it should add value to our lives, support our behaviours (not change them), and make life that little bit easier and more satisfying. Just because you can connect something to the internet doesn't mean that you should. The most successful companies (and marketers) in the IoT will understand this.

Take a minute to reflect

Think back to 2000 and reflect on the impact that the internet has had on your life since then. Think about the products and services that you take for granted today. The following were all launched between 2000 and 2010;

they disrupted the ways that we do business, interact socially and go about our daily lives:

- 2000: Asos, Ocado, Rightmove, TripAdvisor;
- 2001: Wikipedia;
- 2002: LinkedIn, Skyscanner, Xbox Live;
- 2003: iTunes, Skype;
- 2004: Facebook, Flickr;
- 2005: Google Maps, YouTube;
- 2006: Spotify, Twitter;
- 2007: Kindle, iPhone, iPlayer, Netflix;
- 2008: Airbnb, App Store, Dropbox;
- 2009: Kickstarter, Uber, WhatsApp;
- 2010: iPad, Instagram, Pinterest.

Now, reflect on how marketing has evolved alongside the internet. Many of the subjects covered in this book – such as social media, mobile and content marketing – were born out of our need to leverage the internet's capability to connect with people.

The impact of the IoT

What new products and services will emerge out of the IoT? What impact will they have on people's lives and the world of marketing? It is almost impossible to predict – just as we couldn't have predicted the emergence of services such as Facebook, Spotify and YouTube – but there are two areas to watch closely:

- *Big data*: billions of IoT devices will be collecting vast amounts of data on how people interact with the world around them. This will give you better insights into your audience and the ability to target them in increasingly sophisticated ways, but you will need to be mindful of data privacy.
- *IoT products and services* will give you new ways to reach your audience. Right now, this could include wearables such as the Apple Watch, but in time it will extend into a whole ecosystem of products and services; from smart homes to smart cars, to places of work and leisure, and into many other areas of people's lives.

▶

This will not be an overnight phenomenon, but one day we will look back and marvel at how the IoT crept into our lives. Until then, as marketers, we need to identify the products and services that emerge out of the IoT and add value in people's lives, and why this is the case. Only then can we use them effectively to target and reach our audience. One way of doing this is to look at the discipline of user experience.

How to understand the people in the IoT

User experience (UX) is often associated with the design of digital products and services, but it is not limited to the digital world. UX considers all of the experiences that people can have before, during and after a specific interaction, and in any context of use. Over the next few pages we are going to take a number of approaches and techniques from UX and put them in a framework for understanding the people in the IoT:

1 Research the context of use: what activities and experiences are people having in a specific environment?

2 Model the context of use: turn your research into something tangible and practical.

3 Model the people: make sense of people's behavioural characteristics.

4 Write needs, then requirements: a list of instructions on how to connect with people.

5 Use the requirements: to consider the optimal method for connecting with your audience.

Through this framework you will gain a deep understanding of the people in the IoT and how they fit into your marketing strategy; you will have the evidence you need to drive decisions on how to connect with your audience in the most effective way possible, through the IoT or otherwise.

Research the context of use

The first step is to conduct 'context of use' research. This is where you observe the natural behaviour of people in a specific environment. Why bother? Because if you want to connect with people you need to understand them first; only then can you find the most effective way to engage with them and build a relationship. So by doing this research you will gain insights into the:

- *Activities* that people perform as they try to accomplish their goals.

- *Environments* in which these activities take place, both physical and digital, noting the time of day and any social dynamics.

- *Objects* that people interact with, both physical and digital – eg an app (digital) on a smartphone (physical).

- *Data* that is generated, processed, accessed or shared as a result of people's activities.

- *Systems* that support people's activities, both 'front of house' (seen) and 'back of house' (unseen by people).

There are many established techniques that you can use when researching contexts of use; the following qualitative techniques are particularly effective:

- *Observation*: passively observe the natural behaviour of people in an environment, taking note of the activities they perform and the objects, data and systems they come into contact with.

- *Participation*: actively embody the role of someone to gain a first-hand experience of the activities they perform, including the objects, data and systems they come into contact with.

- *Guided tour*: actively follow people as they perform their activities and come into contact with objects, data and systems. Gain additional insights by asking them questions as you go, but remember that this will interrupt the natural flow of the experience (which is not ideal). Use this technique to augment another.

- *Moderated testing*: observe people (in context) performing activities that are associated with a specific object, data or system; assess the usability and ask open-ended questions that probe their experience. This is a useful technique for gaining deeper insights into a specific area of the context of use.

- *Interviews*: ask people a series of questions about their activities, and the objects, data and systems they came into contact with in a specific environment. Interviews can either be prearranged or you can intercept people as they go about their activities (but they will be less willing to talk openly in these situations).

▶

Model the context of use

Your research will generate a lot of data, so you need to 'model' (make sense of) your findings and produce something more tangible and practical to use. The following outputs will give you three different perspectives and a range of insights:

- *Activity maps*: chart the key activities that people perform in a context of use. These are often broken down into phases and stages, and use flow charts to outline the activities and their variations.

- *Journey maps*: chart the journeys that people take through the physical and digital environments; highlighting key activities and objects, data or systems that they come into contact with. Journey maps often use a combination of floor plans, flow charts and data analytics.

- *Experience maps*: chart the emotional levels of people as they perform their activities in a context of use. They often use a linear timeline with a five-point scale to chart the experience (with 'pain points' at the bottom and 'delighters' at the top).

These three maps will tell you what members of your audience are doing, and how they feel about it. You can use this information to consider where and when to connect with the people in a context of use (eg as they perform key activities, or in a specific location, or during a pain point), but you cannot prioritize these decisions until you understand the people better.

Model the people

Much like before, if you want to understand the people in a context of use, you need to 'model' (make sense of) your research findings. There are a number of approaches you can take, all of which explore the following characteristics:

- *Motivations*: the reasons why people act and behave in certain ways.

- *Goals*: the intended outcomes of people's activities – they can be very specific or more aspirational; limited to the present or open to the future.

- *Needs*: the prerequisites that are necessary for people to accomplish a goal. Importantly, needs are not tied down to any one method. For example, let's say you need to travel (the prerequisite) in order to go on holiday (your goal). You have the option of travelling by plane, train or car (the methods). Therefore, your need to travel is not exclusive to any one method.

- *Behaviours*: the way that people go about performing their activities. Patterns of behaviour will often form as activities are repeated.

- *Attitudes*: the beliefs and opinions that people form about our behaviours, based on first-hand experiences and external influences.

- *Wants*: the aspirations and desires that people have as they journey towards their goal – eg wanting fun, or efficiency.

- *Fears, frustrations and anxieties*: the range of negative emotions that people may feel before, during or after an activity.

- *Pain points*: the moments in an activity where people experience particularly negative emotions; they are the lowest points in their experience.

- *Delighters*: the opposite to pain points; the moments in an activity where people experience particularly positive emotions; they are the highest points in their experience.

When modelling people, 'personas' are the ideal starting point. Before we look at what personas are, it is important to understand what they are not: marketing segments.

Segments are useful for categorizing a market by demographic (age, gender, income, etc), as well as forecasting the likelihood that they will buy a product or service, but they do not tell you about people's behaviours.

For example, based on demographics alone, Prince Charles and Ozzy Osbourne are the same. They are both white males born in the UK in 1948; they are on their second marriage; they have an income over £1 million; and they have at least two children. Their demographics may read the same, but in real life they are clearly two very different people.

This is where personas come in. Personas are fictional people. They often have a name, age and other demographics, but they are archetypes of people, consolidating patterns of behavioural characteristics.

You will usually end up with between three to six personas, but the process is not an exact science. What is more important is to identify your 'primary persona'. This is who you will focus your marketing efforts on.

It is not uncommon to build upon personas with other techniques (such as scenarios and mental models), which deepen your understanding of people even further. But even on their own, personas can be used to make informed decisions on how to connect with people. You just need to extract their needs and requirements first.

▶

Write needs, then requirements

Needs and requirements are essentially a list of instructions. Needs describe the prerequisites that are necessary for a person to accomplish their goal. Requirements build upon these from the perspective of a possible solution.

For example, let's look at needs, and imagine that our primary persona is called Susan. She is in an airport departure lounge and inside a shop that doesn't display any boarding gate information: 'Susan needs to know when the boarding gate opens and how far away it is, so that she can board her flight in time.' Requirements that could be built on this include:

- 'Susan must have access to boarding gate information while inside a shop that doesn't provide this information.'

- 'Susan must know when her boarding gate opens and how far away it is, so that she can manage her time.'

- 'Susan must have the option of being told when she should leave for her boarding gate, and what route to take, so that she can board the flight in time.'

The differences between these requirements are subtle, but they do provide different perspectives on Susan's need – eg being told when she should leave. What is important to note is that none of these requirements specify a solution: they do not mention any specific technology or functionality, product or service. Their purpose is to provide the basis for you to consider specific solutions.

Use the requirements

UX designers will use requirements to consider the optimal product or service solution. Marketers can use requirements to consider the optimal method for connecting with their audience.

For example, let's say you wanted to target Susan in the departure lounge and you have the option of using an IoT platform – perhaps a beacon network linked with an app on her smartphone and watch. You can use her requirements to consider when to reach out to her, and when not to. If Susan has plenty of time she may appreciate offers from the shops near her boarding gate; perhaps some information on her destination too (this might build some excitement). However, if she is tight on time these methods might cause frustration and contribute to feelings of anxiety. The skill is in weighing up the options.

These are the sorts of decisions that make understanding your audience in the IoT so important. The worst thing you can do is make decisions based on assumptions and opinions. You need to use the evidence gathered through your research to ensure that people are at the heart of your decision-making process – it will maximize your chances of success.

In summary

When you consider how complex marketing is today, imagine what it is going to be like when we have a pervasive network of IoT products and services; it's only going to get harder.

In an ideal world, before you start an IoT initiative you should use the framework presented in this book. It will help you to formulate the optimal approach for connecting with your audience, before you commit valuable resources. However, in the real world you don't always have this luxury. You are more likely to be asked to retrofit the IoT into an existing strategy, or work from the assumptions and opinions of others.

Either way, it is advisable that you include a degree of research that considers the people in the IoT. The insights you gain will refine your approach and provide the evidence you need to make important decisions.

A final thought, and a warning about working in silos

As a final thought to this section, it is going to be imperative in the years to come that organizations think holistically about their service offering in relation to their customers – and this advice is not limited to the world of marketing.

It is a common problem that departments within organizations work in silo; in fact, it is a common problem for teams within the same department. They work on projects without knowing what other people are up to; they don't communicate with each other; they don't benefit from shared knowledge and experience. This can cause inefficiencies and wasted resources, but it can also lead to a disjointed service offering that negatively affects the overall customer experience (and therefore repeat business).

In the coming years, as the IoT starts to link together previously separate services, working in silos is not going to be an option. Take airlines, for example – the IoT will enable them to capture data on their customers from the moment they search for a holiday, right the way

▶

through to their plane flight. This holistic view will enable them to link their services together – from website to plane flight – and refine the overall customer experience. That is, if they don't work in silos.

The truth is, it is not easy for organizations to knit together the separate parts of their business. But, as the IoT starts to embed itself into our lives, and as new companies are launched to take advantage of what the IoT has to offer, working in silos is going to become a real problem for organizations – they will fall behind the competition.

In the short term, the approach of understanding the people in the IoT will be essential to the success of IoT products and services. In the long term, organizations will need to prioritize a holistic understanding of their customers across their service offering and in the ways that they work.

Industry concerns

According to HP's 2014 Internet of Things Research Study, 70 per cent of the most commonly used IoT devices contain vulnerabilities involving password security, permissions and encryption.

Although an increase in consumer data is great for brands and marketers, it is not so good for consumer privacy and security. 'The internet-connected modules installed on various devices (eg cars, toys, home appliances, etc) can be used for unlawful surveillance,' says Daniel Dimov, security researcher at InfoSec Institute: 'For example, an internet-connected door lock can be used to monitor when a person enters or leaves their home.' If the security company that owns the internet-connected door lock was compromised, this could leave the consumer vulnerable to burglary.

Here I worked with Steve Waite from security experts GlobalSign to discuss the concerns within IoT and how to address this in your digital marketing strategy.

Expert view

Industry concerns and impacts of the IoT
Contribution by Steve Waite, managing director, GlobalSign

IoT industry concerns

This section will address some of the IoT industry concerns that digital marketing professionals must be aware of as they start to build IoT marketing strategies. The proliferation of devices connected to the internet, coupled with the need to keep devices and services secure and personal data private, presents some critical challenges. Marketers must know the impact of these concerns and how they ultimately affect data privacy, user experience and brand reputation – critical components of any marketing strategy.

Today, depending upon who you ask, there are now an estimated 10 billion connected devices worldwide. These devices range from PCs and servers to mobile devices to consumer wearables to home automation to connected automobiles to industrial equipment and so much more. By 2020, estimates are that 50 billion devices will be connected. That represents some amazing growth and also introduces a magnitude of concerns and challenges. At the root of some of these concerns is security and what needs to be done to ensure that devices, communications and transactions are secure, data privacy is properly addressed and the all-important user experience is not compromised. Marketers need to be aware of how an IoT security strategy can positively and/or negatively impact how a company goes to market with their products, how to protect critical customer/user data, and how to ensure the company's brand integrity.

In order to go to market today, IoT device manufacturers need to begin implementing security in the early design phases of their products. Security can no longer be an afterthought as it has been in the past. Trying to retrofit security into devices already in use can be difficult, costly and a burden on the users. In the past, consumers often shunned security because of poor user experiences and the stigma that setting up identities and passwords was both difficult and a nuisance. However, because of the many high-profile data breaches and sensational device-hacking news stories, consumers are becoming much more accepting of security and privacy measures and what needs to be done to secure devices and their own identities and personal data.

▶

As a result, for the manufacturers and developers of connected devices, security is now being positioned by some as a competitive advantage. Consumers are now looking to purchase devices that they know will not expose them to security issues. These consumers want assurance that they can securely use their devices and transact with services where their data will remain private. Marketers should also be using security to their advantage to build messaging that differentiates the products they are marketing from the ones that are not embracing a security strategy today.

Here, we will address some specific IoT concerns related to security that marketers should have an understanding of and how to overcome them when building their marketing strategies and plans.

Mitigating risk and ensuring privacy and security

Everything that is connected to the internet is also a point of vulnerability. Targeted attacks, viruses and malicious software, phishing scams, identity spoofing and much more introduce various degrees of risk that must be mitigated. How a company chooses to address IoT security throughout the product life cycle (from product development to consumer use to ultimately end-of-life of the product) will be a critical decision in the go-to-market strategy. Will a company be able to provide its customers with the confidence they need to make informed buying decisions and that the products and/or services ensure security and privacy?

Consumer device market

In the consumer market, privacy may be the most important concern. Unfortunately, consumer identity, personal information and credit-card data theft are all too common these days. Privacy concerns will only continue to escalate as more and more consumer devices go online and massive amounts of data is collected. Devices and services must be secured to ensure that identities and financial data are not stolen. Consumers are generally more at risk to security issues because of the public nature of their device usage and transactions. Additionally, the average consumer often does not have advanced knowledge of security measures and processes that can help protect them. They must rely on the device manufacturers and service providers to offer the level of security and privacy they need. This represents an opportunity for marketing professionals to leverage the security message when marketing products, in order to help gain the trust of their targeted consumer base.

Privacy concerns can be particularly worrisome in the consumer device market. Devices are already connecting to home, corporate and public networks left, right and centre and it is not entirely clear to the consumer what information and data are being collected, where they are being stored, how they are being used, whether the personal data is being protected, how long it will be kept and what eventually happens to it. When choosing these devices, consumers are often enamoured by the novelty of the device and don't comprehend the risk of introducing data collectors into their homes, workplaces and even their bodies. To protect privacy, how will IoT providers assure consumers, what regulations are in place and who is checking that they are in compliance?

The two hottest areas of the consumer IoT market are home automation devices and wearables, with what seems like new devices being introduced on a daily basis. Consumers will overlook the security and privacy risks of such devices because of the 'cool' factor and perceived personal and financial benefits being marketed to them. Here are a couple of examples...

The connected thermostat is one of the most useful and beneficial IoT devices in the market today. We as consumers see it as a device that can help us to reduce energy consumption and save us money. These thermostats collect temperature data, manage energy usage to keep our home warm or cool and some even monitor when we are home or away in order to optimize when energy is consumed. We easily forget that these devices are connected to the home network and communicate to cloud services. Beyond the security risk of being a vulnerable entry point into your home network with just a simple username and password, do we know who has access to the data being collected? If energy providers purchase or gain access to this type of data, could they use it to change rates during peak or off-peak hours to increase their profits? Maybe this results in fewer cost-saving benefits to the consumer – going against why the device was purchased in the first place.

Wearable devices get even more personal and the data being collected can have a dramatic and/or drastic impact on our lives. For example, fitness devices are great for monitoring our activity level and health data as we look to improve our lifestyles. The data being collected and transmitted by these devices is highly personal, including age, weight, activity times, sleep habits, locations and more. If left unregulated, this

▶

private data could affect how we get insurance, our coverage plans and the rates we can get. Could an insurance company actually raise our rates because we are not getting enough sleep or choose not to offer us life insurance because of a lack of tracked physical activity?

In both these examples, we can offset the negatives with positives, especially around the 'knowledge is power' concept, with the things we interact with in our lives. IoT devices can enable us to be more efficient, save money, get healthier, get to places quicker and easier, be more informed and aware, and so much more. We can also build our own profiles that would enable marketing efforts to be very relevant to us based on time, location, and personal preferences and needs. As marketers, this information is a goldmine of opportunity, but the data must be used appropriately, with consent, and must be protected.

Industrial IoT (IIoT) market

Traditionally, in the industrial market, manufacturing and other equipment systems have been connected in closed or controlled environments and security has not really been an issue with no exposure to the outside world. However, more and more devices and equipment are now connecting to the internet to share data for operational efficiencies, maximize manufacturing and production capabilities, and save time and money in processes that contribute to a stronger bottom line for the company. While keeping critical data secure and private is important, there are additional risks to be aware of. One of those risks is safety.

If a manufacturing device or service is compromised, the safety of the company's workers using the device can be at risk. Malicious attacks can make nearly undetectable changes to how manufacturing equipment operates and functions. Maybe the equipment runs a little hotter than it should or the electric voltage is increased beyond the equipment's capacity. Scenarios such as these can put the safety of the workers at risk and put the manufacturing company and their equipment providers at risk as well.

Additionally, the safety of the consumers who are purchasing the products being made by IoT device manufacturers is another area of concern. What if an attack on the manufacturing process and connected equipment leads to a single screw being left out of devices that grounds the internal wiring inside them? This defect could go undetected even through comprehensive quality assurance tests. When the products then hit the market, consumers can be at risk and potentially harmed if the products fail when being used.

In both of these safety scenarios, the resulting public relations nightmare is the type of negative news that journalists love to expose. How to address and overcome it will be part of a critical marketing exercise that needs to be properly planned for if a crisis arises.

User experience is essential

Why we decide to buy is often tied to the user experience. A positive user experience generally leads to a decision to make a purchase and, more importantly, to repeat the purchase or buy more products and services. Consumers are very loyal to companies and brands when they have exceptional experiences and will not hesitate to look elsewhere when they do not. We as marketers all know how hard it is to win new business and the extremely high costs associated with acquiring new customers – not to mention trying to win them back. Building and sustaining customer loyalty are key to business success. However, a single negative user experience can be a business killer. Consumer IoT devices must present customers with a positive user experience and maintain it as they continue to interact and use the product – and even as they retire the product.

While the importance of building security into a product at the early stages of the design process was touched upon earlier, how security impacts the user experience throughout the product life cycle must be analysed and tested before releasing a product. Securing devices and service must be made easy so that the user experience remains strong.

What happens when setting up an account and linking the device to a service doesn't go smoothly? What happens when users cannot remember their security credentials and can no longer log into the service or application to manage their devices? What happens when the device is lost or compromised? What happens when a user chooses to sell the device to someone else or retire the product? These are all things to consider when bringing IoT devices to market.

Additionally, because consumer UX expectations have set a precedent on how we interact with retail devices and services, the user experience in the industrial market is also changing. We as consumers now expect that same type of experience even when interacting with the products and services that enable us to do our jobs. Positive user experiences and ease

▶

of use can lead to more productivity and workforce efficiency. Businesses understand this and will seek to purchase products that deliver the best user experiences.

Brand reputation and protection

A single security event can have an extremely detrimental impact upon a company. Beyond the financial ramifications, it is the reputation with customers that is most at risk. Our access and how we consume and socially share news can quickly escalate any negative event into a catastrophe.

In the consumer world, one security event or breach can have significant and long-lasting impacts on consumer brands. Just ask Target about the many months it has taken the company to win back its customers' confidence after its highly publicized security breach in 2013. Even today, it is still a work in progress, years after the breach occurred. Target is lucky to have survived. Some consumer brands simply would not be able to recover from such an event. Hot start-up IoT device manufacturers that do not properly address security and do not have the strong financial fortitude and previous established customer loyalty of a company like Target can quickly be forced out of business if they were to experience a similar security scenario.

While it is easy to see the impact of a security event on a company's brand reputation, another area of concern is making sure the devices being manufactured and marketed are legitimate. Counterfeit or knock-off devices in the marketplace can also hurt a company's reputation if problems are mistakenly attributed to the original equipment manufacturer. There are ways to protect the brand from these types of issues. Eventually, every device will need to have a unique identity that can be used to check its integrity when the device authenticates to a service. This could help manufacturers more effectively to secure their product inventories and supply chains to better protect their brands by assuring their products meet the quality standards they have put in place.

IOT security frameworks and future proofing

Today, there is a lack of clearly defined standards for the IoT market. IoT products and services generally fit within an ecosystem where standards may address certain parts of the technology. There are organizations that are working with standards bodies and manufacturers to help provide a set of best practices when bringing IoT products to market.

Organizations such as the Online Trust Alliance (OTA) and Industrial Internet Consortium (IIC) are actively creating frameworks to assist manufacturers with how they implement security into their connected devices. The OTA focuses primarily on consumer goods, including wearables and home automation, while the IIC works within the industrial IoT space. These are just a couple of examples of manufacturers coming together to develop working IoT security frameworks. How we best secure the IoT is still being flushed out and there are many other organizations and standards bodies working on similar types of frameworks. It is hard to say if there will ever be a true winning IoT security framework or if there will continue to be multiple sets of best practices to follow.

The importance of these frameworks will address:

- How users securely interact with IoT devices and services.

- How critical and personal data remains secure and private on devices and services.

- How security and privacy can be sustained throughout the life cycle of the IoT device and application, including when the device is no longer being used, transferred to another user, retired or recycled.

What does the future hold?

Just like every user, every connected device will also soon have a unique identity. Building security and identities into devices during the design and manufacturing stages is essential to addressing issues today and in the future. The amount of data that will be collected will only continue to increase. Big-data capabilities will also play more of a role in how this data will be used and potentially monetized. While the benefits of this data to future marketing efforts could truly enable the holy grail of one-to-one marketing, we as marketers must be aware of the privacy implications and what is the best and most appropriate way to use this information.

CASE STUDY   Airport customer experiences

Bunnyfoot – the UK's leading UX consultancy since 1999 – researched customer experiences at Heathrow and Gatwick airports. Their goal was to identify 'pain points' (notable moments of frustration or anxiety) caused by the airport services and systems, in order to identify where IoT services could be used to improve the customer experience.

13.1   13.2   13.3

Location

Heathrow Airport, Greater London, UK; Gatwick Airport, West Sussex, UK.

Target audience

- Customers flying home over the Christmas period.
- Economy-class tickets.
- Short- and long-haul flights.

Method

'Context of use' research was carried out to capture the natural behaviour and experiences of customers in Heathrow and Gatwick airports. The research focused on the six stages in a departure journey: 1) travelling to the airport; 2) arriving at the airport; 3) check in/bag drop off; 4) security; 5) departure lounge; 6) reaching and boarding the plane.

A 'mobile ethnographic' approach – using a dedicated mobile app and micro camera – captured the highs and lows of the experiences as they happened. Outputs include 'experience maps', which chart the experiences and highlight pain points, alongside a report with recommendations on how IoT services could address pain points.

Figure 13.4

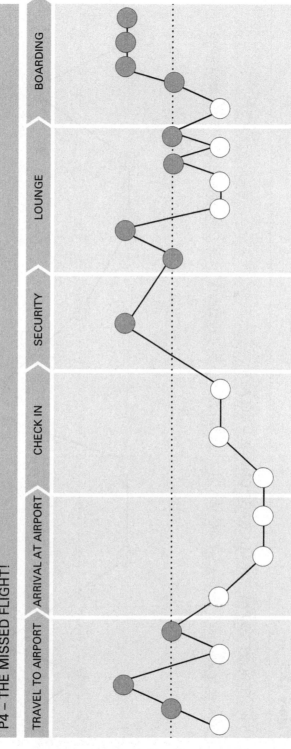

P4 – THE MISSED FLIGHT!

TRAVEL TO AIRPORT | ARRIVAL AT AIRPORT | CHECK IN | SECURITY | LOUNGE | BOARDING

Figure 13.5

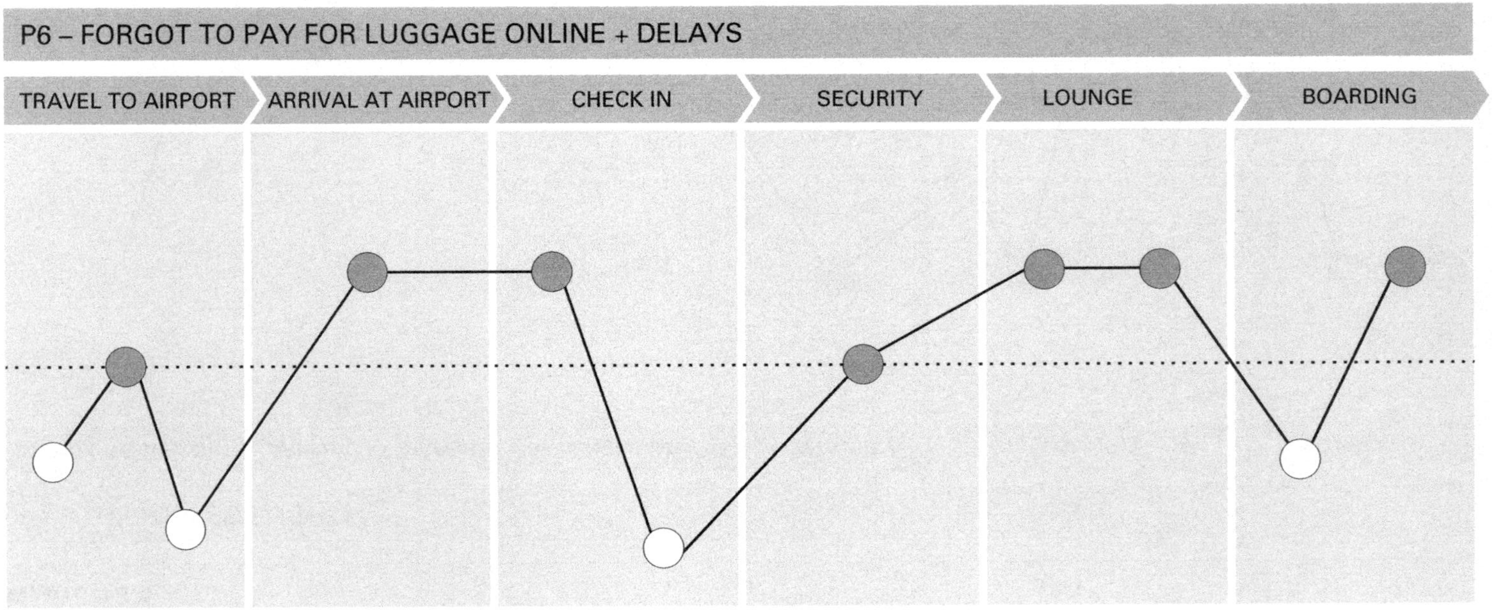

P6 – FORGOT TO PAY FOR LUGGAGE ONLINE + DELAYS

TRAVEL TO AIRPORT | ARRIVAL AT AIRPORT | CHECK IN | SECURITY | LOUNGE | BOARDING

Results

- Photographic evidence of each customer journey, from the moment they left home through to boarding the plane.

- Diary of touch points, documenting the experiences as they happened.

- Experience-map insights and recommendations across the six stages of the departure journey.

- Recommendations on how IoT services could provide personalized, context-specific notifications and services, based on customer needs and pain points.

- The experience maps were also overlaid in order to identify clusters of negative or falling customer experiences. Three key stages in the departure journey were identified:

  - Arrival at the airport and check-in: customers need real-time, personalized, contextual information – such as check-in locations and directions within the terminal, walking distances, current queue times, etc.

  - Departure lounge: customer expectations need to be managed with real-time, personalized, contextual information – eg their boarding gate, what shops will be available, the transit time and advance warning of queues.

  - Boarding gate: customers need to be notified of any boarding issues before they travel to the gate, such as their flight being busy or if they will need to check in their hand luggage. Customer experiences can also be improved through personalized information based on their destination.

Links

www.bunnyfoot.com/about/clients/bunnyfoot-airport-research.php
www.bunnyfoot.com/blog/2014/11/mobile-ethnography/

Figure 13.6

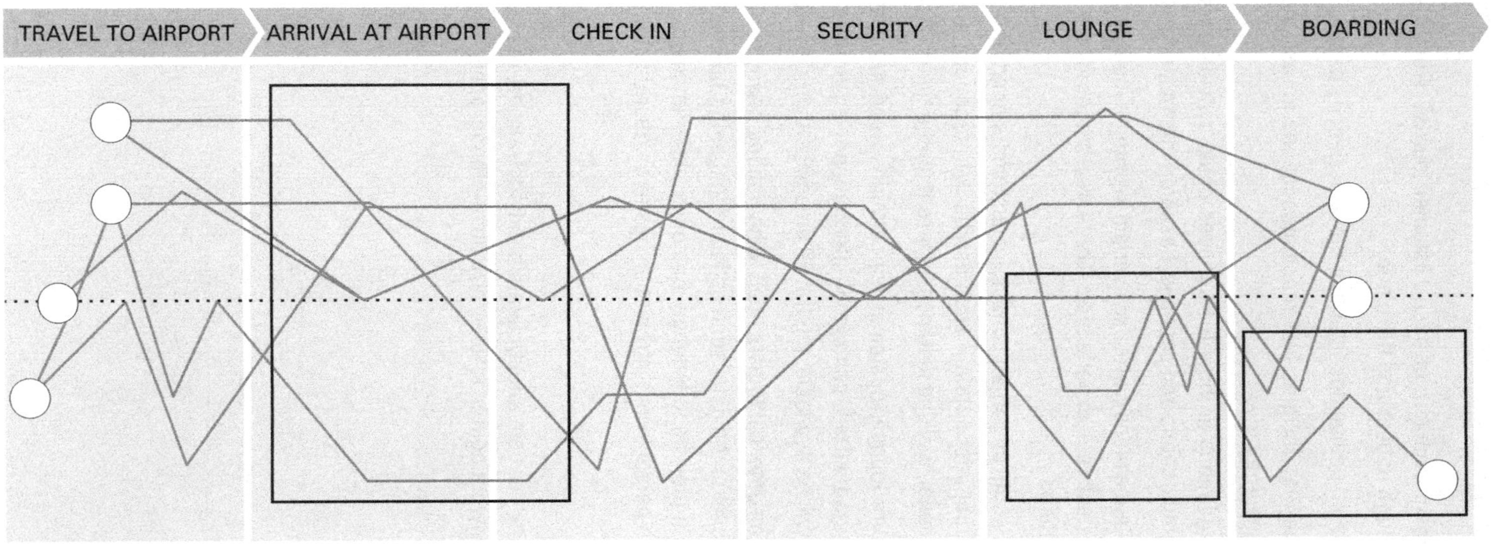

Bonus online-only chapter

Digital transformation 101: a journey of change towards a transformed customer experience

Industry expert Ricky Wallace of Clearpeople guides us through his views on digital transformation, inside out.

To read this chapter, please go online to:

www.koganpage.com/understanding-digital-marketing

Optimizing the customer and user experience

14

OUR CHAPTER PLEDGE TO YOU

When you reach the end of this chapter you will have answers to the following questions:

- What is user experience (UX)?
- How do you achieve good UX?
- What considerations do I need to make in my UX design?
- What is persuasion?
- How can I measure the effectiveness of my UX design?

Contributor note

I worked on this chapter with Dr Jon Dodd, CEO and co-founder of UX consultancy Bunnyfoot. Jon holds a DPhil in Visual and Computational Neuroscience from Oxford University. Jon spends his days helping people to create great experiences by applying the brainy bits from science and psychology, along with best practice and techniques from disciplines such as usability, human–computer interaction (HCI), ergonomics and user-centred design.

User experience (UX)

A lot of digital marketing budget and effort is spent getting people, prospects or customers to a website or service. This is of course vital, but what do you do with them once you get them there? What are they experiencing as they view and interact with what you have provided? This falls within the remit of UX design, where the aim often is to 'convert' them. Conversion could mean getting them to sign up or buy a product, and/or could mean less immediately commercial intents such as empowering them, delighting them or engaging them, with the aim of creating enthusiastic advocates who love what is provided, and tell their friends about it.

UX is about the enhancement of the behaviour and thoughts that a person experiences when interacting with your business, your service, your interactive systems. It is about 'how' it does something not just 'what it does'. The digital entity could be a website, an app, software, a kiosk, or the whole host of things that will shape our digital lives in the future such as virtual reality, augmented reality and the connected devices of the internet of things (IoT). For the purposes of this section I will assume that we are mostly talking about web experiences but the great thing about UX is that, being rooted in the understanding of humans – their psychology, physiology, capabilities etc – much of what we can learn and many of the techniques we can employ are largely invariant over both time and the medium by which we supply the experience. By this I mean that what you might learn below might apply to your current website and will largely apply to whatever unbeknown way we will all be interacting with our customers in 10 years' time.

What is UX?

It is fairly true to say that there is much debate even from those who purport to practise UX about what is involved in UX and how to describe it. It has become a popular thing to tout on CVs and company service descriptions, such that it is at risk of becoming a devalued term. Its current trendiness has meant that many people now claim to be 'user experience designers' when in fact they have none of the skills, experience or knowledge of what should actually be done to execute a good interactive experience. I speak from bitter experience of trying to sift through CVs, and sit through interviews with potential consultants for my UX consultancy. If nothing else, hopefully some of the information that follows will enable you to filter out the pretenders from the real deal if you are recruiting someone to do it for you – hopefully it will also help empower you or your team to investigate the possibilities and begin to execute more of the good stuff yourselves.

Definitions and what it takes

ISO 9241-210 (2010) is an international standard on ergonomics and human system interaction that has evolved since the 1980s. It contains some great guidance on UX and all the other things that go with it (although it is rather a heavy read and expensive so I don't suggest you dive in unless you are feeling particularly enthusiastic). It defines UX as: 'A person's perceptions and responses that result from the use or anticipated use of a product, system or service.'

This 'holistic' viewpoint emphasizes the consideration of what happens before, during and after an interaction, and includes all the users' emotions, beliefs, preferences, perceptions, physical and psychological responses, behaviours and accomplishments. This is summarized in Figure 14.1, which shows also the key role of usability (from another part of the ISO 9241 standard – see later in the chapter) in delivering a good experience.

Figure 14.1 UX considers the user before, during and after the interaction. Usability, an essential component of UX, is considered during actual use of the system/interface

BEFORE USE	DURING USE	AFTER USE
'anticipating'	'using'	'digesting'
Imagining the use of the product without actually having used it (subjective expectations)	Effective, efficient and satisfactory completion of goals (evaluation while using)	Identification with or dissociation from the product (reflective thoughts/feelings)

Usability
(ISO 9241-11)

User Experience
(ISO 9241-210)

The ISO also lists three factors that influence user experience and that you must have a good handle on if you are going to try to design a truly good experience; they are:

- the system – its capabilities and constraints;
- the user – who they are, their goals, needs, expectations, capabilities etc;
- the context of use – the environment (the where, when and how) of how something will be used.

Many other definitions also exist, just try googling – one of my favourites is from Mike Kuniavsky in his book *Smart Things: Ubiquitous computing user experience design* (2010):

> The user experience is the totality of end-users' perceptions as they interact with a product or service. These perceptions include effectiveness (how good is the result?), efficiency (how fast or cheap is it?), emotional satisfaction (how good does it feel?), and the quality of the relationship with the entity that created the product or service (what expectations does it create for subsequent interactions?).

While the User Experience Professionals Association (UXPA) defines user experience as:

> Every aspect of the user's interaction with a product, service or company that make up the user's perceptions of the whole. User experience design as a discipline is concerned with all the elements that together make up that interface, including layout, visual design, text, brand, sound and interaction. User experience works to co-ordinate these elements to allow for the best possible interaction by users.
> Source: https://uxpa.org/resources/definitions-user-experience-and-usability

And actually in the real world we know that great UX comes at the sweet spot where user needs overlap with business/organizational needs. Generally, the more overlap the better the result – too much either way and no one is going to be happy.

So as you can see (and I hope that those who apply for UX jobs with nothing more than proficient use of Photoshop can also see) there is quite a lot that goes into it – but don't let that make you run for the hills – if you adopt the right mindset, and start building in UX practices, you can achieve much and continue improving.

Below I will outline some of the things to think about if you want to improve the UX that you offer and achieve the benefits that come with doing so (not least improving conversion). Whole tomes have been written about all of this stuff so it is naturally a fairly high-level view but it should get you started. If you then want to progress further I provide a recommended list of books at the end of this section – these are ones that I reference in the courses I run on UX and that all my staff are actively encouraged to read – enjoy!

How do you achieve good UX?

As we saw above, to create a good user experience you really need to know your user (and the system and the context of use). A commonly accepted method of ensuring you gain that understanding and design according to user needs, capabilities and context is to employ some form of user-centred design (UCD) process (see Figure 14.2).

UCD places the user of the eventual product or service at the heart of the design effort. The user is considered, explicitly referenced and researched at each stage. This ensures that design is driven forward based on evidence rather than assumption or speculation. How many times have you had those endless debates in design meetings about how a design should be? This aims to end all that. It might seem like a big effort but the time spent up-front on research and defining the users and the problem pays big dividends later on. A greater authority than me sums this up nicely:

> If I were given one hour to save the planet, I would spend 59 minutes defining
> the problem and one minute resolving it.
> Albert Einstein

Executing a successful UCD programme of work requires a variety of different skills in a team, and typically includes roles such as designers, researchers, information architects, marketing experts, business analysts, programmers and project managers. Sometimes an individual may fulfil multiple roles.

A UCD approach that includes iterative usability/UX testing fits with traditional 'waterfall' approaches to development and also with more modern and increasingly popular lean/agile approaches. In an iterative development process, research, design, prototyping and testing may be revisited and refined a number of times (the iterations) before a final product is released.

There are many different models and representations of UCD but all follow roughly the same stages as in Figure 14.2. Some of the methods that you might want to investigate are listed below but, importantly, you don't have to do them all – you can investigate and cherry pick those that might be suitable for your particular circumstances. Over time you might start to add more.

1. Research

At this stage you carry out activities and research to understand the needs of the business and its stakeholders, and crucially to understand user needs and the context of use.

Figure 14.2 A potential user-centred design (UCD) approach for a web design project. The user (your customer) is at the heart of the process and is considered/ tested at each stage. Some stages might have multiple iterations

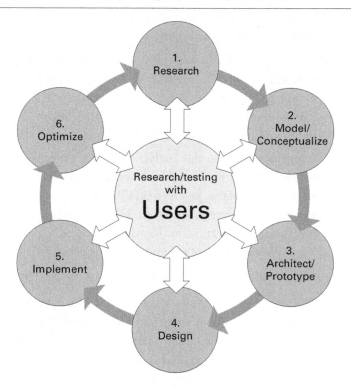

The key with user insight research is to attempt to observe behaviour if you can rather than ask people direct questions at the outset and fall prey to their opinions or hearing what they think you want to hear. People are very bad at both accurately reporting their past behaviour and predicting their future behaviour. For past recollections people may assume knowledge, forget details and see the past through rose-tinted spectacles. For future behaviour, many of our decisions, including purchase decisions, happen non-consciously, so asking our conscious mind about them can be fruitless at best, highly misleading at worst. So don't ask questions – observe real behaviour whenever you can.

Some methods you might employ here are:

- *Contextual research*: you might see the terms 'contextual inquiry' or 'ethnography' bandied about, but basically this is observing and/or interviewing people whilst they go about their normal business of doing the things that interest you in the environment they usually do them.

Many methods for this exist, including more recently the use of mobile phones and other recording devices to help, but you could do worse than just watching people in a shop that sells what you sell, or listening in to call-centre enquiries. Once they have done what they would spontaneously do you can then, if needs be, ask them why they did it.

- *Observed browsing*: similar to a usability test that is described later, you can put people in front of your existing site/design, competitor offerings, or even rough new concepts for things you are considering. Again, don't ask for their opinion on the design (and ignore it if they offer it) but see what they actually do and understand and infer their needs from their actions.

- *Live site testing/analysis*: use the analytics of your current site to infer what people are doing, or you could even set up what is or appears to be a real site, or a minimal viable product (MVP) and find out what people's actual responses are to your proposition. One of the problems here, of course, is that you might learn what they do but not necessarily why – so you should use other qualitative techniques to help triangulate this.

- *Use the research that informs all your other digital marketing activities.*

In practice you might not be able to get away from asking people direct questions, but be careful with interviews, surveys and focus groups, as unless they are very well designed and executed you may get poor levels of insight or, even worse, the wrong answer. This is a huge topic, but below are some short tips to help you do them yourself or assess the quality of those doing the research for you:

- *Interviews*: avoid stilted question-and-answer-type interviews – instead you want to guide a free-flowing conversation/discussion about a recent real event (such as the last purchase of a product, or how they used something) whilst at the same time making sure you cover everything that you wanted to find out. Avoid closed (yes/no) and leading questions. Ideally you should just set them off and listen, and encourage them to continue ('tell me more about that').

- *Surveys*: because they are easy and cheap to produce, surveys are very popular (a host of powerful online tools such as SurveyMonkey or SurveyGizmo is available). Unfortunately surveys are often misused and poorly designed, making them practically worthless from an insight perspective. If you are going to produce one then you would do well to read some of the advice you can find online about how to construct a good survey, then try it on a small number of people to test that: 1) they are answering the questions you think you are asking (the English language is highly interpretable – the same question may mean many things to many different people); and 2) the results you get are actually useful to help inform what you are trying to do – if they are not, don't bother your customers with the survey.

- *Focus groups*: good focus groups are hard to do well – this is for a whole host of reasons, including poor moderation, 'group think', not hearing from shrinking violets, and people being asked to opine or speculate on something shown to them rather than experience it. Not all focus groups are bad but I generally find that, particularly if you want insights about something specific such as how to improve your landing-page concept or your site proposition, you would be better spending your time and money on one-to-one observations, tests or interviews. So if you are currently doing focus groups you might want to seriously consider some alternatives and see how they compare.

Even if you cannot afford to do much research – try to do *some*. It need not take long – just a day spent watching what people do will give you valuable information and inspiration to make what you are doing now much better.

2. Model/conceptualize

Activities in this stage distil the research into useful design tools such as:

- Personas: descriptions of who the users are, their goals and priorities.
- Mental models: how the users might approach using the site/system.
- Scenarios: descriptions of different contexts and uses of the system.
- User flows: step-by-step descriptions or diagrams of key paths through a site or system.
- User experience maps: often detailing the full before, during and after experience and mapping on aspects/insights such as what people are thinking, feeling, saying and doing, key triggers or motivators, potential blockers, etc.
- … and many more – see some of the books at the end of this section to find out more about these and how to use them appropriately.

The goal of these is to drive insight and deep understanding about who your user is and how what you provide might empower them – they drive the next stage of the process and may be useful reference points throughout the whole process. They are great communication devices to get the full team – from management to developers – on board with the same common understanding about who you are designing for and what you are trying to do.

A risk at this stage that we see sometimes is producing deliverables for deliverables' sake, so select what you are going to do on the basis of how they can help you – you might also want to read the book *Lean UX* (included in the list at the end of this section) for some more advice on this.

3. Architect/prototype

Activities at this stage include detailing the overall structure of the system (information or system architecture) and researching/testing it using methods such as card sorting or tree testing, and producing prototypes that demonstrate and simulate how the system will be used (interaction design).

Often during this stage you might explore multiple alternative solutions to a design brief (informed by your research and your modelling) using various ideation techniques – these are designed to produce a high number of potential ideas using 'divergent thinking'. Look it up! It is essentially like brainstorming (without the bad reputation) and is a process you can use to get you out of your current rut, pet solution or temptation to copy your competitors. You work with your colleagues to feed off each other to create new ideas – some of which will be rotten but may have the sparks that lead to something good and new. Read the book *Gamestorming* (included in the list at the end of this section) for a good starter.

Prototypes can be of varying degrees of fidelity, from hand-drawn early prototypes, through to black-and-white 'wireframe prototypes', through to dynamic functional prototypes. Start on paper first before the temptation to go electronic – you will achieve a lot more in a shorter time. When you think you have nailed the basic design then you might want to consider one of the many online prototyping tools available (there are loads of them but I tend to use Balsamiq or Axure), these help you to create realistic simulations quickly and you can add interactivity. Some of the advanced tools like Axure allow you to simulate things like responsive design, complex interactions, animations, and also pass data through the prototype – but you probably should avoid getting carried away with these as you will want to spend the time designing not programming a throw-away prototype – only add the interactions that help you to demonstrate the features or test the parts that will be useful to test. Leave the programming to the coders – indeed in more agile environments it may be appropriate to go straight from sketch to proper code – use what works best for you and what costs the least.

Importantly you can test with real customers at any stage of the process – and the earlier you test the better (see later in the chapter for a brief description of how to do a UX usability test). I find that people are often derisive or scared of testing something half-finished or rough looking on real customers – but why waste time and money on polish if you can get the answers earlier and cheaper? In fact, often precisely because the prototype looks a bit rough, test participants actively engage with the information rather than getting distracted by elements of the creative (you will test these later). Testing early also lets you be more edgy and creative as you can test a whole host of potential alternatives quickly and cheaply, select what works and throw out what doesn't without any of the inertia or emotional attachment you might get with crafting the 'perfect' design.

So next time you are changing something like your landing page, home page, or even a process like checkout – create a number of potential alternatives sketched out on paper and take these out to your customers and see what they would do with them – remember, don't ask them what they think, but see what they do. If it's a website give them a pencil to stand in for the mouse; when they press with the rubber, that's a click; if they need to type anything then get them to write it in pencil. After a click give them the page that it would lead to and see what they would do with that. Similarly you can simulate a mobile experience, complete with tapping and dragging, by using a picture of a phone or tablet with the screen cut out to create the viewport of the device. You then move a piece of paper behind it with your sketch design on it to simulate what appears.

You can learn a lot, quickly and cheaply, by doing this – don't be afraid to give it a go.

4. Design (visual/creative design)

All that you have been doing in the previous couple of stages is design, but this is where the application of branding and fine-scale visual design takes place, resulting in the precise look and feel that the final product will have. Obviously this is vital for the overall experience but it should be built on a sound foundation that you have previously designed and tested. There is not space here to go into details of this (except for some of the information below on visual perception) but there are important decisions to be made regarding style, form, imagery (perhaps the emotional impact), colour psychology, typeface and so on, which can all be informed by your research and modelling. You can, and should, also test these with real users where possible.

5. Implement

This is where the coding occurs, leading ultimately to the launch of the product. In a more agile approach the implementation may be incorporated tightly with the other stages in short bursts (or sprints) leading to viable products that incrementally improve or extend features. It is beyond the scope of this chapter to go into any more detail but you probably want to investigate responsive/adaptive design and frameworks to understand the impacts this might have on what and how you design – and consider this early on!

6. Optimize

Often post-launch performance will be assessed and then changes made to the design to make improvements or address deficiencies. Performance might be assessed using a whole range of methods, including website analytics and regular usability/UX testing. Live tests of the effects of tweaks or alternative designs may be performed using split testing (often A/B testing) or multivariate testing (MVT) techniques.

A short(ish) note about UX/usability testing

A key part of the UCD approach (and indeed any approach that seeks to really produce something that works for its audience) is incorporating usability/UX testing to help improve designs by identifying issues that would decrease the overall experience. As this is a touch point with users, though, you might also find insights to inspire more far-reaching changes than just fixing problems. A testing session can take a number of forms and indeed a number of different exercises can be mixed in to a session – it is precious time with your audience so it's best to make the most of it.

It is tempting to think you might need a formal lab, complete with one-way glass, eye-tracking devices, cameras, picture-in-picture recording and the whole shebang – but in reality all you really need is a computer (not even that if you are paper prototype testing), some willing participants and the intention to give it a go. You will not achieve all you could if you employed expert UX/usability consultants but you will learn some essential things that will lead to improvements (or help decision making about competing solutions). Rather than no testing, almost any testing is beneficial – and it doesn't have to break the bank.

Steve Krug provides an excellent DIY guide for usability testing in his book *Rocket Surgery Made Easy: The do-it-yourself guide to finding and fixing usability problems* (2009) – and if you are going to do it then I suggest you start there. Some quick tips though:

- You can do one-on-one face-to-face testing using just a computer (or tablet or phone) and record what goes on using various screen-recording programs or apps (a quick search will reveal many, and some are free).

- You can test one-on-one remotely using various screen-sharing programs – such as Skype or Gotomeeting.

- You can do 'remote unmoderated' tests – I like to think of these as 'posh surveys' – in which essentially you send people a link to the test, they answer a couple of questions (usually about them and their experience), then they do a task, and then when either they complete the task or they give up they answer a few more questions about their experience. You can get specialized software to run this for you, all with different features and price points – for instance, some will record a video of the user interacting with the site; some will just show the clicks and the path they took; some will provide advanced stats on things like timing, number of clicks etc.

- If you are running a test then avoid the temptation to say too much and risk leading the witness – generally say as little as possible, just set up an appropriate task or scenario and let them run with it. If they ask you questions then reflect the questions back at them, eg 'What does this link do?' – your reply: 'What do you think it does?'

- You can spend a lot of time structuring a testing session with many tasks for participants to do – but avoid it being a mechanical exercise, and avoid asking them to do stuff they would never do in real life. I generally talk to them beforehand, find out what they would be looking for in practice and let them do that.

- Ideally your participants should be representative of your audience (if you have personas they should reflect those) but, to be honest, any testing is better than no testing.

- To find useful issues you need only to test with a small number of people (people in UX still argue about the ideal numbers – but I don't want to go into all that here) – I suggest you try with four or five people per round of testing.

- Testing sessions can be short and sweet (even just a couple of minutes) – the shorter the better, as you get the best stuff early on anyway. So make sure you focus your tests on the essential things you want to know – don't put too much demand on your participants (absolute maximum of one hour).

Doing the design bit

The above discussed a UCD approach as a framework for delivering good UX – below I want to show some of the considerations and resources you might want to take advantage of in order to actually deliver (or improve) your current and future designs. You can use some of this to help you design from scratch or to help you evaluate existing designs or designs that others are doing for you. Similarly to UCD this is a huge topic, but I hope to whet your appetite to investigate further whilst also giving you some things you can probably use immediately.

Levels of design considerations

Figure 14.3 shows a diagram I often use to help explain to people (and clients) the things that we consider when trying to design an interface or an experience, particularly one that is trying to create an action such as 'add to basket'. If you are familiar with Maslow's hierarchy of needs, it is kind of like that in that there is no point executing the higher levels until you have satisfied the lower levels (although, to be honest, persuasion and emotion can be highly interlinked so their separation and order are largely arbitrary but useful in many cases to consider separately).

Figure 14.3 A hierarchy of design considerations

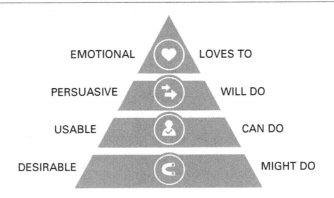

The levels shown in Figure 14.3 are explained below:

- *Desirable*: to create a successful interaction with a user (or customer) the product or service you are providing has to be fundamentally desirable – if it is not then there is not much point concentrating on anything else. There are things you can do to investigate this (eg qualitative research (discussed above) and quantitative research techniques such as conjoint analysis) and things you can do to manipulate this (eg changing the price). Let's assume you have your proposition nailed and it is desirable to your target audience – if so then they 'might' interact with you.

- *Usable*: if your product/service is desirable then you have to make sure that the infrastructure that delivers it is accessible and usable – essentially you have to make sure people can do the things they are trying to do (such as buy your product) without confusing them or wasting their time.

  Designing for usability is informed by established principles from fields such as ergonomics, cognitive psychology, perceptual psychology, human–computer interaction (HCI) and usability engineering – it is a big topic and we will touch on some of the immediately useful stuff in a section below.

  If you manage to make your site or service usable then your target audience 'can' now interact with you (eg buy your product!) – but it doesn't mean they will. This is where considering the next layers comes in.

- *Persuasive*: persuasion is about influencing people to think or behave in a desired way. Online this could mean reducing procrastination and stimulating action, such as pressing the 'buy now' button and completing a purchase. There are actually much more considered definitions and things like context to take into account – but for our purposes here we will just take a simplistic 'increasing conversion' approach, as this is probably most relevant to you.

  How to design for persuasion is informed by fields such as social psychology and behavioural economics, and it is ultimately rooted in how our brains make decisions at a non-conscious level. Basically, most of the time, our brain does the heavy lifting of our decision making in the background for us, without our conscious awareness. To do this the brain takes shortcuts in information processing (so-called heuristics) that determine our decisions. These swift, non-conscious, heuristic-based decisions usually work well for us (otherwise they would not have evolved). It is the understanding of these heuristics, and then the manipulation of them, that can be used to influence decision making, creating persuasion.

  In a section below I will present some of the basic persuasion principles that you could probably start to investigate and make use of straight away.

  If your persuasive design is successful then your customer 'will' interact with you.

- *Emotional*: our emotions have a large influence on our thoughts, our decision making and our memories. Being able to stimulate an appropriate emotional response in our target audiences is an important factor for creating products and services that people will engage positively with and, who knows, even ultimately 'love'. There is not space here to do this topic any justice whatsoever, so we point you to read Donald Norman's book *Emotional Design* (2004), where amongst other things he establishes three dimensions: the visceral, the behavioural and the reflective, which are useful for you to consider and focus on to create emotional impact. A more recent book by Trevor van Gorp and Edie Adams, *Design for Emotion* (2012), addresses the whole topic of emotional design in much more depth – not for the faint hearted but gold dust if you put in the effort.

Usability is something you can define and measure

Usability is about making interfaces easier to use, and matching them closely to the needs and requirements of the people who will actually utilize them (the 'users'). There are a number of ways to define usability but one of the best-known definitions comes again from the International Standards Organization, this time ISO 9241-11, which defines usability as:

> The extent to which a product can be used by specified users to achieve specified goals with effectiveness, efficiency and satisfaction in a specified context of use.

Although it might seem a bit dry, the above definition is robust and still highly relevant even though it has been around since the 1990s. The important components are:

- *Effectiveness*: the degree to which the users complete their goals (or tasks) successfully to completion. Often measured as a percentage of completed tasks.

- *Efficiency*: the amount of effort users must expend in completing their goals. Often measured in time or number of clicks/taps.

- *Satisfaction*: what the users actually think about the experience of using the product/system. Often measured with a subjective questionnaire – a good simple one that will be familiar to you marketeers is the Net Promoter Score.

Importantly, all the above three components are measurable (albeit they are not mutually exclusive measures) and are affected by the users, their goals and the context of use. Other definitions of usability do exist but tend to cover the above components from the ISO definition and add aspects such as:

- *Learnability*: how easy it is for users to perform tasks the first time they encounter the product.

- *Memorability*: after a period of non-use how easy it is for users to get back to their previous performance level.

- *Error tolerance*: how many errors the users make during a task. How easy it is to recover from errors made.

Again, these things can be measured (often in a usability test). The importance of this and why I have troubled you with it here is that this makes usability not just a vague, 'hand wavey' thing about making something more 'user friendly' but instead something that can be planned for and measured. You can determine usability benchmarks for yourself and track the effects of changes you make in a systematic way so you have more of an idea of whether something has worked and what 'good' looks like. You can also benchmark yourself against your competitors, which might help you to determine what to spend your time and effort on improving.

Further reading

Adlin, T and Pruitt, J (2010) *The Essential Persona Lifecycle: Your guide to building and using personas*

Ariely, D (2008) *Predictably Irrational: The hidden forces that shape our decisions* (a good book for insights on persuasion)

Cooper, A, Reimann, R and Cronin, D (1995) *About Face: The essentials of interaction design*

Few, S (2006) *Information Dashboard Design*

Goldstein, N, Martin, S and Cialdini, R (2007) *Yes!: 50 scientifically proven ways to be persuasive*

Gothelf, J and Seiden, J (2013) *Lean UX: Applying lean principles to improve user experience*

Gray, D and Brown, S (2010) *Gamestorming: A playbook for innovators, rulebreakers, and changemakers*

Hanington, B and Martin, B (2012) *Universal Methods of Design: 100 ways to research complex problems, develop innovative ideas, and design effective solutions*

Johnson, Jeff (2010) *Designing with the Mind in Mind: Simple guide to understanding user interface design rules*

Krug, Steve (2000) *Don't Make Me Think: A common sense approach to web usability*

▶

Morville, P, Rosenfeld, L and Arango, J (2015) *Information Architecture: For the web and beyond*, 4th edition

Norman, D (1988) *The Design of Everyday Things*

Norman, D (2004) *Emotional Design: Why we love or hate everyday things*

Ogilvy, D (1983) *Ogilvy on Advertising*

Raskin, J (2000) *The Humane Interface*

Stickdorn, M and Edgar, M (2012) *This Is Service Design Thinking: Basics, tools, cases*

Van Gorp, T and Adams, E (2012) *Design for Emotion*

Young, I (2008) *Mental Models: Aligning design strategy with human behaviour*

Weinschenk, Susan (2011) *100 Things Every Designer Needs to Know About People*

How to design for usability

Figure 14.4 Levels of design guidance and rules

Vague/high level	Flexible yet tangible	Strict
Principles/heuristics	Design Patterns	Guidelines/prescriptions
eg Nielsen and Molich, Norman; short 'rules' without much advice on how to design	Hands on advice, yet flexible in implementation. Recommendations based on best practice	eg *Apple Human Interface Guidelines* Fixed rules or prescriptions
Human based Universal Resilient	Somewhat technology based	Technology based Focused Not Resilient

There are rules and principles to guide you on how to design (or evaluate what you already have) for usability. I like to think of these as existing at three levels (see Figure 14.4):

- *Principles*: (sometimes called heuristics) that establish fundamental overriding 'rules' that should be considered when trying to design anything that a human will interact with. Most bad interactive design or bad usability can usually be attributed to breaking one of these fundamental rules. Often, using them gives you a more objective way to evaluate a design, express issues with a design and what needs to be done to fix it. They are useful because they are short, easy to remember lists, they let you take a holistic overview to creating or evaluating a design, and they avoid you getting swamped in detail or taking a mindless 'tick box' adherence to lists-of-rules approach. A further benefit is that because they are based on the psychological or physical capabilities of humans (your target audience) they are universal and resilient to change. Learn them once and use them for ever more. For example, the ones I present below from Donald Norman were detailed in his book *The Design of Everyday Things*, originally published in 1988 – they are still as relevant now as they were then (pre-internet as we know it and pre-mobile, touch etc) and will also guide the successful interfaces of the future.

- *Design patterns* are, at their most basic level, examples of common types of interactive elements (or combinations of elements) where the thinking has already been done for you. There is a lot more to it than this, but to begin with you might want to consider them as a useful source of good practice. They show why, where and how design elements should be used, and explain the usability and interaction principles upon which they are based. Importantly, patterns themselves are somewhat flexible in their specific design interpretation – they show you what to do, but do not dictate exactly how you must do it. For instance, you may get a pattern for an element such as 'product carousel' that defines certain must haves that a carousel must exhibit, shows five different potential examples, but still allows you to design your own specific interpretation to fit your needs. Many people use patterns to assist them to design their own interfaces, to help evaluate the interfaces provided by others, or even to help specify standards that designs must adhere to. A number of the more UX-savvy organizations have developed their own domain-specific 'pattern libraries' for use by different internal divisions – these help avoid common pitfalls and set a common basic standard whilst still allowing flexibility and individuality. A web search for 'usability design patterns' will reveal many sites (and books) offering collections or libraries of design patterns. I would advise you to generally look at more than one in order to triangulate the guidance they are giving you.

- *Strict guidelines/prescriptions* are platform/technology-specific and specify in detail (often to the pixel level) how an interface element should appear and behave. If you are designing for a specific platform (eg iOS, android, windows etc) knowledge of these rules (and where you can deviate from them) is a must. You will get a lot of this online and also in books. Being familiar with a wide range of different interface guidelines can also help you to get an all-round knowledge of good design practice. Being strict and prescriptive these are often subject to frequent change and, therefore, unlike patterns and principles will have to be reviewed and revised regularly.

Whatever guidance you follow it is important of course to base your designs on the needs of your specific audience and test them. Creating good design is not about mindless following of rules, but rather being cognizant of the rules, principles and guidelines – and if you need to break them, then break them from a position of knowledge rather than ignorance.

Some useful design principles

Norman's design/interaction principles – if nothing else, learn these!

Six of the principles below were first described in Donald Norman's book *The Design of Everyday Things* in 1988, with a further one, 'signifiers', added some time later to help clarify some confusion. They are highly useful high-level things to keep in mind when designing anything interactive, and because they are based on human needs and capabilities, are as relevant now as they were a quarter of a century ago, and they will still be relevant for whatever technologies come in the future (see Figure 14.5).

Figure 14.5 Based on Donald Norman's design/interaction principles, 1988

Visibility	Affordance	Signifiers	Mapping
Controls or information easy to locate and see	Physical form dictates or directs function	Visual form directs function	Logical and clear correspondence of control to effect

Constraints	Feedback	Consistency
Minimize options to direct action/ remove error	Action confirmed clearly and immediately	Aesthetically and functionally, internally and externally

1 *Visibility*: this is quite simply can the user easily see and recognize the thing they are meant to interact with? For example do the links or buttons stand out and look clickable? I am still amazed after doing professional evaluations for over 16 years this is still an issue (links not looking like links!).

2 *Affordance*: this is actually a physical property and does not strictly relate to digital media. Think of a door handle that you pull only to then see the 'push' sign above it. This is an example of bad affordance.

3 *Signifiers*: this is about how what people can see gives them cues about what they or the interface can do. For example if you look at a web page and there is a picture peeking up from 'below the fold' this tells you there is more to be had by scrolling. Meaningful labels on icons are another example.

4 *Mapping*: this is about the relationship of controls and the effect they have – is it clear and obvious what will happen? For example, a 'next' button would tend to be on the right, and the 'back' button to the left, giving good natural mapping. A classic example of bad mapping is many stove tops where it is not immediately clear which dial turns on which burner.

5 *Constraints*: these are usually restrictions on a user's interactions in an effort to minimize error. For example constraining the date format with drop-downs or a calendar to minimize potential input error. Whilst constraints can be useful they can also be annoying so must be selected with care – think of trying to plug a scart lead into the back of a TV and you might realize the potential frustrations with constraints.

6 *Feedback*: when a user performs an action is it clear to them that the action has taken place? If not they may think the system is broken or take inappropriate actions. For example if a user presses 'add to bag' the design must make it very clear that the item has been added otherwise they are likely to press it again (this kind of thing still happens a lot). Following submitting a search or loading a page the design must communicate that something is happening.

7 *Consistency*: do things behave in a way that is consistent with how they generally work elsewhere? People get used to the way things work so unless there is good reason then things should be designed to be consistent with other similar things out there in the world, and in particular consistent within the thing you are providing – eg people should not have to work out how to use each new page in a website or application.

Nielsen and Molich's web usability heuristics

Explained and paraphrased below from their original, are the 10 'heuristics' (or rules of thumb) developed by Jakob Nielsen and Rolf Molich in 1990. Although these were developed prior to the digital world we know today they are still highly relevant and useful to help drive good usable design, or evaluate existing designs. You should keep these in mind as you are designing or critiquing a design; they also give you a more objective way of describing issues or recommending improvements:

1 *Visibility of system status*: users should always be informed about what is going on, through appropriate feedback within reasonable time. They should know where they are in a site or process and what their options are.

2 *Match between system and the real world*: the system should speak the user's language, with words, phrases and concepts familiar to the user, rather than jargon. Follow real-world conventions, making information appear in a natural and logical order. Use appropriate metaphors where useful (but don't overdo it).

3 *User control and freedom*: the most important part of this is to support undo (and redo), but also avoid locking people in to a long process (like a wizard), instead support 'playfulness', eg for a quotation rather than a long wizard ask a few essentials then permit the user to see cause and effect by altering sliders, or similar.

4 *Consistency and standards*: users should not have to wonder whether different words, situations or actions mean the same thing. Follow common conventions. Don't reinvent the wheel unless with very good reason.

5 *Error prevention*: design carefully to prevent problems from occurring in the first place. Eliminate error-prone conditions where possible, eg for date entry, instead of a free text entry use drop-downs or a calendar control.

6 *Recognition rather than recall*: minimize the user's memory load by making objects, actions and options visible. The user should not have to remember information from one part of the site or application to another. This is why 'graphical user interfaces' came to prominence over their 'command line' predecessors.

7 *Flexibility and efficiency of use*: think about accelerators that may often speed up the interaction and therefore efficiency for the expert or frequent user. Allow users to tailor frequent actions – keyboard shortcuts, favourites and quick login all come into play here.

8 *Aesthetic and minimalist design*: increase the signal to noise ratio. Screens should not contain information that is irrelevant or rarely needed.

9 *Help users to recognize, diagnose and recover from errors*: **error messages** should be clearly visible, expressed in plain language (no codes or jargon), precisely describe the issue and constructively suggest a solution.

10 *Help and documentation*: even though it is better if the system can be used without documentation, it may be necessary to provide help and documentation. Any such information should be easy to locate, focused on the user's task, list concrete steps to be carried out and be concise.

Other principles

Many others have also looked at design and interaction principles and a quick web search will show you other listings from both academia and practitioners (eg for more recent ones look at Johnson (2010) – included in Jon Dodd's list of further reading earlier in this chapter; also Ben Schneiderman *et al*'s *Designing the User Interface*, first published in 1986 and now in its fifth edition). Most overlap extensively with the two I have listed above, but it can be a useful exercise to create your own from a combination of these lists. Just be careful to keep the list short (10 or fewer) and use language most relevant to you and your design space.

There is a whole host of other principles that you can also investigate and use to drive better design. These include the principles of perception such as 'Gestalt laws' and 'pre-attentive coding' principles; consider also colour perception, colour psychology, contrast and sizes sensitivity, and, whilst we are at it, how we read and how our memory works. An excellent book if you want to get into all this is Jeff Johnson's *Designing With the Mind in Mind* (2010).

Persuasion and the persuasive layer

As explained above, I like to think that persuasion, particularly when practised online, is about reducing procrastination and stimulating action – getting your user (or customer) to do what they wanted to do, but to do it with you. If you are doing any sort of conversion rate optimization then you should probably investigate persuasion as a matter of urgency.

Thinking about and designing for persuasion have become very popular in recent years; some key names to look out for include Daniel Kahneman, B J Fogg, Dan Ariely and Robert Cialdini, and it also has strong links with things like 'gamification'. By way of an introduction I am going to just focus below on Cialdini's six persuasion principles – these are a good start and you can probably think about ways to use them straight away.

Cialdini's six principles of persuasion

Figure 14.6 Robert Cialdini's six principles of persuasion (or influence)

Cialdini first described the six principles in his 1984 book *Influence: The psychology of persuasion*, and they are still relevant today because they are routed in the fundamental psychology and resultant behaviour of humans. They are simple yet fundamentally powerful and you will be able to apply them tactically (on, say, landing pages) or more strategically if you are designing persuasion paths in highly controlled customer journeys.

The six persuasion principles are:

1 *Reciprocity*: we are fundamentally wired to return favours and repay our debts. This means that if you offer something first, people will feel a psychological indebtedness and be more likely to do what you subsequently request them to do. So think of 'no strings attached' things you can provide for your users; this could be information, tools, free shipping etc. It doesn't always have to be tangible gifts and, in fact, research has shown that making people feel special is one of the most powerful gifts we can supply.

2 *Scarcity*: we value things more when they are in short supply and exclusive – we are drawn to them and want to obtain them. Many experiments have shown that scarce things are actually perceived as being better than their identical readily available counterparts – they taste better, they seem to have higher quality, etc. This is also linked to a fundamental bias of 'loss aversion' – we hate to lose things or lose out on the opportunity to obtain things. You can trigger your customers' sense of scarcity using the following:

- Signal the limited number – 'only two rooms left'.
- Signal the limited availability – 'offer ends 11.59 pm, 2 January 2017' (tip: if communicating deadlines make them precise as this increases conversions).
- Signal exclusivity – 'members only'.
- Signal competition for the item – '20 people are looking at this hotel right now'. Note that scarcity often goes hand in hand with some aspects of social proof (see below).

3 *Authority*: even in our cynical times we tend to follow the lead of experts or people in positions of authority. This can also be linked to fundamental factors of trust or credibility. Signal your authority and trustworthiness by showing your expertise, your awards, your longevity, the respected people or brands you work with or supply. Endorsements from trusted sources work well.

4 *Commitment/consistency*: we tend to behave in a way that is consistent with our prior actions or thoughts – and particularly if we have made our position or behavioural intent public. This means it can be hard to make people change their behaviour or attitude. The way to use this is to encourage a small action (the commitment) that is very easy to take, and then follow up with more in that same general direction – the so-called 'foot in the door and then ask for more' method. This can be something as simple as pressing a single button, or filling out just an e-mail address, or rating you on a single scale. Once you have that initial action you can build on it. You also want to encourage public commitments (likes, sharing etc) as then they will be less likely to change their mind.

5 *Social proof*: we tend to follow what the crowd is doing, and more so if the crowd is more like us. Typically this manifests itself as social proof through data: 'x people bought this', '9.8/10 customer rating', '100,000 downloads', or narrative such as customer quotations, case studies, etc. It can be more subtle though, such as implying group choice or activity, eg 'most popular', 'if the lines are busy please call again'. When signalling social proof try to make the proof come from a group most readily identifiable with your target customer – this is why, for instance, many hotel sites will show ratings from different groups such as 'business travellers' and 'families'.

6 *Likability*: quite simply we are more likely to comply with requests from people we like. This can manifest itself in all sorts of ways, from the style and tone of a site or system, use of humour, providing direct and open contact (eg through social channels), similarity and empathy.

There is much more to persuasion than these six principles but they make a good start. You might want to investigate things like 'framing'; 'the contrast principle'; 'the paradox of choice'; 'anchoring'; the power of the words 'Free', 'yes' and 'because'; 'the decoy effect'; gamification; and reward/motivation systems.

Summary

Delivering a great user or customer experience, and reaping the associated benefits, is complex and there is a lot to consider, and we have only really touched the surface here. There are, however, established frameworks (such as UCD) and robust principles, patterns and guidelines to help – even incorporating some of these aspects will help you to deliver more effective design, and you can build in more as you develop. Testing your designs with your target audience is essential – take just a day to do this, you will be amazed by the insights you get.

The future of digital marketing

15

The future is always difficult to predict but as Peter Drucker said, 'The best way to predict the future is to create it,' and that is just what we in digital marketing need to do. Marshall McLuhan, the inspiration behind this book, often referred to 'retrieval' – how lessons in the past have helped us to shape the future. In the opening chapter of this book I explored the past and demonstrated how this led to the world of digital marketing that we find ourselves immersed in today. It is important to acknowledge what has failed to survive too… be they browsers, devices, sites or practices that have become obsolete. Adopting McLuhan's 'media tetrad' also helps to imagine how best practices today may shift their shape and ultimately 'reverse' themselves into something completely new in the future – a world where perhaps the best digital marketing techniques have yet to be invented. Writing the future chapter is also fun. It is the only part of the book where I get some level of creative freedom and, in previous editions, I have been prone to some wild predictions – most of which have been wrong but that doesn't stop me thinking and hypothesizing about the future of digital marketing. As George Bernard Shaw once said: 'a lifetime making mistakes is better than doing nothing at all'. In the third edition of *Understanding Digital Marketing* I worked with Professor Mike Berry, a real stalwart of the digital marketing academic arena and now a successful author too. In this edition I've been honoured to work with Simon Kingsnorth – a former contributor to this book and author of *Digital Marketing Strategy*, published in 2016 by Kogan Page. I'm going to kick off the chapter with my thoughts and predictions and then Simon will take over to focus on the three symbiotic elements of technology, behaviour and organizational approach that will drive change.

Trust will be *the* commercial advantage

Who are the most trusted members of society? Doctors? Teachers? And who are the least trusted…?

Bobby Duffy, director of the Social Research Institute at Ipsos MORI, said the following in 2015–16:

> Public trust in politicians remains steadfastly low, at the very bottom of the list of professions alongside journalists, government ministers and estate agents. But it's good to remind ourselves that this is not a 'new crisis of trust' – from this long-running survey we can see that public trust has been an issue for politicians for at least the past 33 years.

He added:

> Most notably public trust in the ordinary man or woman in the street is at the highest level we've ever recorded. All generations have increased their level of trust – which is encouraging and important.
>
> Source: https://www.ipsos-mori.com/researchpublications/researcharchive/3685/ Politicians-are-still-trusted-less-than-estate-agents-journalists-and-bankers.aspx

I couldn't agree more. The survey did not include digital marketers per se but it does show a very low rating for business leaders. In relation to brand trust there are various surveys in the marketplace, including Nielsen's 2015 work, which shows that the most trusted brand in the United States by men is Band Aid, while women place their trust in Ziplok bags. According to ClickZ the most trusted brand in the UK is the AA followed by the Post Office, Boots and Google. I predict that digital marketers will recalibrate their 'trust' efforts to a level never before seen by the marketplace. I foresee massive investment in this area, combined with social media channels, as brands and marketers drop their defences and seek to truly become engaged with consumers. By now marketers MUST accept that consumers are empowered like never before… they don't care about digital transformation issues, they want peace of mind. They need to know and believe and trust that their data is safe and their chosen coterie of brands will behave and engage according to their preferences.

Censorship and privacy issues will destroy the internet as we know it

The internet is broken – it's true. The sonic-speed search for success has been chosen over the evolution of a democratized network that will allow citizens of the world to be connected together. It is a throwback to the telephone, telegraph and every other medium that collides with money-making priorities over the true vision held of the internet back in the day. There is massive mistrust. Advertising is fraught with crappy tactics, hacking is rife and some countries will seek to build and protect their own internets in line with their cultures, laws and nationalistic sense of identity. It is too late to do anything about this. Fundamentally I believe the days of the internet as we know it are numbered.

The good internet and the bad internet

From the ashes will arise a new internet – it's true. Because it will be impossible to reboot the current internet (due to trust and ownership issues) we will be faced with a technology dilemma. The impact of IoT and consumer demand for seamless and invisible time/money-saving tech will eventually collide with the driving demons of mistrust and a growing trend to be disconnected from this 'matrix' – it's the perfect storm. I predict the dawn of a new internet. Without boundaries, without owners, with complete transparency over data, privacy, unhackable, unabusable – the impact for digital marketers will be life changing. It may exist on 'tin' that has yet to be invented, it may come at a greater price for marketers to compete and will inevitably bring about a new constitution for the internet – it may have a greater price for consumers too. Would you be prepared to pay if you knew it was safe? Maybe this is the subject matter for my next book, but I sincerely see a separation in our immediate future where brands and consumers can decide if they want to be part of both internets or just 'be good'…

The power of voice and thought

I want an internet where I can think of something and it is done. The technology already exists to vocally command devices to complete certain tasks but we are a long way off. Once again IoT will be our saviour in this regard but let's really think what it is we want:

- Hey digital marketer we don't want to complete your lousy online forms any more – make it seamless. You know who I am because of my voice (or fingerprint or retinal scan) – you don't need any more of my valuable time to complete the task. Be the ultimate concierge… be invisible, be helpful and be good.

- We want things to happen instantly... 'book a table at one of my favourite restaurants for tonight and have a car ready outside my house exactly two minutes after I have brushed my teeth...' Is this doable? Absolutely it is. The toothbrush, the restaurant, the car and my preferences are connected to the net.

The future successful digital marketer is identifiable today because of their curiosity and commitment to investigate IoT. You can start by reading the new Chapter 13 in this edition of *Understanding Digital Marketing*. Think about all the things you have done today and imagine how much easier things could be if people could catch up with technology, harness its power and start to make it really really useful.

Chief digital officers lead to the rise of the data scientists

According to *Harvard Business Review* the 'sexiest job in the 21st century' is the data scientist – a unique blend of skill sets encapsulating analyst, advisor, data engineer and marketer. In previous editions I talked about the rise of the 'chief digital officer' (CDO) – this is relatively old hat now and we can see the CDO is a precursor to a whole raft of specialist new functions within marketing that require a rethink.

Life without Google?

As I write, the investors and speculators are hovering over Yahoo!. Leading the pack is Verizon, a sleepy old telco who acquired AOL in 2015... however, Verizon has 113 million mobile phone subscribers in the United States and Yahoo! might provide that extra oomph required to monetize a combined AOL/Yahoo!/Verizon offering to compete with Google and Facebook, who together control over half of digital advertising dollars in the US market. I can see why marketers and their agencies want to see more choice and more spread of investment but problems of identity... will nations want their own search hero?

The three key pillars of digital marketing's future

Contribution by Simon Kingsnorth, digital marketing leader and author of *Digital Marketing Strategy* (Kogan Page)

The future of digital marketing will be determined by three key pillars: technology, consumer behaviour and organizational approach. Each both pulls the others and is pulled by the others.

Technology

There is no doubt that we are in the technology age. Tech continues to develop at extreme pace with devices available today that were in the realms of sci-fi just 10–15 years ago. Let's explore each of these areas and how they are relevant to the future of digital now. Autonomy is something that many of us long for. Toothbrushes aside, the ability to act free from controls or significant influence. Thus it is an area of tech that has been moving at some pace in recent years. The highest profile of these is autonomous cars. The Google car. An autonomous car itself is not a digital marketing tool but it does significantly change behaviour. If the primary traveller no longer needs to drive the car then they are open to any other activity. This could be an activity produced by the car itself or more time spent on your smartphone or tablet. Another area of autonomy that will accelerate in the near term is artificial intelligence (AI). Systems such as Siri from Apple have been developing for some time to interact directly with voice controls. There are many systems now in development that will become far more sophisticated. AI will begin to be a key form of interaction for us moving forward. Consumers will want to get their answers quickly from a logical system and AI will provide that. An example of this is robo-advisors. Robo-advisors have become increasingly used in financial services in recent years but have a long way to go before they become commonplace. They are effectively financial advisors that exist as an algorithm rather than a human. They are most common in the United States but have spread widely and this will certainly continue. This will of course mean that consumers will need to accept a non-human advisor and that cultural change may take time.

Internet of things

Damian, we're on the same page. IoT is a phrase known to many of us now, although according to Accenture around 87 per cent of us still don't

▶

understand it. Whether it's a nest system for your heating, or controlling your home alarm system through your smartphone, these services and devices are becoming increasingly commonplace. The question is how far this will go. Advertising should go the same way, with an understanding of how the adverts you are seeing are affecting your shopping behaviour and therefore tailoring those that are shown to you in future on all devices. This in turn means that understanding data across all touch points and having a multichannel strategy in place is going to become increasingly vital to success.

Wearables and implants

Wearables have been a mixed bag so far. There are many fitness-focused wearables that have become hugely popular; Google Glass never came close to being mainstream in its first iteration and the Apple Watch has had a mixed reception. As wearables become more common, which is ultimately a question of mainstream developments, behaviours will change again. Wearables are likely to offer even less opportunity for typing than a smartphone, which suggests voice control is the answer – but will users walk around talking to their wearables all day? The world would become a very noisy and confusing place. Implants are in use now in a few specialized areas and it may take some time before society is willing to accept them but there are certainly some great advantages to the technology and these are advancing quickly. Being able to lock and unlock doors, start cars and login to systems without the need for keys and passwords is one, ie convenience. As I write this there has recently been a story in the news about a paralysed man who, through the use of implant technology, has been able to use his fingers to the extent that he can actually play guitar.

Man–machine interfaces

This category is becoming increasingly broad. We have for a long time communicated with technology though biometrics is also an interesting area here. We have seen finger-print recognition becoming commonplace, largely thanks to Apple. Iris recognition has long been featured in spy films but may well see an increase. As with any personal information this brings privacy and data concerns, which we will touch on briefly below.

Personalization

We have seen a rise in more targeted advertising and personalized messaging in recent years. Programmatic advertising, intelligent content platforms and omni-channel marketing all fall into this bracket. The consumer is increasingly less willing to accept broadcast messages that are hit and miss and more willing to listen to, watch and read highly targeted pieces.

Consumer behaviour

Tech is often created to solve the needs of the consumer such as voice-controlled devices for hands-free usage, but tech often drives changes in consumer behaviour too, such as touch screens that were not a genuine consumer need when the iPhone launched but are now becoming the standard interface.

Engagement

Above we have looked at some of the technology-driven changes we will see in how consumers interact with us over the coming years. The ultimate goal for many businesses today is increased engagement. Many other metrics play a part in the success of our digital strategies but this is probably the metric that has seen the most significant increase in focus in the last 10 years. When we talk about engagement today we primarily look at social media metrics, content sharing, website dwell time, feedback and community activity. To further understand the engagement we might cut this data by the 'W' questions such as who, where, when, what and why. This gives us a picture of our engagement, which in turn gives us a guide to our content strategy and even brand and advertising strategies. If we step back from this though, there are still a lot of missing pieces. If someone is reading our content does that mean they think it's fantastic – we don't know. If they always absorb our content on mobile does that mean it's their favourite device – we don't know. If it is mostly women aged 35–50 reading our content does that mean it is most appealing to that audience – we don't know. Sentiment analysis can go some way to understanding feeling but it can't answer everything.

As we move further into the 21st century and some of the above technology developments begin to take hold we can expect to see users become much more in control of who they engage with and where. There will be less time wasted on the wrong sites. I'm sorry to say this, Google (although I suspect you are well ahead of me on this one), but people will no longer be searching for a collection of words and phrases and clicking on titles that look about right to find the content they want. The right content will increasingly go to the consumer at the right time in the right

▶

place. Today consumers are already beginning to see this happening to a small extent – this journey has begun. Engagement will therefore increasingly be defined by how much consumers truly engage with what is given to them at the right time. This means how they interact with it and how they rate it, rather than whether they clicked on something you pushed out on your channels. Indeed the concept of channels will increasingly decline as there will be only one channel – the consumer.

Research and reviews

This concept of rating content leads us nicely on to the very clear trend in the last 10–15 years of rating and recommending. Entire businesses are built on this premise, such as Rotten Tomatoes, and many businesses heavily rely on it such as Netflix and Amazon. Let's cut straight to the point here – this behaviour is not going away. If you do not ensure your products, service, pricing and other front-line features are first class you will suffer the consequences.

As we move forward we can expect these reviews and recommendations to increasingly form the research phase of many shoppers' behaviours and they will also become increasingly interactive. At the moment most of these consist of star ratings and perhaps short written reviews. Increasingly these will be video, audio (check out feefo. com) and I believe will, perhaps less often, also enable direct contact with the reviewer if they choose to allow it. Imagine considering buying a car and seeing mixed reviews: it's a big purchase and I think I like it but there are a few reviews here that I'm not sure about. If I could just have a quick video chat with that reviewer on my digital watch to check a couple of facts and that reviewer earns a small fee from me for the advice then I could be reassured or put off completely. This is incredibly powerful and something we should expect to see in coming years.

Digital natives

Millennials are built into many digital strategies now as the digital natives, the group that truly understands digital as they have never known anything else. This is true but we have to acknowledge that we are no longer in a time when we can dismiss sections of society for not being technology literate due to age. A significant percentage of people well into their seventies, eighties and older are regularly online and using smartphones and tablets regularly. In fact, according to Pew Research Centre, 74 per cent of 65–69 year olds regularly go online and even at age 80+ over one-third of people still regularly go online. When we consider that an 80-year-old in 2016 was 64 in 2000 during the dot.com boom we can see that they were still in work then and so are likely to be technology literate to some degree.

We cannot dismiss any age groups now. What we can say is that some channels and technologies such as social media and mobile apps may not be regularly used by these age groups, and even the 40+ age group may not be fully appreciating many social channels. Even then we cannot assume that people in this age group are not extensive users. Statista reports that 10–15 per cent of social media users are in the 45–54 age range and 3–9 per cent in the 55–64 range. This therefore still accounts for around one-quarter of all users. That may not be relevant to your target audience and it does of course differ by platform, but we have to acknowledge that these numbers are only going in one direction. Expect to see the graph shift to the right as users of social media age over the coming years.

Organizational approach

How organizations adapt to the above and try to stay ahead of the competition will be key to how digital marketing changes. Being big will increasingly become a disadvantage where it has historically been an advantage. The small and nimble will win. Agile approaches to development and cycles of continuous improvement, alongside the solid principles of test and learn, lead to organizations that are able to stay ahead of the competition by understanding the landscape and reacting quickly to the changes they see.

Big data has been a buzz word in digital for many years now and the phrase was coined long before it was widely used. It has been a buzz word for so long in fact that many organizations are already starting to become disillusioned with it, but it is a concept that businesses need to embrace. If we forget the name for a minute we can all appreciate that there are many disparate data sets within our organizations that cause issues around data management, consistency and integration. Getting our data sets to fit together in a coherent manner that we can manage is a true challenge and one that, for the organizations that get it right, can pay enormous dividends. The 'BIGness' of the data is not important, it is the complexity and variety that are the true issue. Data comes from various sources already, including client, financial, servicing, web analytics, social analytics, apps, research and many other sources. Once we begin to

▶

consider data from IoT devices, robots, implants, autonomous machines and many more areas we can see that the challenge is likely to grow. Even just considering today's scale, we perform 40,000 Google search queries every second and send over 31 million Facebook messages per minute. That is probably why 73 per cent of organizations have already invested or plan to invest in big data by 2016. The important part of the puzzle is not collecting the data but using it. In fact, at the moment less than 0.5 per cent of all data is ever analysed and used, which goes some way to explaining that the thinking is more important than the gathering. In tackling big data we mustn't ask *why* but *how* we should solve this problem. Building a data strategy has never been more important.

Structure and transformation

Many businesses are still not set up for digital. Some know they need to take digital seriously but don't know how, some know how but are resistant to upsetting the status quo. There are very few organizations now that don't see the value of digital. The key is transformation. This is a word that gets thrown around a lot in digital conversations but it is vital for every organization to be set up correctly for the digital future as it will be the present before we know it. Organizational structure changes and this is something we should expect to be more common. Change. As new technologies arise and behaviours change (as we have explored above) organizations need to adapt. Social media teams are well established in many organizations but none existed just 10 years ago. Mobile development labs are relatively common but again this was not a consideration for most businesses until recently. Not only are these two examples new but they have often changed priority and focus over this period, with many organizations, for example, struggling to decide if social media should be managed by marketing, HR, public relations, customer service or a combination of these.

The most important point to transformation is that it is not simple. This is not the exercise of rebadging a technology team as digital or simply including 'we are digital first' as one of your business values. The product of transformation must be that digital becomes inherent in everything you do. Your values, your mission, your goals, servicing, brand and product strategies – to name a few. It must not be an afterthought or an area of the business that is brought into some conversations where other departments deem it relevant. Everyone must live and breathe digital. The concept of a digital department is likely to fade over the next 20 years as digital becomes integral to everything we do – and organizations must prepare for this now. It's not simple and it's not painless but it's far preferable to being left behind, which is what will happen without this transformation taking place.

Strategy

There are two key reasons why many of the larger organizations of the world struggle with digital and those are legacy issues, such as technology and process, and the lack of a strategy. Conversely, younger businesses tend to have clearer strategies and no legacy issues, but less resource and experience. Creation of a robust digital strategy is key to success. You cannot move forward with digital improvements within your organization on a pure tactical basis. Digital is a truly symbiotic discipline with the digital marketing channels all feeding from each other. Content strategy creates social engagement, which improves SEO performance, which drives more traffic to your site, which is impacted by your UX, which sends further SEO signals out, and so on.

Summary

As Tolkien put it, the world has changed. More importantly it will never stop changing and the pace of that change seems to quicken every year. In order to be prepared for the future you don't need to understand what is going to happen next but you do need to be ready for it when it does happen. Staying in touch with trends in technology and changes in consumer behaviour are all useful methods of keeping your finger on the pulse, but the most important is setting up your organization to be flexible and ready to evolve. Remain agile in your development processes and structure your organization to embed digital into everything you do.

The last word

Thanks to Simon and thanks to you for reading this latest edition of *Understanding Digital Marketing*… almost 10 years of writing and thought have gone into this book. I would like to think that if it has given you just ONE new idea to improve your digital marketing activity then I've done my job.

My work on this edition of the book has taught me some valuable lessons and provided *me* with ONE new idea already! It's this:

I spend an increasing amount of time with digital marketers who want to succeed and become part of the next generation of digital business leaders. Having all the knowledge in the world about digital marketing is not enough to achieve these ambitions. I would urge digital marketers to take more time to become brilliant at the basic, primary tools of business too – understanding people, adopting a winning mentality and investing in their personal as well as professional development. What will set digital business leaders apart from their counterparts and competitors in the future will not be their ability to parrot about 'understanding digital marketing'… it will be their ability to communicate, persuade and deliver while remaining passionate and curious about this whole big thing called 'digital'.

Damian Ryan

GLOSSARY

Throughout the book we've avoided technical jargon wherever possible and have tried to present information in plain, clear English. Where specific digital marketing terminology was unavoidable we provided a brief definition in the text itself. To supplement the definitions in the text and to give you a handy reference for digital marketing terms, we've included the following glossary, reproduced here with permission from the UK's Internet Advertising Bureau (www.iabuk.net).

abandon   When a user does not complete a transaction.

ad impression   An advertisement impression transpires each time a consumer is exposed to an advertisement (either appended to an SMS or MMS message, on mobile web (WAP) page, within a video clip, or related media).

ad serving   Delivery of online adverts to an end user's computer by an ad management system. The system allows different online adverts to be served in order to target different audience groups and can serve adverts across multiple sites. Ad technology providers each have their own proprietary models for this.

ad unit   Any defined advertising vehicle that can appear in an ad space inside an application. For example, for the purposes of promoting a commercial brand, product or service.

advertiser   Also called merchant, retailer, e-retailer or online retailer. Any website that sells a product or service, accepts payments and fulfils orders. An advertiser places ads and links to their products and services on other websites (publishers) and pays those publishers a commission for leads or sales that result from their site.

affiliate marketing   An affiliate (a website owner or publisher) displays an advertisement (such as a banner or link) on its site for a merchant (the brand or advertiser). If a consumer visiting the affiliate's site clicks on this advertisement and goes on to perform a specified action (usually a purchase) on an advertiser's site then the affiliate receives a commission.

algorithm   The set of 'rules' a search engine may use to determine the relevance of a web page (and therefore ranking) in its organic search results. See also *organic search results* and *search engine optimization*.

application service provider (ASP)   An online network that is accessible through the internet instead of through the installation of software. It is quickly integrated with other websites and the services are easily implemented and scalable.

avatar   A picture or cartoon used to represent an individual in chat forums, games or on a website as a help function.

bandwidth   The transmission rate of a communication line – usually measured in kilobytes per second (Kbps). This relates to the amount of data that can be carried per second by your internet connection. See also *broadband*.

banner   A long, horizontal, online advert usually found running across the top of a page in a fixed placement. See also *universal advertising package, embedded format*.

BARB   Broadcasters' Audience Research Board is responsible for the measurement of TV viewing.

behavioural targeting   A form of online marketing that uses advertising technology to target web users based on their previous behaviour. Advertising creative and content can be tailored to be of more relevance to a particular user by capturing their previous decision-making behaviour (eg: filling out preferences or visiting certain areas of a site frequently) and looking for patterns.

blog   An online space regularly updated presenting the opinions or activities of one or a group of individuals and displaying in chronological order.

broadband   An internet connection that is always on and that delivers a higher bit rate (128Kbps or above) than a standard dial-up connection. It allows for a better online experience as pages load quickly and you can download items faster.

buffering   When a streaming media player saves portions of file until there is enough information for the file to begin playing.

button   A square online advert usually found embedded within a website page. See also *universal advertising package, embedded format*.

cache memory   Used to store web pages you have seen already. When you go back to those pages they will load more quickly because they come from the cache and do not need to be downloaded over the internet again.

call to action (CTA)   A statement or instruction, typically promoted in print, web, TV, radio, on-portal or other forms of media (often embedded in advertising) that explains to a mobile subscriber how to respond to an opt-in for a particular promotion or mobile initiative, which is typically followed by a notice (see *notice*).

click-through   When a user interacts with an advertisement and clicks through to the advertiser's website.

click-through rate (CTR)   Frequency of click-throughs as a percentage of impressions served. Used as a measure of advertising effectiveness.

click to call   A service that enables a mobile subscriber to initiate a voice call to a specified phone number by clicking on a link on a mobile internet site. Typically used to enhance and provide a direct response mechanism in an advertisement.

commission   An amount of income received by a publisher for some quantifiable action such as selling an advertiser's product and/or service on the publisher's website.

content sponsorship   Advertiser sponsorships of content areas (eg entire website, home page or a specific channel) to include the total value of the package including any embedded or interruptive formats. This category also includes revenue related to e-mail advertising or prioritized listing of results in search engines that are included as part of the sponsorship deal.

contextual advertising   Advertising that is targeted to the content on the web page being viewed by a user at that specific time.

conversion rate   Measure of success of an online ad when compared to the click-through rate. What defines a 'conversion' depends on the marketing objective, eg: it can be defined as a sale or request to receive more information, etc.

cookie   A small text file on the user's PC that identifies the user's browser and hence the user so they are 'recognized' when they revisit a site, eg: it allows usernames to be stored and websites to personalize their offering.

cost per acquisition (CPA)   Cost to acquire a new customer.

cost per action (CPA)   A pricing model that only charges advertising on an action being conducted, eg a sale or a form being filled in.

cost per click (CPC)   The amount paid by an advertiser for a click on their sponsored search listing. See also *PPC*.

cost per mille (CPM)/cost per thousand (CPT)   Online advertising can be purchased on the basis of what it costs to show the ad to 1,000 viewers (CPM). It is used in marketing as a benchmark to calculate the relative cost of an advertising campaign or an ad message in a given medium. Rather than an absolute cost, CPM estimates the cost per 1,000 views of the ad (Wikipedia definition).

CRM   Customer relationship management.

deep-linking advert   Linking beyond a home page to a page inside the site with content pertinent to the advert.

demand-side platform (DSP)   Software that allows ad buyers to manage and purchase ad space.

display advertising on e-mail   Advertising that appears around the unrelated editorial content of e-mail newsletters. This can take the form of embedded formats such as banners, or as sponsorship, and includes both opt-in (sent to customers specifically requesting it) and opt-out (sent to customers with the option to be removed at their request) e-mails.

domain name   The unique name of an internet site, eg www.iabuk.net.

downloading   The technology that allows users to store video content on their computer for viewing at a later date. Downloading an entire piece of media makes it more susceptible to illegal duplication.

DRM   Digital rights management is a set of technologies used by publishers and media owners to control access to their digital content. Access can be limited to the number of times a piece of content is accessed from a single machine or user account; the number of times access permissions can be passed on; or the lifespan of a piece of content.

D2C   Direct to consumer.

dynamic ad delivery   Based upon predetermined criteria, dynamic ad delivery is the process by which a mobile advertisement is delivered, via a campaign management platform, to a publisher's mobile content.

e-commerce (electronic commerce)   Business that takes place over electronic platforms such as the internet.

electronic programme guide (EPG)   The electronic version of a television schedule showing programme times and content on the television screen or monitor. In the case of VOD, an EPG displays the content of all of the services available to a subscriber.

e-mail bounced   Those e-mails sent as part of a mailing distribution that did not have a valid recipient e-mail address and so generated a formal failure message (ABC Electronic jargon-buster definition).

embedded format   Advertising formats that are displayed in set spaces on a publisher's page. See also *banner, skyscraper, button*.

emoticons   Emoticon symbols are used to indicate mood in an electronic mode of communication, eg e-mail or instant messenger. ☺

encoding   The conversion of an analogue signal to a digital format.

EPC (average earnings per 100 clicks)   A relative rating that illustrates the ability to convert clicks into commissions. It is calculated by taking commissions earned (or commissions paid) divided by the total number of clicks times 100.

expandable banner/skyscraper   Fixed online advertising placements that expand over the page in the response to user action, eg mouseover. See also *rich media*.

firewall software   Provides security for a computer or local network by preventing unauthorized access. It sits as a barrier between the web and your computer in order to prevent hacking, viruses or unapproved data transfer.

flash   Web design software that creates animation and interactive elements that are quick to download.

flash impression   The total number of requests made for pages holding flash-based content by users of that site in the period being measured (ABC Electronic jargon-buster definition).

geotargeting   The process of only showing adverts to people on a website and in search engines based on their physical location. This could be done using advanced technology that knows where a computer is located or by using the content of the website to determine what a person is looking for, eg someone searching for a restaurant in Aylesbury, Buckinghamshire.

GPRS   General Packet Radio Service or '2.5G' is an underlying mechanism for the networks to deliver internet browsing, WAP, e-mail and other such content. The user is 'always connected' and relatively high data rates can be achieved with most modern phones compared to a dial-up modem. Most phones default to using GPRS (if capable), and Incentivated is able to develop services that utilize this delivery mechanism.

graphic banners A graphic mobile ad represented by a banner featuring an image. Similar to a web banner but with lower size constraints. (See *banner*.)

GSM Global Standard for Mobiles. The set of standards covering one particular type of mobile phone system.

hit A single request from a web browser for a single item from a web server.

hot spotting The ability to add hyperlinks to objects in a video that enable viewers to tag a product or service. Hot spotting can be used as a direct response mechanic in internet video.

HTML Stands for HyperText Markup Language, which is the set of commands used by web browsers to interpret and display page content to users (ABC Electronic jargon-buster definition).

image ad An image on a mobile internet site with an active link that can be clicked on by the subscriber. Once clicked the user is redirected to a new page, another mobile internet site or other destination where an offer resides.

impressions The metric used to measure views of a web page and its elements – including the advertising embedded within it. Ad impressions are how most online advertising is sold and the cost is quoted in terms of the cost per 1,000 impressions (CPM).

instant messaging Sending messages and chatting with friends or colleagues in real time when you are both online via a special application.

Integrated Services Digital Network (ISDN) High-speed dial-up connections to the internet over normal phone lines.

Internet Protocol TV (IPTV) The use of a broadband connection to stream digital television over the internet to subscribed users.

internet service provider (ISP) A company that provides users with the means to connect to the internet, eg AOL, Tiscali, Yahoo!.

interruptive formats Online advertising formats that appear on users' screens on top of web content (and sometimes before the web page appears) and range from static, one-page splash screens to full-motion animated advertisements. See also *overlay, pop-up*.

interstitial ads These appear between two content pages. Also known as splash pages and transition ads. See also *rich media*.

IPA Institute of Practitioners in Advertising is the trade body representing advertising agencies in the UK.

IP address The numerical internet address assigned to each computer on a network so that it can be distinguished from other computers. Expressed as four groups of numbers separated by dots.

keyword marketing The purchase of keywords (or 'search terms') by advertisers in search listings. See also *PPC*.

LAN (local area network) A group of computers connected together, which are at one physical location.

landing page (jump page) The page or view to which a user is directed when they click on an active link embedded in a banner, web page, e-mail or other view. A click-through lands the user on a jump page. Sometimes the landing page is one stage upstream from what would ordinarily be considered the home page.

lead When a visitor registers, signs up for, or downloads something on an advertiser's site. A lead might also comprise a visitor filling out a form on an advertiser's site.

link A link is a form of advertising on a website, in an e-mail or online newsletter, which, when clicked on, refers the visitor to an advertiser's website or a specific area within their website.

location-based services (LBS) A range of services that are provided to mobile subscribers based on the geographical location of their handsets within their cellular network. Handsets do not have to be equipped with a position-location technology such as GPS to enable the geographical trigger of service(s) being provided, since the location of the cell-site can be used as a proxy. Assisted GPS combines cell-site information with satellite positioning for a more accurate read. LBS include driving directions, information about certain resources or destinations within the current vicinity, such as restaurants, ATMs, shopping, movie theatres, etc. LBS may also be used to track the movements and locations of people, as is being done via parent/child monitoring services and mobile devices that target the family market.

locator An advertisement or service through which an advertiser's bricks-and-mortar location can be identified based on proximity of the consumer or their preferred location (can be LBS or user-defined postal code).

log files A record of all the hits a web server has received over a given period of time.

meta-tags/-descriptions HTML tags that identify the content of a web page for the search engines.

micro-site A sub-site reached via clicking on an ad. The user stays on the publisher's website but has access to more information from the advertiser.

MMA The Mobile Marketing Association (MMA) is the premier global non-profit association that strives to stimulate the growth of mobile marketing and its associated technologies. The MMA is an action-oriented association designed to clear obstacles to market development, to establish standards and best practices for sustainable growth, and to evangelize the mobile channel for use by brands and third-party content providers. The MMA has over 500 members representing 40-plus countries.

mobile data services Includes SMS, MMS, WAP, LBS and video.

mobile internet advertising A form of advertising via mobile phones or other wireless devices (excluding laptops). This type of mobile advertising includes mobile web banner ads, mobile internet sponsorship and interstitials (which appear while a requested mobile web page is loading) as well as mobile paid-for search listings. Mobile internet advertising does not include other forms of mobile marketing such as SMS, MMS and shortcode.

MPEG File format used to compress and transmit video clips online.

MP3 A computer file format that compresses audio files up to a factor of 12 from a .wav file.

MSISDN Mobile Subscriber Integrated Services Digital Network. The mobile phone number of the participating customer.

multiple purpose units (MPU) A square online advert usually found embedded in a web page in a fixed placement. Called 'multiple purpose' as it is a flexible-shaped blank 'canvas' in which you can serve flat or more interactive content as desired. See also *rich media, universal advertising package.*

natural search results The 'natural' search results that appear in a separate section (usually the main body of the page) to the paid listings. The results listed here have not been paid for and are ranked by the search engine (using spiders or algorithms according to relevancy to the term searched upon). See also *spider, algorithm, SEO.*

notice An easy-to-understand written description of the information and data collection, storage, maintenance, access, security, disclosure and use policies and practices, as necessary and required of the entity collecting and using the information and data from the mobile subscriber.

NVOD Near video on demand service is the delivery of film and television programming from a server via a cable network or the internet. Like VOD these services are nonlinear and navigated via an EPG. Programming must be downloaded and the majority of existing services require the same amount of time to download as the duration of the selected programme.

OB Outside broadcast unit known as a 'production truck'. In the United States an OB unit is a truck containing a mobile TV production studio.

off-portal Point of sale/access on the mobile network, but outside the operator's 'walled garden'/portal/deck, where consumers can access/purchase information and mobile products/content/utilities.

online HD Is the delivery of high-definition streamed video media. This typically conforms to 720p standards where 720 represents 720 lines of vertical resolution and p stands for progressive scan.

online video advertising Video advertising accompanying video content distributed via the internet to be streamed or downloaded onto compatible devices such as computers and mobile phones. In its basic form, this can be TV ads run online, but adverts are increasingly adapted or created specifically to suit online.

on-portal   Point of sale/access within the operator's 'walled garden'/portal/deck, where consumers can access/purchase information and mobile products/content/utilities.

opt-in   An individual has given a company permission to use his/her data for marketing purposes.

opt-out   An individual has stated that they do not want a company to use his/her data for marketing purposes.

organic search results   The 'natural' search results that appear in a separate section (usually the main body of the page) to the paid listings. The results listed here have not been paid for and are ranked by the search engine (using spiders or algorithms) according to relevancy to the term searched upon. See also *spider, algorithm, SEO.*

overlay   Online advertising content that appears over the top of the web page. See also *rich media.*

paid-for listings   The search results list in which advertisers pay to be featured according to the PPC model. This list usually appears in a separate section to the organic search results – usually at the top of the page or down the right-hand side. See also *organic search results, pay per click (PPC).*

paid inclusion   In exchange for a payment, a search engine will guarantee to list/review pages from a website. It is not guaranteed that the pages will rank well for particular queries – this still depends on the search engine's underlying relevancy process.

paid search   See *PPC.*

pay for performance programme   Also called affiliate marketing, performance-based, partner marketing, CPA, or associate programme. Any type of revenue-sharing programme where a publisher receives a commission for generating online activity (eg leads or sales) for an advertiser.

pay per click (PPC)   Allows advertisers to bid for placement in the paid listings search results on terms that are relevant to their business. Advertisers pay the amount of their bid only when a consumer clicks on their listing. Also called sponsored search/paid search.

pay per lead   The commission structure where the advertiser pays the publisher a flat fee for each qualified lead (customer) that is referred to the advertiser's website.

pay per sale   The commission structure where the advertiser pays a percentage or flat fee to the publisher based on the revenue generated by the sale of a product or service to a visitor who came from a publisher site.

pay per view (PPV)   An e-commerce model that allows media owners to grant consumers access to their programming in return for payment. Micropayments may be used for shorter programming whilst feature films may attract larger sums.

personal video recorder (PVR)   A hard-disc-based digital video recorder (most use MPEG technology) that enables viewers to pause and rewind live TV. PVRs also interact with EPGs to automatically record favourite programmes and have led to an increase in the number of consumers watching 'time shifted' TV and skipping advertising breaks.

pharming   An illegal method of redirecting traffic from another company's website (such as a bank) to a fake one designed to look similar in order to steal user details when they try to log in. See also *phishing*.

phishing   An illegal method whereby legitimate-looking e-mails (appearing to come from a well-known bank, for example) are used in an attempt to get personal information that can be used to steal a user's identity.

placement   The area where an advertisement is displayed/placed within a publisher's mobile content.

podcasting   This involves making an audio file (usually in MP3 format) of content – usually in the form of a radio programme – that is available to download to an MP3 player.

polite loading   Fixed online advertising placements that load and display additional flash content after the host page on which the advert appears has finished loading. See also *flash*.

pop-under   An ad that appears in a separate window beneath an open window. Pop-under ads are concealed until the top window is closed, moved, resized or minimized.

pop-up   An online advert that 'pops up' in a window over the top of a web page. See also *interruptive formats*.

portal   A browsable portal of links to content, preconfigured usually by the network operator, and set as the default home page to the phone's browser.

post-roll   The streaming of a mobile advertising clip after a mobile TV/video clip. The mobile advert is usually 10–15 seconds.

pre-roll   The name given to the adverts shown before, or whilst an online video is loading. There can be more than one and, although they all vary in length, they average 21 seconds in duration.

PSMS   Premium SMS. A text message that is charged at a premium over the standard rate.

publisher   Also referred to as an affiliate, associate, partner, reseller or content site. An independent party, or website, that promotes the products or services of an advertiser in exchange for a commission.

query string formation   In a search engine, a query string is the set of words entered into a search engine by an individual. For example, a search for 'search engine marketing information'. Query string formation is simply the process of thinking of the correct query string to get the results required.

reach   The number of unique web users potentially seeing a website one or more times in a given time period expressed as a percentage of the total active web population for that period.

real time   No delay in the processing of requests for information, other than the time necessary for the data to travel over the internet.

real-time bidding (RTB)   An auction where ad inventory is bought and sold through a bidding system that occurs in the milliseconds before a web page is loaded by a user.

really simple syndication (RSS)   Software that allows you to flag website content (often from blogs or new sites) and aggregate new entries to this content into an easy-to-read format that is delivered directly to a user's PC. See also *blog*.

rich media   The collective name for online advertising formats that use advanced technology to harness broadband to build brands. It uses interactive and audio-visual elements to give richer content and a richer experience for the user when interacting with the advert. See also *interstitial ads, superstitials, overlay* and *Rich Media Guidelines*.

Rich Media Guidelines   Design guidelines produced by the IAB for effective use of rich media technologies in all forms of internet advertising. They aim to protect user experience by keeping them in control of the experience, eg encouraging clearly labelled close, sound and video buttons.

sale   When a user makes a purchase from an online advertiser.

sales house   An organization that sells advertising on behalf of other media owners. These sales houses typically retain a percentage of the revenue they sell in exchange for their services. These organizations may combine a number of websites together and sell them as different packages to advertisers.

search engine marketing (SEM)   The process that aims to get websites listed prominently in search engine results through search engine optimization, sponsored search and paid inclusion. See also *PPC, SEO* and *paid inclusion*.

search engine optimization (SEO)   The process that aims to get websites listed prominently within search engines' organic (algorithmic, spidered) search results. Involves making a site 'search engine friendly'. See also *organic search results*.

serial digital interface (SDI)   A dedicated digital video interface used to carry broadcast-quality video content.

server   A host computer that maintains websites, newsgroups and e-mail services.

session   The time spent between a user starting an application, computer, website, etc and logging off or quitting.

SIM   Subscriber identity module. A removable part of the mobile phone hardware that identifies the subscriber.

simulcast   Watching an existing TV service over the internet at the same time as normal transmission.

site analytics   The reporting and analysis of website activity – in particular user behaviour on the site. All websites have a weblog that can be used for this purpose, but other third-party software is available for a more sophisticated service.

skyscraper   A long, vertical, online advert usually found running down the side of a page in a fixed placement. See also *universal advertising package.*

SMPP   Short Message Peer-to-peer Protocol – used for exchanging SMS messages.

SMS   Short Message Service.

SMSC   Short Message Service Centre. A network switch for routing SMS traffic.

sniffer software   Identifies the capabilities of the user's browser and therefore can determine compatibility with ad formats and serve them an advert they will be able to see/fully interact with (eg GIF, flash, etc).

Solus e-mail advertising   Where the body of the e-mail is determined by the advertiser, including both text and graphical elements, and is sent on their behalf by an e-mail list manager/owner. Solus e-mail advertising is conducted on an opt-in basis where the recipient has given their consent to receive communications.

spam   Unsolicited junk mail.

spider   A programme that crawls the web and fetches web pages in order for them to be indexed against keywords. Used by search engines to formulate search result pages. See also *organic search results.*

sponsored search   See *pay per click (PPC).*

sponsorship   Advertiser sponsorships of targeted content areas (eg entire website, site area or an event) often for promotional purposes.

SS7   Signalling System 7. A worldwide standard for telecommunications hardware to talk to each other.

stickiness   Measure used to gauge the effectiveness of a site in retaining its users. Usually measured by the duration of the visit.

streaming media   Compressed audio/video that plays and downloads at the same time. The user does not have to wait for the whole file to download before it starts playing.

superstitials   A form of rich media advertising that allows a TV-like experience on the web. It is fully pre-cached before playing. See also *rich media, cache memory.*

supply-side platform   (SSP) Software that enables publishers to manage their advertising-space inventory.

tenancy   The 'renting' out of a section of a website by another brand who pays commission to this media owner for any revenue generated from this space, eg dating services inside portals or bookstores inside online newspapers.

text ad   A static appended text attached to an advertisement.

text link   Creative use for mobile advertisements – represented by highlighted and clickable text(s) with a link embedded within the highlighted text. Usually limited to 16–24 characters.

traffic   Number of visitors who come to a website.

UMTS   Universal Mobile Telephony Service or '3G' offers comprehensive voice and multimedia services to mobile customers by providing very high data rates and new functionality such as data streaming. 3G phones are backward compatible and can access all the services that 2 and 2.5G phones can, except that in this case data can be transferred a lot quicker. This means that any service that Incentivated can currently provide will work on the newer phones whose experience can be enhanced specifically based on handset type.

uniform resource locator (URL)   Technical term that is used to refer to the web address of a particular website. For example www.iabuk.net.

unique users   The number of different individuals who visit a site within a specific time period.

universal advertising package   A set of online advertising formats that are standardized placements as defined by the IAB. See also *banner, skyscraper, button, MPU* and *embedded format*.

universal player   A platform-agnostic media player that will allow video and audio to be played on any hardware/software configuration from a single source file.

user-generated content (UGC)   Online content created by website users rather than media owners or publishers – either through reviews, blogging, podcasting or posting comments, pictures or video clips. Sites that encourage user-generated content include MySpace, YouTube, Wikipedia and Flickr. See also *blog, podcasting*.

video on demand (VOD)   Allows users to watch what they want, when they want. This can be either 'pay per view' or a free service usually funded by advertising.

viral marketing   The term 'viral advertising' refers to the idea that people will pass on and share striking and entertaining content; this is often sponsored by a brand that is looking to build awareness of a product or service. These viral commercials often take the form of funny video clips, or interactive flash games, images, and even text.

VMNO (Virtual Mobile Network Operator)   A company that uses the infrastructure of an existing (licence-owning) telecoms network operator. Tesco and Virgin are two of the largest VMNOs in the UK.

Voice Over Internet Protocol (VOIP)   Technology that allows the use of a broadband internet connection to make telephone calls.

WAP (Wireless Application Protocol)   Standard for providing mobile data services on hand-held devices. Brings internet content such as news, weather, travel, etc to mobile phones and can also be used to deliver formatted content such as wallpapers, ringtones, video, games, portals and other useful links.

Web 2.0   The term Web 2.0 – with its knowing nod to upgraded computer applications – describes the next generation of online use. Web 2.0 identifies the consumer as a major contributor in the evolution of the internet into a two-way medium. See also *user-generated content*.

web based   Requiring no software to access an online service or function, other than a web browser and access to the internet.

web portal   A website or service that offers a broad array of resources and services, such as e-mail, forums, search engines and online shopping malls.

whitelist   An e-mail whitelist is a list of contacts that the user deems are acceptable to receive e-mail from and should not be sent to the trash folder (Wikipedia definition).

Wi-Fi (Wireless Fidelity)   The ability to connect to the internet wirelessly, eg internet 'hotspots' in coffee shops and airports use this technology.

wiki   A wiki is a type of website that allows the visitors themselves to easily add, remove, and otherwise edit and change some available content, sometimes without the need for registration.

wilfing (What Was I Looking For?)   Seven in 10 of Britain's 34 million users forget what they are looking for online at work and at home. Wilfing is an expression referring to browsing the internet with no real purpose.

Wireless Markup Language (WML) aka WAP 1.0   Where the mobile internet started many years ago. Hardly supported any more.

XHTML (Extensible Hypertag Markup Language) aka WAP 2.0   The language used to create most mobile internet sites.

XML (Extensible Markup Language)   Language used by many internet applications for exchanging information.

INDEX

Note: *Italics* indicate a Figure or Table in the text.

CPSIA information can be obtained
at www.ICGtesting.com
Printed in the USA
BVOW06s2305190117
473942BV00015B/5/P